# THE REVOLUTIONARY WORDS THAT FORGED AMERICA

# THE REVOLUTIONARY WORDS THAT FORGED AMERICA

## The Definitive Guide to the Declaration of Independence

JUDGE MICHAEL WARREN

Republic Book Publishers
New York, NY

A REPUBLIC BOOK
ISBN: 978-1-64572-120-8
ISBN (eBook): 978-1-64572-121-5

The Revolutionary Words that Forged America:
The Definitive Guide to the Declaration of Independence


Cover Design by Cody Corcoran based on ideas
generated by Judge Warren's Sons of Liberty



Republic Book Publishers
New York, NY
www.republicbookpublishers.com

Published in the United States of America
1 2 3 4 5 6 7 8 9 10

For my beloveds, Shannon, Leah, and Alex

# CONTENTS

# AUTHOR'S NOTE

Contrary to fashionable trends in American history, this work celebrates (as opposed to condemns) the miraculous American Revolution and Declaration of Independence. In this sense, this work is purposefully countercultural—or rather, pro-American. There is no meaningful attempt to review the subject matter from the Loyalist, British, French, Native American, fascist, communist, or critical race theory perspectives. Indeed, this work is unabashedly biased in favor of the Founding Generation. With only a few exceptions, it is written with their perspective in mind. As such, much of the discussion about the Founders is written in the present tense. Still, I do not ignore their deep flaws but place them in context. As much as possible, I leave ideological analysis aside and let the Declaration of Independence speak directly to you in all its glory, power, and clarity.

To assist the reader, my fantastic editor, Mike DeBruyn, added compelling questions to accompany much of the text. However, because the twenty-eight (not twenty-seven as is commonly believed) grievances of the Declaration do not lend themselves to such inquiries, they are omitted there.

To ease readability, I have Americanized, regularized, and modernized spelling, punctuation, and grammar in nearly all primary and secondary sources. For example, the dreaded "hath" is expunged for "has," "ye" becomes "you," and "draught" is revised to "draft." The colonial and English penchant to capitalize nearly every noun is excised. Similar modernization is throughout. Exceptions to this practice include the Declaration itself, the United States and State constitutions, the Holy Bible, and some publication titles. All references to the Creator (in whatever guise) are capitalized. Following the dominant (but less than uniform) treatment by the Founders, "State" and "States" are generally capitalized when referring to the newly independent former colonies. Congress and Parliament are treated as singular bodies. Similar conventions are deployed throughout the work.

In an admittedly unorthodox editing decision, I have omitted an index and bibliography. Fifty-five chapters track the text of the Declaration of Independence, meaning the book itself serves as a rather complete index of the Declaration. The notes amply support the material and direct the reader to the supporting sources for each phrase of the Declaration, constituting a bibliography for each chapter. For the most part, specific notes are reserved for direct quotations, and many chapters include a "catchall" note that supplies additional sources. To include a standard index and bibliography would not only be highly redundant but would rival the length of the text. An index listing just Thomas Jefferson alone would run scores of pages. In light of these choices, full citations (including some very lengthy titles) are used throughout the notes. Citations to historical dictionaries are mostly omitted as they are easily identified in the text and, as a matter of practicality, such sources uniformly omit page numbers, rendering more specific citations all but impossible.

Enjoy our adventure through the grandest document rendered by the hands of man.

*The independence of America, considered merely as a separation from England, would have been a matter of but little importance, had it not been accompanied by a revolution in the principles and practices of governments. She made a stand, not for herself only, but for the world, and looked beyond the advantages herself could receive.**

Thomas Paine (1792)

# INTRODUCTION

***Why care about the Declaration of Independence?***

- ☆ America is an idea more than a place or a people. That idea is best expressed in the Declaration of Independence.
- ☆ The belief in the First Principles of a free and just government articulated in the Declaration is what unites our country. It forges our common bonds.
- ☆ Because we are forgetting—and many disdain—our First Principles and history, our country is at grave risk of cultural and political suicide.
- ☆ By fully understanding the Declaration, we can renew the spirit of America and preserve our freedoms and liberties.

We could rattle off deeply depressing statistics about our citizens' ignorance of American history and civics or rail about the pathetic way much of American education belittles the American Revolution, simply to a war about tea taxes. We could complain about the fashionable trend of condemning our Founding Generation as worthless, mean-spirited, oppressive hypocrites, deserving to be remembered only for their flaws or to be canceled altogether from our collective memory. This book takes a different path.

Why learning about why the Declaration of Independence is important is unrelated to statistics, studies, and educational fads. Rather, it goes to the heart of the human condition. Although arising in a unique historical context, the Declaration expresses universal First Principles that shatter an old world built on inequality, oppression, and arbitrary rule. The Declaration's First Principles of the rule of law, equality, unalienable rights, limited government, the Social Compact, and revolution (the right to alter or abolish oppressive government) turn the world upside down. At a pivotal time in human affairs, men and women who believe in those First Principles are willing to risk everything to fight for them. They break the shackles of tyranny and declare to the entire globe why it must be so. Those principles fundamentally change the world.

If you want to be a better person, live a better life, and be a constructive, positive influence in the world, the Declaration is among the best sources to follow. It is a guidebook of values. For those of us living in the United States of America, it is the foundation of our freedom, liberty, and equality. For those of us living elsewhere, it should be.

John Adams asked,

> What do we mean by the revolution? The war? That was no part of the revolution. It was only an effect and consequence of it. The Revolution was in the minds of the people, and this was effected, from 1760 to 1775, in the course of fifteen years before a drop of blood was drawn at Lexington.*

As Adams so eloquently explains, the American Revolution is not one of blood and tears—it is of the mind and soul. The American People take seriously the First Principles as articulated in the Declaration of Independence. When the American colonists understand that Great Britain is inexorably attempting to crush their unalienable rights, the colonists pledge their lives, fortunes, and sacred honor to defend these rights. The American Revolution is born. As Patrick Henry so immortally puts it, "Give me liberty or give me death!" This is no trite expression. They mean it. Many die; great fortunes are ruined. And sacred honor is maintained.

Like no other document, the Declaration expresses the true essence of our peculiar American Revolution. Despite this, the Declaration is barely understood in its birthplace. It is occasionally referenced or summoned, and most people recognize a phrase or two, but to understand it—to really understand it—is all but lost. Many recent books spend hundreds of pages discussing how it is drafted, but hardly a page on what it means. Books deeply dive into the events and key historical figures of the American Revolution but ignore *why* we declare independence.

The Declaration brilliantly lays out for all to read the underlying First Principles that the Founding Fathers and Mothers embrace, the historical circumstances that compel the Founders to revolt from the British Empire, and the ideological justification for the legitimate independence of America. More plainly, the Declaration announces to the world that the American People have a duty to revolt and fight for their God-given rights against a tyrannical king and parliament.

This is not myth or idle chatter. This is not some hindsight justification for white male slaveholders to protect their slaves and property. Such slanders and slurs are often politically motivated distortions of history. This work is intended to remind us why America is the greatest nation in world history—even when we take a blunt accounting of our troubling and sometimes grotesque past.

Many Americans have a vague idea about how the Declaration came to be. That most Americans have ever read the entire text of the Declaration is highly doubtful. At best, few people have a deep understanding of its full philosophical underpinnings. Almost none really know or understand the twenty-eight enumerated grievances warranting revolution. This is hardly a surprise considering how our schools treat the document. As but one stark example, a leading review book for the Advanced Placement examination for the US Government and Politics course dedicates a single three-sentence paragraph to the Declaration.* By my account, this book you hold is the first major work in over a century to analyze the text of the Declaration line by line, phrase by phrase, and often word by word. Even the older works are often superficial, shallow, and inaccurate. For all their faults (and they have many), the Founders gifted us all a guide for preserving our liberties and equality, and it is right here for all to see in the Declaration. Despite its shortcomings, this work intends to remedy this dire situation.

Some might say, what about the Constitution? The Constitution is a specific framework—a formal and delineated governmental structure—embodying the First Principles articulated in the Declaration. As we will explore in text boxes throughout this work, the Declaration is extraordinarily important to the development of the Constitution. This is especially true—and forgotten—in connection with the Declaration's twenty-eight grievances. Yet the Constitution could be altered in many ways without affecting the First Principles and the foundation of our liberties and equality. There could be one senator or five from each state, and their terms could be one or eight years. The minimum age of the president could be eliminated, or the president could be replaced with an executive council. The president could be elected by a direct popular vote. Supreme Court justices could be selected by the House of Representatives for ten-year terms. Increases in taxes could require the approval of three-fifths of Congress, and Washington, D.C., could be granted statehood. None of these changes would do serious injury to the underlying foundation of our freedoms or equality. After all, there are twenty-seven constiutional amendments, and we remain a free people. In fact, those amendments collectively make us a more equal, free, and just society. But to disregard the First Principles of the Declaration is fatal. This work illuminates how.

Broadly speaking, the Declaration includes several parts:

First, an introduction—an eloquent explanation from the Second Continental Congress why it is issuing the Declaration. The first paragraph is a magnificent, poetic passage setting the stage for the entire document.

Second, a proclamation of the founding First Principles of a free and just government, including the rule of law, unalienable rights, limited government, the Social Compact, equality, and revolution. The second paragraph's elucidation of our First Principles forever changes the hopes and aspirations of all humankind.

Third, a list of injuries and usurpations, often referred to as *grievances*, against the British Empire for violating those founding First Principles in the American colonies. These are critical to understanding why the Revolution is justified.

Fourth, a proclamation that the former British colonies in North America are becoming free and independent States. These last two paragraphs of the document also wax poetic and evoke serious emotion. Just before them are several short transitional paragraphs explaining how the Founders' appeals to the people of Britain to assist the colonies go unheeded. These last paragraphs form the closing argument about why independence is necessary and how the new nation will proceed in war and peace.

Fifth and finally, a concluding mutual pledge of the signers of their lives, fortunes, and sacred honor to support the Declaration. They fulfill this pledge, often to their grave injury.

Nearly all modern scholarship ignores the bulk of the Declaration. For example, the twenty-eight grievances that made it a duty for Americans to engage in the Revolution are often overlooked. Many think reviewing these grievances is boring, tedious, and irrelevant to modern society. Not so, for without the grievances, the rest of the Declaration is just a beautiful, empty shell of wonderful poetry. The Declaration comes alive in the grievances. Americans are rebelling against a bloody tyranny, and the grievances explain why. Furthermore, many of the issues that confront the Founders in the grievances in 1776 echo through the ages, to even today. We are fools to ignore the lessons of history.

If you are to become the best person you can be, the Declaration is a spectacular guide for you to better understand your place in this universe and to improve yourself and others. If we are to become the best people we can be, the Declaration is a wondrous, vital pathway. If we are to preserve our republic, it is the only way.

Book One of this work is the full text of the Declaration. Usually, the text of the Declaration is stuck at the back of a book as an appendix or omitted altogether. Not here. The text comes first. Book Two is a line by line (often word-by-word) explanation of the Declaration. This comprehensive review is the heart of this work. The Epilogue presents two major recommendations about what to do with the knowledge you have gained. When you finish the book, you will know the true story of the American Revolution; why, in Abraham Lincoln's words, America is "the last best hope of earth"; and how you can help save America.

# BOOK ONE

# *The Text of the Declaration*

**In Congress, July 4, 1776**
**The unanimous Declaration of the thirteen united States of America,**

When in the Course of human events, it becomes necessary for one people to dissolve the political bands which have connected them with another, and to assume among the powers of the earth, the separate and equal station to which the Laws of Nature and of Nature's God entitle them, a decent respect to the opinions of mankind requires that they should declare the causes which impel them to the separation.

We hold these truths to be self-evident, that all men are created equal, that they are endowed by their Creator with certain unalienable Rights, that among these are Life, Liberty and the pursuit of Happiness.—That to secure these rights, Governments are instituted among Men, deriving their just powers from the consent of the governed, —That whenever any Form of Government becomes destructive of these ends, it is the Right of the People to alter or to abolish it, and to institute new Government, laying its foundation on such principles and organizing its powers in such form, as to them shall seem most likely to effect their Safety and Happiness. Prudence, indeed, will dictate that Governments long established should not be changed for light and transient causes; and accordingly all experience hath shewn, that mankind are more disposed to suffer, while evils are sufferable, than to right themselves by abolishing the forms to which they are accustomed. But when a long train of abuses and usurpations, pursuing invariably the same Object evinces a design to reduce them under absolute Despotism, it is their right, it is their duty, to throw off such Government, and to provide new Guards for their future security.—Such has been the patient sufferance of these Colonies; and such is now the necessity which constrains them to alter their former Systems of Government. The history of the present King of Great Britain is a history of repeated injuries and usurpations, all having in direct object the establishment of an absolute Tyranny over these States. To prove this, let Facts be submitted to a candid world.

> He has refused his Assent to Laws, the most wholesome and necessary for the public good.
>
> He has forbidden his Governors to pass Laws of immediate and pressing importance, unless suspended in their operation till his Assent should be obtained; and when so suspended, he has utterly neglected to attend to them.
>
> He has refused to pass other Laws for the accommodation of

large districts of people, unless those people would relinquish the right of Representation in the Legislature, a right inestimable to them and formidable to tyrants only.

He has called together legislative bodies at places unusual, uncomfortable, and distant from the depository of their public Records, for the sole purpose of fatiguing them into compliance with his measures.

He has dissolved Representative Houses repeatedly, for opposing with manly firmness his invasions on the rights of the people.

He has refused for a long time, after such dissolutions, to cause others to be elected; whereby the Legislative powers, incapable of Annihilation, have returned to the People at large for their exercise; the State remaining in the mean time exposed to all the dangers of invasion from without, and convulsions within.

He has endeavoured to prevent the population of these States; for that purpose obstructing the Laws for Naturalization of Foreigners; refusing to pass others to encourage their migrations hither, and raising the conditions of new Appropriations of Lands.

He has obstructed the Administration of Justice, by refusing his Assent to Laws for establishing Judiciary powers.

He has made Judges dependent on his Will alone, for the tenure of their offices, and the amount and payment of their salaries.

He has erected a multitude of New Offices, and sent hither swarms of Officers to harrass our people, and eat out their substance.

He has kept among us, in times of peace, Standing Armies without the Consent of our legislatures.

He has affected to render the Military independent of and superior to the Civil power.

He has combined with others to subject us to a jurisdiction foreign to our constitution, and unacknowledged by our laws; giving his Assent to their Acts of pretended Legislation:

For Quartering large bodies of armed troops among us:

For protecting them, by a mock Trial, from punishment for any Murders which they should commit on the Inhabitants of these States:

For cutting off our Trade with all parts of the world:

For imposing Taxes on us without our Consent:

For depriving us in many cases, of the benefits of Trial by Jury:

For transporting us beyond Seas to be tried for pretended offences:

For abolishing the free System of English Laws in a neighbouring Province, establishing therein an Arbitrary government, and enlarging its Boundaries so as to render it at once an example and fit instrument for introducing the same absolute rule into these Colonies:

For taking away our Charters, abolishing our most valuable Laws, and altering fundamentally the Forms of our Governments:

For suspending our own Legislatures, and declaring themselves invested with power to legislate for us in all cases whatsoever.

He has abdicated Government here, by declaring us out of his Protection and waging War against us.

He has plundered our seas, ravaged our Coasts, burnt our towns, and destroyed the lives of our people.

He is at this time transporting large Armies of foreign Mercenaries to compleat the works of death, desolation and tyranny, already begun with circumstances of Cruelty & perfidy scarcely paralleled in the most barbarous ages, and totally unworthy the Head of a civilized nation.

He has constrained our fellow Citizens taken Captive on the high Seas to bear Arms against their Country, to become the executioners of their friends and Brethren, or to fall themselves by their Hands.

He has excited domestic insurrections amongst us, and has endeavoured to bring on the inhabitants of our frontiers, the merciless Indian Savages, whose known rule of warfare, is an undistinguished destruction of all ages, sexes and conditions.

In every stage of these Oppressions We have Petitioned for Redress in the most humble terms: Our repeated Petitions have been answered only by repeated injury. A Prince, whose character is thus marked by every act which may define a Tyrant, is unfit to be the ruler of a free people.

Nor have We been wanting in attentions to our Brittish brethren. We have warned them from time to time of attempts by their legislature to extend an unwarrantable jurisdiction over us. We have reminded them of the circumstances of our emigration and settlement here. We have appealed to their native justice and magnanimity, and we have conjured them by the ties of our common kindred to disavow these usurpations, which, would inevitably interrupt our connections and correspondence. They too have been deaf to the voice of justice and of consanguinity. We must, therefore, acquiesce in the necessity, which denounces our Separation, and hold them, as we hold the rest of mankind, Enemies in War, in Peace Friends.

We, therefore, the Representatives of the united States of America, in General Congress, Assembled, appealing to the Supreme Judge of the world for the rectitude of our intentions, do, in the Name, and by Authority of the good People of these Colonies, solemnly publish and declare, That these United Colonies are, and of Right ought to be Free and Independent States; that they are Absolved from all Allegiance to the British Crown, and that all political connection between them and the State of Great Britain, is and ought to be totally dissolved; and that as Free and Independent States, they have full Power to levy War, conclude Peace, contract Alliances, establish Commerce, and to do all other Acts and Things which

Independent States may of right do. And for the support of this Declaration, with a firm reliance on the protection of divine Providence, we mutually pledge to each other our Lives, our Fortunes and our sacred Honor.

**Georgia**
Button Gwinnett
Lyman Hall
George Walton

**North Carolina**
William Hooper
Joseph Hewes
John Penn

**South Carolina**
Edward Rutledge
Thomas Heyward, Jr.
Thomas Lynch, Jr.
Arthur Middleton

**Massachusetts**
John Hancock

**Maryland**
Samuel Chase
William Paca
Thomas Stone
Charles Carroll of Carrollton

**Virginia**
George Wythe
Richard Henry Lee
Thomas Jefferson
Benjamin Harrison
Thomas Nelson, Jr.
Francis Lightfoot Lee
Carter Braxton

**Pennsylvania**
Robert Morris
Benjamin Rush
Benjamin Franklin
John Morton
George Clymer
James Smith
George Taylor
James Wilson
George Ross

**Delaware**
Caesar Rodney
George Read
Thomas McKean

**New York**
William Floyd
Philip Livingston
Francis Lewis
Lewis Morris

**New Jersey**
Richard Stockton
John Witherspoon
Francis Hopkinson
John Hart
Abraham Clark

**New Hampshire**
Josiah Bartlett
William Whipple

**Massachusetts**
Samuel Adams
John Adams
Robert Treat Paine
Elbridge Gerry

**Rhode Island**
Stephen Hopkins
William Ellery

**Connecticut**
Roger Sherman
Samuel Huntington
William Williams
Oliver Wolcott

**New Hampshire**
Matthew Thornton

*I have often inquired of myself, what great principle or idea it was that kept this Confederacy so long together. It was not the mere matter of separation of the colonies from the mother land; but something in that Declaration* [of Independence] *giving liberty, not alone to the people of this country, but hope to the world for all future time. (Great applause.) It was that which gave promise that in due time the weights would be lifted from the shoulders of all men, and that all should have an equal chance. (Cheers.) This is the sentiment embodied in the Declaration of Independence.*

*Now, my friends, can this country be saved upon that basis? If it can, I will consider myself one of the happiest men in the world if I can help to save it. If it can't be saved upon that principle, it would be truly awful. But, if this country cannot be saved without giving up that principle* [...] *I would rather be assassinated on this spot than surrender it. (Applause.)**

Abraham Lincoln (February 22, 1861)

# BOOK TWO

# *Reading & Understanding the Declaration*

Resolved, *as the Opinion of this Congress, that it will be necessary, that another Congress should be held on the tenth day of May next, unless the redress of grievances, which we have desired, be obtained before that time. And we recommend, that the same be held at the city of Philadelphia, and that all the colonies, in North-America, choose deputies, as soon as possible, to attend such Congress.**

First Continental Congress (October 22, 1774)

# 1

# "In Congress,"

***What is the Continental Congress, and what does it do before the Declaration of Independence?***

- ☆ In 1774, responding to British tyranny, twelve American colonies convene the First Continental Congress to unify their resistance. Congress declares the First Principles of a free and just government, lists a set of grievances outlining British oppression in violation of those First Principles, and adopts a plan of action. Congress also resolves to reconvene in 1776 if British oppression continues.

- ☆ When English oppression continues, all thirteen of the colonies reconvene a Second Continental Congress to lead a more determined and stronger opposition to the empire, climaxing in the Declaration of Independence.

To begin our enterprise, we must understand who drafts and adopts the Declaration. Thankfully, the very first phrase explains that the Declaration is issued "in Congress." But what *is* this "Congress"? Simply put, it is nothing short of a revolutionary government established by the colonies to fend off British tyranny.

To gain true insight into this Congress, we must look back well before independence. As England settles the colonies, they are ruled by the British government based in England. The legislative body is Parliament, which sits in London (to the current day). The hereditary House of Lords and the elected House of Commons comprise Parliament. But the colonists are unrepresented. In fact, not a single person from the colonies will ever serve in Parliament.

The executive branch is commanded by a hereditary king ruling over a global empire, including the thirteen North American colonies on the East Coast. Although London is the ultimate authority, the colonies have legislative assemblies elected by colonists, with governors typically appointed by the Crown. Through a century-long unofficial policy, often dubbed "salutary neglect," the colonies are largely left alone to govern their internal affairs—with the very important exception of trade policy. Salutary neglect is a great boon for the Americans.

This baseline entirely shifts with the French and Indian War (also known as the Seven Years' War). That epic war is a struggle of global proportions, a momentous clash between the British and French Empires. It begins when Virginia Major George Washington sparks a powder keg in the American wilderness that erupts into a worldwide conflagration. To cut very short a complicated and lengthy tale, Great Britain prevails, and France cedes nearly all of its vast North American colonial claims to the British Empire.

Although Great Britain wins, the cost of victory is an enormous governmental debt—double what existed before the war. The interest on the debt alone consumes approximately half of Great Britain's annual revenue. Plus, to securely maintain its new territories, the British resolve to station ten thousand troops in America, requiring an additional, enormous sum of money every year for the foreseeable future.

To help pay for the war debt and new troops, the British government fixes its eyes on the American colonies. Moreover, British ministry officials are concerned that the colonies are drifting away from England toward inevitable independence. The taxes and assertion of control over the colonies serve the dual purposes of raising desperately needed revenue and ensuring a tighter grip on the colonists.

Beginning in 1764, the British Empire begins methodically to enact laws and policies to extract funds from the American colonists while also imposing greater governance over the colonies. The empire repeatedly and relentlessly violates the unalienable rights of the colonists—rights which the colonists passionately believe they possess as Englishmen. These series of oppressive actions, famously referred to in the Declaration as a "long train of abuses and usurpations," will be reviewed in great detail in this work. Each of these twenty-eight grievances is an egregious violation of the unalienable rights of the colonists.

The colonists will have none of it. They vigorously resist, resulting in a dramatic tug-of-war between the seat of the empire and the colonies. One of the most dramatic and famous acts of colonial resistance is the Boston Tea Party (to be explored in detail later in this work), and it provokes Great Britain to enact a cluster of the most repressive measures up to that time—the Boston Port Act, Massachusetts Government Act, Administration of Justice Act, and Quartering Act, collectively labeled the Intolerable Acts in the colonies and the Coercive Acts in England.

On June 17, 1774, to counter the Intolerable Acts and unite the colonies in a single plan of resistance, Samuel Adams steps onto the world stage. He is a distant cousin to his now-more-famous relative, John Adams. He proposes in the Massachusetts House of Representatives a resolution that the representatives of several colonies meet in Philadelphia on September 1, 1774, to determine how to protect their rights and liberties. The Massachusetts House of Representatives adopts the resolution, and soon nearly all the other colonial legislatures concur. Representatives of twelve of the thirteen colonies meet from September 5 to October 26, 1774, at Carpenters' Hall in Philadelphia, Pennsylvania. The First Continental Congress is born.

Although there are fifty-six delegates (with varying numbers from the dozen colonies represented), each colony receives only a single vote. After a great debate, on October 14, 1774, the First Continental Congress approves and issues its Declaration and Resolves that (1) declares the First Principles of a free and just government, (2) lists a set of grievances outlining British oppression in violation of those First Principles, and (3) adopts a plan of action that (a) the colonies not import, consume, or export British goods and (b) Congress send addresses (that is, formal written pleas) to the people of Great Britain, the colonists, and the king, explaining the colonists' position. They also resolve to reconvene in May of the following year if their efforts fail. Congress voluntarily disbands on October 26, 1774—hoping that its measures would be enough to save their liberties and negate the need to meet again.

Alas, the First Continental Congress's hopes are dashed. Since Great Britain continues its oppressive actions, the Second Continental Congress meets on May 10, 1775, at Carpenters' Hall in Philadelphia. This time Georgia joins Congress—all thirteen British colonies are now present. Much has changed since the end of the First Continental Congress. The British double down on their oppression of the colonists: They occupy Boston, and colonial blood is spilled at the Battles of Lexington and Concord less than a month before on April 19, 1775. Patriotic colonists from across the colonies resist by placing Boston under siege.

The Second Continental Congress is the tip of the spear for the united resistance for colonists' rights. Congress, in essence, starts to act as the unitary, national government for the United Colonies. The Second Continental Congress is "Congress" in the first line of the Declaration. Congress is composed of representatives of the thirteen English colonies on the eastern seaboard of North America: New Hampshire, Massachusetts, Connecticut, Rhode Island, New York, New Jersey, Pennsylvania, Delaware, Maryland, Virginia, North Carolina, South Carolina, and Georgia. They are just discerning how to lead the Revolution, and as a representative body, they meet *in* a congress. Today, we do not usually refer to decisions being made "in" Congress but "by" Congress. That is because today, under the federal Constitution, Congress is the official representative legislature vested with very specific powers. In 1776, Congress is solely a gathering of thirteen independent nations, and so they meet *in* Congress. This is more than mere semantics, but a fundamental premise of the governing reality on July 4, 1776.*

*Every spot of the old world is overrun with oppression. Freedom has been hunted round the globe. Asia, and Africa, have long expelled her.—Europe regards her like a stranger, and England has given her warning to depart. O! receive the fugitive, and prepare in time an asylum for mankind.* [...]

*We have the opportunity and every encouragement before us, to form the noblest purest constitution on the face of the earth. We have it in our power to begin the world over again. A situation, similar to the present, has not happened since the days of Noah until now.**

Thomas Paine (1776)

# 2

# "July 4, 1776"

***What happens near and on our nation's birthday of July 4, 1776?***

- ☆ Although the first shots of the American Revolution are fired on April 19, 1775, the Second Continental Congress does not adopt a resolution of independence until July 2, 1776.

- ☆ To justify this resolution of independence, a "Committee of Five" is formed to draft the Declaration. Thomas Jefferson is the primary draftsman and John Adams its primary advocate on the floor of the Second Continental Congress.

- ☆ The Declaration of Independence is adopted by the Second Continental Congress on July 4, 1776.

With the outbreak of fighting in the colonies against British oppression, the empire closes down and dissolves various colonial legislative bodies, including the Virginia House of Burgesses. In response, the leading political leaders of Virginia create the Virginia Convention. In essence, the Virginia Convention is a revolutionary government replacing the House of Burgesses. On May 15, 1776, the Virginia Convention passes a resolution instructing Virginia's delegates in the Second Continental Congress to propose to Congress that it should declare the United Colonies free and independent States, absolved from all allegiance to, or dependence upon, the Crown or Parliament of Great Britain.*

On June 7, 1776, in accordance with Virginia's instructions and egged on by Massachusetts delegate John Adams, Virginia delegate Richard Henry Lee moves that the Second Continental Congress adopts the following resolutions of independence:

> Resolved, that these United Colonies are, and of right ought to be, free and independent states, that they are absolved from all

> allegiance to the British Crown, and that all political connection between them and the state of Great Britain is, and ought to be, totally dissolved.
>
> That it is expedient forthwith to take the most effectual measures for forming foreign alliances.
>
> That a plan of confederation be prepared and transmitted to the respective colonies for their consideration and approbation.*

John Adams seconds the motion to adopt the resolutions of independence. However, the delegates strongly believe the resolutions must be unanimous, and New York, New Jersey, Pennsylvania, Delaware, Maryland, and South Carolina require additional time to consider them. Most everyone in Congress understands that these colonies will approve Richard Henry Lee's motion after a short postponement to allow proper consultation with their respective political leaders. Confidently, on June 10, Congress postpones consideration of the resolutions until July 1. In conjunction with this postponement, Congress also appoints a committee to create a declaration to explain the reasons for independence.

On June 11, 1776, the day after determining that a committee should be formed to draft a declaration justifying independence, Congress appoints five men to serve on the committee: Robert Livingston of New York, Roger Sherman of Connecticut, Benjamin Franklin of Pennsylvania, John Adams of Massachusetts, and Thomas Jefferson of Virginia.

By far the most famous member of the committee, and a worldwide celebrity, is Benjamin Franklin. He is undoubtedly the most notable and famous American in the world. Self-educated from humble beginnings, he ascends to the top of society through force of will, discipline, ingenuity, and hard work. He is a printer, inventor, author, cultural icon, political critic, diplomat, and statesman. Franklin is wildly famous for drawing lightning from the sky, publishing *Poor Richard's Almanack*, establishing a library, creating a fire company, organizing the militia in Quaker (pacifist)-dominated Pennsylvania, establishing an academic society, serving as postmaster general of the colonies and under the Continental Congress, being the first to chart the Gulf Stream, and inventing the Franklin stove, bifocal glasses, and the glass harmonica. He establishes schools for poor African American children in several cities. Franklin will help negotiate the peace with Great Britain.

Roger Sherman is a former judge and extremely active member of Congress who serves on several key committees. He is the only person who signs the Continental Association, the Declaration of Independence, the Articles of Confederation, and the Constitution. He helps negotiate the "Grand Compromise" at the Constitutional Convention, establishing a bicameral Congress with the House of Representatives representing States by population and the Senate representing each State with an equal number of senators.

Robert Livingston actively opposes British oppression as early as the Stamp Act (1765), is likely a New York member of the Sons of Liberty, and is a leading political leader in New York. In 1777, he becomes chancellor of New York, the highest judicial office in the State, and serves in that capacity for nearly twenty-four years. Among other notable accomplishments, he serves as the first secretary of foreign affairs under the Articles of Confederation, as well as minister to France.

John Adams is a farmer and exemplary lawyer by trade. He eminently and successfully defends the British soldiers who commit the Boston Massacre. Ironically, he is a leading Patriot in Boston—the epicenter of colonial resistance to British oppression. He is also the driving force behind the adoption of the resolution of approving independence. Adams later serves as commissioner to France, envoy to the Dutch Republic, and America's first minister to Great Britain after independence. He helps negotiate the Treaty of Paris with Great Britain (ending the American Revolution), authors a groundbreaking and highly influential political treatise entitled *Thoughts on Government* that helps guide the Constitutional Convention, serves as the first vice president of the United States under George Washington, and succeeds Washington as the second president.

Thomas Jefferson chairs the committee because he receives the most votes. A wealthy aristocratic member of the planter class in Virginia, he is only thirty-three years old and quickly catches the attention of Adams and the Continental Congress when, in 1774, he writes a searing indictment of British oppression. Entitled *A Summary View of the Rights of British America*, the pamphlet eloquently attacks the British for attempting to quash freedom in America. He serves as governor of Virginia, minister to France, secretary of State, vice president under Adams, and president after defeating Adams. Among other things, he is the driving force behind one of America's first political parties, world-class author, founder of the University of Virginia, fabulous inventor, and wonderful architect.

The first draft of the Declaration falls to Jefferson. Franklin and Adams are also brilliant thinkers and writers, but Franklin is elderly and not up to the rigors of the assignment. Most pressing, he is suffering a fit of gout that cripples him during the key days of drafting the Declaration. Because he is such an outspoken proponent of independence, Congress likely expects Adams primarily to draft the Declaration. In fact, according to Adams, the five-member committee appoints both Jefferson and Adams to a subcommittee to create a first draft. However, Adams recognizes Jefferson's eloquence. Adams later writes that he and Jefferson discuss the matter and that Adams pointedly tells Jefferson to write it. Jefferson responds by asserting that Adams should do so. Adams relates that the committee:

> appointed Mr. Jefferson and me, to draw them [in other words, the Declaration] up in form, and cloth them in proper dress. The Sub Committee met, and considered the minutes, making such observations on them as then occurred: when Mr. Jefferson desired me to take them to my lodgings and make the draft. This I declined and gave several reasons for declining. 1. That he was a Virginian and I a Massachusettsian. 2. That he was a southern man and I a northern one. 3. That I had been so obnoxious for my early and constant zeal in promoting the measure, that any draft of mine, would undergo a more severe scrutiny and criticism in Congress, than one of his composition. 4thly and lastly would be reason enough if there no other, I had a great opinion of the elegance of his pen and none at all of my own [...]. He accordingly took the minutes and in a day or so produced to me his draft.*

A slightly different but complementary version is conveyed by Adams in a subsequent letter in which he notes that Jefferson first tries to press Adams into writing the Declaration. Adams responds: "I will not. Why? Reasons enough." Jefferson replies, "What can be your reasons?" Adams answers: "Reason first. You are a Virginian, and Virginia ought to appear at the head of this business. Reason second. I am obnoxious, suspected, and unpopular; You are very much otherwise. Reason third: You can write ten times better than I can."*

On the other hand, Jefferson's recall substantially differs from Adams's. He disclaims the creation of a subcommittee and simply believes that the other four members "unanimously pressed on myself alone to undertake the draft."*

Regardless of the exact details, undoubtedly Adams is sincere. He desperately desires Virginia to be in the lead because it is the largest colony, it is geographically in the middle of the colonies, and those in Virginia are seen as less personally invested in the Revolution. Having Virginia in the lead ensures that independence will be motivated and perceived as justified by higher concerns for rights and principles rather than petty local concerns. Massachusetts is the center of Revolutionary agitation. The cause is best served if the American Revolution is led by others.

Either way, Jefferson relents. Not only is Jefferson the best writer in Congress, but he also already possesses two substantial working drafts. The first is his 1774 *A Summary View of the Rights of British America*, detailing a list of grievances against the king and Parliament. The second work is a much more recent creation—a draft constitution for Virginia, penned in June 1776. Literally crafted on the eve of the Declaration, Virginia incorporates much of Jefferson's work into its first State constitution on June 29, 1776. Jefferson's work explains that King George III has "endeavored to pervert" his kingship "into a detestable and insupportable tyranny" through twenty-two specific tyrannical actions.* *A Summary View of the Rights of British America* and the draft Virginia Constitution lay the foundation for the twenty-eight grievances detailed in the Declaration.

At first, Jefferson shares a draft of the Declaration with Franklin and Adams, who make a few suggestions that Jefferson readily adopts. The exact substance of these alterations is lost to history, but scholars agree that they are mostly stylistic. On June 28, the committee presents a final draft of the Declaration to Congress—just two days before the July 1 deadline earlier established for Congress to begin debating independence.

Later, Adams will note that Jefferson's draft "contained no new ideas, that it is a commonplace compilation, [its] sentiments hackneyed in Congress for two years before, and its essence contained in [James] Otis's pamphlet [*The Rights of the British Colonies Asserted and Proved* (1764)]."* Jefferson also noted that Richard Henry Lee "charged it as copied from [John] Locke's [Second] treatise on government."* When responding to Adams's comments, Jefferson simply remarks that "Otis' pamphlet I never saw, & whether I had gathered my ideas from reading or reflection I do not know. I know only that I turned to neither book [n]or pamphlet while writing it. I did not consider it as any part of my charge to invent new ideas altogether & to offer no sentiment which had ever been expressed before."* Whether Jefferson's profession is true is difficult to ascertain, especially since he recounted this understanding forty-seven years after the fact, when he was eighty years old.* However, considering that some of the language of the grievances is nearly identical to his prior draft of the Virginia Constitution, he likely at least borrowed heavily from that tract—perhaps from memory.

In any event, on Monday, July 1, 1776, Congress begins in earnest to consider Richard Henry Lee's resolution. Adams seconds the resolution. Lee is from Virginia, and his lead follows Adams's desire that Virginia takes the first position for independence. Adams is clearly the person most responsible for convincing Congress to adopt independence—including persuading and cajoling congressmen one-on-one, as well as giving a pro-Revolution speech for the ages during the debate. Adams's speech is so powerful that delegates jump to their feet, and the clerk drops his quill. Unfortunately, the speech is lost when the beguiled clerk stops taking notes. Adams is so indispensable that Jefferson dubs him the "Colossus" of independence.*

In addition to considering Lee's resolution for independence, on July 1, a raging debate ensues regarding the exact wording of the draft of the Declaration.

Congress painstakingly reviews Jefferson's draft, paragraph by paragraph, line by line, word by word. While Congress slices and dices substantial portions of the draft, Jefferson never says a word, although the critiques feel like dagger blows. He suffers in silence. On the other hand, Adams vociferously defends the initial draft with all his power. Jefferson later writes that Adams is "the pillar of its support on the floor of Congress; its ablest advocate and defender against the multifarious assaults it encountered."*

But Congress will have its way. It adopts many changes. Some are grammatical; some are for readability or precision. But they almost always improve the flow, tempo, vibrancy, and meaning of the draft.

Other changes are more fundamental. At least one of these is grave and unforgivable—deleting a passage condemning the king for perpetuating the slave trade. Ironically, the slaveholding Jefferson condemns himself alongside the slave traders. However, this passage provokes strong objections from Georgia and South Carolina as going too far, and the passage is struck.

On July 2, Congress concludes its debate on Richard Henry Lee's resolution for independence and unanimously approves it. At this instant, America legally and politically becomes independent of the British Empire. The shackles are shattered. Even if he is obnoxious and unpopular, Adams wins the day. The very next day, Adams writes to his wife Abigail that the anniversary of independence

> ought to be commemorated, as the day of deliverance by solemn acts of devotion to God Almighty. It ought to be solemnized with pomp and parade, with shows, games, sports, guns, bells, bonfires and illuminations from one end of the continent to the other, from this time forward, forever more.*

Adams's prediction comes to pass: Independence Day is still marked with parades, games, and fireworks. But he is wrong on two major points. First, the celebrations center not on July 2, but on July 4. That is because the Declaration, as opposed to the resolution of independence, is officially adopted and announced on July 4. And because the Declaration is such a magnificent document, it overshadows the functional and somewhat perfunctory resolution of July 2.

Second, July 4 is hardly solemn. It has long ago been drained of any true meaning. It is commercialized and hollowed out as a time for barbecues and appliance sales. (This overarching trend of gutting the true meaning of all of our civic holidays is why my daughter Leah pounded on the table as a ten-year-old and demanded a new celebration for America—hence the creation of "Patriot Week."*)

On July 4, the Declaration—as modified by Congress—is ratified. A final engrossed document—i.e., the final version, complete text written in flowing calligraphy on parchment, ready for signature—is drawn up and signed by many of the delegates on August 2. Just to be clear, there are at least four versions of the Declaration of Independence. The first rough draft is by Jefferson alone. A second draft, presented to Congress on June 28, includes the handful of changes suggested by Adams and Franklin. The third draft incorporates the modifications by Congress and is approved on July 4. As president of Congress, John Hancock signs it, along with the secretary of Congress, Charles Thomson. Congress orders that it be promptly printed. That night, a local Philadelphia printer—John Dunlap—creates two hundred copies for public distribution. This version is referred to as the Dunlap Broadside, as it is printed on large "broadside" sheets of paper, which are much longer and wider than what we are used to today. After New York finally approves independence on July 19, 1776, Congress resolves that the Declaration be "fairly engrossed on parchment with the title and style of 'The unanimous declaration of the thirteen united states of America' & that the same, when engrossed, be signed by every member of Congress."* Timothy Matlack, the clerk to the secretary of the Second Continental Congress, handwrites the Declaration. The fourth draft is the final, engrossed version. The Matlack-engrossed document is presented for the signatures of the delegates of the Second Continental Congress on August 2. Anyone in Congress is permitted to sign it, even if they did not vote for it or were not even in Congress on July 4, 1776. Ironically, Robert Livingston, a member of the drafting "Committee of Five," does not sign it because New York recalls him before the Matlack-engrossed version is available for signature. Instead, he continues his public service in New York. One congressman—John Alsop of New York—resigns from Congress rather than sign it. Secretary Thomson's signature is also omitted on the engrossed document.

Fifty-six congressmen eventually sign the Matlack-engrossed Declaration, with forty-nine delegates signing on August 2, 1776, and the other seven over the course of the next few months. The congressmen sign by State, right to left, in geographical order—the North signing first. Hence, the New Hampshire delegates sign first on the top far right and Georgia delegates sign on the far left. However, as president of Congress, John Hancock deliberately places his signature dead center on top of the other signatures, with by far the largest script.

The final, August 2, engrossed version cleans up capitalization, usage of commas, semi-colons, and colons, as well as spelling—some of which have long-lasting consequences. The main grammatical revision is the alteration of the word "inalienable" in Jefferson's version to "unalienable" in the engrossed version. This change is likely purposefully made at the direction of Adams, who is in charge of overseeing the production of the final, engrossed version. This fourth and final version is the commonly recognizable version, marked with the familiar calligraphic flowing script with John Hancock's and scores of other congressmen's handwritten signatures.

In sum, independence is technically established on July 2, 1776—that is, the date when the Second Continental Congress, meeting in Philadelphia, approves Richard Henry Lee's resolution severing all ties with the British Empire and creating a newly independent country. But we celebrate that independence on July 4 because it is on this date that Congress releases the Declaration. We revere the final August 2 text because it eloquently and powerfully explains why we chose to become a new nation completely unique in human history.*

*There must be no pulling different ways. We must all hang together.**

John Hancock (as he signs the engrossed copy of the Declaration on August 2, 1776).

*Yes, we must, indeed, all hang together, or most assuredly we shall all hang separately.**

Benjamin Franklin (immediately responding to Hancock)

# 3

# "The unanimous Declaration of the thirteen united States of America"

***What irrevocable step is taken by the colonies?***

☆ Collectively and independently, each colony agrees to declare independence, unequivocally tying their fates together.

Congress adopts the resolution of independence on July 2 and the Declaration of Independence on July 4. The next phrase of the Declaration adds that it is approved by the "thirteen united States of America." Although all thirteen colonies are represented in Congress, there is no unifying of the thirteen colonies into a new nation. In fact, each colony has been established in a separate fashion and has a unique pre-Revolutionary history. Until their resistance to the long train of abuses and usurpations, the colonies rarely cooperate with each other or coordinate policy.

Moreover, we cannot overlook the fact that on July 2, the colonies become free and independent "States." In essence, each colony becomes an independent nation. The resolution of independence on July 2 does not change the reality that the colonies—now States—are almost entirely independent of each other. Congress is a compact—a coalition—of thirteen independent States acting in concert to oppose British oppression.

The States are thirteen separate republics loosely banded together in Congress. There are no central executives or judicial branches. Congress can only act if all thirteen States agree. Even then, there is no central or national government to enforce the resolutions and acts of Congress.

This is exactly why the phrase "the thirteen united States of America" uses this terminology. Today we refer to the country as "*the* United States of America," not the "*fifty* United States of America," because under the current Constitution, we have a unifying, federal constitutional government—but that is not the case in July of 1776. Congress itself is insufficient to establish a new nation.

The sentence also refers to a "Declaration." This seems rather obvious but is noteworthy. Congress and States are not simply passing a garden-variety resolution or law; they are making a profound pronouncement—for our citizens, our British brethren, and the world.

Although the Declaration of Independence is entirely unique, this is not to say that there are no "declarations" before it in British history. King James I, Lord Protector Oliver Cromwell, the Quakers, William the Conqueror, and King James III all issued declarations on vital issues.

The most pertinent English declaration for our purposes is An Act Declaring the Rights and Liberties of the Subject and Settling the Succession of the Crown, colloquially referred to as the Bill of Rights 1689. Parliament enacts this groundbreaking document in the wake of the Glorious Revolution (to be more fully explored later). It begins with a condemnation of King James II, with a list of fifteen specific grievances, and guarantees the protection of the many rights of Englishmen.

In organizing resistance to British oppression, the colonists follow the technique of issuing a declaration. In particular, the Stamp Act Congress convenes in opposition to the dreaded Stamp Act and approves a Declaration of Rights and Grievances on October 19, 1765, condemning taxation without representation, the suppression of the right to a jury trial, and virtual representation (all topics to be explored in detail below). It also demands repeal of the Stamp Act.

Understanding its power, the Continental Congress issues two key declarations before 1776. On October 14, 1774, the Declaration and Resolves of the First Continental Congress denounces British oppression, which we explored above. On July 6, 1775, the Declaration of the Causes and Necessity of Taking Up Arms of the Second Continental Congress justifies and authorizes violent resistance to British oppression.

Although the declarations are not unique, never has a nation been birthed in such a dramatic fashion, accompanied by such eloquent words deeply rooted in the foundations of truth, freedom, and equality. Certainly, there have been civil wars, wars of conquests, and revolts, but never has such an effort been accompanied by a carefully drafted, considered, debated, and approved declaration with a majesty that rings through the ages—inspiring men and women of each succeeding generation to this very day.

The last word of this phrase to explore is "Unanimous." Of course, that means all the States agree on the Declaration. The vote occurs on July 4, and all the States agree, right? Actually, on July 4, only twelve of the thirteen States approve the Declaration. Although the other colonies all provide their congressional delegates authority to approve independence, the New York delegates do not yet have that approval. Yet, the New York delegation does not oppose independence—New York merely abstains—and the appearance that the Declaration is unanimous is maintained.

On July 9, New York approves the Declaration, and that approval is received by Congress on July 15. On July 19, Congress resolves that the engrossed, final version of the Declaration be produced, and that delegates sign that engrossed copy. Since New York now approves the Declaration, Congress revises the introduction. The original version simply provides:

> In Congress, July 4, 1776
> A Declaration by the Representatives of the United States of America, in General Congress Assembled.*

On July 19, Congress approves this wording:

> In Congress, July 4, 1776
> The unanimous Declaration of the thirteen united States of America,

The rephrasing, especially adding the word "unanimous," is subtle but very important. The world now knows that all thirteen States approve the Declaration. Independence is unanimous.

*Happily for America, happily we trust for the whole human race, they* [the Founding Fathers] *pursued a new and more noble course. They accomplished a revolution which has no parallel in the annals of human society. They reared the fabrics of governments which have no model on the face of the globe.**

James Madison (1788)

# 4

# "When in the Course of Human Events"

***Why do we seek a new and nobler path?***

- ☆ The Declaration is a key part of the march of progress for human equality and freedom.
- ☆ The Declaration is the profoundly considered action of a people controlling their own destiny to improve mankind.
- ☆ Although it is a product of a specific time and place, the Declaration is immensely relevant—even critical to our way of life—today.

The Declaration begins with the simple word "when." This word is easy to skip over. But let's not be so hasty. Why is this seemingly comprehensible and trivial word important to explore? To understand the Declaration, we must understand the specific time that it occurs. The Declaration is deeply embedded in its time and place.

Yet the Declaration is also relevant today. It is tremendously important—perhaps the most important document in American history. It defines the nation then and now. We use it to measure our successes and failures. It inspires generations of men and women across the globe. Indeed, putting aside religious texts, it may very well be the most important text in history. This is so because it is truly revolutionary. It does not merely justify the war of independence; it justifies a revolutionary society. Proving this point is the primary purpose of this work. And to truly understand the Declaration, we need to understand the historical context from which it arises—which this work thoroughly explores.

The first sentence of the Declaration continues, "in the course of human events." This clause also seems simple but is actually complex and vitally important. It reveals the underlying understanding of the Founding Fathers of time and history. For much of ancient history, and for some religions even today, the concept of time is cyclical. Some refer to time as a wheel. We have seasons. Without fail, the seasons repeat annually. Crops are planted at a certain time; they are harvested at another. The next year, the cycle repeats. Generalizing that rhythm to higher realms makes it a universal trait of time. Events repeat on a cosmic scale. Humankind is born, matures, and dies—and this pattern repeats over and over.

However, the Founding Fathers and Mothers reject the cyclical view of time. Jefferson literally and figuratively refers to this idea in his phrase, "When in the course of human events." Modern Western conceptions of time—that is, of European and Judeo-Christian origin—think of time as going only in one direction: forward. It is like a river, flowing in one direction.

The Founding Fathers and Mothers are mostly children and believers of the Enlightenment. They believe in progress—that with the application of reason and science, the human condition will inevitably improve over time. The idea that humankind can advance health, comfort, and knowledge with each passing year, and that living standards will steadily increase with each generation, is deeply embedded in this Enlightenment perspective.

The overarching story of the Talmud and Bible is how God's chosen people advance in the march of history toward salvation. Beginning with Genesis, the Bible reveals the linear progress of God's chosen people. Christianity carries this perspective forward in its scripture regarding the prophets, Jesus Christ, and Revelation. This idea of forward progress is deeply embedded in the Jewish and Christian faiths. Like a great river flowing in one direction, as mentioned earlier, there is a current of history that moves forward toward a better tomorrow.

Inherent in this view is the idea that the people have control over their destiny. The Founders believe that destiny is controlled by *human* events. Certainly, there are natural disasters and other catastrophes outside human control, but generally, we shape our own destiny. Human progress happens because men and women make it so. People investigate, explore, probe, sacrifice, and dedicate their energies, resources, and time to make the improvements we all enjoy. We are not automatons mindlessly wandering the world. We purposefully consider challenges and shortcomings in the world, which could become opportunities to improve life, and then dedicate ourselves to making it so. We control our own fates.

In 1776, the Founders understand that it is their time to make a stand for the world. As James Madison reflects, the Founders must pursue "a new and more noble course." The key question is the following: *Where is the course of human events taking us in 1776?* To revolution! And why is that? We must read on.

*If we wish to be free; if we mean to preserve inviolate those inestimable privileges for which we have been so long contending; if we mean not basely to abandon the noble struggle in which we have so long engaged* [...] *we must fight!**

Patrick Henry (March 23, 1775)

# 5

# "IT BECOMES NECESSARY"

***Why do we make the difficult and irrevocable choice to break away from the king?***

> ☆ The Declaration is not a matter of choice; the Founders understand that they must declare independence or that their freedom—and consequently our freedom—will be lost to tyrants forever.

"When, in the Course of human events, it becomes necessary": The Founders do not write when "convenient," "at our leisure," or "whenever we feel like it." They do not suggest that independence will simply be a "good idea" or the "most preferable option" of many choices. It is not only "justifiable" or "warranted." The Founders carefully select "necessary" because it conveys the immense gravity of the situation they confront. Declaring independence must be done. It is required. There is no choice. Unless they are to forfeit their freedoms, Americans cannot retreat or otherwise remedy the situation. But it is more than just that. Revolution is compelled by Nature and the Creator—it is fate and destiny.

A nearly forgotten key figure of Revolutionary America is the Presbyterian minister Reverend John Witherspoon, a Scottish immigrant to the colonies. In 1768, he becomes the president of the College of New Jersey (now known as Princeton). He serves as a delegate to the Constitutional Congress, signs the Declaration of Independence, serves in Congress, and attends the Constitutional Convention. A few months before he signs the Declaration, he delivers a fiery homily from the pulpit, thundering that resistance to the British is necessary to ensure justice and liberty. In fact, he persuasively proclaims that Americans have a *duty* to resist. It is not a matter of pride but of conviction (a subtlety too often lost in contemporary America). He readily acknowledges that this is his first political speech from the pulpit and explains that he must join the fray. Freedom, including religious liberty, will be lost if the colonists do not resist. "At this season," he preaches, revolution "is not only lawful, but necessary" because "the cause in which America is now in arms, is the cause of justice, liberty, and of human nature."* In full agreement with Witherspoon, the Second Continental Congress carefully chooses "necessary" as the most appropriate word. The universe itself is requiring the Founders to revolt.

As we will explore in this work, the Founders repeatedly seek reconciliation with the British Empire through many means to avoid revolution—speeches, petitions, government resolutions, boycotts, protests, destruction of tea and stamps, and even limited armed resistance. In the end, these all fail. The Revolution is not a matter of choice. It is unavoidable and demanded by freedom and creation. The Founders are fulfilling the demands of Natural Law and the Creator. It is a world-breaking notion that they take seriously—and so will the world.*

*Our forefathers, inhabitants of the island of Great-Britain, left their native land, to seek on these shores a residence of civil and religious freedom. At the expense of their blood, at the hazard of their fortunes, without the least charge to the country from which they removed, by unceasing labour, and an unconquerable spirit, they effected settlements in the distant and inhospitable wilds of America* [...]. *Societies or governments, vested with perfect legislatures, were formed under charters from the crown, and a harmonious intercourse was established between the colonies and the kingdom from which they derived their origin.**

Second Continental Congress (July 6, 1775)

# 6

## "FOR ONE PEOPLE"

***Who exactly are these "Americans"?***

- ☆ With nearly no assistance from Great Britain and through tremendous sacrifice, subjects of the British Empire forge the thirteen colonies out of the wilderness. In doing so, they develop into a new, unified people, separate from the remainder of the empire.
- ☆ This new *American People* is a melding together of immigrants and former slaves (and their descendants) from across Europe and Africa who are fiercely independent and jealously guard their unalienable rights.

Until the Revolution, the colonists are the subjects of the British Empire. Each of the thirteen separate colonies has its own origins, populations, traditions, customs, laws, militia, governors, legislators, and courts. In 1776, colonists include immigrants, indentured servants, convicts, freed slaves, and all their descendants. Others, like the Quakers and Puritans, flee England to escape religious persecution and establish a new "city on a hill"—as John Winthrop puts it—where they can freely worship. The colonies are a great mixing bowl of nationalities, cultures, religions, and classes. Sprinkled (or perhaps more accurately, clumped) throughout the colonies are colonists from areas such as England, Scotland, Ireland, the Netherlands, Sweden, France, Spain, Germany, and Africa. Some colonists, like the Irish, absolutely detest England. Not all the colonies are originally established by England. Nevertheless, by the time of the Revolution, the British govern and dominate all thirteen colonies.

Regardless of how they arrive in the colonies, all colonists are subjects of the British Empire. Despite their diverse origins, the colonists share a common bond of allegiance to the king and Parliament, and they possess all the rights, privileges, and immunities of Englishmen. For the most part, they share a general culture and worldview.

The idea that the colonists are a "people" separate from the British Empire would have been almost certainly rejected by most colonists before the conclusion of the French and Indian War (also known as the Seven Years' War) in 1763. However, after the peace of 1763, as the British become oppressive and colonists actively protect their rights, the idea that the colonists are "Americans" starts to germinate. But even when the fighting explodes in 1775, most colonists consider themselves to be British. They are fighting for the rights of Englishmen to which they are entitled—nothing more and nothing less. This struggle is an internal family squabble, an insurrection to protect their rights or even a civil war of resistance, but it is *not* (yet) a war of independence.

Others, however, are forming a radically different perspective. Thomas Jefferson is unable to attend the First Continental Congress, so he writes a pamphlet for the attending congressmen entitled *A Summary View of the Rights of British America*. In 1774, this remarkable work starts to establish the framework for definitively demonstrating that the colonists deserve to be an independent nation and are now a different people from the British by noting that "America was conquered, and her settlements made, and firmly established, at the expense of individuals, and not of the British public."*

Free from the bondage and oppression of Europe, Americans, through tremendous work and sacrifice, carve a new way in the wilderness. They flourish, enjoying religious, political, and economic liberties and rights far beyond the wildest dreams of the common person in Europe. This fundamentally transforms those who live in America. "What, then, is this American, this new man?" In compelling and prophetic language, J. Hector St. John de Crèvecœur, in his *Letters from an American Farmer*, answers his own question:

> *He* is American, who, leaving behind him all his ancient prejudices and manners, receives new ones from the new mode of life he has embraced, the new government he obeys, and the new rank he holds. [...] Here individuals of all nations are melted into a new race of men, whose labours and posterity will one day cause great changes in the world. [Italics are in the original.]*

(These sentiments ignore the dark, unfathomable torture of the enslaved who are not treated as citizens at all and have none of the opportunities to which he speaks. This is addressed later in this work.)

Let's dwell on what transfiguration the free colonists have undergone. In some way, they purposefully choose to come to America. The trip is dangerous; many die. The survivors struggle under extraordinarily challenging circumstances. This struggle builds up their character and fortitude. They are not servile or weak like those left behind in Europe, but strong, vibrant, robust, and filled with verve. They are independent, spirited beyond anything imaginable in Europe. They take the best England has to offer and leave behind the worst. They fervently hold to the belief in the rights of Englishmen. There is no nobility in America. Religious intolerance and class divisions are much less severe than in Europe. A difficult landscape, hard work, and liberty are the great levelers. Men and women from across the world are forged together in a new type of people who are fiercely independent in spirit, dynamically innovative, and vigorously protective of their unalienable rights. They are a new people. The *American* People.*

*Every thing that is right or natural pleads for separation. The blood of the slain, the weeping voice of nature cries, 'TIS TIME TO PART. Even the distance at which the Almighty has placed England and America, is a strong and natural proof, that the authority of the one, over the other, was never the design of heaven.**

Thomas Paine (February 14, 1776)

# 7

# "To dissolve the political bands which have connected them with another,"

***Why do the colonies permanently break the political connection with England?***

> ☆ England's tyrannical actions have simply gone too far. The colonists determine that the time has come to sever their political ties with the British Empire and their people—Americans must govern themselves.

The Declaration continues with this unusual phrase that the time has come to "dissolve the political bands" between Great Britain and the colonies. The Founders are not addressing cultural, economic, or military bands. As we will explore in this work, those are already dissolved. Therefore, on July 4, 1776, the issue at hand is *political* bands. Who will determine how governments are to be organized and administered? Who will choose and control public officials? Who will pass legislation, execute the laws, and ensure justice? Who governs? Who is sovereign? The political bands between the king, Parliament, and the British People on one side and Congress, colonial governments, and colonists on the other are at a snapping point.

A British immigrant who barely survives the voyage to Philadelphia and is scarcely in the country for a few months makes the closing argument about the need to permanently sever our political ties with the British Empire. On January 10, 1776, Thomas Paine anonymously publishes *Common Sense*. To call it an overnight sensation is a tremendous understatement. The pamphlet rivals the Bible for sales and readership throughout the colonies.

Paine argues, among many other brilliant observations, that independence from the British Empire is already a foregone conclusion—an inevitability. To have a small island thousands of miles away govern a vast continent populated by millions is absurd. Besides, too much divides the people and governments. Most importantly, the British are tyrants.

Paine explains that the time for any kind of peace has long since passed: "Reconciliation is *now* a fallacious dream. [...] For, as [John] Milton wisely expresses, 'never can true reconcilement grow where wounds of deadly hate have pierced so deep.'"* Paine illustrates the point in much more colorful language: "You that tell us of harmony and reconciliation, can you restore to us the time that is past? Can you give to prostitution its former innocence? Neither can you reconcile Britain and America."* Strong words!

Paine declares the obvious—the time for petitions and addresses is over. "Wherefore, since nothing but blows will do, for God's sake, let us come to a final separation, and not leave the next generation to be cutting throats, under the violated unmeaning names of parent and child."*

Before the Revolution, there is a Social Compact among the subjects of the British Empire—including the colonists. This idea of the Social Compact is critical to the American understanding of a free and just government. As will be explored in much more detail later in this work, the Social Compact involves the people joining together to create a government with the specific purpose of providing security and justice to the people. In a state of Nature without a government, all are at risk and vigilante justice reigns supreme. The whole purpose of the government is to stop this chaos and protect the unalienable rights of the people.

Yet, instead of protecting the unalienable rights of the people, the British are tyrannical. Through a long train of abuses and usurpations of the unalienable rights of the people as examined in the twenty-eight grievances in the Declaration, the British are attempting to destroy American liberties. Subverting the very purpose of government, the British forfeit their right to rule. Liberty can only be safe if the American People rule themselves. To defend our unalienable rights, the Declaration revokes that Social Compact between the American People and the rest of the empire. Americans must govern themselves. The political bands between the colonies and the British Empire are dissolved. America will be free.

*That these United Colonies are, and, of right ought to be, free and independent States; that they are absolved from all allegiance to the British crown, and all political connection between them, and the state of Great-Britain, is, and ought to be, totally dissolved.**

Second Continental Congress (July 2, 1776)

# 8

## "AND TO ASSUME AMONG THE POWERS OF THE EARTH, THE SEPARATE AND EQUAL STATION"

***What exactly does "independence" mean?***

☆ By declaring independence, the former colonies become free and independent States on the global stage, vested with all the authority and responsibility of sovereign nations.

On July 4, 1776, the States are independent from Great Britain and from each other. They act in concert through the Second Continental Congress, but that is voluntary. At any time, any new State can chart its own path in war, peace, trade, self-government, and countless other ways. This is hardly inevitable. Founding Father James Wilson lays out four distinct possibilities: (1) unifying as one country, (2) refusing to act together at all—in other words, complete independence, (3) forming two or more groupings or confederacies, and (4) uniting in one federal republic.*

Melding all the States into one "super state" nation is beyond nearly everyone's imagination then—and even today. Completely going on their own paths is just as unthinkable. Likewise, no one contemplates dividing the old thirteen colonies into two or more confederacies. The last thing the colonists need is rival factions between former allies. They also do not create a new federal republic, in which some of the key aspects of State sovereignty (such as national defense, foreign relations, and trade relations) are fully vested in a unified central government. A federal republic will be created, but not until the Constitution is ratified in 1788. In 1776, that prospect is well beyond the horizon. Instead, they remain together in the Second Continental Congress in which the States cooperate on major overarching policies, such as conducting the Revolutionary War and foreign relations. Indeed, Congress does not even have a binding governing document until the Articles of Confederation become effective on March 1, 1781.

Several other options unmentioned by Wilson are also rejected. Once the colonies dissolve their political bands from the British Empire, they do not join a competing empire such as France or Spain. The States do not divide into more States, and no States merge into others. The colonies do not collapse into anarchy or simply dissolve.

Instead, the colonies are now free and independent countries—in the words of the Declaration, they are "powers of the earth." They are not subjects of other powers, and they enjoy the authority of all other independent nations. The States are assuming "the separate and equal station" of independent nations. "Station" is derived from the Latin word for "stand."* The new American States stand in equal rank with the other previously established and recognized nations of the world. They are no longer colonies, subject to the dictates of a motherland across the Atlantic Ocean. They will not be puppets or subservient territories to any empire. They will not pay tribute or be the protectorate of another country. They stand independently and equally. Moreover, the new States *assume* this station. They are not creating a new station or advocating for its adoption. They already possess it as a matter of course, as free and independent States.

*Thus when the Supreme Being formed the universe, and created matter out of nothing, he impressed certain principles upon that matter, from which it can never depart, and without which it would cease to be.* [...]

*Man, considered as a creature, must necessarily be subject to the laws of his Creator, for he is entirely a dependent being.* [...]
*This will of his Maker is called the law of nature.**

Sir William Blackstone (1753)

# 9

# "To which the Laws of Nature and of Nature's God entitle them,"

***Beyond Britain's tyranny, what is the absolute justification for the Revolution?***

- ☆ When the universe was created, the Creator established universal, fixed, immutable laws of Nature that apply to Nature and mankind.
- ☆ We have a sacred obligation to abide by Natural Law.
- ☆ The colonies become free and independent States under Natural Law.

When the States become free and independent and assume their powers, they do so because of the "Laws of Nature and Nature's God." To our modern ears and sensibilities, this text may ring as quaint or antiquated, a phraseology easily passed over as superfluous window dressing.

Nothing could be further from the truth. In fact, "Nature and Nature's God" is the heart of the matter, the foundation on which the Founders base our Revolution and the Constitution. The Founding Generation holds a deeply seated belief in Natural Law. Simply put, the Founders believe that there is the Supreme Being—the single Creator—who created the universe and the laws by which it is governed. More particularly, with a few notable exceptions, the Founders believe in the God revealed in the Old and New Testaments.

Although some may be tempted to downplay or ignore altogether the religious beliefs of the Founding Generation, this is a myopic and historically incorrect view. Almost all the Founders are Christians of the Protestant strain. True, there are some Catholics, Jews, and deists. But there is no question that many of the colonies are established as religious havens from religious persecution, and many of the colonists come to the New World with the avowed purpose of finding liberty in the wilderness to worship the Almighty Christian God as they see fit. These colonies are settled by Protestant dissenters from the Church of England as a sanctuary from repression in the British Isles. The exception is Maryland, which is established to allow Catholic dissenters to exercise their faith free from British persecution.

George Washington, John Adams, Samuel Adams, James Madison, John Marshall, Patrick Henry, Roger Sherman, and many other leading figures in the Founding Generation are fervently religious and consistently express their convictions. Nearly all key public speeches and documents make explicit appeals to Divine Providence, Almighty God, the Creator, the Supreme Lawgiver, the Lord, the Ruler of Nations, Governor of the Universe, or similar expressions of faith in the Supreme Being.

The current prevailing sentiment throughout our society is to downplay or ignore religious motivations. Some scholars even claim that the Founders are not motivated by religious considerations but instead by an Enlightenment philosophy divorced from religious tenets. Worse, others claim the Founders are motivated by greed, power, and bloodlust; America is established to support oppression of whatever critique is fashionable. For example, communists claim that the American Revolution is about perpetuating class oppression, while critical race theorists claim it solidifies racist oppression.

Yet a review of the key Founding documents and other expressions of thinking involved in the American Revolution and the adoption of the Constitution reveals that a religious perspective is an indispensable motivating factor for nearly all that occurs. After all, the first full sentence of the Declaration of Independence begins by invoking the "Laws of Nature and Nature's God." The Declaration also invokes the "Creator," the "Supreme Judge of the world," and "divine Providence." Other critical concepts of the Declaration absolutely depend on a Supreme Being—as we will explore, unalienable rights and sacred honor only have meaning if they rest on the foundation of the Creator. Many essential documents of the Founding era, before and after the Declaration, reflect the same.

Even the likely least religious of the Founders express devotion to a supreme deity and justice that flows from God's decrees. Thomas Jefferson, considered by most scholars to be a deist who denies the divinity of Jesus, includes almost all the references to the Creator and Natural Law in his initial draft of the Declaration. Thomas Paine virulently attacks organized religion but frequently refers to the "Almighty" and similar expressions of a Godhead. Overwhelmingly, the Founders are firm in their beliefs, statements, and practice that there is an Almighty Creator.

That the Founders believe in a creator is not at all unusual for their time. During the Founding era, belief in a "Supreme Judge of the world" is commonplace across the globe. Much of Europe, Asia, Africa, and the Americas do not question that there is a creator (or some form of divine creators).

The fact that there is a creator, however, does not end the matter—it is just the beginning. The Declaration also refers to the "Laws of Nature." After all, God's existence does not necessarily mean much about the governance of the universe. One view is an absent clockmaker. English clergyman William Paley writes that there must be a God because the design of the universe is so complicated that it could only spring from a greater intelligence and power.* God created the earth—like a watchmaker creates a clock—and put the universe in motion. Paley uses the analogy that if you were to find a watch in the forest, you could not rationally come to believe that the random forces of Nature had simply formed this complex structure. Reason reveals that a higher being must have designed it. Even so, some argue that on a day-to-day basis, God is no longer present. Just like a person who inherits a timepiece, the watchmaker no longer controls what happens with the watch. The watch, in one sense, is simply perpetual. The watchmaker is missing. God is absent.

The Founders believe quite differently, and they express this in their ideas of the "Laws of Nature" and "divine Providence." Not only did the Supreme Being create the cosmos, but He is an active agent in the lives of men and women. That this God actively intervenes in today's affairs will be explored more thoroughly later.

Regardless of whether the divine is actively engaged or an absent watchmaker, the Founder's perspective includes the idea of the "Laws of Nature." Many of the Founders who sign the Declaration are lawyers, and they, along with most colonists, look to British legal giant Sir William Blackstone in connection with defining the law. Blackstone writes a fundamentally important work—*Commentaries on the Laws of England*—which deeply influences Americans' understanding. In defining the law, Blackstone writes it "signifies a rule of action; and is applied indiscriminately to all kinds of action [...] which is prescribed by some superior, and which the inferior is bound to obey."* Put simply, there are rules that govern everything: energy, matter, life, and people. When the Supreme Being created the universe, He created these fundamental laws. The Founders have a baseline: God created the universe, and He established the rules that everything in the universe must follow. This is *Natural Law*, created by the hand of divinity. This understanding is entrenched in the Founding Generation.

James Wilson is a signer of the Declaration, key member of the Constitutional Convention, and United States Supreme Court justice appointed by George Washington. He explains there are only two kinds of law: divine and human.* As trite but illuminating examples, the speed limit on your street or the rate of your income tax is hardly defined by God. Although the Declaration later delves into violations of man-made law, here it is reflecting that Nature's God promulgated Natural Law.

Unlike man-made law, Natural Law is unalterable and fixed. The Founders' understanding of the law is also especially informed by the French jurist Charles-Louis de Secondat (Baron de Montesquieu) and his monumental work *The Spirit of the Laws.* Montesquieu notes that Natural Laws "cannot [...] change" and they "are never to vary" because they are "the best."* Man-made law can be improved because we can learn from the past and current experience, or circumstances may change. But Natural Law is fixed because time and experience will not change its value or efficacy. Since the Supreme Being created the Natural Law, and the Supreme Being is perfect, there is no evolution of the Natural Law. Blackstone concurs. In his *Commentaries,* Blackstone explains that Natural Laws "are the eternal, immutable laws of good and evil."*

In addition, James Wilson explains that "The law of nature is universal." Quoting the Roman statesman Cicero, he continues that the law "'is the same eternal and immutable law, given at all times and to all nations: for God, who is its author and promulgator, is always the sole master and sovereign of mankind.'"* James Otis expresses it succinctly: "[T]he laws of nature are uniform and invariable. The same causes will produce the same effects, from generation to generation."*

Underlying the idea of God-made, immutable, and universal law is that Natural Law exists before man and is superior to the law of man. Alexander Hamilton comments that Natural Law existed "prior to any human institution whatsoever."* Existing before government or any similar organization of mankind, Natural Law applies to us all. Since no person is superior to God, Wilson comments, God's law must prevail whenever there is a conflict between man and God.* Indeed, Elizur Goodrich explicates in a Connecticut 1787 Election Day sermon that attempts by rulers to oppose Natural Law is both folly and madness, because "[i]t is no more in the power of the greatest earthly potentate to hinder their operation, than it is to govern the flowing and ebbing of the ocean."* To oppose Natural Law is as futile as shouting at the ocean to stop its currents.

Dr. Jonathan Mayhew addresses a similar theme in a 1750 sermon in Boston, which is later published as *A Discourse Concerning Unlimited Submission and Non-Resistance to the Higher Powers.** John Adams notes that the *Discourse* is "read by everybody."* Mayhew lays out that the people have a right—a duty—to disobey man-made law that violates Natural Law:

> [N]o civil rulers are to be obeyed when they enjoin things that are inconsistent with the commands of God: All such disobedience is lawful and glorious; [...] All commands running counter to

> the declared will of the supreme legislator of heaven and earth, are null and void: And therefore disobedience to them is a duty, not a crime.*

When the law of man conflicts with Natural Law, men and women have a duty to disobey it. Indeed, such disobedience is "lawful and glorious."

The Founders boldly stake out the position that Natural Law entitles the people in the former colonies to become an independent nation. "Entitle" here means that they have a right. Noah Webster's 1828 *An American Dictionary of the English Language* provides context: "The labor of the servant entitles him to his wages. Milton is *entitled* to fame [italics added]." The former colonies have a right under Natural Law to become free and independent States.

*Resolved, That the consideration of the first resolution* [Richard Henry Lee's resolution for independence] *be postponed to Monday, the first day of July next* [July 1, 1776], *and in the mean while, that no time be lost, in case the Congress agree thereto, that a committee be appointed to prepare a declaration to the effect of said first resolution, which is in these words: "That these United Colonies are, and of right ought to be, free and independent states; that they are absolved from all allegiance to the British crown; and that all political connection between them and the state of Great Britain is, and ought to be totally dissolved."**

Second Continental Congress (June 10, 1776)

# 10

# "A DECENT RESPECT TO THE OPINIONS OF MANKIND REQUIRES THAT THEY SHOULD DECLARE THE CAUSES WHICH IMPEL THEM TO THE SEPARATION."

***Why publish the Declaration of Independence for the world to read?***

- ☆ Because people are majestic creations of the Almighty, their opinions deserve respect. The Second Continental Congress determines that humankind deserves to know the reasons why the colonies are declaring independence.

- ☆ British oppression pushes the Founders into revolution as a matter of necessity.

The Founders are compelled to explain to the world why they are declaring independence. Remember, two days before the Declaration, the colonies adopt the resolution establishing independence. They could have left it at that. But in this sentence, they explain the reason they adopt the Declaration.

Over the millennia, many people rebel against their rulers. Civil wars, wars of secession, and revolts are commonplace in ancient civilizations, during the Middle Ages, and in the modern age. What sets the American experience apart is that the Founders explain the need for their war for independence. Historians agree that the Declaration is the first time in history that revolutionaries issue a formal statement justifying their revolution.* Reflecting on days past, Thomas Jefferson writes to fellow Founding Father Henry Lee that "an appeal to the tribunal of the world was deemed proper for our justification. This was the object of the Declaration of Independence."* Why do they do so?

The Founders need to justify their Revolution not only to the English Parliament and king, the people in the colonies, and the people of the British Empire—they must also justify to all mankind as to why independence is necessary. As the remainder of the Declaration reveals, the American Revolution is based on a worldview that each person is important and unique in the world. Because each individual is formed by the Creator, he or she is imbued with what George Washington terms a "celestial fire" and deserves to be treated with respect and dignity.* Accordingly, the opinions of the people across the globe matter.

Jefferson comments that the Declaration was "neither aiming at originality of principle or sentiment, nor yet copied from any particular and previous writing, it was intended to be an expression of the [A]merican mind, and to give to that expression the proper tone and spirit called for by the occasion."* Its explanation must be clear, easily understandable, and persuasive. It is not striving for originality but for something much more important—truth.

In addition, a few months before the Declaration is adopted, Thomas Paine in *Common Sense* suggests the colonists should adopt and forward a "manifesto" to foreign countries to ensure peace and obtain trade support.* The Declaration strongly serves Paine's purpose. Not only will the world know the reasons for independence, but the Declaration itself is an overture of peace and friendship with foreign nations. As we will discover, several key passages of the Declaration directly make such appeals.

There is another key concept in this clause: "the causes which impel them to the separation." This word choice of "impel" is not casual and should not be overlooked. This word is a purposeful expression of the Founders' view that they are being forced to revolt. The nearly contemporaneous Noah Webster's 1828 *American Dictionary of the English Language* defines "impel" as the following:

> To drive or urge forward; to press on; to excite to action or to move forward, by the application of physical force, or moral suasion or necessity. A ball is impelled by the force of powder; a ship is impelled by wind; a man may be impelled by hunger or a regard to his safety; motives of policy or of safety *impel* nations to confederate. [Italics are in the original.]

Pursuing independence is not a matter of discretion, convenience, or desire. British oppression is forcing the Founders forward toward Revolution—just like a ball being shot out of a cannon.

*The human understanding is a revelation from its Maker which can never be disputed or doubted* [...]. *This revelation has made it certain that two and one make three; and that one is not three; nor can three be one* [...]. *Miracles or prophecies might frighten us* [...] *to lie; to say that we believe that 2 and 2 make 5. But we should not believe it. We should know the contrary.**

John Adams (1813)

# 11

## "We hold these truths to be self-evident"

***What is truth? Does it change with time and context?***

- ☆ Truth exists and can be discovered through intuition, reason, and science. Moral truth exists alongside scientific truth.
- ☆ Truth is universal and fixed in meaning for all people and at all times.
- ☆ Some truths are so obvious that they need not be justified or defended—they are self-evident.
- ☆ The opposite belief—that there is no truth or that truth changes depending on one's personal viewpoint—enables massive injustice and even evil to run amok.

As reviewed earlier, the "We" in this sentence refers to the Second Continental Congress.

Congress *holds* certain truths. "Hold" here basically means to believe, to firmly grasp, to embrace.

And what does Congress "hold"? "Truths" which are "self-evident." At first glance, this seems to be a simple concept to understand and accept. The Founders believe that truth is real. What is true can often be easy to see—open and obvious. Some truths are so obvious that they do not require additional proof or justification; in other words, they are "self-evident." Webster's 1828 *An American Dictionary of the English Language* definition captures the Founders' definition: "Evident without proof or reasoning; that produces certainty or clear conviction upon a bare presentation to the mind; as a *self-evident* proposition or truth. That two and three make five, is *self-evident* [italics in the original]."

The Founders believe that some truths are so obvious that no one must explain why they are true—they are clear and unmistakable without additional proof or discussion. Some playfully obvious examples: George Washington was not a tree. If a mammal stops breathing, it will die. A circle is not a square. A rock cannot have elephant babies.

Undoubtedly, many truths can be discovered through observation, reason, scientific exploration, and similar means. However, at some point reason does not help us to discover the truth—it just exists. As John Locke explains, some ideas spring from "intuitive knowledge"—they cannot be refuted.* This is knowledge "which is certain, beyond all doubt, and needs no probation, nor can have any; this being the highest of all human certainty."* For example, "the mind perceives that an arch of a circle is less than the whole circle,"* that "two are not three, that white is not black, that a triangle is not a circle."* Any such truth "cannot be mistaken; it is clear and visible there, like the light of bright sunshine [...] and needs no other proof but its own evidence."* As Alexander Hamilton observes, it "commands the assent of the mind."* These are the foundational truths upon which everything else rests.

Such truths are not limited to math and science but also include basic morality. Except for genocidal maniacs and pathological murderers, we all know murder is wrong—as is rape. So is torturing a newborn baby. Why? Because we know it. We feel it in the very fiber of being. It is innate; our conscience tells us so. It is written on our hearts. James Wilson reflects that at bottom, "investigation must stop; reasoning can go no farther. The science of morals, as well as other sciences, is founded on truths, that can't be discovered or proven by reasoning."* It will be "equally unintelligible, as the term *color* [italics in the original] to one who was born and has continued blind."* Unfortunately, some are born blind—but there is color. Likewise, some are born without (or at least never find) a moral compass, but that does not negate the reality of self-evident moral truths.* Thomas Jefferson likewise confirms that, in connection with the American Revolution, "[w]e had no occasion to search into musty records, hunt up royal parchments, or to investigate the laws and institutions of a semi-barbarous ancestry. We appealed to those of nature, and found them engraved on our hearts."*

Moreover, truth never changes; it is always the truth. And the truth is the same for everyone. "Nature and the truth, or rather truth and right are invariably the same in all times and in all places," reflects John Adams. "[A]nd reason, pure unbiased reason, perceives them alike in all times and in all places."*

Despite the Founders' strong convictions, the entire concept of truth has been under assault since ancient times. Perhaps one of the most famous illustrations of this point is found in a biblical passage involving an exchange between Jesus and Pontius Pilate, in which Pilate, presiding over the trial of Jesus, asks, "What is truth?"* Questioning what is truth, and whose truth, has been with us for thousands of years.

But the battle over truth does not begin with Judeo-Christian scripture. Well before Jesus walks the earth, the ancients wrestled with truth. Perhaps the most renowned work of antiquity involving this topic is penned by Plato about four centuries before Jesus. Plato is dubbed one of the fathers of Western philosophy for serious reasons. He is a monumental philosopher and renowned teacher. An Athenian, Plato is perhaps the greatest thinker of the classical age. His influence over Western thinking could hardly be more important. He writes of the overarching importance of truth: "Truth is the beginning of every good to the gods, and of every good to man."*

Plato adds another vital component. Lying—perpetuating the opposite of the truth—is not only the opposite of good, it poisons the soul: "[F]alse words are not only evil in themselves, but they infect the soul with evil."* During his recitation of the trial of Socrates, who is tried for corrupting the youth (among other things), Plato recounts that Socrates explains that he is falsely accused and that his persecutors hate him precisely because he tells the truth:

> And this, O men of Athens, is the truth and the whole truth; I have concealed nothing, I have dissembled nothing. And yet, I know that my plainness of speech makes them hate me, and what is their hatred but a proof that I am speaking the truth?—this is the occasion and reason of their slander of me, as you will find out either in this or in any future enquiry.*

The internet is full of paraphrases of this eloquent passage, which all boil down to "[n]o one is more hated than he who speaks the truth."*

Protagoras is an ancient Greek philosopher who holds a position diametrically opposed to Plato's. Protagoras claims that there is no truth whatsoever: "Man [...] is the measure of all things—white, heavy, light: there is nothing of this sort of which he is not the judge; for he has the criterion of them in himself, and when he thinks what he feels, he thinks what is [...]."* In other words, each person—not a higher, objective reality—decides what is true. Everything is subjective in the eye of the beholder. People, not Nature, define the truth. Plato's teacher Socrates restates Protagoras as, "[T]hat things are for me such as they appear to me, and for you such as they appear to you?"* The Bible expresses a similar sentiment in the book of Judges, which recounts a dismal period when Israel is ruled by judges and morality is collapsing. Anarchy prevails; everyone is free to act as they wish. "In those days there was no king in Israel: every man did that which was right in his own eyes."* The result is an absolute disaster.

Under this paradigm, there is only opinion, no facts. Everyone is the center of his or her own universe. Some call it "global positioning syndrome." That is, the world rotates around you. Actually, it is even more powerful. Not only does the world revolve around you, but you set the rules. *You* determine what is right, what is wrong, what is reality, and what is fantasy.

This summary accurately reflects the perspective held by many today. This view is made fashionable by brilliant philosophers as well as tin-pot academics. On the brilliant side, Friedrich Nietzsche writes, "Facts are precisely what is lacking, all that exists consists of interpretations."* And with no truth comes the demise of good and evil. After all, good and evil require an overarching truth.

The rejection of truth is the opposite of the Judeo-Christian worldview firmly embraced by the Founding Generation. It is also contrary to the secular United Nations' Universal Declaration of Human Rights, adopted on December 10, 1948. Without relying on religion but instead on universal maxims of morality, the Universal Declaration recognizes a set of human rights that all people in the world should enjoy.* Like the Declaration, the Universal Declaration presupposes there is truth and that these rights are recognized by that truth.

To the modern Protagoras, this is nonsense. In fact, at the time the United Nations is debating the Universal Declaration, it is opposed by some who think truth is a dangerous concept. Of all groups, the American Anthropological Association, in 1947, publishes the "Statement on Human Rights" opposing the Universal Declaration. These anthropologists argue that

> [s]tandards and values are relative to the culture from which they derive [...].
>
> What is held to be a human right in one society may be regarded as anti-social by another people, or by the same people in a different period of their history. The saint of one epoch would at a later time be confined as a man not fitted to cope with reality. Even the nature of the physical world, the colors we see, the sounds we hear, are conditioned by the language we speak, which is part of the culture into which we are born.*

In one sense, nothing could be more reasonable than what the American Anthropological Association illustrates. Clearly, societies have differed in their views of the truth over time and among each other. Still, the downright disdain for any kind of universal absolute truth is stunning, especially since it is written in the wake of World War II, the Holocaust, and the mass oppression and annihilation of hundreds of millions under Nazi, Japanese, and Soviet tyrannical states. Given the proximity of the "Statement on Human Rights" to the events of the late 1930s and early 1940s, the logical conclusion of this perspective is that no society is better than any other, no matter how oppressive or murderous. This view means that the totalitarian, genocidal dictatorships of Mao Zedong, Pol Pot, Adolf Hitler, Hirohito, and Joseph Stalin are as valid and good as the western democracies of the United Kingdom, France, Canada, Sweden, and the United States. Genocide, liquidation of disfavored peoples, concentration camps, and a police state are the moral equivalent to free elections, equality, due process, and protecting unalienable rights such as life, free speech, free press, and religion. Today, the republic of the United States of America; authoritarian Communist China; the Kingdom (literally, with a hereditary king) of Saudi Arabia; the military junta of Myanmar; the authoritarian, dictatorial Russia; and the dynastic (hereditary) dictatorship of North Korea—they are all of equal worth. We should respect cultural practices that include genital mutilation, subjugation of women, honor killings, suppression of religion, censorship, purges, political prisons, concentration camps, assassinations, purposeful mass starvation, and similar barbaric practices because those cultures are just as good as ours. Who are we to judge? The lack of a universal, timeless, objective truth justifies the most vicious, barbaric, and evil regimes in history.

Some take it one step more and argue that all societies are equal and to be valued, *except* the republics of the West.* In their view, the American and Western civilizations are racist, sexist, elitist, and oppressive, and should be undermined, subverted, and destroyed. This "liberation" will somehow result in justice being spread throughout the world, and a utopia will spring into existence. Of course, this view was firmly held in different guises by the communists of the Soviet Union and Mao's China, which led to the liquidation of tens of millions of their own citizens and unprecedented police states that crushed all freedoms and liberties. Again, this is not a new perspective. The numerous hair-raising, brutal stories contained in the book of Judges are too lengthy to recount here, but this scripture reveals that when each person is his or her own judge of right and wrong, the outcome is murder, anarchy, civil war, tyranny, and mass slaughter.

These views of truth—or the lack of truth—and the attacks on Western perspectives are diametrically opposed to the Declaration. When the Founders declare that "we hold these truths to be self-evident," they clearly believe that there is a discoverable, fixed, timeless, universal truth. They understand that not all agree on what the truth is, and most of them clearly believe that determining the truth is no easy task. Nevertheless, they also believe that, despite these difficulties, there is a truth, but it will take a determined effort to be discovered through intuition, reason, logic, and science. As noted earlier, John Adams writes to Thomas Jefferson that "[m]iracles or prophecies might frighten [...] us to lie; to say that we believe that 2 and 2 make 5. But we should not believe it. We should know the contrary."* Adams makes this simple. Put aside the Creator for a moment. No matter what a multiculturalist or relativist says, 2 + 2 will never equal 5. There is an indisputable truth.

Another example of indisputable truth is brilliantly illustrated by Dr. Jordan B. Peterson: pain. "You try to argue yourself out of pain, and see how far you get. [...] I'll watch you when you're in pain, and every single one of your actions will indicate that you believe in it. And not only that, that you can't not believe in it."* And let us not forget thirst. And hunger. You cannot deny those things exist. If you do not drink or eat for long enough, you will die. Even a multiculturalist or Protagoras will die of hunger, terminal cancer, or a bullet. You cannot disbelieve your own demise. Truth is real.

But the Founders go well beyond math, science, pain, hunger, and death. They believe that truth reveals good and evil, morality and immorality. Not only does such an objective reality exist, but man can discover it. John Adams explains that God had given him, and by extension all people, "nobler powers of intelligence and reason. He has given me reason to find out the truth, and the real design of my existence here."* In other words, by our very nature, humanity is able to discover the truth. The multiculturalist and Protagoras are wrong. By examining the world and using reason, we can discover Natural Law, justice, good, evil, and how to live a fulfilling life. Thomas Jefferson writes to Adams "in all cases to follow the truth as the only safe guide."*

Adams and Jefferson clearly articulate the worldview of the Founding Generation. Being inherently flawed, individuals will inevitably fall short of the grand ideals of natural justice, and that has been the reality since the origin of man. But falling short does not render the truth false. Truth and morality exist and should be the polestar for behavior. If not, we all end up in an endless cycle of error that is a path of destruction.

Unlike the cynics who attack the whole idea of the truth, the Founding Generation lives and dies by it. Unlike those who think that truth is whatever whoever says it is, the Founders believe that truth is immutable. Murder is a crime. Adultery is a sin. Pedophilia is despicable. Theft is immoral. Taxation without representation is enslavement. Trial without jury is oppression. Closure of legislative assemblies is tyranny. Burning innocent towns is barbarism.

They also believe truth is fixed, not subject to change based on popularity or fashions. The great nineteenth century American Frederick Douglass illuminates this idea at a speech at Hillsdale College in Michigan: "There is no such thing as new truth; error might be old or new, but truth is as old as the universe."* British Prime Minister Winston Churchill also encapsulates this idea in the twentieth century when he addresses the House of Commons: "The truth is incontrovertible. Panic may resent it, ignorance may deride it, malice may distort, but there it is."*

The Founders reject the belief system of the past and adopt as self-evident truths a set of revolutionary ideals that forever change the world. They reject the passionate, subjective rule of men and instead embrace the rule of principled truth. They do this by staring down King George III, Parliament, and British nation—indeed, nearly the entire world. They become traitors to their own empire so they can honor the truth. Plato's paraphrased admonition that "no one is more hated than he who speaks the truth" certainly applies to the Founders. They are definitely hated by the British and many tyrants across the world. However, today they are beloved across the globe by uncounted millions.

This idea of the truth moving the world strongly resonates even today. Martin Luther King, Jr., explains that "unarmed truth and unconditional love will have the final word in reality. This is why right temporarily defeated is stronger than evil triumphant."* As modern philosopher Roger Scruton quips, "a writer who says that there are no truths, or that all truth is 'merely relative,' is asking you not to believe him. So don't."* To hold otherwise is the path of madness.

*[A]ll men are by nature equally free and independent.**

The Virginia Declaration of Rights, Section I (1776)

# 12

## "THAT ALL MEN ARE CREATED EQUAL"

***How do the Founders break with thousands of years of inequality?***

- ☆ As the creation of Nature's God, every person is reflective of the majesty of the Almighty and equally valuable.
- ☆ America is the first nation founded on this self-evident truth. Slavery and Hinduism's caste system are examples of the regimes and institutions based on inequality. America rejects this past prevailing reality and embraces a new path forward.
- ☆ America in 1776 falls short of realizing the First Principle of equality, as evidenced by, among other things, slavery, racial discrimination, and gender discrimination. Although the journey is difficult and unfinished, the Declaration's unabashed, revolutionary commitment to equality makes possible tremendous strides toward equality.

Because the Founders believe that all of mankind is the creation of the Supreme Being, they also embrace the idea that every individual is created equal. Today, most may take for granted this commitment to equality. In fact, much criticism is leveled at the Founding Fathers for failing to live up to their ideal of equality. Much of this criticism is warranted; this principle is not a lived experience in 1776. The Founding Generation is not perfect—far from it. They declare the First Principle of equality as a self-evident truth and then in many ways live their lives exactly opposite from what they declare. Some of the Founders (but by no means all) enslave others. Nearly no women have political or economic rights. Even men without land are generally unable to vote. Native Americans generally are excluded from the body politic because they are treated as members of a separate body politic—their Native American nations.

Despite these deep flaws, the Founders' commitment to equality is a remarkable, quantum leap for mankind. America is exceptional in its embrace of equality as a First Principle. Really? Yes. To truly comprehend how revolutionary our commitment to equality is in 1776, we need to investigate how societies are organized over the ages.

Our first example of inequality is slavery. Today, many people in the United States seem to only focus on slavery in pre-Civil War America, as if it never existed anywhere else. This is a natural impulse. Americans are fond of introspection and pointing out our own flaws—especially when we fall short of our announced ideals. Nevertheless, to focus solely on American slavery tremendously minimizes the phenomenon. Slavery is not an American creation or in any fashion unique to our shores. Major societies embed slavery in their laws, cultures, and economies. In fact, "slavery was a nearly universal institution."* It is hardly the exclusive domain of the European empires, English colonies, or the American South. It infects every major civilization at nearly all times. Most historians agree that organized, institutionalized slavery begins at the dawn of civilization in ancient Mesopotamia and Sumer. Slaves are often the bounty of war and commonly an essential part of the workforce. Slavery is common throughout Asia, Africa, the Americas, and Europe for thousands of years. Ancient Greece and Rome are no exception. Slavery is a fact of life in pre-Islamic Arabia and the Middle East.* Just like Christianity does not halt slavery, neither does the rise of Islam. Instead of abolishing it, Muslims create a massive slave trade to enslave Christians and other non-Muslims.

Likewise, slavery is no stranger to the Western Hemisphere before Europeans arrive. Author Andrés Reséndez explains that "[n]ative peoples such as the Zapotecs, Mayas and Aztecs took captives to use as sacrificial victims; the Iroquois waged campaigns called 'mourning wars' on neighboring groups to avenge and replace their dead. [...] Native Americans had enslaved each other for millennia."*

Leaping well ahead of 1776 to the 1900s, slavery rears its ugly head. The Japanese enslave thousands of Korean and Chinese women during World War II as "comfort women"—sex slaves for the imperial troops.* Nazi Germany uses slave labor—nine million people are sent to concentration camps, and those not immediately exterminated are enslaved.* In fact, the world only decides to outlaw the institution after World War II. In 1948, the United Nations General Assembly finally adopts the Universal Declaration of Human Rights, which declares that there is a universal human right to be free from slavery and prohibits it. Still, slavery persists in Saudi Arabia and Yemen until 1962 and Mauritania until 1980—and some challenge whether it has really been abolished there.* Outright slavery appears again with the Islamic State (otherwise known as ISIS and Daesh) in the mid-2010s* and the Islamic terrorist group Boko Haram.*

Unfortunately, there are many more instances of slavery throughout history. The idea that large swaths of humanity are destined to be enslaved and that their enslavers will be protected by the law is a long, dismal tradition, spanning across millennia and across the globe. Simply put, inequality via slavery is pervasive when the Founding Generation embraces the idea of equality.

A second vivid example of inequality is the caste system of Hinduism. Many scholars consider Hinduism to be the world's oldest religion, with its roots and customs dating back more than four thousand years. Today, it is the world's third-largest faith, with over a billion followers. Approximately 92 percent of Hindus live in India, the world's most populous nation. As one scholar succinctly explains, "Caste is the basis of Hindu society."* According to the sacred *Ṛgveda Saṃhitā*,* India's most ancient text, the caste system arises as a necessary consequence of the very creation of man. In particular, mankind is spawned from the sacrifice and splitting of the cosmic, primordial individual into all of the constituent parts of humanity. Since mankind is inherently divided into these divinely imposed tiers of society, the caste system is implemented in both religion and law to ensure adherence to the naturally ordained order of things.* The caste system is hereditary. You are a member of the caste of your parents, and your children inherit your caste. The law enforces the system for many centuries. A person's caste assignment is of paramount importance in the trajectory of one's life:

> Hindu society is divided into [...] castes, which are regarded as high and low according to their position in the social scale, and that members of the same caste eat and drink together but not with members of an inferior caste. Another fact [is that] some castes have a common hereditary occupation or handicraft. [...] [T]he most important and distinctive feature of the caste system is [...] that of marriage with the caste, the rule of endogamy, according to which men must marry women of their own caste and no other. [...]
>
> So far from being a homogeneous whole, a caste is generally subdivided into sections called sub-castes, most of which are replicas of the main caste both in the matter of food and drink and nearly all in the more important matter of intermarriage, for members of each sub-caste marry only fellow-members of the sub-caste.*

Stated more simply, "Hinduism lends weighty support to the hierarchy of caste by declaring that a man's caste is the exact index of his soul's behavior and piety in previous births."* Hinduism's four main castes are divided into about three thousand castes with twenty-five thousand sub-castes. Each sub-caste dictates the key aspects of all person's rights and responsibilities. Then there are the untouchables, *below* the caste system. There is no equality in the caste system. Inequality is ordained by the divine not just for one lifetime, but throughout the ages.

Fortunately, the caste system was officially abolished in India under the constitution adopted after independence from British colonial rule. The country marks another leap of progress with the passage of the Untouchability (Offenses) Act in 1955, which in essence is a civil rights act for these oppressed members of society. However, many argue that the hard, cold reality is that the caste ethic is still pervasive in Indian society. The caste system is ingrained in Hinduism because of the faith's cardinal belief that all men and women are reincarnated.

Other examples of inequality can be easily cited across time and the globe, including feudalism, France's estate-based ancien régime, communism's class-based divisions, South Africa's race-based apartheid regime, Tibet's feudal theocracy, China's Fēngjiàn class regime, the Mayan Empire's stratified feudal system, the Islamic Republic of Iran's treatment of religious minorities and women, the Aztec Empire's King Itzcoatl's strict social hierarchy, and the Nazi's Germanic race-based nightmare. Whether based on class, caste, religion, race, gender, tribe, ethnic group, economic status, language, party membership, eugenics, or otherwise, nearly all governments throughout world history maintain rigid divisions among individuals and social groups—granting special favors to those at the top and saddling those on the bottom with unjust burdens. With few exceptions, these partitions are woven into societies' basic law, religion, economies, and culture. Such governments are based on the proposition of the self-evident truth, in their eyes, of the inherent inequality of the people.

Regretfully, the idea of embracing inequality as the hallmark of society has not vanished. Quite to the contrary, in Communist China, North Korea, Laos, Vietnam, and Cuba, party members are superior, and in many countries, the majority ethnic groups openly oppress minorities.

The Founders reject this world view. They embrace the Judeo-Christian understanding of the Supreme Being by which all are created equal: Each person arises from His handiwork, and every person embodies His blessing. In Genesis 1:26–27, scripture reveals that God made men and women in His own image.

The Judeo-Christian belief embraced by the Founders invests men and women with equality. Regardless of physical and mental differences between individuals, and despite sometimes yawning disparities in wealth or station, each individual, as someone engendered by the Creator, is equally precious in His eyes. Because each person is made in His image, each person has inherent, true dignity before God; no person is elevated above his fellow man. Each is loved equally by the Creator, and each judged by his or her deeds and intentions. Each individual has an equal opportunity to obtain redemption from sin or damnation, and each chooses his or her own path. The great historian Russell Kirk encapsulates the understanding concisely when he reflects that "[t]hey [the men of the Continental Congress] subscribe to two venerable concepts of equality: equality before the law, and equality in the judgment of God."*

Directly contrary to the historical reality of millennia, America rejects the deliberately inequitable regimes dominating the globe in their time. From its very founding, America aspires to embody the First Principle that all men are created equal. The Declaration expressly affirms this principle. So do the State constitutions that are drafted and ratified following the Declaration. Those constitutions consistently recognize in some form "[t]hat all men are by nature equally free and independent."* In 1863, Abraham Lincoln reaffirms this founding First Principle in the Gettysburg Address when he articulates that the nation is "conceived in liberty and dedicated to the proposition that all men are created equal."*

This equality of each individual is one of rights, opportunities, and equal treatment under the law. Individuals are never equal in intellect, physical talent, strength, stamina, creativity, empathy, leadership, and countless other differences. Nor are they equal as moral agents. James Wilson explains that "[w]hen we say, that all men are equal; we mean not to apply this to equality in their virtues, their talents, their dispositions, or their acquirements."* He further observes that the diversity of talents and intellect can come together to serve the greater interest. By leveraging our comparable strengths, we all improve.

This inherent inequality does not justify governmental discrimination based on class, race, gender, ethnic group, religion, or creed (belief). As the Fourteenth Amendment to the United States Constitution recognizes, each person is entitled to the "equal protection of the laws." This equal protection does not require that the government attempt to equalize the social status, wealth, and property of individuals. The government is not some great leveling machine that should chop down everyone to the same height or size. Equality before the law only requires that each individual, regardless of race, color, creed, nationality, wealth, social status, religion, and similar characteristics, be treated equally under the law. Wealthy white, cisgender, heterosexual, Lutheran men, therefore, should be subject to the same treatment under the law as poor, Black, homosexual, Hindu women, and vice versa. Combined with the rule of law, this First Principle requires that each person be treated equally under the law and that equal protection of the laws be afforded to all.

Equality demolishes the various divisions that dominates mankind for eons. No longer will the great mass of humanity be repressed by kings and nobility, slavery, caste, and other such discrimination. It also renounces the infamous class divisions of communism and racial segregation. The standard, prevailing view that the general population is inferior and should be relegated to a permanent underclass of slaves, serfs, peasants, or untouchables is totally rejected. The Declaration reflects a watershed moment in human history. Americans embrace the idea that the poorest and most unfortunate people in society are, as John Adams puts it, "by the unalterable, indefeasible laws of God and nature, as well entitled to the benefit of the air to breathe, light to see, food to eat, and clothes to wear, as the nobles or the king. All men are born equal."* James Wilson similarly expresses that "[a]ll men are, by nature, equal and free."*

This understanding shakes the very foundations of the Old World. The axiomatic premise that the world is divided between the privileged and the oppressed breaks apart. "Is not the change we have seen astonishing?" remarks John Adams less than a month after the Declaration is adopted. "Idolatry to monarchs, and servility to aristocratical pride, was never so totally eradicated, from so many minds in so short a time."* Adams is not engaging in hyperbole. The people are now citizens, not subjects. Prominent South Carolinian historian and political figure David Ramsay summarizes the transformation of America he witnesses firsthand in the wake of the American Revolution. He explains that a subject "means one who is under the power of another; but a *citizen* [italics added] is a unit of a mass of free people, who, collectively, possess sovereignty."* Citizens control their own destiny.

These might be worthy sentiments, but what does it really matter in practical terms? *Everything.* The transformation is astonishing. Americans begin to radically alter the legal landscape. In 1776, the Virginia Declaration of Rights, written by the somewhat overlooked—but enormously influential—Founding Father George Mason, specifically eliminates nobility and any hereditary privileges of property or political advantages. Soon, all the States follow. Thomas Jefferson also leads the abolition of ancient privileges provided to landowners that had allowed them to hoard property among the landed gentry, thereby cracking open the ability of men of merit to purchase property. As he writes in his *Autobiography*, America replaces the "aristocracy of wealth [...] to make an opening of the aristocracy of virtue and talent."* As nobility and class divisions are repudiated, a meritocracy begins to take hold.

Equality, according to David Ramsay, becomes the "life and soul" of America.* Before 1776, "he that can best please his superiors, by the low arts of fawning and adulation, is most likely to obtain favour," but in America, one can succeed on his or her merits.* What matters is hard work, industry, intelligence, dedication, innovation, frugality, creativity, honesty, integrity, and resilience—not bloodlines, flattery, and corruption. Charles Cotesworth Pinckney, a leading political leader from South Carolina, likewise can accurately declare at the Constitutional Convention "equality is [...] the leading feature of the United States."* No Divine Right, no caste here.

Because of the nature of the New World, land is more widely distributed in colonial America than anywhere else in the world. With the overthrow of British tyranny, almost all male landowners possess the right to vote. This vastly broadened electorate is well beyond anything since ancient Greece. Nevertheless, it is undoubtedly a small segment of the population; women, slaves, racial minorities, the landless, and sometimes religious minorities are excluded from the franchise. Native Americans are considered members of foreign nations. But for its time, it is absolutely a quantum leap. Putting aside the ancient democracies in Greece, America is the first society in the world to bring ordinary people into government as meaningful participants.

Moreover, this equality extends far beyond voting rights. Unalienable rights are respected and guaranteed by the government. Ordinary people can speak their minds, practice their religions, freely assemble, bear arms, own property, serve in the militia, petition the government, publish freely, join associations, and run for and serve in political office. Other than slaves (and too often racial minorities), individuals are provided impartial, due process regardless of their status in society. A home—no matter how modest—is the homeowner's castle that even a king cannot enter without a duly authorized warrant.

In fact, some of the leading lights of the Founding Generation would have been considered human trash in other societies. Crispus Attucks, a free African American, is martyred in the Boston Massacre and celebrated thereafter.

Alexander Hamilton is an outcast orphan immigrant from a tropical island. With charity from some, and amazing self-honed talent and dedication, he becomes one of the most important figures in American history. Hamilton is the aide-de-camp to George Washington, leads troops in the siege of Yorktown (the battle that clinches victory in the American Revolution), coauthors *The Federalist Papers* (writing more than any other contributor), and is the first secretary of the Treasury.

Thomas Paine sails across the sea from England in his middle age. He is nearly penniless. Prior to his passage, he is a failure at most everything he tries—including tavern keeper, merchant, and tax collector. His likely unconsummated marriage is a wreck; his wife basically bribes him to leave Great Britain. He barely survives the voyage to America and is nursed back to health by America's leading physician, Dr. Benjamin Rush. About a year later, he sets the world on fire with *Common Sense*. He also writes the remarkable *The American Crisis* (which inspires American troops to stay in the fight in the Revolutionary War's darkest hours) and the groundbreaking *Rights of Man* (which has a global effect in enlightening the world toward freedom and liberty). He is so influential that several French districts elect him as a delegate to the National Convention during the French Revolution.

John Adams comes from what we would consider at best a middle-class background. He becomes "the Colossus of independence," a leading political figure for generations, vice president under Washington, and Washington's successor as president.

Roger Sherman, a cobbler and small farmer, signs the Declaration and plays a key role in the Constitutional Convention.

Benjamin Franklin's father makes soap and candles, and Franklin is apprenticed to his older brother as a printer because he was too poor to pay for the education to be a minister or a cutler (in other words, a maker of knives, forks, and spoons). By sheer talent and tenacity, he, essentially a runaway, becomes a leading scientist of the age and the most famous American on the globe before the American Revolution.

Suffice it to say there are also plenty of influential rich landowners—like Thomas Jefferson, George Washington, and Patrick Henry. Yet leadership in abundance springs from the ranks of the poor and middle classes. A meritocracy is born. This commitment to equality spreads like wildfire. Soon, indentured servitude disappears, and most States abolish property and religious qualifications to vote. Eventually, Article I, Section 9 of the Constitution will abolish nobility.

Undoubtedly slavery, racial discrimination, gender and sexual orientation discrimination, and the mistreatment of Native Americans are still prevalent and often crushing. Contrary to some currently fashionable but misinformed beliefs, the Founding Fathers do not uniformly embrace these forms of discrimination. Many hold radical views for the times. They recognize the dreadful nature of at least some of these sins and advocate for eliminating the scourge of slavery. But others are not so farsighted. These issues split the Founding Generation, and the country, for many decades to come.

Still, America's advancements during the Revolutionary era are a remarkable phenomenon in world history. America's commitment that equality will be its polestar is extraordinary. America becomes a beacon of hope for the world. For those for whom this promise of equality is denied within America, they challenge that injustice by harkening back to the Declaration's recognition of that self-evident truth that all are created equal. Indeed, that is exactly what happens.

As they fight for their own liberty, many in the Founding Generation develop a new awareness of the plight of slaves. The great Frederick Douglass—a runaway slave and force of nature for abolitionism decades after the American Revolution—accurately reflects that

> [t]he anti-slavery movement has little to entitle it to being called a new thing under the sun, in the view of any just historical test. [...] The patriots of the American Revolution clearly saw, and with all their inconsistency, they had the grace to confess the abhorrent character of slavery, and to hopefully predict its overthrow and complete extirpation. Washington, and Jefferson, Patrick Henry, and Luther Martin, Franklin, and Adams, Madison, and Monroe, and a host of earlier statesmen, jurists, scholars, and divines [clergy] of the country, were among those who looked forward to this happy consummation.*

But the hindsight of Douglass is unnecessary. At the time of the American Revolution, the enslaved are quite aware of what the Revolution has wrought. Although omitted in most history texts, on the eve of the American Revolution, many enslaved in Massachusetts are petitioning and demanding emancipation.* Some, like Jenny Slew, even sue for their liberty and obtain it.*

Even as the colonies are hurtling toward Revolution, the first abolitionist society in the world, demanding the emancipation of slaves, is formed in Philadelphia in 1775. Benjamin Franklin (a former slave holder who changes his position after visiting a school for African Americans in 1763) eventually heads the organization. Franklin establishes free schools for African American children in several cities and forwards an antislavery petition to the new Congress under the Constitution in February 1790, just two months before he dies. Leading Founding Father Dr. Benjamin Rush, who encourages Thomas Paine to write *Common Sense* (Rush even recommends the title), also leads the American Society for the Abolition of Slavery. Others Founding Fathers, such as Thomas Paine, John Jay, Alexander Hamilton, John Laurens, and John Adams, are fierce abolitionists. Abigail Adams, wife of John and a remarkable woman in her own right, originally is disinclined to support the cause of such zealous African Americans,* but as the Revolution proceeds, she completely embraces emancipation. She writes to her husband,

> I wish most sincerely there was not a slave in the province; it always appeared the most iniquitous scheme to me to fight ourselves for what we are daily robbing and plundering from those who have as good a right to freedom as we have.*

This sentiment is strongly held in various pockets of the new States. For example, many prominent leaders from New York's Hudson Valley vigorously oppose slavery. Among these were Gouverneur Morris (the "penman of the Constitution" and future United States senator), John Jay (diplomat, contributor to the *Federalist Papers*, governor of New York, drafter of New York's first constitution, chief justice of New York, and the nation's first chief justice of the Supreme Court), Alexander Hamilton, George Clinton (diplomat, governor of New York, leading Anti-Federalist, and vice president [under two presidents]), and Daniel Tompkins (governor of New York and vice president).* However, early vigorous attempts during and following the American Revolution to emancipate slaves are defeated through various parliamentary procedures and political posturing.* Undeterred, Jay becomes the first president of the New York Manumission Society,* and members include many leading figures in New York, including Alexander Hamilton and United States Senator Rufus King.*

Understanding its sinful nature, George Washington emancipates his slaves upon his wife's death. Prominent slaveholders such as Thomas Jefferson and James Madison are remarkably troubled by slavery, recognizing it to be sinful and often—perhaps hypocritically—condemning it. No one of any influence in the Founding Generation argues that slavery is a positive good, and most hope and expect that it will slowly be eliminated. The American Revolution makes many revolutionaries reexamine the widespread assumption that slavery was part of the natural order of things. Most believe that with time, slavery will disappear.

In the wake of the American Revolution, that expectation is coming true for many. As historian David Hackett Fischer summarizes the analysis of pioneering Professor Jackson Turner Main, "As late as 1774, [...] about 80 percent of African Americans in New England were slaves [...]. By 1800, less than 5 percent remained slaves throughout the entire region—a sweeping revolution in status within the span of one generation." Fisher reflects that "[i]t was achieved not by gradual emancipation acts, but by the acts and choices of individual slaves and masters, on a very broad scale. And the slaves often took the initiative."* In other words, large swaths of the Founding Generation are putting into practice the principles of the American Revolution. By their own will, slavery is perishing.

But then the unexpected invention of the cotton gin changes the course of history. A new generation of Americans become deeply wedded to the evil. Some enslavers even argue that slavery is a positive good for the slaveowner and slave alike and that the institution should be perpetuated forever. Of course, that viewpoint and history is despicable—and well beyond the reach of nearly all the Founders and this work.

However, the Declaration's unabashed commitment to equality becomes the primary weapon and the indispensable idea with which to later attack slavery. Abraham Lincoln's Gettysburg Address roots his commitment to emancipation on the principle of the Declaration's dedication to equality.

As noted earlier, the Declaration's First Principle of equality is embodied in Article I, Section 9's abolition of nobility. America will have no royalty. The three great amendments to the United States Constitution adopted in the wake of the Civil War and during Reconstruction make unprecedented strides for this First Principle. The Thirteenth Amendment forever abolishes the despicable stain of slavery. The Fourteenth Amendment guarantees that "all persons born or naturalized in the United States, and subject to the jurisdiction thereof, are citizens of the United States and of the State wherein they reside." Citizenship—a wild fantasy for generations of the enslaved—is a constitutional right. The Fourteenth Amendment also ensures that "no State shall make or enforce any law which shall abridge the privileges or immunities of citizens of the United States; nor shall any State deprive any person of life, liberty, or property, without due process of law; nor deny to any person within its jurisdiction the equal protection of the laws." The government must treat all Americans equally—discrimination is dead. Equal protection is the order of the day. The Fifteenth Amendment provides that "the right of citizens of the United States to vote shall not be denied or abridged by the United States or by any State on account of race, color, or previous condition of servitude." All have the right to vote regardless of race. Groundbreaking civil rights legislation strengthens these protections throughout society.

Reverend Martin Luther King, Jr.'s "I Have a Dream" speech repeatedly refers to and echoes the Declaration's principle that all men are created equal. The suffragettes' call in 1848—the Seneca Falls Declaration of Sentiments and Resolutions—propels the woman's suffrage movement into the consciousness of America and the world by literally reciting the Declaration with modifications to advocate for gender equality (for example, "We hold these truths to be self-evident, that all men *and women* [italics added] are made equal").

The Fourteenth Amendment also applies to women. They are citizens and entitled to equal protection and due process. Although coming generations later, women win a major advancement for their constitutional equality when the Nineteenth Amendment guarantees the right to vote for women. Subsequent civil rights legislation also ensures gender equality in many arenas of American life.

Generations of abolitionists, suffragettes, civil rights leaders, and activists call upon Americans to live up to the ideals of the Declaration. These are just a few profound illustrations among countless others. The very idea of equality creates opportunities for all citizens—regardless of their immutable characteristics, origins, and social station—to be protected by the same law so they can exercise their unalienable rights, own property, obtain a livelihood, pursue happiness, participate in politics, and hold office, including as legislators, judges, governors, and presidents. Simply put, the Declaration's commitment to equality is truly revolutionary, shattering the millennia-old commitment to inequality, and continues to pave the way for greater equality even today. Of course, this is no easy task, and the journey is hardly over, but it is the Declaration's unabashed, revolutionary commitment to equality that makes any of this progress even possible.

*The sacred rights of mankind, are not to be rummaged for among old parchments or musty records. They are written, as with a sunbeam, in the whole volume of human nature, by the hand of the divinity itself, and can never be erased or obscured by mortal power.**

Alexander Hamilton (1775)

# 13

## "THAT THEY ARE ENDOWED BY THEIR CREATOR WITH CERTAIN UNALIENABLE RIGHTS,"

***What does it mean to have "unalienable rights"? Who or what grants these rights? Can they be taken from us?***

- ☆ Each person is born with the same unalienable rights.
- ☆ Governments do not give us unalienable rights—they come from the Creator.
- ☆ Unalienable rights cannot be given away by individuals or taken away by the government.
- ☆ America is the first and only country in world history to declare unalienable rights as the foundation of its government.
- ☆ China, Social Darwinism, and eugenics illustrate the dominant thinking that denies that every person has equal, unalienable rights.

The Declaration's pronouncement that we base our government on our possession of unalienable rights is unique in the course of human history. Before 1776, very few societies even recognize the idea of rights at all, and no government is established with the foundation that those rights are vested in us by the Creator and are unalienable.

"Unalienable" means that the rights cannot be transferred, sold, given up, or taken away. The term "alienable" is simply an old-fashioned word that means a person has the authority to sell or give something away.* In other words, if you own your home, you have the right to sell it—it is "alienable." "Unalienable" (some prefer "inalienable") means that you do not have the power to sell or transfer something. Thus, we are born with certain rights that cannot be sold, transferred, given up, or taken away by the government.*

From the perspective of the Founding Fathers, unalienable rights fit squarely within their understanding of Natural Law and the Creator. Unalienable rights make no sense without a creator, because the Creator binds those unalienable rights inherently into mankind. Today, many argue or presume that you can have rights without a creator. True enough, rights can be justified through reason, culture, agreements, contracts, social conditions, tradition, custom, biology, and myriad other theories. However, that is not the Founders' conception, and we will leave those alternative theories to others. More importantly, those other theories of rights are based on fragile, shifting sands that can be swept away with the currents of cultural change, evolving social conditions, and scientific advances. In other words, none of the other theories are permanent, because rights are then based on particular circumstances and understandings at a specific time. What is a right on any given day can be lost the next day and vice versa. Such rights do not have the bedrock foundation of unalienability. This flies in the face of the American understanding.

For example, your unalienable right to the free exercise (or avoidance) of religion does not depend on prevailing sentiments. Governments can come and go, the popularity of the religion you practice can ebb and flow, society's general hostility toward religion can rise and fall, robust disagreements among your religion's doctrines can persist or fade, science can undermine or affirm your religious beliefs, and younger generations can be deeply cynical or supportive of your values. Changing winds do not undermine unalienable rights. You will always possess the intrinsic unalienable right to the free exercise of your religion. The same holds true for the freedom of speech, freedom of press, freedom of association, right to petition, and our other unalienable rights. No matter how unpopular, hated, or despised your opinions and organizations you belong to might be at any given time, you have the unalienable right to express yourself and join others in doing so.

The Founders hold as a self-evident truth that since all people are created by Nature's God with the same rights, everyone (regardless of social status, privilege, race, gender, belief system, and so forth) enjoys the same unalienable rights.* Thomas Paine eloquently expresses the idea that whatever your station in life, "the floor of freedom is as level as water."* We not only have liberty, but we all have the *same* liberties.

Although the notion of unalienable rights is central to the Founders' beliefs, today we skip over any meaningful discussion of it. Nearly everyone in American society today seems to clamor for rights. They do so based on constitutional text, statutory provisions, executive orders, court precedents, notions of fairness, and other similar sources. Yet, reference to *unalienable* rights is scarce indeed. But to ignore this fundamental foundation of our rights is false history, rotten political science, and poor philosophy. By ignoring the unalienability of rights, we endanger them. If rights are not unalienable, they can be irreparably lost. For example, if your religion suddenly becomes unpopular, a government could suppress it through the raw exercise of power. The same for unpopular speech and press—censorship can easily override your rights if they are not fixed and unalienable. Nothing is more common in human history.

The principle of unalienable rights is nurtured in the Founding Fathers by John Locke and other English Natural Law philosophers. Locke writes in his *Second Treatise of Government* that all men possess the unalienable rights to life, liberty, and property. Sir William Blackstone, an English jurist and legal scholar extraordinarily influential with the Founders, writes in his 1765 *The Commentaries of the Law of England* that "the principal aim of society is to protect individuals in the enjoyment of those absolute rights, which were vested in them by the immutable laws of nature."* Despite Locke's brilliant *Second Treatise of Government*, Blackstone's amazing *Commentaries*, and similar works, no society in world history is based on this belief—until 1776.

That such a nation of unalienable rights would ever be established is hardly inevitable. In fact, at the beginning of American resistance to British oppression, the colonists only argue that they are being deprived of their rights as Englishmen. At that time, the colonists view themselves as Englishmen entitled to the protections of the unwritten English Constitution, Parliamentary statutory enactments, kingly decrees, legal rulings, traditions, and customs. Such protections include the right to a jury trial, the necessity of a court-issued warrant before searching someone's home, the prohibition of cruel and unusual punishments, and taxation only with representation. These are *English* concepts enjoyed by *English* subjects—not unalienable rights enjoyed by everyone. When resistance breaks out in the colonies in 1764, no one argues that these English rights apply to all of mankind throughout time and history. Instead, the colonists fight to maintain the rights they are entitled to as Englishmen. The Russians, French, Germans, Japanese, Egyptians, Ethiopians, and Chinese have nothing to do with it.

Had the British made a course correction in 1764 or 1765, the colonists would likely never have harkened to unalienable rights. As British oppression increases and American resistance to this treatment persists, the view of the colonists begins to transform. The key idea of protecting English rights gives way to protecting the unalienable rights of all. The Founders begin to realize that their rights are not dependent on an amiable king and Parliament. At birth, the Creator endows everyone with their sacred rights. The king and Parliament have nothing to do with it.

Former President John Quincy Adams (and son of John Adams) illuminates this transformation when he notes that following 1776, Americans' "charter was the Declaration of Independence. Their rights, the natural rights of mankind."* The transformation is fundamental. The rights of Englishmen are no longer the nexus for the American Revolution. Instead, as Thomas Jefferson explains, "a free people [claim] their rights, as derived from the laws of nature, and not as a gift from their chief magistrate."* John Dickinson, an early and highly influential American colonial opponent of the tyrannical British, eloquently expresses this understanding well before most in the colonies even begin to defend the rights of Englishmen:

> We claim them [rights essential to happiness] from a higher source—from the King of kings, and Lord of all the earth. They are not annexed to us by parchments and seals. They are created in us by the decrees of Providence, which establish the laws of our nature. They are born with us; exist with us; and cannot be taken from us by any human power, without taking our lives.*

Likewise, John Adams powerfully explains that the people possess rights "antecedent to all earthly government—Rights, that cannot be repealed or restrained by human laws—Rights derived from the great Legislator of the universe."*

The British Empire never recognizes this theory. With independence, for the first time in history, governments begin to embody the Revolutionary understanding of unalienable rights. When the bonds of allegiance are severed by the Declaration, each State needs to create a new fundamental law—a new constitution—to organize and govern its affairs. That this principle of unalienable rights forms much of the philosophical bulwark of our founding is evidenced by its recognition not only in the Declaration, but in the State constitutions enacted during and after the Revolution. The Virginia Declaration of Rights is drafted by the influential Revolutionary leader George Mason and adopted just prior to the Declaration of Independence. Like many of the Revolutionary-era State constitutions, it proclaims,

> all men are by nature equally free and independent, and have certain inherent rights, of which, when they enter into a state

> of society, they cannot, by any compact, deprive or divest their posterity; namely, the enjoyment of life and liberty, with the means of acquiring and possessing property, and pursuing and obtaining happiness and safety.*

> The Preamble of the federal Constitution recognizes our unique perspective when it explicitly recognizes that the Constitution is adopted to "secure the *Blessings* [italics added] of Liberty." By its very nature, blessings require the divine—the Creator.

We could span the whole course of human history before 1776 and find no society embracing unalienable rights as understood by the Founding Generation. In point of fact, governments embrace the exact opposite.

The great civilization of China is one vital example. "In the case of China," Professor Deborah Cao of Griffith University observes,

> there was an absence of a linguistic sign for "rights" in classical Chinese for either legal rights or moral rights, i.e., no word or equivalent concept existed in classical Chinese close to the Western idea of "rights." There were no equivalent intellectual discussions and debates about natural rights in early Chinese history.*

Simply put, the concept of unalienable rights is alien in China. China is a highly complex, developed, and sophisticated civilization spanning perhaps five thousand years. The Chinese culture comprises a wide array of art, advanced transportation, cutting-edge technology, and unparalleled architecture. Yet despite its accomplishments, China lacks one of America's fundamental, revolutionary First Principles. Scholar Frank Li reports that

> [t]he concept of natural rights has been consistently alien to the Chinese mind. One can hardly argue that the majority of the governing and intellectual elite in China from the middle of the nineteenth century to the present day had a basic understanding of the philosophy expounded by the Declaration of Independence, let alone aspired to see it realized.*

In 1776, the Chinese hold no belief whatsoever in the idea of unalienable rights.

Further, highly influential modern doctrines outright repudiate unalienable rights. Social Darwinism and its partner, eugenics, highlight this repudiation. In 1859, Charles Darwin turns the world on its head. Instead of static species directly created from the Hand of God, Darwin proposes the theory of evolution in that species change and evolve based on changing environmental conditions and genetic mutations. He terms it "Natural Selection," but recognizes "the expression often used by Mr. Herbert Spencer [English biologist, sociologist, philosopher, among many other things] of the Survival of the Fittest is more accurate, and is sometimes equally convenient."*

Although Darwin is initially discussing the animal kingdom, he subsequently applies natural selection to humanity. He then recognizes that society is acting against the theory of natural selection by preserving the weak and infirm through artificial means. Advanced, humanitarian efforts to improve and save lives, such as medical advancements and a social safety net, dilute the progress of the species. Civilization and mankind will be strengthened if plagues, poverty, insanity, and similar curses are allowed to simply run their course to cull out the weak, which enables the strong to propagate the species:

> With savages, the weak in body or mind are soon eliminated; and those that survive commonly exhibit a vigorous state of health. We civilized men, on the other hand, do our utmost to check the process of elimination [...]. Thus the weak members of civilized societies propagate their kind. No one who has attended to the breeding of domestic animals will doubt that this must be highly injurious to the race of man.*

Seemingly reluctantly, Darwin acknowledges that we have a noble instinct of sympathy, which helps save the weaker members of the species.* As Darwin notes above, the English philosopher and sociologist Herbert Spencer also argues that the "Survival of the Fittest" applies to mankind, societies, and individuals, and that letting this take its course will result in the greater perfection of mankind:

> The forces which are working out the great scheme of perfect happiness, taking no account of incidental suffering, exterminate such sections of mankind as stand in their way, with the same sternness that they exterminate beasts of prey and herds of useless ruminants.*

Taken to its logical extreme, Social Darwinism holds that, as a matter of public policy, the government should not just sit back and let the survival of the fittest run its course. Instead, the government should actively intervene and help the strong prevail. Note that Darwin's theory of evolution—that species evolve due to the interaction of mutations and environmental conditions—is not at issue here. After all, many of the Founders, such as Benjamin Franklin, Thomas Jefferson, Thomas Paine, Benjamin Rush, and even George Washington are leading inventors and scientists. The Founders' perspective is not anti-evolution, but it is diametrically opposed to Darwin's sinister belief that human kindness somehow violates what would otherwise be a perfect system.

The theory of eugenics is the fulfillment of this dark thinking. It takes various forms in many places, but basically it asserts that the government should eliminate flawed genes and individuals and cultivate superior genes and individuals. In ancient times, the Greek city-state of Sparta builds the most powerful fighting force in the ancient world by not only training its young men as soldiers, but by murdering babies who are considered inadequate for the rigors of combat.

Jump a few thousand years and Sparta's instinct is confirmed by Darwin's science. In truth, eugenics is a respectable, modern theory for generations. In the decades before World War II, it is widely popular in England, continental Europe, Latin America, and even the United States.* Scientists advocate for putting into practice Darwin's theory. The weak, infirm, and socially undesirable elements should be eliminated—just like diseases. Soon, public health policy in many advanced, industrial nations strongly embrace eugenics, supporting the policy that "defectives" should be prevented from breeding through custody in asylums or compulsory sterilization. Following this theory, many nations engage in vigorous sterilization campaigns leading to the sterilization of 3.5 million persons.* Nazi Germany fulfills the "promise" of eugenics by exalting the supposedly superior Germanic race above all others and by attempting to subjugate and even exterminate inferior Slavic and Jewish races through mass murder and the Holocaust.*

The theories of evolution, Social Darwinism, eugenics, and Nazism are diametrically opposed to unalienable rights. Under those systems, no one has rights. Nothing is unalienable or beyond the reach of government. The imperative is to follow Nature and the survival of the fittest—to perfect the human race, no matter the carnage.

As embodied by China, ancient civilizations do not recognize unalienable rights. Other powerful exemplifications include ancient Rome (recognizing privileges [not rights] based on customs, traditions, and laws), Athens (an all-powerful majority dominates all decisions without regard to rights), and Persia (the only person with rights is the absolute dictator). Before 1776, no nation authentically embraces unalienable rights. Later, Darwin, eugenics, and Nazism explicitly reject it. The same can be said of Marxism (the class struggle simply does not recognize rights), Progressivism (experts are empowered to better society without regard to rights), and utilitarianism (policies that support the most good for the most people must be pursued, regardless of individual liberties). In the end, 1776 America is the one true beacon of light that embraces unalienable rights—surrounded by the darkness of prior and subsequent history.*

*That all men are born equally free and independent, and have certain natural, inherent and inalienable rights, amongst which are, the enjoying and defending life and liberty, acquiring, acquiring, possessing and protecting property, and pursuing and obtaining happiness and safety.**

Pennsylvania Declaration of Rights (August 16, 1776)

# 14

## "THAT AMONG THESE ARE LIFE"

***What is the humane yet nonetheless radical commitment to life undertaken by the Founders?***

- ☆ Governments murdering their subjects—as opposed to protecting life—is a recurring theme in ancient and modern history. Governments across time and the globe, including Aztec and Soviet exemplars, fail to protect the unalienable right of life. Instead, they murder their own citizens.

- ☆ The Declaration declares as a self-evident truth that all men are endowed by their Creator with the unalienable right of life.

- ☆ We are the first nation in world history to recognize the unalienable right of life as a foundation for our government.

America is the first and only country to establish its government on the foundation of unalienable rights. The next natural question is: *What* are those rights? The Declaration specifically delineates three: "Life," "Liberty," and "the pursuit of Happiness." In contemporary America, these words may seem trite. But they are no such thing. The idea that life, liberty, and the pursuit of happiness are unalienable rights that should be protected by government is another truly revolutionary concept of the Founding Generation.

"Life" seems like a simple enough concept. People are alive and have a right to live. Who can argue with that? Contrary to our naive current expectations, life is quite expendable throughout all of human history—including the present. Indeed, the phenomenon of humans killing humans is as old as humanity. Ancient archeological research proves this beyond a doubt.* The Declaration's proclamation that people are born with the unalienable right to life is truly focused on the responsibility of the government to protect the lives of its own citizens from external enemies and from each other within the society. In other words, the Founders believe that a key purpose of government is to protect against foreign invaders, keep the peace, and maintain order within the society.

The Founders' view contradicts the brutal facts of history. Governments committing mass murder of their own people is commonplace across cultures and times. Likewise, government policies that indirectly result in mass death are common. Death of innocents at the hands of the government is ubiquitous across the globe and time. To help understand how that could be possibly be true, Professor R. J. Rummel coins the term "democide" as "the murder of any person or people by a government, including genocide, politicide [politically motivated killing], and mass murder."* This expansive definition captures deaths caused by capital punishment, wars with other countries, civil wars, crusades and religious conflicts, purposefully created famines, medical experimentation, concentration camps, forced labor, and torture. It also includes genocide, that is, the purposeful annihilation of an entire ethnic group, race, religion, or other targeted group. By Professor Rummel's count, 262 million people are the victims of democide in the twentieth century alone. This count includes 50 million killed by imperial powers against their colonial subjects, over 60 million decimated by the Soviet Union, and over 76 million exterminated by Communist China.*

The Americas before colonization are a fitting starting point for further exploring the unalienable right to life. For instance, the Aztecs worship many gods, each of whom requires some kind of human sacrifice, and each god has its own particular requirements. The Aztecs believe that the sun god Huītzilōpōchtli conducts an unending war against darkness. Huītzilōpōchtli needs human hearts and blood to continue to beat back the darkness. If the sun god loses, the world will end. Human sacrifice is part of everyday life to save the world. Historian Caroline Dodds Pennock explains the bloody scene:

> As they mounted the pyramid, captives saw their colleagues brutally dispatched, their hearts torn from their chests and offered to the gods. The lifeless, bloodied, corpses rolled past them down the pyramid steps as they climbed toward their fate.*

At Templo Mayor, conquistadors found towers and racks of thousands of skulls.

Considering the brutality of this scene, the natural reaction might be that this gruesome ritualization of sacrifice is a fabrication or anti-indigenous people propaganda. However, archaeologists at the National Institute of Anthropology and History confirm the reports of the conquistadors.* The annual number of sacrifices is estimated from a minimum of 25,000 to as much as 250,000. The Aztecs are not alone, just perhaps the most robust and vivid in their practices.*

Another deadly example is the Soviet Union's murder of its Ukrainian citizens. Managed by Nikolai Bukharin in 1932 and 1933, the Soviet Union's actions orchestrate the death of between six to twelve million people concentrated in the Ukraine. Dubbed the *Holodomor* (in Ukrainian, "death by hunger" or "killing by hunger"), this genocide is perpetrated to crush the people of the Ukraine, in particular the peasant class. Ironically, the Ukraine is the breadbasket of the Soviet Union, and it is pillaged by the Soviets with the direct purpose of starving their political opponents. The Soviets cut off escape routes by shutting down train service, surrounding communities with barricades, and shipping back anyone who escapes. The Soviets also target other areas within the USSR. Historian Timothy Snyder describes the hellish situation:

> Survival was a moral as well as a physical struggle. A woman doctor wrote to a friend in June 1933 that she had not yet become a cannibal, but [she] was "not sure that I shall not be one by the time my letter reaches you." The good people died first. Those who refused to steal or to prostitute themselves died. Those who gave food to others died. Those who refused to eat corpses died. Those who refused to kill their fellow man died. Parents who resisted cannibalism died before their children did.*

The Soviet Constitution of 1924 makes no mention of rights at all—including the right to life. At least they are not outright hypocrites.

The urge to use governments to murder—as opposed to protect life—is a long-standing and recurring theme in ancient and modern history. From ancient Aztecs to the USSR (and so many more), governments across time have not protected the unalienable right of life. Instead, they execute just the opposite policy: They murder their own citizens.

America, however, is founded on the belief that life is an unalienable right endowed in each person by the Creator. Once again, the Founding Fathers turn history on its head. To the extent that it can, the government has a duty to stop murder and punish it. Government has a sacred duty to defend against foreign invaders. This is why we have the military, border protection, criminal law, police, a criminal justice system, prisons, and judges. In short, the purpose of the government is not to kill, but protect life.

This understanding flows from the foundation of the Ten Commandments given to Moses in the desert by the Hebrew God. The sixth commandment prohibits murder. This commandment is the basis of the conviction that the government is responsible for protecting life. The Founders more specifically embrace the exposition of this belief by the English philosophers Thomas Hobbes and John Locke. Hobbes explains in his magnum opus, *Leviathan*, that "[t]he right of nature [...] is the liberty each man has, to use his own power, as he will himself, for the preservation of his own nature; that is to say, of his own life."*

In other words, each person has the right to self-defense. Locke writes two treatises to justify the Glorious Revolution of 1688, but much of them also justify the American Revolution. In his *Second Treatise of Government*, he echoes Hobbes's observation that Natural Law vests in each person the right to life. Locke reasons that since we are all made from the Creator, it is His will that we exist, and that no one should subvert the Creator's will by murdering one of His creations.* In fact, Locke confirms that not only should we not harm others, but every person should, as much as possible, "preserve the rest of mankind, and may not, unless it be to do justice on an offender, take away or impair the life, [...] the liberty, health, limb, or goods of another."* The right to life is an unalienable one, vested by the laws of Nature and Nature's God.*

Indeed, Hobbes and Locke agree that the whole point of joining into a society under a government is the "preservation of their lives, liberties, and [...] property."* Government must protect our unalienable rights because that is a key purpose justifying its existence. Otherwise, we might as well live in the wild, free of government dictates. This is a matter of Natural Law, and the government is duty bound and accountable to God to protect the people under its care.*

Not only should the government act to protect its people, but it has a duty to teach its populace what is right and wrong, especially in connection with the safety of individuals and criminal justice. Hobbes propounds that "the people are to be taught, to abstain from violence to one another's person, by private revenges."* This helps explain the view held by Thomas Jefferson, Benjamin Rush, and other Founders that government has an obligation to provide for the free education of children. They want to ensure that future citizens understand history and the Constitution, as well as to instill the moral values and habits of a free republic.

The idea that the natural, unalienable right of life should be protected by law is starting to take root in England before the American Revolution. William Blackstone writes that "[l]ife is the immediate gift of God, a right inherent by nature in every individual."*

The Founders take this theoretical English idea and make it a core pillar of America. The Declaration unequivocally declares that government is created to protect the unalienable right to life. The State constitutions adopted in the wake of the Declaration proclaim similar sentiments. For example, Article 1 of the

Declaration of Rights of the Pennsylvania Constitution, adopted in 1776, provides that among the "natural, inherent and inalienable rights" we possess is the "enjoying and defending of life and liberty."*

Unlike most of the rest of the world, where this sentiment is considered bizarre, and England, where it is only tentatively believed by some, in America this view is nearly universal. James Wilson is a leading legal scholar and a key member of the Constitutional Convention from Pennsylvania. Beginning in 1790, he delivers a series of legal lectures that accurately summarize the state of the law in America. The audience for Wilson's inaugural lecture includes the president, vice president, and the Pennsylvania legislature. That audience would almost certainly make an ordinary person nervous. But Wilson is extraordinary. Among many accomplishments, he signs both the Declaration and the Constitution and serves as one of the first justices on the United States Supreme Court. During his lecture series, Wilson explains that life is an unalienable right given to man as a gift from heaven, as "life, and whatever is necessary for the safety of life, are the natural rights of man. [...] By the law, life is protected not only from immediate destruction, but from every degree of actual violence, and in some cases, from every degree of danger."*

The importance of the unalienable right to life is reflected in our federal Bill of Rights. The Fifth Amendment to the United States Constitution provides "nor shall any person [...] be deprived of life, liberty, or property, without due process of law." In other words, the right to life cannot simply be snatched away without adhering to strict judicial proceedings, including notice of charges, the right to contest any criminal charges at a trial with an impartial jury or judge, and a verdict based on the law and evidence.

The Founders' embrace of life is directly contrary to many regimes throughout history. In addition to the Aztec and Soviet examples, the Ottoman Empire commits the Armenian genocide, the French Revolution's Terror slaughters tens of thousands, Communist China's Great Famine starves between twenty to forty-five million, and the Rwandan genocide murders up to a million Tutsis. Unfortunately, there is so much more. By exalting the First Principle that individuals are endowed with an unalienable right to life, America breaks once again with the past (and future) and moves mankind forward in a tremendous, unprecedented fashion.

*Give me liberty or give me death!**

Patrick Henry (March 23, 1775)

# 15

# "Liberty"

***What is personal freedom, and why do the Founders believe it to be so fundamental to the role of government?***

- ☆ Before 1776, no government embraces the unalienable right of liberty. Quite to the contrary, ancient civilizations such as Babylon and Greece, and more modern regimes such as Fascist Italy and ISIS, are tyrannies that violate the unalienable right of liberty.

- ☆ We receive the unalienable right of liberty from Nature and Nature's God, not government.

- ☆ Liberty is to be free from the arbitrary rule of the government and to be free to do what you choose, so long as you do not interfere with the unalienable rights of others. Paradoxically, liberty is protected by the rule of law.

- ☆ Liberty is at the heart of the American Revolution.

Harvard Professor Orlando Patterson observes that "non-western peoples have thought so little about freedom that most human languages did not even possess a word for the concept before contact with the West."* Aside from a small number of Greek city-states, liberty is unknown in ancient cultures. For example, Babylon's Hammurabi's Code has no reference to a free person. There are slaves and masters. But even masters are not free. They are simply the subjects of the monarch; the king controls all.*

The ancient Greek city-states have many different types of governments, most of which lack democracy or liberty. For those few ancient city-states that are a democracy, it is a tyranny of the majority. The Greek philosopher Aristotle explains that

> [o]ne principle of liberty is for all to rule and be ruled in turn, and indeed democratic justice is the application of numerical not proportionate equality; whence it follows that the majority must be supreme, and that whatever the majority approve must be the end and the just.*

Liberty is found *in* majority rule. A majority vote determines what liberties people possess. The majority determines what the society does and what is justice. If the majority, for example, determines to criminalize the worship of Zeus, they are fully empowered to ban the free exercise of religion. If the majority votes to execute an old philosopher for corrupting the youth, he is executed. Of course, this is exactly what happens to Socrates—Aristotle's (indeed, the West's)—philosophical grandfather. The rule of the majority is a splendid system—until you are outvoted. Then you may very well lose your property, liberty, and life. No minority rights are protected under this system. No rights are unalienable, quite the opposite. All rights are entirely dependent on the will of the majority.

Contrary to the ancients, the Declaration declares that *all* men have unalienable rights. Moreover, everyone has the *same* rights. Your rights are not dependent on your social status, your family bloodline, or your wealth. Simply by virtue of being a human being, you have these rights.

But what exactly is "liberty"? On occasion, one better understands what something *is* by understanding what it is *not*. Consider two countries from the relatively recent past in which there is no liberty.

Our first historical example is Fascist Italy. Affectionately known as *Il Duce* ("the Leader"), Benito Mussolini is the founder of fascism. He takes power as the prime minister of Italy on October 29, 1922, by marching into Rome at the head of his own proto-army—the infamous Blackshirts. Over time, they intimidate the government into vesting Mussolini with absolute power. Mussolini defines the proper role between individuals and the state—individuals are entirely subservient to the state. The state is *everything*:

> Anti-individualistic, the fascist conception of life stresses the importance of the state. It affirms the value of the individual only in so far as his interests coincide with those of the state, which stands for the conscience and the universal will of man in history [...]. Fascism stands for the only liberty worth possessing: the liberty of the state and of the individual within the state [...].

> No individuals outside the state; no groups (political parties, associations, trade unions, social classes) outside the state.*

The state is all, the individual nothing. In the view of Mussolini, liberty is not something possessed by individuals, groups, or the people at large. Liberty is something owned and provided by the state.

In action, the Italian Fascists are cruel and brutal. Although their leaders are significantly less demonic than in Nazi Germany, Communist China, or the Soviet Union, individual liberties are severely suppressed in Fascist Italy. Once Mussolini consolidates his power, he replaces local elective leaders with his appointees, crushes opposition parties, arrests and tortures political opponents, cancels elections, and establishes kangaroo courts to persecute political opponents. Unauthorized meetings, assemblies, parades, and demonstrations are banned—even for the Fascists. Opposition party leaders are tried and imprisoned or simply murdered on the streets. Mussolini eviscerates free speech, controls the media, and shutters all non-Fascist papers. He takes control of radio and film production. Phone tapping is widespread. The Fascists control the schools. He outlaws unions and strikes and replaces them with Fascist syndicates. Industry and monetary policy are under Il Duce's thumb. He institutes forced deportations and issues "shoot to kill" orders at the borders. Even the opera and the boy scouts are controlled. The church and military are co-opted. Police spy on citizens, and citizens inform on their neighbors, friends, and family members. This is all done under the color of law.

The Italian government changes the language—literally banning the use of the formal pronoun *Lei* and replacing it with *Voi*. Foreign words, streets, and places are replaced with Latin and Italian names. Suits, top hats, and afternoon tea are all but banned, and Roman numerals replace Arabic numbers in connection with dates. Mussolini resurrects the ideal of Roman glory, including banning the handshake and replacing it with the Roman salute. This is so compelling that the Nazis borrow it.* Propagandistic Fascist slogans blanket Italy, such as "Mussolini is always right" and "Better to live one day as a lion than 100 years as a sheep."* Enthusiastic crowds chant "Il Duce is always right!" and "Believe, obey, fight!" Like so many governments before and after it, the Italian Fascists reject the idea of individual liberty and instead insist that humanity should serve the state.

To prove the adage that it can always get worse, in 2014, ISIS conquers large swaths of Iraq and Syria. A militant terrorist group and unrecognized state, it brutally enforces a fundamentalist, Salafi-jihadist doctrine of Sunni Islam. ISIS members believe they know Allah's will, and to achieve worldwide domination to implement it, they are willing to kill anyone who stands in their way. When ISIS wins territory, it proclaims itself as the Muslim caliphate (successor to the Ottoman Empire), pretending it has authority over Muslims across the globe.

ISIS imposes a theocracy of the most pernicious type. It requires everyone to follow its interpretation of scripture, Wahhabism, an extreme form of Islam. The United Nations Commission on Human Rights finds that ISIS "seeks to subjugate civilians under its control and dominate every aspect of their lives through terror, indoctrination, and the provision of services to those who obey."* ISIS enforces its dictates through reeducation, recruitment, a general police force, and morality police forces (known as Al-Hisbah and the Al-Khansaa Brigade). Its judicial system butchers nonbelievers. It creates a religious police state that punishes failure to attend religious services, neglect of religious practices, and what it considers to be vice. It destroys non-Sunni religious buildings and widely employs capital punishment. Beheadings of enemies, enslavement of girls and women as sex slaves, and the destruction of cultural heritage sites are the harvest they sow. German journalist Jürgen Todenhofer, embedded with the group for ten days, reports that its goal is to "conquer every country" and kill anyone who does not agree with their extremist theology. ISIS members believe that "all religions who agree with democracy have to die,"* which will necessarily lead to the killing of "hundreds of millions" of people.*

This work could spend thousands of pages on tyrannies throughout history. After all, tyranny (in its many guises) is the dominant mode of governance in human history. However, the Founding Generation turns the world topsy-turvy by boldly declaring that men have an unalienable right to liberty and founding a government on that belief.

Before 1776, the colonists are considered Englishmen. England has a long tradition of recognizing certain rights and privileges. However, as noted earlier, these are not understood as universal, unalienable rights. Instead, English rights and privileges are recognized as the result of centuries of conflict between the Crown and Parliament, by which the elite scratch and claw power away from the monarchy. Accordingly, most rights and privileges at first protect only Parliament or the nobility, but over time, some of them are extended to more and more of England's common people.

The most famous example of the acknowledgement of these rights is the Magna Carta of 1215. The king, appropriately known to history as "Bad King John," squares off against his nobles in a protracted power struggle. Intensely arrogant King John aggressively attempts to steal away from the nobility a great deal of their ancient authority. He has the added disadvantage of being incompetent. Most of the noble class respond to King John's efforts to take their power with armed resistance. In the end, the resisting nobles outmatch the king's royal forces. Bad King John finds himself in a very bad spot and is on the verge of losing his throne—if not his life—unless he concedes certain rights to the nobles. At Runnymede, England, near Windsor, on June 15, 1215, he signs the Magna Carta Libertatum ("the Great Charter of Freedoms").

The Magna Carta of 1215 has several unique aspects. First, it is written. A written document is basically unprecedented in connection with establishing rules of conduct that limit government authority. Second, it acknowledges that the monarchy will be bound by certain rules and limitations into perpetuity. Third, it lists specific rights guaranteed to the noble class. Fourth, it establishes a twenty-five-member council of barons to ensure that its commitments are implemented.

Not all its promises last long, but it sets a compelling precedent that reaches across the centuries. In fact, some of the rights it establishes are protected to this day. For example, it recognizes the right to the due process of law. In other words, life, liberty, and property cannot be taken unless it is authorized by a legitimate law and taken pursuant to preset procedures. It also guarantees to the English Church religious freedom. It also has the kernel of the prohibition of cruel and unusual punishment. It protects certain property from being seized without consent. Section 39 is a truly groundbreaking provision:

> No free man shall be seized or imprisoned, or stripped of his rights or possessions, or outlawed or exiled, or deprived of his standing in any way, nor will we proceed with force against him, or send others to do so, except by the lawful judgment of his equals by the law of the land.

In other words, this provision establishes a trial by jury by fixed laws. In addition, Section 40 includes the origin of the right to a speedy trial. It also protects the right to leave and return to the kingdom "unharmed and without fear [...] except in time of war." However, most of these protections apply solely to barons, and many are eventually ignored or discarded. Nevertheless, they set a marker for liberty that eventually expands for all.*

More than four centuries later, another clash between the king and Parliament results in an expansion of liberty. King Charles I and Parliament struggle over the direction and funding of a war with Spain. This results in the issuance of the Petition of Right of 1628. The brainchild of Sir Edward Coke, the greatest jurist of the age, the Petition of Right is just that: a petition by Parliament of demands to the king. It declares that "no man, of what estate or condition that he be, should be put out of his land or tenements, nor taken, nor imprisoned, nor disinherited nor put to death without being brought to answer by due process of law." Thus, due process is afforded to all, not just nobility. This expansion of due process to *all* men is a true watershed moment in the all-too-slow march of liberty. The Petition of Right also declares that no one should be forced to pay a tax "without common consent by act of parliament." In other words, no taxation without representation. It further proclaims that no soldiers should be quartered among the citizens, and martial law is barred in times of peace. The Petition of Right also claims that the king has violated several of these rights and "humbly" prays that the king would heed the rights it sets forth and stop any future violations of those rights.*

When King Charles I accepts it (in essence, implicitly agreeing to abide by its terms), the Petition of Right of 1628 becomes a vital link in expanding liberty in the constitutional law of England. Like the Magna Carta of 1215, on occasion it is ignored. Still, it is a monumental acknowledgement of the rights of Englishmen.

Most scholars point to the Habeas Corpus Act 1679 as the next vital link in the expansion of English liberty. The Latin term "habeas corpus" means "you shall have the body." The idea is that any prisoner has the right to be brought before a court and be released by the court if he or she is unlawfully imprisoned. A "writ of habeas corpus" is a judge-issued order that requires governmental authorities to bring the imprisoned person before the court, at which time the court will determine if the prisoner should remain in custody or be released.

Another magnificent step to protecting liberty is the Bill of Rights 1689, which Parliament enacts in the wake of the Glorious Revolution. In quick, Parliament deposes King James II, whom the majority of Parliament views as a dangerous tyrant. Parliament basically invites the King's Protestant daughter, Mary, and her Dutch husband, William, to invade England to depose King James II. To ensure that the cure is not worse than the disease, in 1689, Parliament passes An Act Declaring the Rights and Liberties of the Subject and Settling the Succession of the Crown. A key portion of the act includes the Bill of Rights 1689, which expands constitutional protections for Parliament and the people. It bars the monarch from suspending, discarding, or refusing to enforce the law and requires Parliament to approve the spending of any government funds. The Bill of Rights 1689 also establishes the people's right to petition for a redress of grievances. Moreover, it prohibits a standing army without the consent of Parliament, as well as guarantees the right to bear arms (albeit limited to Protestants). Free elections of members of Parliament are guaranteed, the king is barred from frequently dissolving Parliament, and members of Parliament are immune from prosecution for whatever they say in Parliament. It also provides a major step forward in criminal justice and the protection of unalienable rights when it proclaims that "excessive bail ought not to be required, nor excessive fines imposed, nor cruel and unusual punishments inflicted."*

As Englishmen, the American colonists believe in the core of their souls that they possess these rights and liberties. In practice, they have far less to fear from London than anyone in England. In the New World, they are generally left alone from imperial interference. This long-standing practice of "salutary neglect" makes it the public policy of the empire to allow the colonies to run their own internal affairs. The American colonies are likely the freest people in world history. Consequently, they thrive. Early American historian David Ramsay succinctly observes that the colonists "shared in every privilege belonging to her native sons, and but slightly felt the inconveniences of subordination."* Before 1764, very few in England or the American colonies question this arrangement. Likewise, the understanding that the English subjects of the colonies possess the rights of any Englishmen in the empire is unchallenged.

As noted earlier, with English oppression, Americans shift their thinking away from defending the rights of Englishmen and toward defending unalienable rights endowed by the Creator in all men. Among these natural rights is *liberty.** English philosopher Thomas Hobbes explains what this means in his magnum opus, *Leviathan or the Matter, Forme and Power of a Commonwealth Ecclesiasticall and Civil:*

> By liberty, is understood [...] the absence of external impediments: which impediments, may often take away part of a man's power to do what he would; but cannot hinder him from using the power left him, according to his judgment, and reason shall dictate to him.*

Subject to certain limits, Natural Law provides the liberty to do, or not do, what one pleases. Hobbes explains that the first law of Nature is the right to self-defense. The second law of Nature is basically the Golden Rule—do unto others as you would have them do unto you.* When the Golden Rule is applied to society at large, it generally means that within certain social norms, the government leaves you free to do what you desire, so long as you do not interfere with the rights of others.* Hobbes explains that liberty is to be free from constraint, and a freeman "is he, that in those things, which by his strength and wit he is able to do, is not hindered to do what he has a will to."* John Locke echoes this sentiment in his *Second Treatise of Government* when he explains that Natural Law vests in each person the right to liberty* so long as the exercise of that liberty does not harm another.* Thomas Jefferson adds that liberty includes "the rights of thinking, and publishing our thoughts by speaking or writing: the right of free commerce: the right of personal freedom."*

Liberty is central to the American founding. As we have learned, America is mostly settled by those seeking liberty from the oppressive governments that otherwise dominate the world. In a stirring sermon, Minister Simeon Baldwin preaches:

> Liberty was the darling object of the first settlers of this country. Animated with the hope of enjoying those civil and religious rights, which Heaven designed for the virtuous, they bade adieu to the joys of a more social life, and, surrounded with the horrors of death in a thousand different shapes, they took possession of the fair territory we now inhabit. In the anticipation of liberty, plenty and peace, they braved all dangers and all hardships.*

In the American context, the understanding of what constitutes liberty seems to be an ever-evolving and expanding notion. In 1776, liberty clearly includes the rights recognized in the Magna Carta of 1215, Petition of Right of 1628, and the Bill of Rights 1689. The Founding Generation also embraces Locke's idea of liberty. At the time of the founding, the heart of liberty is the ability to self-govern. As Locke observes, to have true liberty, the government must be based on the consent of the governed:

> The natural liberty of man is to be free from any superior power on earth, and not to be under the will or legislative authority of man, but to have only the law of nature for his rule. The liberty of man, in society, is to be under no other legislative power, but that established, by consent, in the commonwealth; nor under the dominion of any will, or restraint of any law, but what that legislative shall enact, according to the trust put in it.*

Stated in more modern language, in a state of Nature, people are free because there is no government. When a government is established, individuals can only be free if the government acts within the authority given to it by the people. Consent is a prerequisite to liberty.

This understanding, however, does not allow a tyranny of the majority. To be free, individuals cannot be subject to the arbitrary power of the government, untethered from duly enacted laws. This is the rule of law—that the people are to be governed by known laws, appropriately established by the government, that apply to everyone equally. Locke further explains that an established, known law is necessary for liberty. For with no known, governing law, we are subject to the whims and wrongs of others at any given time. Within the rule of law, we have the liberty to follow our dreams.

Indeed, Hobbes and Locke agree that the whole point of joining into a society and forming a government, in the language of Locke, is the "preservation of their lives, liberties, and estates, which I call by the general name, property."* The bundle of constitutional rights we consider second nature are bound up in this idea of liberty protected by the rule of law.

Most famously expressed in several protections in the original, unamended Constitution, as well as amendments codified in the Bill of Rights, these protections include the free exercise of religion, freedom of speech, freedom of the press, the right to assemble, the right to petition government, the right to bear arms, the prohibition of quartering of troops in homes, due process of law, the right to counsel, the right against self-incrimination, the prohibition of searches and seizures without a duly issued warrant, the right against double jeopardy, the right to a public trial, the right to a speedy trial, the prohibition of cruel and unusual punishments, the protection against ex post facto laws (Latin for "after the fact"—in other words, laws that criminalize retroactively what was legal at the time), the right to trial by an impartial jury of your peers, the prohibition of bills of attainder (in other words, specific legislative acts finding individuals guilty of crimes), and the prohibition of the taking of private property by the government unless for public use and with just compensation. This is truly a stupendous and historically unique assortment of rights.

On the other hand, Americans recognize that the law can also be an instrumentality of severe oppression. When the government acts under the guise of lawful authority to violate the unalienable rights of the people, it is no longer a force for good, but evil. When the British clamp down on the colonists, the colonists move from the old British understanding that the right to liberty was protected as an English right and transform it into a universal right of men, granted by the Creator. They take Locke and Hobbes seriously. They also realize that under British rule, the government is not protecting unalienable rights. To the contrary, the British are subverting the whole purpose of government. Thomas Jefferson reflects that "law is often the tyrant's will, and always so when it violates the right of an individual."* In a very real sense, this is what the Declaration is all about: rebelling against the law that is subverting—as opposed to protecting—the unalienable rights of the people.

The revolutionaries resolve that this unalienable right of liberty is worth fighting and dying for. On March 4, 1775, Son of Liberty Samuel Adams writes that the revolutionaries must "resist the tyranny which threatens us" and that "[t]he public liberty must be preserved though at the expense of many lives."* With such expressions, Samuel Adams musters unruly crowds to physically protest and resist British oppression in the streets of Boston. He exhorts that liberty is more precious than personal pleasures and comfort, American martyrs should not be forgotten, and those unwilling to sacrifice for liberty deserve scoffs and disdain:

> You abandoned minions of an infatuated ministry; if peradventure any should yet remain us!—Remember that a Warren* and Montgomery* are numbered among the dead.—Contemplate the mangled bodies of your countrymen—and then say, What should be the reward of such sacrifices?—Bid us and posterity bow the knee, supplicate the friendship, and plow and sow, and reap to glut the avarice of the men who have let loose on us the dogs of war to riot in our blood, and hunt us from the face of the Earth.—If ye love wealth better than liberty, the tranquility of servitude, [better] than the animating contest of freedom, go home from us in peace.—We ask not your counsels or arms—crouch down and lick the hands which feed you—May your chains set lightly upon you, and may posterity forget that you were our countrymen.*

Although Samuel Adams is unparalleled in organizing political resistance on the street and has a dramatic and powerful ability to rouse the crowd with uplifting speeches, Patrick Henry is undoubtedly the most eloquent and powerful orator for the cause. A member of Virginia's colonial legislature (the House of Burgesses), Henry defines the moment and the stakes in an unforgettable fashion. On March 23, 1775, he stands before the Second Virginia Convention, the successor to the now disbanded House of Burgesses. The body is forced to convene at St. John's Church in Richmond, Virginia. About a month later, on April 19, shots are fired at Lexington and Concord between colonial militia and English regular troops. Today, the world remembers the first shot fired at Lexington, Massachusetts, as the "shot heard round the world," which sparks the American Revolution. The reality on the ground and at the time was in some dimensions much different. The British crackdown is centered on Boston and Massachusetts. The Southern colonies are ignored. At the time, most in England and many in America hold grave doubts that the other colonies will rally to Massachusetts's defense. There stands Patrick Henry at St. John's Church—nearly four hundred miles away from Boston—several days if not a week's journey away. No one in Virginia has been threatened with military force. Immaterial. Henry thunders that the time for peace efforts with England has passed for all of America. The time has come to risk all of their lives for liberty:

> Sir, we have done everything that could be done, to avert the storm which is now coming on. We have petitioned—we have remonstrated—we have supplicated—we have prostrated ourselves before the throne, and have implored its interposition to arrest the tyrannical hands of the ministry and parliament. Our petitions have been slighted; our remonstrances have produced additional violence and insult; our supplications have been disregarded; and we have been spurned, with contempt, from the foot of the throne. In vain, after these things, may we indulge the fond hope of peace and reconciliation. *There is no longer any room for hope.* If we wish to be free—if we mean to preserve inviolate those inestimable privileges for which we have been so long contending—if we mean not basely to abandon the noble struggle in which we have been so long engaged, and which we have pledged ourselves never to abandon, until the glorious object of our contest shall be obtained—we must fight! I repeat it, sir, we must fight!! An appeal to arms and to the God of hosts, is all that is left us! [Italics are in the original.]

Henry's riveting conclusion resounds throughout the ages:

> There is no retreat but in submission and slavery! Our chains are forged. Their clanking may be heard on the plains of Boston! The war is inevitable—and let it come!! I repeat it, sir, let it come!!!
>
> It is in vain, sir, to extenuate the matter. Gentlemen may cry, peace, peace—but there is no peace. The war is actually begun! The next gale that sweeps from the north will bring to our ears the clash of resounding arms! Our brethren are already in the field! Why stand we here idle? What is it that gentlemen wish? What would they have? Is life so dear, or peace so sweet, as to be purchased at the price of chains and slavery? Forbid it, Almighty God! I know not what course others may take; but as for me... give me liberty or give me death!*

An eyewitness illustrates the overwhelming power of the speech: "Imagine you heard a voice as from heaven uttering the words, 'We must fight!' as the doom of fate,—and you may have some idea of the speaker, the assembly to whom he addressed himself, and the auditory of which I was one."* The effect is stunning:

"Men leaned forward in their seats, with their heads strained forward, their faces pale, and their eyes glaring like the speaker's. His last exclamation, 'Give me liberty, or give me death!' was like the shout of the leader which turns back the rout of battle."* The war will come, and Henry welcomes it. Henry is far from alone. His speech leads Virginia to pass a resolution placing the colony on a war footing. Other colonies soon follow suit. The colonies are unifying and stiffening their resolve that they will risk their lives to protect their liberties. Everyone who takes up arms against the British literally takes Henry's commitment to heart.

This is a very special movement. Insurrections, civil wars, rebellions, and revolts throughout human events are usually motivated by riches, lust for power, political or ethnic separation, religion, cults of personality, resources, class divisions—there is barely a mention of liberty. But not in the American Revolution. It is all about liberty. As Henry reflects several years later, "Liberty. [T]he greatest of all earthly blessings—give us that precious jewel, and you may take every thing [*sic*] else!"*

This Revolutionary fever is widespread—even in what modern readers might consider to be unexpected corners, people join the resistance. At Lexington and Concord, at least forty African Americans (most of them slaves) from eleven Massachusetts towns join the colonial forces in battle. A couple of months later at Bunker Hill, at least 150 slaves defend American liberty. When George Washington crosses the Delaware River in a victorious surprise attack in brutal conditions, many former slaves, now free men, participate in the victory that saves the American Revolution. At least four hundred join colonial forces at the first major American victory at Saratoga, and over eight hundred are at the Battle of Monmouth on June 28, 1778. Many slaves gain their freedom because of their courageous service. As a Southern slaveholder, Washington is originally opposed to African American participation in the Patriot forces and even orders them out of the Continental Army. However, New England officers refuse these orders and Washington relents, leaving recruitment of free African Americans to the discretion of the officers. It is a wise choice, as African Americans are vital to the War of Independence. Eventually, the First Rhode Island Regiment possesses entire companies of free African Americans. African Americans also play a prominent role in New York's Continental Army regiments, fulfilling instrumental roles in various engagements. The Bucks of America in Massachusetts is another all-African American fighting force. Scholars estimate that during the course of the American Revolution, up to ten thousand African Americans fight for the American cause, rising from perhaps 1 percent in 1776 to up to 10 percent of all American forces by 1781.

Washington's understanding of the bravery and skill of African American troops softens his heart about the justice and necessity of slavery. As historian David Hackett Fischer summarizes,

> [w]ith these events, and much encouragement from his friend the Marquis de Lafayette, Washington's thinking on race and slavery changed during the war. And after the war, he corresponded with antislavery leaders in Britain and Europe, received their writings and read them. He stopped the use of whipping at Mount Vernon, ceased selling slaves on principle, and ordered that all his slaves be freed at his death. Of ten slaveholding presidents, Washington was the only one to do so. [...] Washington increasingly linked the conduct of the War of Independence to the expanding principles of the American Revolution. Agents of that expansion were often American soldiers of African ancestry.*

Other Americans clamor for the freedoms that were won in the American Revolution to be bestowed upon the enslaved. They understand the rank hypocrisy of slavery in the land of the free. The march of abolitionism begins with the American Revolution. In a Fourth of July address delivered a few years after the Revolution, Simeon Baldwin announces the thinking of many of the Founding Generation:

> The labours of the patriot and the friend of humanity are not yet completed. It is their talk to remove those blemishes which have hitherto sullied the glory of these States. We may feed our vanity with the pompous recital of noble achievements—[...] we may boast of the anticipated glories of the western continent:—But virtue will mourn that injustice and ingratitude have, in too many instances, had the countenance of law—Humanity will mourn that an odious slavery, cruel in itself, degrading to the dignity of man, and shocking to human nature, is tolerated, and in many instances practiced with barbarian cruelty.—Yes, even in this land of boosted freedom, this asylum for the oppressed, that inhuman practice has lost its horrors by the sanction of custom.
>
> To remedy this evil will be a work of time.—God be thanks it is already begun.*

Later, enslaved persons find great inspiration from the revolutionaries. Gabriel's Rebellion in Virginia is a slave uprising in 1800. At trial, one of the leaders declares in "a manly tone of voice" that "I have nothing more to offer than what George Washington would have had to offer, had he been taken by the British and put to trial by them. I have adventured my life in endeavouring to obtain the liberty of my countrymen, and am willing to sacrifice to their cause."*

The State revolutionary governments embed liberty into their fundamental law. The new States adopt constitutions in the wake of the Declaration of Independence, which proclaim commitments to liberty paralleling the Declaration. As just one example, the Preamble of the 1777 Constitution provides

> all government ought to be instituted and supported, for the security and protection of the community, as such, and to enable the individuals who compose it, to enjoy their natural rights, and the other blessings which the Author of existence has bestowed upon man; and whenever those great ends of government are not obtained, the people have a right, by common consent, to change it, and take such measures as to them may appear to be necessary to promote their safety and happiness.*

The United States Constitution later exults the importance of liberty in its Preamble, when it proclaims that securing the "Blessings of Liberty" is one of the major reasons for its adoption. Indeed, preserving liberty is nearly the whole point. The constitutional structure—establishing three separate branches of government, each with distinct, limited enumerated powers, along with checks and balances against each other—is carefully designed to stop tyranny. Under Article I, Section 9, persons accused of a crime are guaranteed the right of habeas corpus—that is, they can demand that a court order their release if they are illegally detained. Under the same section, bills of attainder—that is, legislation that specifically finds named individuals guilty of crimes—are prohibited.

Additionally, the Bill of Rights (the first ten ratified amendments) expressly checks the power of the federal government by protecting individual liberties. The First Amendment declares "Congress shall make no law respecting an establishment of religion, or prohibiting the free exercise thereof; or abridging the freedom of speech, or of the press; or the right of the people to peaceably assemble, and to petition the Government for a redress of grievances." We are free to express our thoughts and opinions individually and with others, even highly critical ideas against and to the government, without censorship or retribution; we can worship (or not) the Creator in the manner we believe the divine demands without suppression, even if that worship is in direct contradiction of prevailing norms.

The Second Amendment ensures "the right of the people to keep and bear Arms, shall not be infringed." With force of arms, we can protect our lives, families, property, and—if it comes to it—freedom. The Third Amendment prohibits the quartering of troops in peacetime. No military locusts will descend on our homes. The Fourth Amendment guarantees the "right of the people to be secure in their persons, houses, papers, and effects, against unreasonable searches and seizures, shall not be violated, and no Warrants shall issue, but upon probable cause, supported by Oath or affirmation, and particularly describing the place to be searched and the persons or things to be seized." Persons, homes, and property cannot be searched unless the government has solid evidence that a crime has been committed and the person to be arrested or the place to be searched is connected to the crime.

The Fifth Amendment bars a federal prosecution without "a presentment or indictment of a Grand Jury," and prohibits placing a criminal defendant in double jeopardy (being tried again for the same crime even if first acquitted), self-incrimination (being forced to testify against oneself), and the deprivation of "life, liberty, or property, without due process of law." These are key protections against oppressive government practices. The same amendment requires that any taking of private property by the government be only for "public use" and with "just compensation." The government cannot arbitrarily take our property and must pay for it if such a move is actually necessary.

The Sixth Amendment guarantees "a speedy and public trial, by an impartial jury of the State and district wherein the crime shall have been committed," the right to confront witnesses, and the right to counsel. The government bears the burden to prove crimes, the accused is armed with key rights to defend against the charges; and the prosecution must operate under the watchful eye of the people and prove its case to a fair jury. These are key protections from oppression and for justice, as we will learn in great detail.

The Seventh Amendment also guarantees a jury trial as existed at common law in civil cases, ensuring the parties and the people have the right to have disputes decided by the collective wisdom of the community under law as expressed by a panel of fair citizens. The Eighth Amendment prohibits excessive bail or fines as well as "cruel and unusual punishments." These provisions ensure that the accused are not crushed under oppressive practices before and after trial.

The Ninth Amendment guarantees those rights not otherwise expressly protected in the first eight amendments. The Founders understand that as a matter of practicality, not all unalienable rights are listed, and they are not forfeit just because they are omitted. Many unalienable rights are not expressly protected because it is unthinkable that they will be violated. Vital unalienable rights such as the right to travel within and outside of the United States, the right to direct the education of your children, the right to pursue a living, the right to own property, and the right to marriage are all safe despite not being enumerated in the Bill of Rights.

The Tenth Amendment embodies enumerated powers and federalism by reserving all "powers not delegated to the United States by the Constitution, nor prohibited by it to the States [...] to the States respectively, or to the people." Being closest to the people, the States are substantially better equipped to address most governmental concerns (they actually understand the issues and their practical solutions), and they are much more accountable to the people than a distant federal government. Federalism also more robustly protects the Social Compact and ensures that the people's right to consent to government policies is not unnecessarily diluted to nearly nothing. Moreover, by dividing power between the States and the federal government, the probability that a tyrannical government will take hold drops dramatically. In fact, the States are strong counterweights to federal overreach and oppression. Together, this is the strongest protection of liberty in human history—then and now.

Protecting the unalienable right to liberty is the heart of the Declaration and the American Revolution. As this work reviews the grievances of the Declaration, the truth of this observation will become unassailable.*

*That all men are by nature equally free and independent, and have certain inherent rights, of which* [...] *they cannot, by any compact, deprive or divest their posterity; namely, the enjoyment of life and liberty, with the means of acquiring and possessing property, and pursuing and obtaining happiness and safety.**

Virginia Declaration of Rights (June 12, 1776)

# 16

# "AND THE PURSUIT OF HAPPINESS."

***How are virtue and morality related to the Founders' concept of happiness?***

- ☆ For the first time in history, the Declaration of Independence declares as a self-evident truth that all men are endowed with the unalienable right to the pursuit of happiness.
- ☆ Governments do not give us the unalienable right to pursue happiness—it is bestowed upon us by Nature and Nature's God.
- ☆ The unalienable right to the pursuit of happiness includes your right to acquire and transfer assets, to pursue your own occupation and career, and to live your life as you please—so long as you do not hurt others.
- ☆ To truly obtain happiness, its pursuit must be tempered by virtue. Broadly speaking, virtue means pursuing the good and restraining your immediate passions for the long-term welfare of yourself, your family, and society. The lack of virtue is a grave threat to individuals, families, and society.
- ☆ South African apartheid, Communist North Korea, and many other forms of government squelch the right to pursue happiness.

Although it is a major pillar of American freedom, the unalienable right to the pursuit of happiness is poorly understood. This misunderstanding begins with the very origin of the phrase. Today, the common understanding seems to be that Thomas Jefferson revised an old formulation written by John Locke—that we have the unalienable rights of "life, liberty, and property." Conventional wisdom holds that in a stroke of unique genius, Jefferson swapped out the word "property" with the phrase "pursuit of happiness."*

Those who so heavily rely on Locke do so with mixed results. As we explored, Locke, along with other philosophers—most famously Thomas Hobbes in his masterpiece *Leviathan*—postulates that governments are created by men to protect their unalienable rights. In accord with the conventional wisdom, one of those rights Locke termed the right to *property.* But what Locke considers "property" and what modern parlance considers "property" are remarkably and crucially different. When Locke uses the term "property," he did not only mean what most of us think of today, which are the assets we own. Some examples of our assets include real estate, homes, personal goods (clothes, food, appliances, jewelry, furniture, televisions, computers, cell phones, bikes, cars, books, and games), investments (gold, silver, commodities, cash, and bonds), and intangible rights (stocks, bonds, insurance, patents, trademarks, and copyrights). Locke refers to these assets as a person's "estate." Locke's idea of property is much more expansive than just one's estate. In addition to your estate, it includes the right to control your life, your body, and the fruits of your labor.

Locke also elaborates that because (1) every person has a right to his or her own property and (2) every person has a right to the fruits of his or her labor, then when an individual works to add value to raw materials, the resulting product or service is also property that should be protected.* People who improve on Mother Nature gain ownership over the resulting products and services they create. These improvements include food, clothes, homes, farms, cars, boats, appliances, computers, books, poetry, music, computer applications, paintings, energy, roads, bridges, canals, and an infinite number of other creations for improving our lives.

As Hobbes and Locke so vividly explain, in a state of Nature, we cannot possibly defend ourselves individually against violence, theft, fraud, and similar wrongs from everyone else in the world. So, we band together under government to protect our lives, liberties, and estates. In fact, Locke, in his *Second Treatise of Government,* writes that the "chief end" of government "is the preservation of property."* Locke advances a step further and writes that "government has no other end but the preservation of property."* Remember, in Locke's view, property means control over your body, your labor (and its fruits), and your liberty.

Having said all that, Locke does not even mention the pursuit of happiness in the *Second Treatise of Government.* If that is your sole point of reference, you could easily think that Jefferson did indeed brilliantly swap out the "property" in Locke's trinity of "life, liberty, and property" for "the pursuit of happiness." That view, however, ignores Locke's explicit reference to the pursuit of happiness in another marvelous work—*An Essay Concerning Human Understanding,* published in 1689.

Locke even entitles section 50 of book II, chapter 21 of this essay "A constant determination to a pursuit of happiness, no abridgment of liberty."* Locke observes that "the highest perfection of intellectual nature lies in a careful and constant pursuit of true and solid happiness; so the care of ourselves, that we mistake not imaginary for real happiness, is the necessary foundation of our liberty."* He even argues that the "unalterable pursuit of happiness [...] is our greatest good."*

During Locke's time, the idea that people have an unalienable right to pursue happiness as such is not yet embraced by any society. Ancient civilizations have no conception of unalienable rights. Locke does have such a conception of unalienable rights, but he does not expressly include among them the right to pursue happiness per se—although it could be seen as being enveloped by the right to property (as defined by Locke). In any event, Locke and his fellow thinkers lay the soil in which that idea will take root in Revolutionary America.

Nearly a century after Locke's writings, the Scottish jurist and philosopher Henry Home (better known to history as Lord Kames), in his influential *Essays on the Principles of Morality and Natural Religion*, lays down another layer to what would become the foundation of an unalienable right to pursue happiness. However, it is only mentioned in passing, during the conclusion of the work, in what might best be characterized as a hymn or prayer in which he enjoins "[w]hile man pursues happiness as his chief aim, you bend self-love into the social direction."*

The key point is that Lord Kames espouses the idea that people are endowed in their Nature with the desire to pursue happiness, and that when they examine the world, they will learn that the Creator is responsible for its beauty and goodness. In this context, the pursuit of happiness is joined with the idea that the Creator bends our personal disposition to seek our own happiness away from our selfish desires and toward helping to improve the happiness of everyone in society. It is not so much an individual unalienable right than an internal motivation to act in a way that benefits society as well as the individual. Kames's passage is written in 1751, a little more than a decade before the passage of the Stamp Act by Great Britain.

Jefferson owns Lord Kames's books, and some scholars surmise that Jefferson borrows Kames's phrase for the Declaration of Independence.* On the other hand, as we have learned, Locke uses the phrase a century earlier, and Jefferson owns those books, too. Another extremely influential authority with the Founding Generation is Ireland's Francis Hutcheson. One of the leading philosophers of the Scottish Enlightenment, he is well known by Benjamin Franklin, Jefferson, and other Founders. In 1747, just before Kames, Hutcheson writes that the pursuit of happiness is embedded in our very souls:

> The parts or powers of the soul, which present us with a more glorious view, are of various kinds: but they are all reducible to two classes: the *Understanding* and the *Will*. The former contains all the powers which aim at knowledge; the other all our desires pursuing happiness and eschewing misery. [Italics are in the original.]*

Yet others (most notably constitutional law expert Jeffrey Rosen) argue that Jefferson and his fellow Founders derive their thinking from the ancient Greeks and Romans, as well as those who follow them.* In truth, the kernel of the idea of the pursuit of happiness begins with various Greek and Roman political and philosophical thinkers. Regarding the ancients, the Founding Fathers are heavily influenced by Pythagoras, Socrates, Epictetus, Epicurus, Marcus Aurelius, Seneca, Plutarch, Cicero, and similar thinkers.* Of course, the libraries of Jefferson and other Founders are well stocked with these sources.* In the end, we can safely surmise that Jefferson was likely pulling from most or all of these sources when drafting the Declaration.

Much of this academic debate joins with—if it is not overshadowed by—the practical reality in pre-Revolutionary America. In the context of the English colonies, almost entirely ungoverned by the British Empire, the colonists are free to satisfy this desire embedded in their very souls to pursue happiness—without constraint—and to avoid misery. This philosophical belief in the pursuit of happiness as being intrinsic to mankind is actualized in America.

This actualization begins with immigration. Although the British colonies are colonized over several centuries by men and women encompassing a wide mix of nationalities, political beliefs, religions, and customs, a universal thread binds them together. They flee Europe for a refuge of freedom in America. Putting aside the awful and unforgivable exception of the enslaved, many seek American shores with the hope of building a new, better life. Regardless of reason and origin, those who voluntarily immigrate to America are creating liberty in the wilderness, forging together new societies by their sacrifices, hard toil, treasure, and dedication. They are the very embodiment of the pursuit of happiness.

Dr. Joseph Warren is a Son of Liberty with Samuel Adams and other leading Patriots. Dr. Warren is slain at the Battle of Bunker Hill and becomes the first prominent political leader martyred in the American Revolution. A spellbinding orator, he is also a most compelling writer. He explains the practical reality of the colonists as a magnet for freedom-seeking immigrants:

> Our fathers having nobly resolved never to wear the yoke of despotism, and seeing the European world, at the time, through

> indolence and cowardice, falling a prey to tyranny; bravely threw themselves upon the bosom of the ocean, determined to find a place in which they might enjoy their freedom, or perish in the glorious attempt. Approving heaven beheld the favorite ark dancing upon the waves, and graciously preserved it until the chosen families were brought in safety to these western regions.*

Dr. Warren expresses the prevailing thinking when he announces that "[t]he colonist found himself free, and thought himself secure: He dwelt *under his own vine, and under his own fig tree, and had none to make him afraid.* [Italics are in the original.]"*

The actualization of happiness becomes deeply rooted as the colonists self-govern. This is not to say life is easy. Life in the frontier is difficult; threats abound. Likewise, this is not to say that all vestiges of aristocracy vanish—an aristocracy of sorts quickly takes hold. Slavery is unquestionably an unabashed, malignant stain to the idea and reality of self-government. Women possess few rights. Native Americans are excluded from the Social Compact. But for the free, common man, there is no freer place in all of human history. For them, happiness is truly becoming a way of life.

Whatever philosophical beliefs may have existed before the colonists arrive, with each passing year, the idea that the purpose of government is to ensure the happiness of the people takes deep root in America. The opposition to the Stamp Act generates a torrent of colonial political writing, much of which robustly explores the concept of happiness in earnest. The political awakening that begins with the passage of the Stamp Act only elevates the importance of the government's role in promoting happiness. Daniel Shute, a Congregationalist minister in Massachusetts, provides colonial and then State leadership for decades, including serving as a delegate to the Massachusetts Ratification Convention that ratifies the United States Constitution. In his 1768 Election Day sermon, he begins with the proposition that "[t]he communication of happiness" is "the end of creation," and that the "[p]lan of the creator being thus manifestly adapted to promote the happiness of his creation," certain obligations of mankind therefore follow.* In other words, to fulfill the divine plan, each person has a duty to find happiness and to promote the happiness of others. Shute declares that the purpose of government is

> to promote, not only barely to secure to their subjects the cardinal privileges of human nature, but also kindly endeavor to heighten their happiness in the enjoyment of them. Those methods which will be most conducive to the preservation and prosperity of the

> *whole* are to be studiously devised, and faithfully urged by them. [Italics are in the original.]*

Richard Bland serves in Virginia's House of Burgesses and is widely acknowledged as the leading authority on colonial legal history in his age. He addresses the topic in his 1766 pamphlet *An Inquiry into the Rights of the British Colonies.* He explains that individuals possess a natural right to leave a society to preserve their happiness:

> Men in a state of Nature are absolutely free and independent of one another as to sovereign jurisdiction, but when they enter into a society, and by their own consent become members of it, they must submit to the laws of the society according to which they agree to be governed; [...] yet they retain so much of their natural freedom as to have a right to retire from the society, to renounce the benefits of it, to enter into another society, [...] and their submission to the public authority of the state, do not oblige them to continue in it longer than they find it will conduce to their happiness, which they have a natural right to promote. This natural right remains with every man, and he cannot justly be deprived of it by any civil authority.*

This is an amazingly bold statement. The colonists take it very seriously. After all, we declare independence.

In 1776, John Adams writes a letter to two North Carolina delegates in the Continental Congress recommending how new State governments should be organized in the wake of the dissolution of the British colonial governments. The letter is later transformed into a longer pamphlet and published at large. Its pithy title is *Thoughts on Government, Applicable to the Present State of the American Colonies, In a Letter from a Gentleman to His Friend.* This work is enormously influential in the development of American constitutional law, both in the States and the federal government. Adams unequivocally argues that the happiness of society is the purpose of government:

> We ought to consider what is the end of government, before we determine which is the best form. Upon this point all speculative politicians will agree that the happiness of society is the end of government, as all divines and moral philosophers will agree that the happiness of the individual is the end of man.

> From this principle it will follow that the form of government which communicates ease, comfort, security, or, in one word, happiness[,] to the greatest number of persons and in the greatest degree is the best.*

*Thoughts on Government* is first drafted in February of 1776, not even six months before the Declaration of Independence.

Today, when we think of the pursuit of happiness, many believe that means that they have an unbounded right to do what makes them happy regardless of its morality or long-term consequences. As long as their actions do not directly affect others—or so many seem to think and act—it is no one else's business, and they should and can do whatever they want to with their money, body, and soul.*

This libertine attitude is almost diametrically opposed to the 1776 understanding of the pursuit of happiness. At that time, almost all colonists believe that a republican form of government will only work if citizens and government officials are infused with *virtue*. Locke warns that we need to carefully consider whether pursuing our desires is actually

> inconsistent without our real happiness; and therefore till we are as much informed upon this inquiry, as the weight of the matter, and the nature of the case demands, we are, by necessity of preferring and pursuing true happiness, as our greatest good, obliged to suspend the satisfaction of our desire in particular cases.*

What might seemingly make you happy now may very well lead to your long-term suffering. Thus, the pursuit of happiness must be tempered with a thorough and honest examination of whether succumbing to the desires of the moment will result in long-term, authentic happiness. This is a bit like deciding whether guzzling beer, devouring a delicious calorie-heavy cake, gambling your savings, or playing rapturous video games for days on end—as opposed to the discipline of healthy eating, learning, spending quality time with your family, and frugality—is really in the best interest for your health, career, and retirement. Fleeting, temporary pleasures may very well destroy your long-term, genuine happiness, resulting in permanent misery.

Indeed, Jefferson observes as a matter of fact that "the order of nature [is] that individual happiness shall be inseparable from the practice of virtue."* Summarizing Greek philosopher Epicurus, he also reflects that "[h]appiness [is] the aim of life"* and that "[v]irtue [is] the foundation of happiness."* "The whole frame of our nature shows that we are destined for action," Hutcheson comments, "and that in virtuous action alone we can find the highest happiness, in comparison with which all sensual pleasures appear despicable."* George Washington notes in his brilliant first inaugural address that "there is no truth more thoroughly established, than that there exists in the economy and course of nature, an indissoluble union between virtue and happiness."* Virtue is indispensable to the true happiness of the individual, the family, and society at large.

But what is this "virtue"? It is an ancient idea originally formulated by Roman and Greek (especially Spartan) philosophers and political leaders. Religious leaders and Enlightenment thinkers build on these ancient traditions to explain how a good person should live his or her life. Based on these and other sources, Jefferson succinctly summarizes virtue (derived from Epicurus) as "1. Prudence. 2. Temperance. 3 Fortitude. 4. Justice. To which are opposed, 1. Folly. 2. Desire. 3. Fear. 4. Deceit."* Early in his career, Franklin goes much beyond Jefferson and describes a person of "consummate virtue" embodying "habits of virtue":

> His aspect is sweetened with humanity and benevolence, and at the same time emboldened with resolution, equally free from a diffident bashfulness and an unbecoming assurance. The consciousness of his own innate worth and unshaken integrity renders him calm and undaunted in the presence of the most great and powerful, and upon the most extraordinary occasions. His strict justice and known impartiality make him the arbitrator and decider of all differences that arise for many miles around him, without putting his neighbors to the charge, perplexity and uncertainty of law-suits. He always speaks the thing he means, which he is never afraid or ashamed to do, because he knows he always means well; and therefore is never obliged to blush and feel the confusion of finding himself detected in the meanness of a falsehood. He never contrives ill against his neighbour, and therefore is never seen with a lowering suspicious aspect. A mixture of innocence and wisdom makes him ever seriously cheerful. His generous hospitality to strangers according to his ability, his goodness, his charity, his courage in the cause of the oppressed, his fidelity in friendship, his humility, his honesty and sincerity, his moderation and his loyalty to the government, his piety, his temperance, his love to mankind, his magnanimity, his public-spiritedness, and in fine, his *consummate virtue*, make him justly deserve to be esteemed the glory of his country. [Italics are in the original.]*

Of course, as exemplified among Jefferson and Franklin, the precise parameters of virtue are open to robust discussion. Nevertheless, however precisely or imprecisely it is defined, in 1776 the Founding Generation agrees that virtue is indispensable for a person to live a good life. Franklin aptly summarizes the view when he observes that "*there was never yet a truly great man that was not at the same time truly virtuous* [italics in original]."*

In the American context, pursuing happiness and exercising liberty is decidedly *not* the right to do *anything* you want. Liberty is not anarchy and the unbridled exercise of passion and lust. John Joachim Zubly's sermon at the opening of the 1775 Revolutionary Provincial Congress of Georgia describes how the lack of restraint is not a recipe for freedom, but disaster. Instead, liberty can only be found when it is bound by the restraints of the law:

> [L]iberty does not consist in living without all restraint; for were all men to live without restraint, as they please, there would soon be no liberty at all; the strongest would be master, the weakest go to the wall; right, justice, and property must give way to power, and, instead of its being a blessing, a more unhappy situation could not easily be devised unto mankind, than that every man should have it in his power to do what is right in his own eyes.*

And virtue is not just vitally important for individuals. Without virtue, the people as a whole can be duped by corrupt demagogues and liars who will subvert their liberties. Licentiousness (as in acting without consideration of morality; degrading, wanton abuse of liberty) is the enemy of freedom. Minister Simeon Howard likewise warns, "If a licentious spirit prevails among a people, a general disposition to trample upon laws and depose government [...] [m]ay as effectively destroy the liberty of a people, as the most despotic government."* Equally terrible, a corrupt majority of the people can abuse their power to violate the unalienable rights of a political minority of their fellow citizens. Likewise, a licentious people are easy prey for an invasion since they will not have the capacity and willpower to band together to repulse an invading force.*

As such, there is a conjoined expectation with happiness and responsibility. Governments are formed to promote happiness, and the government—as well as the people who elect them—must be virtuous. In other words, the pursuit of happiness is not a blank check to engage in a corrupt, prideful, hedonist, and unjust life. It must be tempered by integrity, humility, prudence, honor, and self-responsibility.

Henry "Light-Horse Harry" Lee is an American Revolutionary War hero who prevails in many battles and witnesses Lord Charles Cornwallis surrender at

Yorktown. He serves in Virginia's House of Representatives and in the First Continental Congress, as governor of Virginia, as a major general in the Continental Army, and in the United States House of Representatives. He may be most famous, however, for drafting the congressional resolution marking Washington's death, including the immortal line, "First in war, first in peace, and first in the hearts of his countrymen."* During the Constitution's ratification debate in the Virginia Constitutional Convention, Lee observes that the Constitution is "necessary to provide against licentiousness, which is so natural to our climate. I dread more from the licentiousness of the people, than from the bad government of rulers."* This is a remarkable statement for someone who literally risked his life in battle to throw off the yoke of British oppression.

But we are jumping ahead of the story. Jefferson's initial draft of the Declaration specifically refers to the unalienable right to the pursuit of happiness, and it is untouched by the Committee of Five assigned to draft the Declaration, and untouched again by Congress as it revises and adopts the Declaration. And yet, despite having a lineage to the ancients, it is truly revolutionary.

As we have discussed earlier, the colonists are originally fighting for the rights of Englishmen, but by the time of the Declaration, they transform their fight into one for the unalienable rights of all mankind. Literally just weeks before the Declaration is written, George Mason moves along the prior thinking into a rendition much closer to Jefferson's. Mason drafts Virginia's Declaration of Rights, which is adopted on June 12, 1776, and it foreshadows the Declaration:

> That all men are born equally free and independent and have certain inherent rights, of which, [...] they cannot, by any compact, derive or divest their posterity; namely, the enjoyment of life and liberty, with the means of acquiring and possessing property, and pursuing and obtaining happiness and safety.

Although some historians claim that Jefferson relies heavily on Mason's wording, Jefferson's draft does not use Mason's "obtaining" and there is no reference to "safety." In fact, Jefferson specifically disclaims having referred to any documents when he writes the Declaration. He also observes that he does not intend to create anything new, as he is simply distilling American thought at the time. For the most part, this is undoubtedly true. As we have seen, Locke repeatedly writes that the purpose of government is to protect the rights of life, liberty, and property. Jefferson chooses not to refer to "property"; he selects the "pursuit of happiness." Before 1776, happiness is considered the goal and purpose of government, but the pursuit of happiness is not expressed as an unalienable right. Jefferson reformulates the original proposition that happiness is the goal of government by recasting it into an unalienable right. He also purposefully does not declare that the people have an unalienable right *to be* happy. The Declaration carefully uses the phrase the *pursuit of* happiness. One is not entitled to be happy, just to seek it.

The Declaration is the first time a nation declares that the pursuit of happiness is an unalienable right endowed in man by God and that right is to be protected by government. Even Mason's rendition does not declare that governments are instituted to protect the unalienable right to happiness. Jefferson takes the final step. The change, although seemingly subtle, is monumental. In his drafting, Jefferson undoubtedly tips the scales of history. Only in America in July 1776, and from Jefferson's hand, could the somewhat vague idea of mankind's desire to pursue happiness (and the governmental purpose to support that desire) finally be recognized as an unalienable right to the pursuit of happiness. Simply put, Jefferson's draftsmanship makes it immortal.

That a privileged, vast plantation owner dependent on slave labor unlocks "the pursuit of happiness" is more than a bit ironic. This ethos of the pursuit of happiness—that men and women should be free to pursue their own occupation and acquire property as possible—is diametrically opposed to slavery. Abraham Lincoln highlights this terrible contradiction in a wonderful speech delivered in 1860:

> To us it appears natural to think that slaves are human beings; *men,* not property; that some of the things, at least, stated about men in the Declaration of Independence apply to them as well as to us. [...] I say [...] that this Charter of Freedom applies to the slave as well as to ourselves, that the class of arguments put forward to batter down that idea, are also calculated to break down the very idea of a free government, even for white men, and to undermine the very foundations of free society. [Italics are in the original.]*

Lincoln also explains that the idea of the pursuit of happiness is the essence of a meritocracy. It empowers the poor to become wealthy and the wealthy to become poor, based on what they do, not to whom they are born:

> Some will get wealthy. I don't believe in a law to prevent a man from getting rich; it would do more harm than good. So while we do not propose any war upon capital, we do wish to allow the humblest man an equal chance to get rich with everybody else. [...] When one starts poor, as most do in the race of life, free society

> is such that he knows he can better his condition; he knows that there is no fixed condition of labor, for his whole life.*

Lincoln comes from a very poor family. Through hard work, grit, intellect, curiosity, wit, and self-education, he undertakes a slow, steady march to reach his station: store clerk, bartender, postmaster, surveyor, rail splitter, lawyer, state legislator, congressman, and president. At the time this is unthinkable anywhere else in the world—and that is basically the truth today. Lincoln reflects on his personal experience:

> I am not ashamed to confess that twenty-five years ago I was a hired laborer, mauling rails, at work on a flat-boat—just what might happen to any poor man's son! [Applause] I want every man to have the chance—and I believe a black man is entitled to it—in which he *can* better his condition—when he may look forward and hope to be a hired laborer this year and next, work for himself afterward, and finally to hire men to work for him! [Italics are in the original.]*

Lincoln is a living example of what we now call the "American Dream." This thinking of Lincoln and Jefferson is now second nature to Americans. There is no question that the ability to pursue happiness does not necessarily mean that any particular person will achieve happiness. It does not deny that whole swaths of the population start life in either a disadvantaged position or in a privileged position. And we know that plenty of disadvantaged people become raging successes and very happy, and many privileged people become raging failures and miserable. But that is not the point. The point is that you and everyone else even has the opportunity to try. That idea has been denied in most societies throughout human history. America is the first to recognize the pursuit of happiness as a self-evident, unalienable right, the protection of which is the very purpose of government.

If we apply what we have learned about Hinduism, Nazi Germany, Communist China, Social Darwinism and eugenics, the Aztec Empire, and the Soviets, we know that there was no recognition of the pursuit of happiness—quite the opposite. The Buddhist island nation of Sri Lanka and the religiously diverse nation of Ethiopia also have severe caste systems suffocating the pursuit of happiness.

On the African continent lies another poignant example of a society which suffocated the pursuit of happiness—the now defunct system of apartheid in South Africa. Dutch settlers establish a colony in 1652, although the British subsequently take power. Regardless of which European imperialist nation governs, racial segregation is fiercely enforced. For centuries, this is mostly done through customs and government policies. However, with the election of 1948, the Nationalist Party comes to power. Mostly composed of Dutch descendants (known as Afrikaners), the Nationalist Party platform includes imposing a strict racist legal regime separating whites and non-whites. Quickly after their electoral victory, "[t]he maze of laws and regulations which afflicted the lives of urban Africans was steadily enlarged and their severity increased."* As a matter of course, non-whites have no political rights. Non-whites cannot vote and have no rights of petition, press, assembly, or speech. South Africa is what political scientists term a "Herrenvolk democracy," a democracy for a single race that governs the political system and excludes all others. In South Africa, this system is called "apartheid," which in Dutch means "separating, setting apart."

This is all the more confounding in light of the demographics of South Africa. At the time of apartheid's implementation, only about 20 percent of the population is white. Approximately 68 percent is Black, and the remaining 12 percent is Indian, Asian, or mixed race. Often a Herrenvolk democracy involves a racial majority oppressing racial minorities, but South Africa turns this formula on its head; the small minority oppresses the massive majority. To ensure that non-whites do not compete with whites for lucrative jobs, laws exclude non-whites from labor unions, unemployment insurance, and all other labor protections. Apartheid also oppresses non-whites in key areas of life, such as marriage, recreation, travel, and culture. A severe racial regime exploits non-whites. "Segregation in South Africa stood out for the range and extent of its discriminatory legislation, which affected every possible sphere of life (for example, work, education, health, transport, recreation, politics, sexual relationships)."* The apartheid system is intended to "create a society in which the African majority is pegged to poverty and servitude."*

In the 1990s, after years of resistance and international sanctions pressure from the West, the government ends apartheid and allows for free elections. The history of South Africa is very complex, but for our purposes, it illustrates a ruinous, poisonous society dedicated to squelching the pursuit of happiness for a majority of its citizens.

Although apartheid joined the ash heap of history, our last example still reigns: North Korea and its tyrannical communist regime. A true relic from the Cold War, North Korea is a totalitarian communist dictatorship, with a cult of personality that surpasses anything else in modern times. Unlike the totalitarian cult-like regimes of the Soviets, Chinese Communists, and Nazis, North Korea's tyranny is akin to a hereditary monarchy. Kim Il Sung, the country's first communist dictator, is honored as the "Great Leader" and "Eternal President" of North Korea, even after his death. His dictatorship is inherited by his son Kim Jong Il, entitled the

"Supreme Leader." The current Supreme Leader, Kim Jong Un, ascends to power after the death of his father.*

This hereditary cult of personality puts to shame Joseph Stalin, Mao Zedong, Adolf Hitler, and similar totalitarian dictators. To perpetuate the rule of the Supreme Leader, the communist party prolongs and strengthens a class system called the *Songbun*. This system of classification takes full effect in the wake of the Korean War. On May 30th, 1957, each person is assigned a loyalty classification. If an individual or his or her family sacrificed for the fatherland during the Korean War, he or she is favored. Those who did not sacrifice, returned prisoners of war, or are viewed as sympathetic to South Korea are treated as "enemy" class. Many of them are "relocated to isolated mountain areas secluded from population centers, forced into hard labor, and subjected to intensive surveillance for the remainder of their lives."* Just like the caste system, feudalism, and the estates system of the French ancien régime, these inherited classifications are devastatingly important:

> At birth, a baby's Songbun classification system is assigned after an examination is conducted on their parent's status. The consequences began early in school, [where] grades were determined by Songbun and not performance. Songbun controls every aspect of their lives[,] what jobs they can do after school[,] to their ability to travel, how much food or health care they receive and even who they can marry. The [United Nations] commission found that the "Songbun system leads to structural discrimination whereby generations become locked into disadvantage and social mobility is not possible." Once assigned, the baby's status is theirs for life barring any acts of wrongdoing[,] or in limited cases[,] they rise to a higher status. Losing status is much easier; all it takes is a political crime as determined by the state.*

North Korea is an almost cartoonish caricature of the worst of communism, totalitarianism, monarchy, and cults of personality, all wrapped up into one cosmic horror. It is something you might expect to read about in a nightmarish novel by George Orwell, Aldous Huxley, or Franz Kafka. Unfortunately, it is not fiction, but an appalling reality. The entire nation is an open-air prison, with a massive, militarized surveillance state. Famine grips the country for years, killing millions. A police state replete with famine, executions, and oppression is there for the world to see. And the pursuit of happiness? Nonexistent.*

America, on the other hand, embraces as part of its very essence the pursuit of happiness. Perhaps no American embodies this spirit more than Theodore

Roosevelt. Throughout his larger-than-life adventure, he plays poet, author, game hunter, mountain climber, New York State Assembly member, New York City Police commissioner, assistant secretary of the Navy (in most respects he manages the Navy), volunteer soldier (he organizes his own force and fights in Cuba, including leading the famous courageous charge up San Juan Heights to a glorious victory), governor of New York, vice president, president (upon the assassination of President William McKinley), and founder of a third national party (the Bull Moose Party), as well as an unsuccessful third-term candidate for president.* His remarkable figure is sculpted on Mount Rushmore. One of his many talents is to cut to the chase in simple, yet powerful ways. In connection with the pursuit of happiness, he does so brilliantly in a letter penned in 1912:

> In this country we cannot permanently succeed except upon the basis of treating each man on his worth as a man. We can fulfill our high mission among the nations of the earth, we can do lasting good to ourselves and to all mankind, only if we so act that the humblest among us, so long as he behaves in straight and decent fashion, has guaranteed to him under the law his right to life, to liberty, to protection from injustice, his right to enjoy the fruits of his own honest labor, and his right of the pursuit of happiness in his own way, so long as he does not trespass on the rights of others. Our only safe motto is "All men up" and not "Some men down."*

The pursuit of happiness is protected by the federal Constitution's guarantees of equal protection, due process, and liberty. The First Amendment guarantees the freedoms of speech, press, petition, assembly, and the free exercise of religion while barring a government church. We are able to speak and express our minds—even the most unpopular ideas and vigorous dissent against the government—and worship our God, however despised, without fear of retribution. The Second Amendment guarantees the right to bear arms. We can defend ourselves, families, property, and homes against criminals, and if necessary, our liberties, against a tyrannical regime. The remainder of the Bill of Rights provides a protective buffer against governmental repression. The Thirteenth Amendment prohibits slavery and involuntary servitude. We control our own destinies. The first section of the Fourteenth Amendment provides: "All persons born or naturalized in the United States, and subject to the jurisdiction thereof, are citizens of the United States and of the State wherein they reside. No State shall make or enforce any law which shall abridge the privileges or immunities of citizens of the United States; nor shall any State deprive any person of life, liberty, or property, without due process of law; nor deny to any person within its jurisdiction the equal protection of the laws." Class distinctions are eliminated—all are equal under the law to blaze their own path in life. Each individual's rights to life, liberty, and property are protected by due process of law. The privileges and immunities of citizenship are defended. Combined, individuals have the unalienable right to pursue happiness without governmental intrusion.

In 1776, America rejects the past and future as embodied by feudalism, the ancien régime, caste systems, fascist tyrannies, and communist totalitarianism. The Herrenvolk democracy? That we initially fumbled terribly, much to our great shame. But, for all our faults (and there are many we must not overlook), unlike any other nation in world history, we declare as a self-evident truth that all men and women possess the unalienable right to the pursuit of happiness. America's social mobility and fulfillment of human potential is novel in human history. The pursuit of happiness is a key, indispensable feature of our society. This understanding revolutionizes the world, even today.

*All men are naturally in a state of freedom, and have an equal claim to liberty. No one, by nature, not by any special grant from the great Lord of all, has any authority over another. All right therefore in any to rule over others, must originate from those they rule over, and be granted by them. Hence, all government, consistent with that natural freedom, to which all have an equal claim, is founded in compact, or agreement between the parties;—between rulers and their subjects, and can be no otherwise.**

John Tucker (1771)

# 17

# "—That to secure these rights, Governments are instituted among Men,"

***What is the true (and only) purpose of government?***

- ☆ Before 1776, no national government was founded on the First Principle of the Social Compact, in other words, that the people join to create a government to protect our unalienable rights.

- ☆ The Founders reject force theory, Divine Right, and many other alternative theories of government when they adopt a government founded on the Social Compact.

The Declaration of Independence recognizes as a self-evident truth that government is established to protect our unalienable rights. In fact, it goes a step further and declares that the very *origin* of government is the protection of those rights. Once again, the Declaration recognizes as a self-evident truth an ideal that no other nation in world history considered either self-evident or a truth.

Before we explore the Founders' thinking, we must examine other theories about the origins and purpose of government to contextualize and appreciate America's unique embrace of the First Principle—that government is formed as a Social Compact to protect unalienable rights. We will explore in detail two competing theories of the origin of government that existed at the time of the American Revolution.

## Force Theory

Grounded more in practical reality than philosophy, this idea is simple: Raw power dictates who rules. Whoever has the bigger club (or bigger gun) takes power, establishes the rules, and imposes a system that is maintained through force, coercion, and fear. Also dubbed "conquest theory" (which is more aptly a term of art for how some nations or people conquer others through warfare), it means "might makes right."*

An early expression of this idea is illustrated by the character Callicles in the ancient Greek philosopher Plato's *Gorgias* dialogue. In Plato's brilliant work, he explores truth by having characters debate age-old questions. Callicles is a foil for Socrates (Plato's mentor) in the dialogue. Clearly Plato disfavors Callicles's viewpoint, but he poignantly explains the thinking of many ancient Greeks. Callicles begins by declaring that the law is made by the weak to check the strong, and the weak ingeniously persuade the strong to relinquish their natural superiority for the sake of civilization. This transpires under the "artificial law [through which we take] the best and strongest of us [...] and [tame] them like young lions, and [convince] them that with [...] equality they must be content, and that this is the honorable and the just."* In other words, the law is a scam to keep the powerful in check and enable the weak to exploit the strong under the guise of treating everyone equally regardless of their natural strength. Callicles asserts that the man-made custom of men and women following the rules of civilization (the rule of law) is an affront to the true laws of Nature:

> [N]ature herself intimates that it is just for the better to have the more than the worse, the more powerful than the weaker; and in many ways she shows, among men as well as among animals, and indeed among whole cities and races, that justice consists in the superior ruling over and having more than the inferior. For on what principle of justice did Xerxes [Persian emperor] invade Hellas [Greece], or his father [King Darius I] the Scythians (not to speak of numberless other examples)? They, I conceive, act according to nature; yes, and according to the law of nature.*

Under this view, power should be embraced as the driving force of history. The powerful should rise up and take their rightful, preeminent place in the natural order. Natural justice demands that the strong should rule and lord over the weak. Callicles yearns for the day that the strong "would [...] escape from all this [to] trample under foot all of our formulas and spells and charms, and all of our laws, sinning against nature." In Callicles's vision, "the slave [the strong who have been unjustly held down] would rise in rebellion and be lord over us, and the light of natural justice would shine forth."* The brutal reality is that for thousands of years, this is exactly what happened in most societies.

The idea that "might makes right" is still a force in modernity. Just before the outbreak of World War I, German General Friedrich von Bernhardi writes a chilling book, fittingly entitled *Germany and the Next War*. General von Bernhardi proclaims that government by might and force is biologically compelled and fulfills the law of Nature:

> War is a biological necessity of the first importance, a regulative element in the life of mankind which cannot be dispensed with, since without it an unhealthy development will follow, which excludes advancement of the race, and therefore all real civilization. "War is the father of all things."
>
> The struggle for existence is, in the life of Nature, the basis of all healthy development. All existing things show themselves to be the result of contesting forces. [...] The law of the stronger holds good everywhere. [...] The weaker succumb. This struggle [...] [i]n the human race [...] is consciously carried out, and regulated by social ordinances. [...]
>
> In such cases, might gives the right to occupy or to conquer. Might is at once the supreme right, and the dispute as to what is right is decided by the arbitrament of war. War gives a biologically just decision, since its decisions rest on the very nature of things.*

One only needs to review the history of the world to discover just how many governments have been established, expanded, and defeated with no political theory underlying them—just raw power. Current history is filled with such governments. Just read the headlines (or, more likely, the last few links on a news website). Force theory may be cloaked by its perpetrators, but oppression reigns and wars rage simply because the aggressors believe that they have the right to use their might to conquer the weak.

### Divine Right

Divine Right is the concept that the gods or a singular god anoints a particular person—usually a priest, king, or emperor—to rule over society. Thus, the chosen one is the divine representative of God's rule on earth. In the Middle Ages, this idea takes a strong hold in Europe, and the kings of England, France, Russia, and other nations claim that they have the Divine Right to rule with unlimited power.

By 1776, this perspective is substantially tempered in England. With the Glorious Revolution of 1688, Parliament significantly cabins in the British monarchy through several monumental legislative enactments. The idea of Divine Right in England is mostly finished.

Nevertheless, at the time of the American Revolution, absolutist Divine Right is in full effect in several other great powers. In 1786, Russian Emperor Catherine the Great writes that "[t]he Sovereign is absolute; for there is no other authority but that which centers in his single person, that can act with a vigor proportionate to the extent of such a vast dominion." Catherine explains that "[t]he extent of the dominion requires an absolute power to be vested in that person who rules over it."* More famously, the French monarchy in 1776 derives its power from *la grâce de Dieu* (in other words, "from the grace of God").* The ramification of that perspective is summarized in the absolutist phrase attributed to King Louis XIV (great-great-great-grandfather of King Louis XVI who sits on the throne in 1776 and shares the same view): *"L'État, c'est moi"* *— "I am the state," or, "The state is me."

The Founders reject force theory and Divine Right traditions. They also repudiate other alternative theories such as divine rule (kings and queens are actually gods themselves),* family (families join together into tribes, which eventually become nations),* customs (governments arise from long-term customs and traditions),* exceptional heroes or leaders (the exceptional rise to power),* class conflict (the government is created to protect the property of the rich),* hydraulic civilization (governments form in the East to control water and irrigation),* and evolutionary biology (evolution favors a hierarchy of competency that leads to a competency pecking order embodied in the government).* They also reject anarchy (which attacks all government as corrupt and oppressive).* Instead, they embrace the idea that the people consciously form governments through a Social Compact.

We previously fleshed out what the Founders understand as the meaning of unalienable rights and the purpose of government as traditionally identified with the English philosophers Thomas Hobbes and John Locke. The Social Compact is an interrelated idea in which Hobbes and Locke are again indispensable. *Leviathan* by Hobbes is published in 1651, and *Two Treatises of Civil Government* by Locke is published about twenty-seven years later—which would be about ninety years before the American Revolution. This provides their ideas more than enough time to deeply fertilize the thinking of the Founders.

Hobbes and Locke share the same basic philosophical foundation. As we explored, they both believe in the single, universal Creator, who forms man and Nature. The Creator establishes universal, Natural Laws that rule the world and man. These Natural Laws are immutable and fixed. There are self-evident truths that mankind can discover through reason. The Creator endows unalienable rights in each person, which cannot be taken away without their consent.

Hobbes and Locke also believe that most rights are not absolute. They understand that the right to eat does not permit one to steal another's bread. Yet, in a state of Nature, each person is free to pursue his or her interests—food, lodging, love, family, recreation, employment, career, material goods—without regard to human-established rules of conduct. In utopia, each person will exercise those rights granted by Nature without interfering with the rights of others. However, *Utopia* is St. Thomas More's fantasy,* and conflict is inevitable without established laws and norms of conduct.

Indeed, as related by chapter 4 of Genesis, Cain possesses the right to farm and make offerings to God, but his jealousy over how God favors Abel's animal sacrifices does not grant Cain the right to slay Abel. As the story of Cain and Abel reveals, conflict arises from man's very nature. After all, there is an infinite number of causes for strife: pride, greed, fear, hate, love, competition, desire, lust, frustration, resentment, power, mental illness, addiction, and jealousy being just some of the more obvious examples. And do not forget evil—there *is evil.**

Of course, as Locke observes, a person unjustly assaulted by another may, by the "fundamental law of nature," protect herself, her family, and her property.* Philosophically and theoretically this is more than rational and logical. This all makes great philosophical and theoretical sense. The dilemma is that in real life, when people believe that they have wronged each other, the result is *practically* disastrous. Without a government to govern disputes, the result is chaos and war. In *Leviathan,* Hobbes explains most famously that without a government

> *there is always war of every one against every one.* Hereby it is manifest, that during the time men live without a common power to keep them all in awe, they are in that condition which is called war; and such a war, as is of every man, against every man. [...]
>
> Whatsoever therefore is consequent to a time of war, where every man is enemy to every man; the same is consequent to the time, wherein men live without other security, than what their own strength, and their own invention shall furnish them withal. In such condition, there is no place for industry; because the fruit thereof is uncertain: and consequently no culture of the earth; no navigation, or use of the commodities that may be imported by sea; no commodious building; no instruments of moving and removing, such things as require much force; no knowledge of

> the face of the earth; no account of time; no arts; no letters; no society; and which is worst of all; continual fear and danger of violent death; and the life of man, solitary, poor, nasty, brutish, and short. [Italics are in the original.]*

Hobbes masterfully captures the practical reality. Locke agrees that no government means the war of all against all. Forever. This is so because the lack of government "with authority, puts all men in a state of nature; force without right, upon a man's person, makes a state of war."* Without a governmental police force and army to protect you, you must always be vigilant to defend yourself and your family. If you or your family are wronged or injured, you must extract revenge yourself. There is a never-ending cycle of fear and vigilante justice.

Locke and Hobbes expound that government is created to escape and stop the war of all against all. Individuals unite in civil societies and establish government to secure the peace by delegating to the collective their individual authority to protect themselves and obtain justice. Locke observes that there can be "no freedom" without a Social Compact of laws, because "liberty is, to be free from restraint and violence from others; which cannot be, where there is no law."* Later, James Madison reflects this same sentiment in more poetic terms: "If men were angels, no government would be necessary."* But men are anything but angels, Alexander Hamilton adds, and government becomes necessary "[b]ecause the passions of men will not conform to the dictates of reason and justice without constraint."* This understanding is deeply rooted in Western civilization. St. Paul in his Epistle to Timothy preaches that "the law is not made for a righteous man, but for the lawless and disobedient, for the ungodly and for sinners, for unholy and profane, for murderers of fathers and murderers of mothers, for manslayers."*

Thus, paradoxically, legal restraints are necessary to preserve liberty. By giving up certain natural rights of self-defense and retribution, an individual gains greater overall security for his or her individual rights. Without each individual's relinquishment of some of his or her natural rights to the broader society, chaos reigns. To secure one's life, liberty, and pursuit of happiness, one has no choice but to unite with others in a civil society embodied in a government. James Wilson explains in his opening address to the Pennsylvania Ratifying Convention for the federal Constitution that by

> entering into the Social Compact, though the individual parts with a portion of his natural rights, yet, it is evident that he gains more by the limitation of the liberty of others, than he loses by the limitation of his own,—so that in truth, the aggregate of liberty is more in society, than it is in a state of nature.*

Individuals forgo the right to judge and punish others for wrongdoing and instead delegate that authority to law enforcement, judges, juries, and the justice system. Government also establishes a military, secures the border, and generally defends the nation and individuals from harm. The alternative is vigilantism and invasion with all of its accompanying Hobbesian horrors.

The Founding Generation repeatedly observes that they operate within the framework of the Social Compact. Any lingering doubts are readily dispelled by a declaration of the entire federal Constitutional Convention. In the summer of 1787, this Convention meets in Philadelphia, and after months of heated debate, the delegates agree upon a draft Constitution. The Convention then forwards the draft to Congress for its consideration. Accompanying the proposed Constitution is a letter signed by George Washington as the president of the Convention. In essence a cover letter to Congress, it specifically affirms that "[i]ndividuals entering into Society, must give up a Share of Liberty to preserve the Rest."*

In addition to this philosophical theory, the colonists have the historical experience of living in a Social Compact. As we have explored, the New World presents immigrating Europeans a novel opportunity to begin anew. Eager to escape the cruelties of Europe or to find riches, they choose to settle in America (either as free persons or indentured servants) and establish societies in the wilderness. The theory of the Social Compact comes to life in America. While Locke and Hobbes had only theorized about the origins of primordial societies, America becomes a living experiment of societies created through a compact of the governed.*

The Puritans are perhaps the best-known example. They enter into a Social Compact by subscribing to the Mayflower Compact in 1620. Perhaps for the first time in history, the Mayflower Compact places into practice the theory of the Social Compact by establishing a new community government through a written agreement signed by the governed. The Mayflower Compact expressly acknowledges the creation of a government by a Social Compact:

> IN THE NAME OF GOD, AMEN. We, whose names are underwritten [...] [d]o by these presents, solemnly and mutually, in the presence of God and one another, covenant, and combine ourselves together into a civil body politic, for our better ordering and preservation, and furtherance of the ends aforesaid: and by virtue hereof do enact, constitute, and frame, such just and equal laws, ordinances, acts, constitutions, and officers, from time to time, as shall be thought most meet and convenient for the general good of the colony: unto which we promise all due submission and obedience. [Emphasis is in the original.]*

Other colonies also establish havens of freedom based on a Social Compact. Putting aside the shameful, horrific, and dreadful realities of enslaved Africans and the slaughter and displacement of Native Americans (and really, there is no putting those aside), the European immigrants consent to come to America and begin a new life. They do so with an understanding of how their lives are to be governed. They are willing participants in a new Social Compact.

The colonies quickly sprout representative assemblies that are intended to help implement a Social Compact. Although it is by no means a perfect fulfillment of the ideal of the Social Compact, they approach the principle much more than any society in previous history. Perhaps a few ancient cities and short-lived republics operated with a Social Compact of some of the people, but in the modern age, no nation explicitly embraces the principle until the establishment of (at least some) of the colonial governments. The Social Compact is coming into reality in a more robust way than anywhere else in the world.

After the colonies declare independence, the revolutionaries have a fresh opportunity to forge a new Social Compact. Before them is an almost blank slate. When the colonies become free and independent States, the old imperial governing institutions are swept aside. The Founders create new Social Compacts when they establish State constitutions that embody the First Principles of a free and just government. Soon they go a step further by binding the States together under the Articles of Confederation. A few years later, they embrace yet another opportunity to establish a new Social Compact by jettisoning the Articles for the federal Constitution. That does not end the journey. The Social Compact of the Constitution is amended twenty-seven times to date. Plus, the people of many States ratify their own Social Compacts with new State constitutions, and many of these supreme laws of the land are frequently amended via ballot initiatives and similar mechanisms. We can also reconstitute our constitutions through constitutional conventions. These are all embodiments of the Declaration's recognition of the Social Compact as a founding First Principle. The journey of blazing the Social Compact continues to this day.

In the end, the American experience is not only philosophically based on the Social Compact, but it is also experienced as the Social Compact—they and we live it. As Americans, we are extraordinarily fortunate to be blessed to live in a time and place such as this that is dedicated to the Social Compact theory, and not force theory, family, Divine Right, divine rule, Marxism, anarchism, customs, heroes, evolutionary biology, and hydraulic civilization. Those viewpoints often result in tyrannical and unjust rule. Today, we take for granted this remarkable and revolutionary development in history—to our grave danger.

*[T]he origin of all power is in the people, and* [...] *they have an incontestable right to check the creatures of their own creation, vested with certain powers to guard the life, liberty, and property of the community.* [...]

*Man is not immediately corrupted, but power without limitation, or amenability, may endanger the brightest virtue.**

Mercy Otis Warren (1788)

# 18

## "DERIVING THEIR JUST POWERS FROM THE CONSENT OF THE GOVERNED,"

***What is the source and extent of a government's power?***

- ☆ A just and free government requires that the people consent to it.
- ☆ For a government to be just and free, it must be limited to the purpose for which it is formed—the protection of the unalienable rights of the people.
- ☆ A government with unlimited power—even a republic or democracy—inevitably leads to tyranny and the oppression of the unalienable rights of the people.
- ☆ The results of unlimited power are illustrated by the tyranny of dictatorships, police states, the ancient Egyptian pharaohs, and the government in the novel *Nineteen Eighty-Four*. Absolute tyranny can also arise when the people become enchanted and corrupted by a demagogue, elected officials like Benito Mussolini and Adolf Hitler take complete power, and the people directly impose a democratic dictatorship as in ancient Athens and the French Revolution.
- ☆ The Founders establish America on the First Principle of limited government.

The understanding that individuals establish the government through a Social Compact to protect their unalienable rights leads to a corollary: the people must *consent* to living under the government for the government to be considered free and just. James Wilson explains in 1774:

> All men are naturally equal, and naturally free. No one therefore has a right to any authority over another without his consent. All lawful government then must be founded on the consent of those who are subject to it. Such consent was given with a view to ensure and to increase the happiness of the governed above what they could enjoy in an independent and unconnected state of nature.*

Because the people agree to create a government and be subject to it, the government has legitimate authority over the people, and the people have a duty to follow it. Unlike force theory, family, Divine Right, divine rule, a clash of classes, the control of water, and other political origins, a just and free government is founded on the consent of the people it governs.

Of course, in practice, no government directly asks each individual to consent to its governance or to approve each exercise of governmental authority. We do not receive a preprinted form on our eighteenth birthday asking if we consent to the government. Putting aside the rare exceptions of referendums and ballot initiatives, the people do not vote on specific policy proposals and laws. Most agree that implied consent through representative government suffices. Indeed, in America, our consent is very robust. We live in a republic in which the people are the ultimate sovereign, individuals possess protected unalienable rights, citizens are free to emigrate or stay, individuals only pay taxes that are approved by the people or their representatives, and individuals freely take advantage of the security and benefits offered by the government.

The United States Constitution both embodies the consent of the People and ensures it. Pursuant to Article VII, the Constitution is ratified on June 21, 1788, by the representatives of the people through a series of State constitutional conventions. The Constitution only comes into effect with consent. Furthermore, the Constitution ensures that the federal government is based on the people's consent. Article I, Section 1 vests legislative authority in Congress, and the members of Congress are elected by the people (originally senators were elected by State legislatures, but pursuant to the Seventeenth Amendment, they are now directly elected by the people). Under Article II, Section 1, the president is vested with the executive power and is chosen by electors who are chosen by the people. Under Article II, Section 2, the judges who exercise the judicial power are nominated and approved by the president and the Senate—in other words, representatives of the people. The people not only vote, under the First Amendment, they have the right to petition the government, speak and publish freely about political matters, and assemble to affect the government. Under Article V, the people have the right to amend the Constitution and call for a new constitutional convention. America actualizes the First Principle of the Social Compact.

At first glance, the declaration that government derives its just powers from the consent of the governed seems simply a reiteration of the Founders' perspective on the origin of government. Yet, there is more to the issue. Just because a government is organized by the consent of the people does not mean that the government has limited power. The key word in the Declaration's phrase of "deriving their just powers" is "just"—a *just* government stays limited to the purpose for which it is established.

The First Principle of the Social Compact generates two logical possibilities regarding the scope and reach of governmental authority: (1) Because the people have consented to the government to preserve the peace and maintain order, the government is all-powerful, or (2) because the government is granted its power to preserve the unalienable rights of individuals, the powers the government possesses are limited to those necessary to the accomplish that aim. At its extreme, the choice becomes either an absolute, tyrannical government or a limited, free government.

Thomas Hobbes's vision is clear: absolute power. According to Hobbes, because individuals consent to be ruled by the government, the government can do no wrong. The power of the government has no limit. Hobbes sums it up concisely: "*Nothing done to a man by his own consent can be injury* [italics in original]."*

Hobbes's conception of consent simply requires an individual to consent to being a member of society. As such, an individual need not consent to particular governmental powers, policies, or specific actions; the individual simply submits to the rule of the government for all purposes. In short, Hobbes advocates the view that the sovereign has control over all things, including life, liberty, the pursuit of happiness, and justice.

An illuminating example of unlimited power is ancient Egypt. Pharaohs begin ruling Egypt in approximately 3000 BC and govern for nearly three thousand years. About thirty dynasties hold Egypt in their thrall for millennia. Lasting at least ten times longer than our relatively young republic, rule by the pharaoh is an extremely powerful and stable form of rule worthy of our attention.

During the Old Kingdom, which lasts several centuries, the pharaohs are considered to be living gods—not anointed by God to rule (such as Divine Right in Europe), but actual living gods of the divine rule variety. Accordingly, the pharaohs possess vast power over everything. During the Middle Kingdom, which lasts for centuries after the Old Kingdom, the pharaohs are understood to be representatives of the gods—of the Divine Right variety—but still possess unlimited power. Historian Lewis Mumford explains:

> By this union of cosmic and earthly powers the ruler became at once a living person and an immortal: he was born and died like other men, yet would be reborn, like his other self, Osiris [perhaps the most powerful Egyptian god], even as his power was renewed each day, like that of the returning sun, Atum-Re. [...] [T]he words coming forth from the king's mouth brought a world into existence; and when he uttered a command, he must be obeyed. Not merely did he hold the powers of life and death over the community, but he was the living incarnation of that community [...] his health, its health. The community lived and flourished vicariously, through the king.*

Political power? Although the pharaoh has advisors, the pharaoh's command is law. Nothing is under debate once the pharaoh decides. There is no legislative assembly. The pharaoh does not share power or bargain with interest groups. There are no elections or pandering to public opinion—no veto, no separation of powers, no checks and balances, no Bill of Rights, no federalism. There is no Constitution. What the pharaoh commands, happens.

Economics? There is no private property. The pharaoh owns the kingdom and everyone's personal property, including homes, land, livestock, agriculture, modes of transportation, and precious metals. The pharaoh takes what the pharaoh wants and leaves the remains for the rabble. With a snap of a finger, the pharaoh can make you rich or impoverished.

Justice? The pharaoh has the power to resolve any dispute. No need to consult laws or legislative intent. No constitutional doctrines. No considering the opinions of independent judges. No appeals. The pharaoh's decision is final.

Religion? The pharaoh is a living god (in the Old Kingdom) or an intermediary between the people and the gods who rule the universe (in the Middle Kingdom). The "high priest of every temple," the pharaoh assists those who die to pass through the afterlife. There is no free exercise of religion. After all, God is ruling.

True, the society is divided into classes: nobles, priests, scribes, skilled workers, unskilled workers, and slaves. But that is important just for dealing with each other. The king-god-pharaoh lords over everything. This absolute, unaccountable, and massive power is alien to us. Yet, for thousands of years, one of the greatest civilizations of all of world history persists (and flourishes) under that regime.

*Nineteen Eighty-Four* is a fictional account of future unlimited power written by English novelist George Orwell. Near the end of this masterpiece, the protagonist Winston Smith is caught trying to join a revolutionary resistance to the massive totalitarian surveillance state (of which he is a part). The enigmatic O'Brien tortures Winston and explains the underlying motivation of the all-powerful government:

> We are different from all the oligarchies of the past in that we know what we are doing. [...] The German Nazis and the Russian Communists came very close to us in their methods, but they never had the courage to recognize their own motives. They pretended, perhaps they even believed, that they had seized power unwillingly and for a limited time, and that just round the corner there lay a paradise where human beings would be free and equal. We are not like that. We know that no one ever seizes power with the intention of relinquishing it. Power is not a means; it is an end.*

"Power is *not a means*. It is an *end*": Power for power's sake. The end of government is not to protect the rights of the people but to perpetuate the state like an insatiable monster devouring everything—merely for the sake of devouring everything. As Lewis Mumford relates in connection with kings,

> Apart from murder and rape, the most horrendous crimes punished by civilized authority stem back to the "unpardonable sin" of kingship: disobedience to the sovereign. Murderous coercion was the royal formula for establishing authority, securing obedience, and collective booty, tribute, and taxes. At bottom, every royal reign was a reign of terror.*

Whether an ancient kingship or modern totalitarian state, unlimited power brooks no dissent and viciously punishes opposition—terror and death are the instrumentalities of absolute power for power's sake.

Yet, there is another danger you might not normally consider: the people. Unlimited power is not defined by the form of government. True, unlimited power is often wielded by kings, dictators, totalitarian states, theocracies, and military juntas, but it can also arise from republics and democracies. The Founding Generation generally believes that the people, if left to their own devices, are likely to kill off liberty by collapsing into anarchy (leading to a dictator) or electing a dictator. During the debate about the ratification of the federal Constitution, influential Anti-Federalist Cato (the pen name of likely New York Governor George Clinton) observes that Americans are just as susceptible to tyranny as any other People:

> Americans are like other men in similar situations, when the manners and opinions of the community are changed by the causes I mentioned before, and your political compact inexplicit, your posterity will find that great power connected with ambition, luxury, and flattery, will as readily produce a Caesar, Caligula, Nero, and Domitian in America, as the same causes did in the Roman empire.*

There is no shortage of examples in history where a democracy or republic degenerates into an authoritarian regime. Germans electing Adolf Hitler and Italians electing Benito Mussolini are just two of many republics committing suicide by electing dictators.

Other insightful historical examples are those in which the people themselves run amok. The archetype the Founders well understand is the very birthplace of democracy: the ancient Greek city-state of Athens. At the time, Athens is a true democracy, in which the people govern through majority rule.* From approximately 508 BC until 322 BC, all male citizens of Greece have the right to make the law through public gatherings where the majority rules. The key power is the assembly of *demos*, the *ecclesia*, composed of nearly all Greek male citizens. To be a citizen, you must be a biological man who, at the age of eighteen, serves two years as a military cadet. That is all. It is 100 percent sexist and excludes slaves, but is by far the most democratic and inclusive form of government for many thousands of years. Depending on the time, the ecclesia is composed of between thirty thousand and sixty thousand men. Generally, the ecclesia is all powerful—it can propose and do all. Any citizen can propose anything, and the whole assembly can ignore, defeat, or approve whatever is proposed. Anyone can speak.

There is no constitution, although some laws are difficult to change because the law itself provides it so. The majority rules. Since the assembly's power includes everything, the most important aspects of government are decided by majority rule: war, finances, trade, food supplies, foreign policy, and spending money. The assembly impeaches and even executes generals. The ecclesia also handles mundane matters, like the proper qualifications for a ferry boat captain.

With rare exceptions, justice is administered by the popular courts, the *Heliaea*.

Although scholars debate its exact operations, there appears to be up to six thousand members, but usually it meets in smaller groups of 501 or more, the *dikasteria*. Every day, at least 501 jurors are chosen by lot. Like legislation, a majority decides a case—including criminal charges with death penalties. As a pure democracy, no judge presides over the trial. Cases are brought by citizens, and they basically manufacture their own charges and claims. The parties do not have attorneys; they prosecute or defend themselves.

Although Athens is a democracy, it is militant and often launches war. At times, it turns its aggression upon its own. Putting aside the trial and execution of Jesus, perhaps the most infamous perversion of justice in history occurs at the hands of the Athenian popular court. To observe that Socrates is a fountainhead of Western civilization is no exaggeration. He develops critical thinking to a state never before recorded, and he creates groundbreaking philosophy. Rationality and inquiry are almost his inventions. Surely he will be protected as he pursues the truth in a city-state governed by the people.

But telling the truth is always dangerous, especially in an unfettered democracy. As an old man, Socrates is hauled before the democratic court and stands trial. Xenophon, a leading Greek light in his own right, summarizes the charges: "Socrates commits an injustice by not believing in the gods in which the city believes and by bringing in new and different divine things (*daimonina*); he commits an injustice also by corrupting the young."* Socrates also questions elections for the basis of selecting leaders. Although Socrates's position is anti-democratic, it is the prevalent means of thinking in the ancient world. Further, his accusers charge that Socrates convinces his students that he is the best teacher in Greece, he riles up young people to disrespect their parents, and his students robustly criticize the status quo. Socrates is on trial for his life for core political speech and sparking teenage angst.

Socrates is defiant. He defends his actions as no crime. As reported by his greatest student, Plato, Socrates explains that he is under attack for seeking and telling the truth, which generates enemies as a matter of course. He exclaims that he would rather die than perpetuate lies and submit to censorship. His sacred duty to God mandates that he retain his freedom to speak the truth:

> [I]f you were therefore to say to me, "Socrates, this time [...] we will let you go; but on this condition, that you cease from carrying on this search of yours, and from philosophy; if you are found following those pursuits again, you shall die:" I say, if you offered to let me go on these terms, I should reply: "Athenians, I hold you in the highest regard and love; but I will obey God rather than

> you: and as long as I have breath and strength I will not cease from philosophy, and from exhorting you, and declaring the truth."*

Socrates's gambit fails. Unlike today's due process protections, there is no presumption of innocence and no requirement that the charges be proven beyond a reasonable doubt. A verdict need only be rendered by majority vote. The jury votes 280 to 220 to convict. After further proceedings, he is sentenced to death by a lopsided vote of 360 to 140. Although there is plenty of opportunity to escape his fate, he keeps to his convictions and dies by drinking the poison hemlock—and becomes immortal.

What is the lesson of Athens? A democracy with unlimited power can crush a man just as easily as any pharaoh, emperor, or totalitarian surveillance state. If the government itself has unlimited power, the form of government will not stop tyranny. During the trial, Socrates strikes upon the truth when he comments that "[t]here is no man who will preserve his life for long, either in Athens or elsewhere, if he firmly opposes the wishes of the people."*

The Founders understand this lesson quite well. In the *Rights of Man*, Thomas Paine warns that an elective tyranny is still a tyranny:

> It is not because a part of the government is elective, that makes it less a despotism, if the persons so elected, possess afterwards, as a parliament, unlimited powers. Election, in this case, becomes separated from representation, and the candidates are candidates for despotism.*

Such despotism is not limited to oppressing a single man. The French Revolution is a poignant, more modern example that occurs in the wake of the American Revolution. Under the ancien régime that governs for centuries before the French Revolution, French society is divided into three major estates. The First Estate is the clergy, and the Catholic church possesses huge land holdings, is exempt from taxation, and holds tremendous political power. The Second Estate is the nobility, with hereditary privileges, wealth, and power. The Third Estate includes everyone who is not fortunate enough to be in the First or Second Estates, about 87 percent of the population, who have no privileges or power. Lording over all three estates is the king. Emulating King James I, the king in France is the embodiment of the Divine Right of kings. Over time, momentous societal, cultural, and economic pressures—along with an enormous debt and poor leadership—places insurmountable pressure to reform the ancien régime. King Louis XVI convenes the Estates General, an assembly which represents each of the three estates to consider new taxes and financial reforms, and in great measure gets the ball rolling toward the

French Revolution. The Estates General eventually transforms into the French Constituent Assembly.

As the old French order is crumbling, on August 26, 1789, the National Constituent Assembly adopts the Declaration of the Rights of Man and of the Citizen. It declares that "[m]en are born and remain free and equal in rights." It affirms that liberty, property, security, and resistance to oppression are "natural and imprescriptible rights." It protects due process, equality, freedom of speech and press, and prohibits taxation without public consent. Property is declared sacred and inviolable, and religious freedom guaranteed.

Fundamental reforms of the ancien régime are enacted, including the adoption of the Constitution of 1791, which establishes a constitutional monarchy—it includes the separation of powers among the executive, legislative, and judicial authorities. However, it is stillborn. On August 10, 1792, under pressure from Parisian mobs, the French Legislative Assembly (successor to the French Constituent Assembly) suspends King Louis XVI's power, arrests him, and calls for a national convention to draft yet another new constitution and govern France until this new constitution is effective. The National Convention is elected by universal suffrage—the most democratic election in a major country since ancient Greece. The Legislative Assembly dissolves itself on September 20, 1792, and the elected delegates of the National Convention of 1792 meets for the first time that very day. The next day, the National Convention abolishes the monarchy. Soon the king is tried and convicted of conspiracy to commit crimes against the nation. He is guillotined on January 21, 1793, unequivocally ending the ancien régime.

A few years earlier in 1789, Abbe Emmanuel Sieyès is a member of the First Estate, but very sympathetic to the Third Estate. He is elected as a member of the Third Estate in the Estates General. Sieyès's influential pamphlet, *What Is the Third Estate?*, argues that the people should control everything. "[I]t is sufficient for its will to be manifested for all positive law to vanish before it. In whatever form the nation wills, it is sufficient that it does will: all forms are good, and its will is always the supreme law."*

In 1792, Sieyès's pamphlet becomes reality. The National Convention replaces the absolute power of the king with the absolute power of the nation; the will of the people nullifies any laws, constitutional barriers, and unalienable rights; their will is "*always* the supreme law." Unlike in Great Britain with the House of Commons and the House of Lords, or in the United States with the House of Representatives and the Senate, the French possess a single-chamber national legislature that rules by a simple majority. The French also have no independent executive like the king of England or the president of the United States. This enables the legislative body to enact the unfettered will of the people.

Yet determining this will of the people is not so simple. The National Convention quickly divides into different factions, akin to informal political parties. One faction is the Jacobins (also called "The Mountain," based on how they appear when they sit in the National Convention); another is the Girondins (based on the locale that spawns most of their leaders). Most deputies are independent and rest in the middle (often referred to as "The Plain").

In reaction to threats against the government, on March 19, 1793, the National Convention put aside its divisions and unanimously passes a decree proclaiming that anyone participating in rebellions or demonstrations against army recruitments is to be summarily executed within twenty-four hours of capture. The despotism of the people is far swifter and more draconian than any king. In 1793, the new Declaration of the Rights of Man and Citizen specifically provides that "any person who may usurp the sovereignty be instantly put to death by free men." Be accused, and you have the right to die—instantly.

On April 6, 1793, the National Convention creates the Committee of Public Safety. On June 2, 1793, the National Convention expels from its ranks many Girondin "enemies of the people."* A few months before, the Girondins lead the Assembly. Now, they are its enemies. Several Girondin leaders are quickly executed. American Thomas Paine, a member of the National Convention, is aligned with the Girondins and arrested, but by a quirk of fate, he escapes execution.

The Jacobins quickly turn on themselves. Radical leaders attack their former allies when they find them too moderate in their revolutionary zeal. Maximilien Robespierre, a rising star of The Mountain, declares that France must have a "Government of Terror."* On September 5, 1793, the National Convention declares that "terror is the order of the day."* It suspends the recently enacted Constitution of 1793; passes the new Law of the Maximum (in other words, price controls), a violation of which is treason and punishable by death; reconstitutes a Committee of General Security, which hunts down traitors through a network of spies (so-called guardians of the people); and enacts the new Law of Suspects, by which anyone, through actions, remarks, writings, or similar conduct, will be deemed an "enemy of liberty" and accused of treason.

Flush with power, Robespierre and his allies yearn to create a "republic of virtue." To prove it, they execute Queen Marie Antoinette and a set of moderate revolutionaries, several of whom are heroes in the early days of the French Revolution. The National Convention and the Committee of Public Safety appoint "representatives-on-mission" with sweeping powers, including supervising local governments and dictating strategy to generals. They are empowered to dismiss any military commanders, local officials, and judges, they create new courts and order executions, and otherwise, they are all-powerful. The Committee of Public

Safety invests some of these revolutionary agents with "unlimited powers."* The rule of law degenerates completely into the boundless rule of one man, delegated with absolute power by the National Convention.

On October 10, 1793, the National Convention declares that the government is revolutionary until the peace. On February 5, 1794—17 Pluviôse (roughly meaning "rainy"—the revolutionaries even change the names of the months of the calendar)—Robespierre releases the "Report on the Principles of Public Morality," which outlines the grand ambitions for the French Revolution that will result in perfection on earth by "sealing our work with our blood, may we ourselves see at least the dawn of universal felicity gleam before us!"*

Louis Antoine de Saint-Just is Robespierre's strongest ally. Dubbed the "Angel of Death" for his bloodlust against the purported enemies of the French Revolution, he announces that because the will of the people is supreme, political parties or coalitions in opposition to the government, or even individuals who question the government, are criminals guilty of treason and worthy of execution. Since opposition to the government is treason, public safety demands that dissenters be arrested and executed. The National Convention establishes the Revolutionary Tribunal of Paris to preside over treason cases. Naturally, it deploys the guillotine (affectionately nicknamed the "National Razor") to implement public executions. Approximately fifty thousand people throughout the country lose their heads. Other instruments of death are also unleashed. In Lyon, they find the National Razor too slow, so they tie prisoners to stakes and train cannon fire upon them; at Nantes, they tie down enemies of the people on barges and sink them in the Loire River; and in Toulon, they deploy firing squads. Despite popular misconception, up to 60 percent of the executed are peasants or working-class citizens.

Following Robespierre's ambitions, the National Convention drives headlong into recreating society. It declares forfeit lands held by enemies of the state. The National Convention creates the metric system as a rational way to measure and count; plans to create free public schools and a higher education system; establishes a national library and the national museum (the Louvre); revises the calendar, with twelve thirty-day months of three ten-day weeks (and, as noted before, each month renamed as part of the seasons—plus a spit of holidays to end the year); eliminates Sundays and all Christian holidays; and converts churches into secular "temples of reason."* Federalism (in other words, local governance) is outlawed as treason. The National Convention in Paris is all-powerful—politically, economically, socially, and religiously.

The Revolutionary Tribunal orders a leading left-wing opponent of the majority, Jacques-René Hébert, and his allies, to be executed via guillotine on March 24, 1794. Less than a week later, the National Convention arrests revolutionary hero and Jacobin leader Georges Danton and his allies, including key Mountain journalist Camille Desmoulins, who plays an indispensable role in sparking lynchpin moments during the French Revolution. Desmoulins and Robespierre are even close personal friends. It matters not. Danton, Desmoulins, and other key revolutionary figures are executed after a circus show trial that flagrantly tramples their rights—all in pursuit of paradise on earth.

Finally, the National Convention turns on its leaders. On July 28 (9 Thermidor), Robespierre and Saint-Just are arrested. The National Convention does not bother with the pretense of a trial. Robespierre, Saint-Just, and seventy allies are executed on 10 and 11 Thermidor—July 28–29, 1794. The Terror ends.

And soon, so will the Republic. In a few years, Napoleon Bonaparte seizes control of the country, and the remnants of the French Revolution are quashed by a new dictatorship. When it is all said and done, an all-powerful King is replaced by the all-powerful National Convention, which in turn is replaced by an all-powerful emperor.*

Simply put, absolute power in the hands of the people or their representatives can be at least as terrifying as that same power held in the hands of a single tyrant. The French Revolution begins by recognizing various unassailable individual rights and ends with an elected, all-powerful assembly flagrantly infringing on every single right, violating every principle of free and just government and massacring tens of thousands. The revolutionary zeal of human perfection consumes revolutionaries throughout the entire French Revolution—friends massacre each other—while turning society upside down. The revolutionaries do this in pursuit of a "republic of virtue." Their understanding of virtue during the French Revolution and that which is understood by the Founding Fathers in the American Revolution cannot be further apart. Unlimited power in the hands of the representatives of the people makes a mockery of virtue, the rule of law, unalienable rights, limited government, the Social Compact, and equality.

The Founders would not have been surprised. They all but predict what will happen if the people exercise unlimited power. Thomas Jefferson observes in 1774 that "[h]istory has informed us that bodies of men, as well as individuals, are susceptible of the spirit of tyranny."* His reflection is a bit ironic in light of his initial enthusiasm for the French Revolution, but it is no less prophetic in light of the horrors that arise in its wake. In essence, Hobbes justifies the tyranny of the Soviet Empire and Mao Zedong's Communist China—they are supposedly based on the unfettered power of the people. Fascist Italy also subscribes to the principles that the sovereign (in other words, the corporate state) possesses unchecked power. In totalitarian regimes, the authority of the government overrides the rights of all its subjects.

The Founders reject the doctrine of Hobbes and adopt its opposite as a First

Principle--the powers of the government are limited to those necessary to protect the unalienable rights of the people and related necessary auxiliary authority. This First Principle is recognized by the Declaration of Independence when it explains the purpose of government: "[T]o secure these rights, Governments are instituted among Men." After all, Jefferson explains in another context, "[I]t is to secure our just rights that we resort to government at all."*

Although government is necessary, it is not to be relished or encouraged. Thomas Paine's *Common Sense* may best capture for all time the particular American sentiment of robust skepticism regarding the government's role within the Social Compact:

> Society in every state is a blessing, but government even in its best state is but a necessary evil; in its worst state an intolerable one [...]. Government, like dress, is the badge of lost innocence; the palaces of the kings are built on the ruins of the bowers of paradise. For were the impulses of conscience clear, uniform, and irresistibly obeyed, man would need no other lawgiver; but that not being the case, he finds it necessary to surrender up a part of his property to furnish means for the protection of the rest. [...]
>
> Here then is the origin and rise of government; namely, a mode rendered necessary by the inability of moral virtue to govern the world; here too is the design and end of government, [namely] freedom and security.*

In light of this cautionary view of government as a necessary evil, Jefferson and the other Founders follow the path laid down by Locke. Locke reasons that the Social Compact did not vest the government with unlimited power. To the contrary, the government has no more just power than what a single individual has in a state of Nature. Simply because everyone bands together into a Social Compact does not vest the government with more power than held separately by an individual alone. We have consented to the government to protect our unalienable rights and, therefore, have only granted the government such power as it needs to perform that function—nothing more. As Jefferson writes, "[T]he rights of the whole can be no more than the sum of the rights of individuals."*

In other words, the Social Compact does not mean—as Hobbes, the Athenians, and the French Revolutionaries would have it—that the government, even a democratic one, has unlimited power. Indeed, in addressing the American Revolution, Jefferson explains that the Founders are not seeking a representative form of tyranny:

> Can any one reason be assigned why 160,000 electors in the island of Great Britain should give law to four millions in the states of America, every individual of whom is equal to every individual of them in virtue, in understanding, and in bodily strength? Were this to be admitted, instead of being a free people, as we have hitherto supposed, and mean to continue ourselves, we should suddenly be found the slaves, not of one, but of 160,000 tyrants, distinguished too from all others by this singular circumstance, that they are removed from the reach of fear, the only restraining motive which may hold the hand of a tyrant.*

In the years leading up to the Declaration of Independence, the idea of limited government takes a stronghold in the colonies. For example, Minister Daniel Shute's 1768 Election Day sermon reflects that the government cannot infringe on unalienable rights but is bound to protect them. "Civil government among mankind is not a resignation of their natural privileges, but that method of securing them, to which they are morally obligated as conducive to their happiness."*

Because the purpose of government is to secure the unalienable rights of the people, the law is founded on this "great end" of government, and Minister Shute explains that the government can have "no rightful power to act beside or counter to this purpose."* In America, Jefferson explains, "[O]ur rulers can have authority over such natural rights only as we have submitted to them."* Because the only way government officials have authority to rule is through the consent of the people to secure their rights, Shute explicates, public officials "ought to be guardians of the natural and constitutional rights of their subjects; which are here supposed to be so near the same that there is no interfering between them. To form a civil constitution otherwise would be to establish inequity by law."* The government acts despotically when it betrays its mandate to protect unalienable rights and instead violates them.

John Tucker, the pastor of the First Church in Newbury, Massachusetts, conveys similar beliefs in a sermon preached at Cambridge in 1771. Pastor Tucker notes that the government's authority comes from the people and is limited by the Social Compact. To accept the opposite, Hobbesian view that the government is unlimited subverts the whole idea of troubling with a government in the first place—it leads to tyranny:

> To suppose otherwise, and that without a delegated power and constitutional right, rulers may make laws, and appoint officers for their execution, and force them to effect, i.e., according to

> their own arbitrary will and pleasure, is to defeat the great design of civil government, and utterly to abolish it. It is to make rulers absolutely despotic, and to subject the People to a state of slavery.*

Samuel West concurs. He is the leader of the Congregational church at Dartmouth, Massachusetts, and widely understood to be one of the most learned men of this time. West will serve as a member of the Massachusetts Constitutional Convention of 1780 and the Massachusetts Convention that ratifies the federal Constitution in 1788. In an Election Day sermon delivered in Boston in 1776, he takes the idea further and explains that even if a government is somehow vested with unlimited authority by the people, such an attempt is null and void under Natural Law:

> [T]yranny and arbitrary power are utterly inconsistent with and subversive of the very end and design of civil government, and directly contrary to natural law, which is the true foundation of civil government and all politic law. Consequently, the authority of a tyrant is of itself null and void; for as no man can have a right to act contrary to the law of nature, it is impossible that any individual, or even the greatest number of men, can confer a right upon another of which they themselves are not possessed; *i.e.*, no body of men can justly and lawfully authorize any person to tyrannize over and enslave his fellow-creatures, or do anything contrary to equity and goodness. [Italics are in the original.]*

Here is the key point: The American view rejects the French National Convention, ancient Athens, the totalitarian surveillance state, and the pharaoh. Whether placed in the hands of many, a few, or one, absolute power is still tyranny—it violates the foundation of the Social Compact, justice, and Natural Law. The Founders believe that government is instituted to protect unalienable rights, a just government is limited to that purpose, and violating those rights forfeits the authority of the government to rule the People.

In 1778, in response to a proposed Massachusetts constitution, Theophilus Parsons writes *The Essex Result*. This tract is adopted by various Essex County towns and cities. Parsons is an attorney and serves as chief justice of the Massachusetts Supreme Court. *The Essex Result* is an intensely interesting, near preview of *The Federalist Papers*. He explains that not only would an unlimited government be null and void, but it would be better not to have a government at all under such circumstances. When confronted with a tyrannical government,

> [s]urely a state of nature is more excellent than that, in which men are meanly submissive to the haughty will of an imperious tyrant, whose savage passions are not bounded by the laws of reason, religion, honor, or a regard to this subjects, and the point to which all his movements center, is the gratification of a brutal appetite.*

Contrary to Hobbes, at least some of the Founding Generation believe that individuals are better off having no government at all rather than being subjected to tyranny, regardless of whether it is a single or collective tyrant.

In short, power is not an end, but a means to protect the unalienable rights of the people. The power to do good is the power to do evil. Power is seductive and corrupting. Unlimited power must be rejected, no matter the motivations for attempting to gain it. The Founders unequivocally declare that the Social Compact does not justify absolute power but, to the contrary, requires that the government be limited. Any person, group, or government that tries to seize unlimited power must be stopped. As such, power cannot be fully placed in the hands of one person (or group of people). Indeed, the underlying basis of the American Revolution is to prevent absolute power from taking control.

However, we must understand that power in itself is not necessarily evil, so long as it is exercised with humility and self-restraint, and most importantly, limited by external constraints. To be useful and capable, government needs substantial power to protect our unalienable rights. That is the whole point of the rule of law and the Social Compact. The lesson is not that power itself is corrupting and evil, but that unaccountable, unconstrained, and absolute power is. This is why we have the separation of powers, checks and balances, federalism, a Bill of Rights, enumerated powers, judicial review, and similar limits on governmental authority in the federal and State constitutions. The Founders embrace the fundamental proposition that to be just, a government must be limited. The Declaration of Independence stands against absolute power. Limited government is a First Principle of the new American order.

*We have counted the cost of this contest, and find nothing so dreadful as voluntary slavery.—Honor, justice, and humanity, forbid us tamely to surrender that freedom which we received from our gallant ancestors, and which our innocent posterity have a right to receive from us. We cannot endure the infamy and guilt of resigning succeeding generations to that wretchedness which inevitably awaits them, if we basely entail hereditary bondage upon them.* [...]

*In our native land, in defense of the freedom that is our birthright, and which we ever enjoyed till the late violation of it—for the protection of our property acquired, solely by the honest industry of our forefathers and ourselves, against violence actually offered, we have taken up arms.**

Second Continental Congress (July 6, 1775)

# 19

## "—THAT WHENEVER ANY FORM OF GOVERNMENT BECOMES DESTRUCTIVE OF THESE ENDS, IT IS THE RIGHT OF THE PEOPLE TO ALTER OR TO ABOLISH IT, AND TO INSTITUTE NEW GOVERNMENT, LAYING ITS FOUNDATION ON SUCH PRINCIPLES AND ORGANIZING ITS POWERS IN SUCH FORM, AS TO THEM SHALL SEEM MOST LIKELY TO EFFECT THEIR SAFETY AND HAPPINESS."

*May citizens be justified in removing or replacing their government?*

- ☆ If a government becomes oppressive by violating our unalienable rights, the people have the right to alter or abolish the government and replace it with another—the people have the right to reform their government or engage in a revolution.

- ☆ America is the first nation in world history to include in its founding document the right to alter or abolish an oppressive government.

The Declaration is truly a revolutionary document—it defends the Founders' revolution in bold and stark terms. Like so much else, the Founding Fathers embrace a novel perspective in connection with resisting governmental oppression. They declare as a self-evident truth that the people have the right to alter or abolish an oppressive government. This reverberates throughout American history, leading to fundamental American constitutional reform such as abolitionism, equal protection, and women's suffrage. We often forget that this perspective is unique. Before 1776, no nation's foundational document included the seeds of its own reform or destruction. And make no mistake: That is the whole point of the Declaration.

This is not to say that Americans are somehow the first to invent revolution. World history is rife with protests, riots, rebellions, civil wars, revolutions, and other forms of political resistance. As but one example, the nearly endless bloody civil wars, revolts, and assassinations of the Roman Republic and Empire are well known by the Founders. Rome is hardly alone. Closer to the Founders' time and lineage, the English War of the Roses (1455–1487), the English Civil War (1642–1651), and the Glorious Revolution (1688) are staples of the Founders' education, as is the Dutch rebellion against Spanish rule in 1566. The Founders likewise dread the return of the religious warfare that tears apart and ravages Europe for generations, such as the devastating Thirty Years' War (1618–1648) in Central Europe. Wars of national liberation from colonizing forces are strewn throughout the ages. Haiti will revolt against French imperial rule during the lifetime of many of the Founders.

The American Revolution is fundamentally different. For the first time in history, the people declare and act on a universal claim that their violent resistance is justified based on universal truths and principles to protect their unalienable rights. To justify their resistance, the Founders again turn to John Locke, Thomas Hobbes, and similar thinkers. Although they theorize about the Social Compact and the creation of a government from the state of Nature, they are no fools. As we have learned, even the thinnest understanding of history reveals that the prevailing situation is not some idealistic government and society that protects the rights of the people but quite the opposite: Governments that oppress the people in violation of their unalienable rights are the norm. Recall the oppression and unlimited authority of the Egyptian pharaohs; the terror of the French Revolution; the societal divisions of the ancien régime; and the genocide of the Soviet Union. That oppressive state of affairs dominates the globe before 1776 and remains true today throughout much of the world. Witness the oppressive regimes holding power in, among others, China, Russia, Belarus, Egypt, Libya, Iran, North Korea, Cuba, Vietnam, Turkey, Mynamar, Sudan, Algeria, Afghanistan, Saudi Arabia, and Nicaragua.

Locke explains that because oppressive governments violate the unalienable rights of the people, they are—in essence—at war with the very people they should be serving and protecting:

> [H]e who attempts to get another man into his absolute power, does thereby put himself into a state of war with him [...] [H]e who would get me into his power without my consent, would use me as he pleased when he got me there, and destroy me too when he had a fancy to it; for nobody can desire to have me in his absolute power, unless it is be to compel me by force to that which is against the right of my freedom, i.e., make me a slave.*

Locke's formulation is not hyperbole. A government acting beyond its just powers enslaves the people. It is a perversion of our unalienable rights and the purpose of government. Instead of bringing peace and security, such a government is our enemy.

We must be on guard to resist any infringement of our natural rights. When an infringement happens, the people have the right to resist the government's actions. After all, when we are in a state of Nature, we have the right to defend ourselves. We have joined a Social Compact to protect our unalienable rights. But if the Social Compact is destroying the very rights it is intended to protect, then we have the God-given right to resist the government that has, in essence, declared war against us. Because the people are sovereign (that is, possessing the highest authority in society), they retain the ultimate authority to rebel against an oppressive government that has gone beyond its just authority:

> [T]he legislative [body] being only a fiduciary power to act for certain ends, there remains still in the people a supreme power to remove or alter the legislative [authorities], when they find the legislative [authorities] act contrary to the trust reposed in them; for all power given with trust for the attuning an end, being limited by that end, whenever that end is manifestly neglected, or opposed, the trust must necessarily be forfeited, and the power devolve into the hands of those who gave it, who may place it anew where they shall link best for their safety and security.*

In other words, as we previously learned, the people are the supreme power even when they create a government. Accordingly, when a government violates the rights of the people, it forfeits the right to rule. Under such circumstances, the people have the right to reform or rebel against the government—with violence if necessary. This is even true in an elected system of government. Where tyranny begins, just government ends, and the right to reform or abolish that government is triggered.

Locke's theory is enthusiastically embraced in the colonies. As radical as it is at the time, this proposition is deeply embedded in the American mindset before the American Revolution. In great measure, this arises from the Founders' view of the Glorious Revolution of 1688 in Great Britain, considered as the epitome of a just revolution. Before 1688, many in Great Britain believe that their Catholic King James II is a tyrant who is subverting English liberty. Shortly after the birth of his son (who many believe will perpetuate despotic Catholic rule), King James II is overthrown by his Protestant daughter Mary and her Protestant Dutch husband, William of Orange. In the aftermath of the Glorious Revolution, Parliament gains many powers against the monarchy, and a groundbreaking Bill of Rights is adopted. This is the context for Locke's *Second Treatise of Government*—the work legitimizes the Glorious Revolution. Among other things, Locke's reasoning becomes part of the philosophical underpinnings of the Whigs (an English political party favoring more individual liberty, a strong Parliament, and a limited monarchy) in England. The often minority perspective of the Whigs in England becomes the prevailing perspective in America.

The colonial clergy are at the forefront of revolutionary zeal and thought. They often deliver stirring sermons that shape and reinforce the political thinking of the day. In the early days of the resistance, Daniel Shute's "An Election Sermon" (May 26, 1768) observes that government leaders must stay within the limits of their due and just powers, and if the government acts "otherwise, the subject can be under no obligation to observe them; but may be morally obliged to resist them, as it must ever be right *to obey God rather than men* [italics in original]."* The people not only have a right to resist oppression, but they have a duty to God to do so. Indeed, if one fails to resist in the face of oppression, the failure to challenge the oppression is itself a defiance of divine will. Worse, compliance with an unjust government is the wicked work of the "Prince of Darkness":

> The doctrine of *passive obedience* and *non-resistance* in the unlimited sense it has been urged by some, came not down from above, as it can be supported neither by reason nor revelation; and therefore if any where, may be urged with a better grace by *the rulers of darkness*, in the regions below, upon those who by the righteous decree of heaven, are excluded the common benefits of creation, than by those *powers that are ordained of God* for the *good* of mankind. [Italics are in the original.]*

One cannot be more direct.

Gad Hitchcock, the minister of the Second Church of Christ (also known as the First Congregational Church) in Pembroke, Massachusetts, reflects and influences American political thought. He is widely acclaimed for his fearless teaching, as well as his knowledge of the Bible, history, and theology. Hitchcock's riveting election sermon in Boston in 1774 is delivered before General Thomas Gage, the newly appointed governor of Massachusetts, and shiploads of British troops. After the Boston Tea Party, Gage is appointed with the specific purpose of crushing Massachusetts's resistance to British oppression. The presence of Gage and the troops might be expected to intimidate Hitchcock. Instead, it likely emboldens him. He takes Shute's theme an extra step and explains that if the people are timid and do not resist oppression, then they are simply inviting tyrants to impose a dreadful enslavement. Only by showing a stiff resolve to oppose tyranny will the people remain free. The failure to teach resistance to oppression will "dispose princes of evil minds, to enslave and ruin the best and most submissive subjects [and will] encourage all tyranny, and all the most intolerable persecutions and oppressions imaginable."*

The Patriots clearly understand that they must resist British oppression if they have any chance of remaining free. This sentiment is widely expressed by clergy and laypersons throughout the colonies. Building on the understanding that the Social Compact is established to protect the unalienable rights endowed in us by the Creator, Samuel West elaborates in his Election Day sermon of 1776. The sermon is delivered before the Massachusetts governing council and House of Representatives. West is the minister of a Congregational church in Dartmouth, Massachusetts, and an active member of the Massachusetts Constitutional Convention of 1780. He declines to serve in the federal Constitutional Convention but participates in the Massachusetts convention that ratifies the federal Constitution in 1788. In the 1776 sermon, West not only rejects Hobbes's position that a government must be obeyed, but he also declares that such a position is all but blasphemy:

> [I]t would imply a gross absurdity to assert that, when magistrates are ordained by the people solely for the purpose of being beneficial to the state, they must be obeyed when they are seeking to ruin and destroy it. This would imply that men were bound to act against the great law of self-preservation, and to contribute their assistance to their own ruin and destruction, in order that they may please and gratify the greatest monsters in nature, who are violating the laws of God and destroying the rights of mankind. Unlimited submission and obedience is due to none but God alone. [...] [A]nd to suppose that he has given any particular set of men a power to require obedience to that

> which is unreasonable, cruel, and unjust, is robbing the Deity of his justice and goodness, in which consists the peculiar glory of the divine character, and it is representing him under the horrid character of tyrant.*

Of course, although this resistance should try to avoid violence, it may become necessary. The people need not idly lie down and accept tyranny. They have the right to use force to protect their liberties. Unitarian Congregational Minister Simeon Howard, who also holds positions at Harvard in addition to his ministry, is thought by contemporaries to be "one of the ablest men New England ever produced."* In "A Sermon Preached to the Ancient and Honorable Artillery Company in Boston" in 1773 (yes, he is preaching to an imperial British artillery company), he announces:

> [T]he experience of all ages has shown, that those, who are so unreasonable as to form designs of injuring others, are seldom to be diverted from their purpose by argument and persuasion alone. [...] And in this case, what is to be done by the sufferer? Is he to use no other means for his safety, but remonstrance or flight, when these will not secure him? Is he patiently to take the injury and suffer himself to be robbed of his liberty or his life, if the adversary sees fit to take it? Nature certainly forbids this tame submission, and loudly calls to a more vigorous defence. Self-preservation is one of the strongest, and a universal principle of the human mind: And this principle allows of everything necessary to self-defense, opposing force to force, and violence to violence. This is so universally allowed that I need not attempt to prove it.*

Similarly to Minister Shute, Minister Howard explains that violent resistance is a duty imposed by God, but not only on individuals; a community or nation must rebel against oppression as well:

> This reasoning is as applicable to a community as to an individual. [...]
>
> Men are also bound, individuals and societies, to take care of their temporal happiness, and do all they lawfully can, to promote it. But what can be more inconsistent with this duty, than submitting to great encroachments upon our liberty? Such submission tends to slavery; and complete slavery implies every evil that the

> malice of man and devils can inflict. Again, the regard which we owe to the happiness of others makes this a duty.*

As these sermon passages reveal, the Founders believe that a whole people, if necessary, should oppose an oppressive government through revolution. After all, the essence of the government is to act as a guardian and fiduciary for the people to protect their rights. When the government betrays that trust, the people are relieved of their responsibility to follow it and have a God-given duty and the right to throw off the oppressive government through revolution.

This theoretical philosophy is put to the test in America. In the years leading up to the Declaration (as we will soon closely examine), the British Empire engages in a long train of abuses and usurpations of the unalienable rights of the colonists. The colonists draw many parallels and lessons from the circumstances resulting in the Glorious Revolution and believe that the same conditions compelling revolution in England a hundred years ago exist in the colonies. The Founding Generation is convinced that Great Britain's rule is devolving into an oppressive tyranny, and the colonists will become the slaves of the empire. Thus, for many years before 1776, the colonists engage in various robust tactics to oppose British oppression, including petitions, protests, proclamations, boycotts, burning tax officials in effigy, tarring and feathering British officials and Loyalists, the Boston Tea Party, and even demolishing the homes of imperial officials. Although this resistance falls well short of revolution, it is deadly serious.

As we explored earlier, two years before the Declaration, the Massachusetts and Virginia legislatures call for a meeting of delegates from the various colonies to devise a coordinated, continental strategy of resistance and reconciliation with Great Britain. Lacking only North Carolina and Georgia, the First Continental Congress convenes in Philadelphia. The importance of Congress is not lost on the colonists. On September 9, 1774, the county of Suffolk, Massachusetts, adopts resolutions written by Bostonian Dr. Joseph Warren, which explain to Congress the hour at hand. Warren is a Harvard-educated physician turned fiery revolutionary orator and leader. On the eve of the Battle of Lexington, Warren sends Paul Revere and William Dawes to warn that the British are coming. He is later martyred as a volunteer soldier at the Battle of Bunker Hill. After the disastrous battle at Bunker Hill, British commander Lord Francis Rawdon takes some solace in Warren's death, noting that he was "the greatest incendiary in all America."* On September 17, 1774, the First Continental Congress adopts Warren's Suffolk Resolves. The preamble is a masterpiece. It invokes the right and duty to resist tyranny:

> On the fortitude—on the wisdom and on the exertions of this

> important day, it suspended the fate of this new world, and of unborn millions.—If a boundless extent of continent, swarming with millions, will tamely submit to live, move and have their being at the arbitrary will of a licentious minister, they basely yield to voluntary slavery, and future generations shall load their memories with incessant execrations.—On the other hand, if we arrest the hand which would ransack our pockets, if we disarm the parricide who points the dagger to our bosoms, if we nobly defeat that fatal edict which proclaims a power to frame laws for us in all cases whatsoever, thereby entailing the endless and numberless curses of slavery upon us, our heirs and their heirs forever; if we successfully resist that unparalleled usurpation of unconstitutional power, whereby our capital is robbed of the means of life, whereby the streets of Boston are thronged with military executioners, whereby our coasts are lined, and harbours crowded with ships of war, whereby the charter of the colony, that sacred barrier against the encroachments of tyranny, is mutilated, and in effect annihilated; whereby a murderous law is framed to shelter villains from the hands of justice; whereby the unalienable and inestimable inheritance, which we derived from Nature, the constitution of Britain, which was covenanted to us in the charter of the province, is totally wrecked, annulled and vacated;—Posterity will acknowledge that virtue which preserved them free and happy; and while we enjoy the rewards and blessings of the faithful, the torrent of panegyrists will roll our reputations to that latest period, when the streams of time shall be absorbed in the abyss of eternity.*

The fate of the world rests on America. The Suffolk Resolves call out England for oppression and urge Americans to live up to their duty to defy such oppression. The document lists a high-level accounting of how the British are oppressing the colonists. It is also an abbreviated preview of the long train of abuses and usurpations that the Second Continental Congress will list as grievances in the Declaration of Independence. They also proclaim the specific reactions the colonists should take short of violent revolution—at least for the time being. They specifically resolve that Massachusetts should convene a new provincial congress. In other words, they call for the creation of a new assembly to represent the people to replace the legislative assembly that had been established under English law. Many other local Massachusetts petitions concur.

Unsurprisingly, the royal governor completely disagrees and forbids the colonial legislature from even meeting. He is hardly persuasive. On October 5, 1774, the colonial legislature meets in defiance of the governor's order. In its final act, it calls for a new provincial congress to convene the next day, and then immediately dissolves itself.

The question then becomes, Now what? Samuel West had addressed this years earlier. When a people overthrow an oppressive government, they "have a right to form themselves into a body politic, and assume to themselves all the powers of a free state."* It should come as no surprise that the very day after the Massachusetts colonial legislature dissolves itself, its call for a new government to meet is realized. With John Hancock as its president, the Massachusetts Provincial Congress convenes. The colonists are revolting against the British Empire and establishing a new government in the form and based on the principles they expect will secure their rights and happiness.

Meanwhile, the English ignore the pleas of the First Continental Congress for the British to adopt policies that will preserve colonial liberties. America and Great Britain edge closer to open warfare. Unknown to the colonists, a week before the Suffolk Resolves are ratified by the First Continental Congress, the king announces that "[t]he die is now cast, the colonies must either submit or triumph."* By November 1774, the king decides that "the New England governments are in state of rebellion, [and] blows must decide whether they are to be subject to this country or independent."* Any hope of a peaceful reconciliation vanishes.

The king's prophecy becomes reality on April 19, 1775, when the first shots of the American Revolution are fired at Lexington and Concord. In the wake of the skirmish, author of the Suffolk Resolves and newly minted president of the Massachusetts Provincial Government, Dr. Warren, publishes a letter on behalf of the new government, explaining that "to the persecution and tyranny of [the king's] cruel ministry we will not tamely submit; appealing to heaven for the justice of our cause, we determine to die or be free."*

For a second time, the Second Continental Congress follows Warren's lead. On July 6, 1775, it approves military action in defense of the rights of the colonists in its Declaration of the Causes and Necessity of Taking Up Arms. Written by John Dickinson (one half) and Thomas Jefferson (the other half), it proclaims that Parliament, having "attempted to effect their cruel and impolitic purpose of enslaving these colonies by violence [has] rendered it necessary for us to close with their last appeal from reason to arms."* The Declaration of the Causes and Necessity of Taking Up Arms affirms for America what Patrick Henry proclaims for Virginia in his "Give Me Liberty or Give Me Death!" speech—and what Warren proclaims in his letter for Massachusetts:

> We do most solemnly before God and the world declare, that, exerting the utmost energy of those powers, which our beneficent Creator has graciously bestowed upon us, the arms we have been compelled by our enemies to assume, we will in defiance of every hazard with unabating firmness and perseverance, employ for the preservation of our liberties, being with one mind resolved to die freemen rather than to live like slaves.*

The momentum for Revolution becomes unstoppable. On October 4, 1774, the town of Worcester, Massachusetts, leapfrogs ahead of the Continental Congress and declares that unless the British reverse course completely, it will dissolve its bands with England. On January 9, 1776, Thomas Paine's thunderous and captivating pamphlet, *Common Sense,* is published, swaying public opinion heavily toward independence.

Thus, when the Massachusetts Provincial Government calls upon its towns for their instructions about the possibility of independence, on May 27, 1776, the town of Malden confidently "renounce[s] with disdain our connection with a kingdom of slaves; we bid a final adieu to Britain."* Malden proclaims that if a declaration of independence is made, "your constituents will support and defend the measure, to the last drop of their blood, and the last farthing of their treasure."* Malden's instructions are not unique. Very soon, all the colonies agree that their freedoms will only be secure if they sever all ties from the British Empire and establish an independent nation founded upon just principles of free government.

In a letter to Thomas Jefferson, John Adams summarizes the American experience:

> What do we mean by the revolution? The war? That was no part of the revolution. It was only an effect and consequence of it. The revolution was in the minds of the people, and this was effected, from 1760 to 1775, in the course of fifteen years before a drop of blood was drawn at Lexington.*

After the Declaration is issued, the practical reality is that the colonies become newly born States and begin to adopt new constitutions. A new government is also being forged between the colonies. The new nation is fulfilling the First Principle of revolution by engaging in revolution and establishing new governments. Indeed, many States integrate the First Principle of revolution in their State constitutions. Several of the State constitutions immediately adopted around or in the aftermath of the Declaration include passages about how they had become free and independent

States as a result of revolution. Later constitutions include passages like this one from New Hampshire's Constitution of 1784:

> Government being instituted for the common benefit, protection, and security, of the whole community, and not for the private interest or emolument of any one man, family, or class of men; therefore, whenever the ends of government are perverted, and public liberty manifestly endangered, and all other means of redress are ineffectual, the people may, and of right ought to reform the old, or establish a new government. The doctrine of nonresistance against arbitrary power, and oppression, is absurd, slavish, and destructive of the good and happiness of mankind.*

Others are more tempered. For example, the oldest written constitution in the world, to this day, is primarily drafted by John Adams. The preamble and Declaration of Rights of the Massachusetts Constitution of 1780 provide a right to reform, alter, or totally change the form of government:

> Government is instituted for the common good; for the protection, safety, prosperity and happiness of the people; and not for the profit, honor, or private interest of any one man, family, or class of men: Therefore the people alone have an incontestable, unalienable, and indefeasible right to institute government; and to reform, alter, or totally change the same, when their protection, safety, prosperity and happiness, require it.*

Other State constitutions that in the past or currently express in some fashion the First Principle that the people have the right to alter or abolish an oppressive government include Alabama,* Arkansas,* California,* Connecticut,* Idaho,* Indiana,* Iowa,* Kentucky,* Maine,* Maryland,* Minnesota,* Mississippi,* Missouri,* Montana,* New Jersey,* New York,* North Carolina,* North Dakota,* Ohio,* Oklahoma,* Oregon,* Pennsylvania,* Rhode Island,* South Carolina,* South Dakota,* Tennessee,* Texas,* Utah,* Vermont,* Virginia,* Washington,* West Virginia,* and Wyoming.* Michigan's 1835 Constitution includes this strong provision:

> Government is instituted for the protection, security, and benefit of the people; and they have the right at all times to alter or reform the same, and to abolish one form of government and establish another, whenever the public good requires it.*

Colorado's original and only constitution has a provision that is entitled (capitalization in the original): "PEOPLE MAY ALTER OR ABOLISH FORM OF GOVERNMENT."*

Although not in quite so vivid terms, the federal Constitution also embodies the right to revolution—albeit in a peaceful manner. First, there are scheduled, bloodless revolutions—elections—that occur every two years for members of the House of Representatives, four years for the president, and six years for senators. Second, Article V provides two mechanisms to reform or abolish the government: constitutional amendments and constitutional conventions. Amendments must be proposed by two-thirds of the House of Representatives and the Senate, and they become effective when ratified by three-fourths of the States. As of 2025, thousands of amendments are proposed and twenty-seven are ratified. Whenever two-thirds of the States apply to Congress, a constitutional convention is convened, and the proposed amendments (which might include wholesale replacement of the Constitution) take effect when ratified by three-fourths of the States. There are many calls for a constitutional convention and precisely none convened.

The right to revolution empowers the people to establish a new government based on the First Principles of equality, unalienable rights, the Social Compact, limited government, and the rule of law. The Founding Generation and subsequent generations firmly believe that the people have the right to alter or abolish an oppressive government, and to replace it with a new one in the form and based on such principles they believe will effect their happiness and safety.*

*When a people, born and bred in a land of freedom and virtue, uncorrupted by those refinements which effeminate and debase the mind, manly and serious in their sentiments, bold and hardy in their nature, and actuated by every principle of liberality, from too sad experience are convinced of the wicked schemes of their treacherous rulers to fetter them with the chains of servitude, and rob them of every noble and desirable privilege which distinguishes them as freemen,—justice, humanity, and the immutable laws of God, justify and support them in revoking those sacred trusts which are so impiously violated, and placing them in such hands as are most likely to execute them in the manner and for the important ends for which they were first given.**

Presentments by grand jury of Cheraw District, South Carolina (May 20, 1776)

# 20

"Prudence, indeed, will dictate that Governments long established should not be changed for light and transient causes; and accordingly all experience hath shewn, that mankind are more disposed to suffer, while evils are sufferable, than to right themselves by abolishing the forms to which they are accustomed. But when a long train of abuses and usurpations, pursuing invariably the same Object evinces a design to reduce them under absolute Despotism, it is their right, it is their duty, to throw off such Government, and to provide

**NEW GUARDS FOR THEIR FUTURE SECURITY.—SUCH HAS BEEN THE PATIENT SUFFERANCE OF THESE COLONIES; AND SUCH IS NOW THE NECESSITY WHICH CONSTRAINS THEM TO ALTER THEIR FORMER SYSTEMS OF GOVERNMENT."**

***Understanding that citizens may abolish their government, what conditions justify this drastic measure?***

- ☆ The people should cautiously consider invoking their right to revolution.
- ☆ The people should only consider a revolution when government oppression is heavy and permanent.
- ☆ Historically, the people will suffer under oppression for many years before they invoke the right to revolution.
- ☆ The people have the right and duty to invoke the right to revolution when there is an unrelenting history of serious government oppression designed to impose tyranny and repeated attempts at nonviolent resistance fail.
- ☆ Because the British Empire oppresses the colonists for years and resistance efforts short of revolution fail, the colonists have the right and duty to engage in revolution.

The Founders explain that the people should only cautiously undertake a revolution. This passage from the Declaration begins with the key word "prudence"—perhaps a neglected term in today's society. Because the meaning of many words changes over the last 250 years, reference to sources more contemporary with the Founding Generation is always the wisest course. Samuel Johnson's 1768 *A Dictionary of the English Language* defines "prudence" as "wisdom applied to practice." The essence of this definition is wisdom applied practically. Using this definition, the Founders are declaring "wisdom, as applied to worldly affairs." Noah Webster's 1828 *An American Dictionary of the English Language* elaborates that "prudent" means acting with due caution and thinking through the possible negative consequences of one's actions or omissions:

> 1. Cautious; circumspect; practically wise; careful of the consequences of enterprises, measures or actions; cautious not to act when the end is of doubtful utility or probably impracticable. [...] 2. Dictated or directed by prudence [...] 3. Foreseeing by instinct [...] 4. Frugal; economical [...] 5. Wise; intelligent.

In sum, prudence is exercising caution, thinking through the consequences of actions, and contemplating the future with a careful, wise plan of action. It is the opposite of impulsivity or rashness.

The Founders are not plunging into the American Revolution out of passion or impulse, but after due, cautious, profound deliberation. That this is no mere idle pronouncement is evidenced by the reality that the Founders reach the Revolutionary climax only after fifteen years of British oppression. Even after this long-standing maltreatment, the Declaration is still hotly contested and debated. Congress even takes its time to materially edit Jefferson's and the Committee of Five's draft. This is no knee-jerk reaction, but the outcome of a slow, deliberative, contemplative process weighing with due caution the advantages and dangers of declaring independence.

The Declaration continues with the phrase, "Prudence, indeed, will dictate that Governments long established." The most instructive definition (from Webster's 1841 dictionary) that is relatively contemporary with the Founders of "dictate" is "[t]o tell with authority; to deliver, as an order, command or direction." Thus, the Founders' original phrase might be reworded as "cautious wisdom commands that governments that have existed for a long time."

The phrase continues that "[g]overnments long established should not be changed for light and transient causes." As defined by Johnson's 1768 dictionary, "light" here means "1. [...] [N]ot heavy, [...] 2. Not burdensome; easy to be worn, or carried, [...] 3. Not afflictive; easy to be endured." As defined by Webster's 1848 dictionary, "transient" means "1. Passing; not stationary; hence of short duration;

not permanent; not lasting or durable [...] 2. Hasty; momentary; imperfect." In other words, we should not take the momentous action of engaging in a revolution based on something that is not overly burdensome or that is temporary, passing, or of short duration. Put together, this phrase expounds that if a government has been established for a long time (like the colonial and English governments), then a temporary, relatively easy burden does not justify a revolution.

The phrase continues, "and accordingly all experience hath shewn, that mankind are more disposed to suffer, while evils are sufferable, than to right themselves by abolishing the forms to which they are accustomed." Unlike the phrases before it, this one is not a declaration of principle—it is a historical observation. The Declaration refers to "all experience hath [shown]," meaning what all of history reveals. A broad claim, but the Founders are on solid ground because they qualify this observation with the next clause: "mankind are more disposed to suffer, while evils are sufferable, than to right themselves by abolishing the forms to which they are accustomed."

A literal interpretation is warranted. The Declaration notes that history has shown that the people are more likely to suffer evils imposed on them for as long as they can suffer them—rather than taking the dramatic action of engaging in an uprising to oppose repression. This makes inherent sense. A revolution risks the careers, homes, and treasures of the revolutionaries and their families, as well as their freedom, health, and very lives. Other reasons for patience abound, including honoring tradition, respect for leaders, the prospect that oppressions will be reversed or minimized by the present leaders, and hope that the intransigent current leaders may be replaced by others who will abandon the oppressions of their predecessors. A key expectation (or at least hope) is that protests that fall short of violence will trigger a change of policy. Considering the costs, a person must be backed in a corner with no better option to pick up arms against an established government. People almost never immediately riot, loot, and revolt when a government imposes a bad—even evil—policy.

Before Lexington and Concord, the British impose on the colonists a series of unjust actions and policies, and the colonists robustly resist in several ways. For example, they boycott British goods through joint action labeled "non-importation agreements." They soundly object to British actions in the newspapers. Colonial legislative assemblies pass resolutions condemning imperial policies and petitioning for their repeal. Protestors take to the streets and intimidate British government officials. Colonial officers and agents refuse to enforce the Stamp Act. Bostonians throw tea laden with unconstitutional taxes into the ocean. Soldiers are harassed and taunted; homes are even demolished. But rarely is anyone gravely hurt. Some stamp and customs agents are tarred and feathered (a very rough way to be treated) but rarely fatally. Some of these resistance activities actually result in the British authorities backing off and revoking inflammatory policies. Such a wide array of resistance reveals that the first reaction to an unjust policy should not be insurrection. Patient, deliberative, organized, and well-reasoned protests and resistance can be highly effective.

Furthermore, the Founders understand that the cost of a violent reaction could very well end up being substantially worse than the policies and actions being opposed. A crackdown by the empire could lead to the loss of more freedoms, properties, and lives. Plus, there is always a high probability that a revolution will simply be crushed. After all, governments typically meet armed resistance with brutality and the widespread suppression of unalienable rights.

The Founders' conclusion that the people are more likely to suffer than revolt is hardly novel. In fact, John Locke expresses this idea in his *Second Treatise of Government*. Locke's critics argue that his faith in the people is foolish because the people are fickle, passionate, and easily aroused to take ill-mannered and unwise actions. Resting the government on the sovereignty of the people is a recipe for tumult, chaos, and disaster. Locke counters that there is no real danger from the people trying to change the government for just any perceived injustice. To the contrary, inertia, tradition, and familiarity with government norms means that the people are very unlikely to make radical breaks with the past. They are reluctant to force change "even when all the world sees there is an opportunity for it," and "[g]reat mistakes in the ruling part, many wrong and inconvenient laws, and all the slips of human frailty, will be borne by the people without mutiny or murmur."*

Poor policies, wrongful actions, foolish directives, and corrupt practices will not usually provoke the people to take to the streets, at least not violently. As heartbreaking and enraging these negative actions or omissions can be, they usually are still not enough to spark a revolution. This is especially true when political leaders can be pressured or replaced and new polices implemented. Elections or changes in administration often ameliorate the people's rage.

This tendency continues. If you align yourself with any particular political party or viewpoint today, you can readily criticize the President, Congress, and Supreme Court in connection with a whole host of executive actions or inaction, legislation or lack of legislation, and Supreme Court rulings or nonrulings that you intensely dislike. You might even characterize some of those actions or omissions as unconstitutional or oppressive. Some may make your blood boil. Republicans tear down Presidents Bill Clinton, Barack Obama, and Joe Biden; Democrats tear down George H. W. Bush, George W. Bush, and Donald Trump. Independents have wide-ranging criticisms of the two major parties. Congress's approval rating is at historic lows. The Supreme Court is vigorously criticized by the left, right, and center, depending on the ruling. The views of the Libertarians, the Green Party, and the Constitution Party are vigorously opposed to many of the policies of the major parties. Independents and moderates seem without a political home.

But this all comes with the territory of having a republic. Sometimes your party is in control, and you love the government; sometimes a different party is in control, and you hate it; sometimes your party is in control, and you hate it anyway. Maybe you do not have a party and love and hate the government or policies as they align with or oppose your positions. Take any hot-button issue today—immigration, crime and criminal justice reform, healthcare, social security and entitlements, government spending, governmental regulations, education, foreign policy, trade policy, abortion, environmental regulations, energy policy, or gun rights—and there are deep divisions. But this does not rise to the level of justifying a violent revolution. Combat comes via the ballot box, petitions, pressure groups, lobbying, demonstrations, mass media coverage, social media, speeches, editorials, pickets, strikes, and constitutional amendments—not by mobs and revolts.

Why not jump to revolt? Because we believe we can effect change within the system—that those in government, no matter how much we disagree with them, are people of good faith, intending to do what they think supports the public welfare. You have the right to critique, lobby, and vote them out. Paraphrasing Thomas Jefferson's first inaugural address, differences in opinion are not differences in principle. We are all trying to reach the same destination of a free and just society but have different solutions for how to best arrive at the destination.

Of course, there are exceptions. Some are self-absorbed, immoral scoundrels oblivious to public welfare. Communists and fascists really do hate the Declaration of Independence and the Constitution. Still, they remain in the minority—for now. Some might say these are unprecedented times, but they ignore the American Revolution and the Civil War, to name just two awful periods of division.

The reality is that the governing paradigm for generations is give-and-take, peaceful reform through the ballot box, constitutional amendments, legislative reform, and Supreme Court rulings. It all boils down to decision-making within the framework of the Constitution. It requires something extraordinary to justify revolution.

With this understanding, there is still more to unpack in this phrase: "[M]ankind are more disposed to suffer, while evils are sufferable, than to right themselves by abolishing the forms to which they are accustomed." "Suffer" is a key word here. Webster's 1841 dictionary defines it as "1. To feel or undergo pain of body or mind; to bear what is inconvenient. 2. To undergo, as punishment. 3. To be injured; to sustain loss or damage."

When you are hurt, injured, punished, or betrayed, you suffer. It can be physical—thirst, hunger, a pulled hamstring, a slap to the face, a cut, a punch to the gut, a shotgun wound, or torture. It can also be mental—emotional abuse, anxiety, sorrow, shame, and terror. This idea of suffering is vitally important to the Founders as well as across the world and religions. For example, Christianity has long focused on Christ's crucifixion and suffering on the cross. Many have been canonized as saints because they suffered for the poor and justice. Buddhism has Four Noble Truths (or "truths of the noble ones") that address suffering's existence, origin, cessation, and pathway to ending. As Buddhists wisely lament, life is suffering.

The Founders are not Buddhists, but they stake a claim in suffering. To have just cause for a revolution, the government must cause the people to suffer. They must be subject to pain or other injury of the mind or body or to the infringements of unalienable rights, the Social Compact, the rule of law, equality, or limited government. In theory, violations of unalienable rights and other First Principles that are painless or cause no injury are insufficient to warrant a revolution. For example, the Founders will not revolt against the mercantilist trading laws that prohibit the colonists from trading with foreign countries because these laws are rarely enforced. The colonists simply ignore them and smuggle what they want. The colonists can hardly be seen as suffering at that point. Small inconveniences fall far short of justifying a revolution. Only truly substantial pain and injury warrant a revolution.

In 1750, highly influential Minister Jonathan Mayhew preaches that patience is indeed the disposition of the colonists. In *A Discourse Concerning Unlimited Submission and Non-Resistance to the Higher Powers,* he explains that mistakes and ill judgment alone do not justify revolution; otherwise, there would be chaos and lawlessness:

> [A]s all men are fallible, it cannot be supposed that the public affairs of any state, should be always administered in the best manner possible, even by persons of the greatest wisdom and integrity. Nor is it sufficient to legitimate disobedience to the *higher powers* that they are not so administered; or that they are, in some instances, very ill-managed; for upon this principle, it is scarcely supposable that any government at all could be supported, or subsist. Such a principle manifestly tends to the dissolution of government; and to throw all things into confusion and anarchy. [Italics are in the original.]*

There is another key word in the phrase "that mankind are more disposed to suffer, while evils are sufferable, than to right themselves by abolishing the forms to which they are accustomed." The Founders purposefully choose the word "evils."

Johnson's 1773 definition of "evil" is straightforward: "1. Wickedness; a crime. [...] 2. Injury; mischief. [...] 3. Malignity; corruption. [...] 4. Misfortune; calamity. [...] 5. Malady; disease." Webster's 1839 definition is more elaborate:

> 1. *Evil* is *natural* or *moral.—Natural evil* is any thing which produces pain, distress, loss or calamity, or which in any way disturbs the peace, impairs the happiness, or destroys the perfection of natural beings.—*Moral evil* is any deviation of a moral agent from the rules of conduct prescribed to him by God, or by legitimate human authority. 2. Misfortune; mischief; injury. 3. Depravity; corruption of the heart, or disposition to commit wickedness; malignity. 4. Malady; as the *king's evil* or scrofula [a swelling of the lymph nodes of the neck supposedly cured by the touch of royalty]. [Italics are in the original.]

In the Judeo-Christian tradition, Satan (in his many guises) is evil incarnate. Evil desires to tempt, disrupt, and poison men and women away from God and toward Hell. Corrupting the souls of individuals is Satan's kingdom and work. The Founders' Judeo-Christian conception is akin to a universal belief. Similar incarnations appear in other cultures: The Philistines have Dagon; the Japanese Emma-O, also known as the Hindu Yama; the Greeks, Demogorgon and Typhon; the Norse, Loki and Fenrir; the Aztecs, Mictlantecutli; the Egyptians, Set; the Muslims, Iblis; and the Zoroastrians, Angra Mainyu.

Historical examples are too long to recount, but none but the most malignant will seriously argue with these lowlights of evil (several of which we have previously addressed in this work): Communist China's murderous Mao Zedong, the Soviet Union's tyrannical Joseph Stalin, Nazi Germany's totalitarian Adolf Hitler, Cambodia's genocidal Pol Pot, Iraq's dictator Saddam Hussein, Ugandan strong man Idi Amin, North Korea's multigenerational cult of personality, the cruel and vicious Genghis Khan, the terror mastermind Osama bin Laden, blood-soaked Attila the Hun, the barbaric Taliban, the lunatic Roman Emperor Caligula, China's brutal "one-eyed tyrant" Fu Sheng, Belgian Congo-crushing King Leopold II, and Vlad III of Romania, better known as "Vlad the Impaler "(the inspiration in part for another evil villain, Dracula).

"Evils" is not a term used casually. The Founders not only find that to throw off government, the people must be suffering, but the suffering must be caused by *evils*. For the Founders, the definition most applicable is the "moral evil" definition of Webster: "Moral evil is any deviation of a moral agent from the rules of conduct prescribed to him by God, or by legitimate human authority."

When the king and Parliament purposefully subvert Natural Law by violating the unalienable rights of the people, undermining equality, breaking the Social Compact, and exploding limited government—these are clear deviations of the moral agents of the people (in other words, the king and Parliament) from the rules of conduct prescribed by the Creator. Those actions also violate the rule of law by violating the legitimate lawful bounds of authority on the government and ignoring the protections afforded to British subjects. Furthermore, violations of the Social Compact, equality, the rule of law, limited government, and unalienable rights are fairly characterized as wicked, mischief, and calamities. Accidents, mistakes, and even willful neglect are not evil. But the king and Parliament are not ignorantly stumbling into their oppressive actions and policies; they are designed, deliberate, and purposeful. They are evils.

The Declaration's phrase also declares that even if you are suffering evils, history has shown that the people are more *accustomed* to suffer those evils while they are sufferable than to revolt over them. Johnson's 1768 dictionary definition of "accustomed" is "[a]ccording to custom; frequent; useful." The Declaration observes that the people are unlikely to break from traditions, habits, and routine practices unless they have no other choice. Again, trivial and temporary problems will be borne by those who were suffering—the people will grin and bear it. Only when the evils are too much, when the people can no longer bear them, will revolution occur. Again, the phrase observes "that mankind are more disposed to suffer, while evils are sufferable." Johnson's 1768 dictionary defines "sufferable" as "[t]olerable; such as may be endured." Webster's 1830 edition is similar: "[t]hat may be tolerated or permitted." Some evils can be tolerated or endured. When this is the case, the people are willing to continue with the form of government that they are used to.

The passage also deploys the phrase, that "mankind are more disposed to suffer, while evils are sufferable, than to right themselves." "Right" in this context is not a noun or adjective, but a verb: "[t]o do justice to; to relieve from wrong"—the applicable definition in Webster's 1830 edition as well as Johnson's 1768 work. The people will not change their form of government, abolish it, or revolt if the evils they face can be endured, tolerated, or rectified.

Next, the Declaration explains when the people must justly invoke their right to revolution:

> But when a long train of abuses and usurpations, pursuing invariably the same Object evinces a design to reduce them under absolute Despotism, it is their right, it is their duty, to throw off such Government, and to provide new Guards for their future security.

This understanding clearly echoes the original pronouncement of the same principle by Locke in his *Second Treatise of Government*:

> But if a long train of abuses, prevarications and artifices, all tending the same way, make the design visible to the people, and they cannot but feel what they lie under, and see whether they are going; it is not to be wondered at, that they should then rouse themselves, and endeavour to put the rule into such hands which may secure to them the ends for which government was at first erected.*

The language of the Declaration more than just echoes Locke; it directly integrates Locke's phrase of "a long train of abuses"—but instead of listing "prevarications and artifices," it deploys "usurpations."

Webster's 1841 dictionary defines an "abuse" as

> 1. Ill use; improper treatment or employment; application to a wrong purpose; as an *abuse* of our natural powers. 2. a corrupt practice or custom; as, the *abuses* of government. 3. Rude speech; reproachful language addressed to a person; contumely; reviling words. 4. Seduction. 5. Perversion of meaning; improper use or application; as, an *abuse* of words. [Italics are in the original.]

Johnson's 1773 dictionary is more concise: "1. the ill use of any thing. [...] 2. A corrupt practice, bad custom. [...] 4. Unjust censures, rude reproach, contumely." The Declaration is addressing the corrupt practice, illegitimate customs, and ill treatment of the colonists by the empire.

"Usurpation" is defined by Webster's 1830 edition as "[t]he act of seizing or occupying and enjoying the property of another without right." Johnson's 1768 dictionary is very similar: "[f]orcible, unjust, illegal seizure or possession."

The Founders explain that the British Empire is abusing its governmental powers, violating the rights of the colonists, and using unjust force upon the colonists. Just how true this is will be explained in exacting detail in our review of the twenty-eight grievances in the Declaration. Still, prudence dictates that not a handful of abuses or usurpations are enough to justify revolution. Instead, there must be a long *train* of such abuses and usurpations—as Samuel Johnson's 1768 dictionary puts it, "a series; a consecution."

"Consecution" is rarely heard today. Johnson's 1768 definition of "consecution" is a series of "consequences; chain of deductions. [...] 2. Succession." When the government is intractable and immoveable (oppressing the people for an extended period through a series of actions) and even knows it is violating the rights of the people (and has no intention of letting up despite the pleas and protests of the people)—this is the time for revolution. The government is no longer fulfilling its function of protecting our unalienable rights. The Social Compact is broken. The rule of law is subverted; constitutional norms are smashed; limited government is vanishing; equality is denigrated. If living under an oppressive government is worse than not having a government at all, now is the time for a revolution.

This understanding takes strong root in the fertile soil of the American colonies before 1776. Minister Simeon Howard's previously quoted sermon lays it out again:

> [T]he experience of all ages has shown, that those, who are so unreasonable as to form designs of injuring others, are seldom to be diverted from their purpose by argument and persuasion alone. Notwithstanding all that can be said to show the injustice and inhumanity of they attempt, they persist in it, till they have gratified the unruly passion which set them to work. And in this case, what is to be done by the sufferer? Is he to use no other means for his safety, but remonstrance or flight, when these will not secure him? Is he patiently to take the injury and suffer himself to be robbed of his liberty or his life, if the adversary sees fit to take it? Nature certainly forbids this tame submission, and loudly calls to a more vigorous defence. Self-preservation is one of the strongest, and a universal principle of the human mind: And this principle allows of every thing necessary to self-defense, opposing force to force, and violence to violence. This is so universally allowed that I need not attempt to prove it.*

Minister Howard makes clear that when the government continues to oppress the rights of the people, the people need not continue to rely simply on protest. That is futile. And they need not flee their homes, for such flight is cowardly and surrenders to the unjust oppression. The law of Nature and Nature's God provides the oppressed with the right of self-defense of their God-given unalienable rights. The victims of government oppression should oppose force with force and violence with violence.

Again, the Founders stress that revolution should be avoided unless there is a long, connected series of abuses and usurpations. However, the Founding Generation qualifies the right of revolution even further, because the phraseology recognizes that the long train of abuses and usurpations must be "pursuing invariably the same Object [which] evinces a design to reduce them under absolute Despotism."

Of course, as Johnson's 1768 dictionary reveals, "invariably" means "[u]nchangeably; constantly." To justify revolution, the government must engage in a succession of connected abuses and usurpations that always have the same object—the same aim, the same purpose, which *evinces* a certain design. According to Johnson's 1768 dictionary, "evinces" means "[t]o prove; to show." In other words, the long train proves a design (a plan, a purpose, a mission, a purposefully created scheme of action), and the goal of that design is to reduce the colonists under absolute despotism.

"Reduce" in this passage does not mean to make smaller; it is much more sinister. Johnson's 1768 dictionary's applicable definitions again provide the elaboration: "4. To bring into any state of diminution [...] 5. To degrade; impair in dignity. [...] 6. To bring into any state of misery or means. [...] 7. To subdue [...] 8. To bring into any state more within reach or power. [...] 9. To reclaim order." The context in this passage is unmistakable. The British Empire is using the long train of abuses and usurpations to degrade, impair in dignity, make miserable, bring into their reach and power, subdue, and reclaim the colonists and colonies. And to what ultimate end? Absolute despotism. The colonists are to become the slaves of the empire. The twenty-eight grievances make this abundantly clear.

When *all* that happens, the Declaration declares, "it is [the colonists'] right, it is their duty, to throw off such Government, and to provide new Guards for their future security." At that point, revolution is not just a right—it is a duty, and the people have the right and duty to create a new government to protect their liberties.

The next issue is *who* is to determine if revolution is justified. Minister Jonathan Mayhew preaches that the people are the correct judges of when tyranny arises. Anyone who challenges this proposition commits treason against the people and God Himself:

> To say that subjects in general are not proper judges when their governors oppress them, and play the tyrant; and when they defend their rights, administer justice impartially, and promote the public welfare, is as great *treason* as ever man uttered;—'tis treason,—not against one *single* man, but the state—against the whole body politic;—'tis treason against mankind;—'tis treason against common sense; —'tis treason against God. [Italics are in the original.]*

Those who oppose the people's opposition to tyranny are complicit supporters of oppression over the minds and liberties of man and support their own enslavement under tyrants. Opposition to revolution "lays the foundation for justifying all the tyranny and oppression that ever any prince was guilty of."*

The rebelling colonists agree this is precisely the situation they face. Hence, the Declaration observes, "Such has been the patient sufferance of these Colonies; and such is now the necessity which constrains them to alter their former Systems of Government."

Note here two more essential words: "necessity" and "constrains." Revolution is not an option; it is a necessity. It must be undertaken. There is no other choice. The right and duty to overthrow a government under these circumstances constrains the colonies to the Revolution. Even if they wish to cower and surrender, they must not. The Revolution arises not from a whimsical passion, boredom, or mere discontent. The colonists must declare independence.*

*A sense of unprovoked injuries will arouse the resentment of the most peaceful. Such injuries these colonies have received from Britain. Unjustifiable claims have been made by the king and his minions to tax us without our consent; these claims have been prosecuted in a manner cruel and unjust to the highest degree. The frantic policy of administration has induced them to send fleets and armies to America; that by depriving us of our trade, and cutting the throats of our brethren, they might awe us into submission, and erect a system of despotism in America, which so far enlarge the influence of the crown as to enable it to rivet their shackles upon the people of Great Britain.* [...]

*Could an accommodation now be effected, we have reason to think that it would be fatal to the liberties of America; we should soon catch the contagion on venality and dissipation, which has subjected Britain to lawless domination.**

Town of Malden (May 27, 1776)

# 21

## “The history of the present King of Great Britain is a history of repeated injuries and usurpations, all having in direct object the establishment of an absolute Tyranny over these States.”

***How has King George III ruled the colonies? Are his actions those of a just government?***

- ☆ As revealed by a year-long, serial pattern of oppression, the king is fixed on forcing tyranny on the colonies.

- ☆ By rejecting colonial overtures of reconciliation, George III has become the enemy of the colonists.

The Second Continental Congress declares that the colonists have a duty to declare revolution, but they have not yet specifically explained why that is so. This sentence sets the stage for a bird's-eye historical journey reviewing why revolution is compelled. It is followed by a candid list of twenty-eight grievances. This list typically gets very short shrift. Other than the grievances of taxation without representation and the quartering of troops, in most classrooms, the other grievances are usually skimmed or ignored—a nearly unforgivable mistake. The glorious beginning and end of the Declaration make no sense without the middle. The Declaration is not just a philosophical statement. It is not an idealist pamphlet or theory. It is a political, legal, and cultural document explaining why the colonies pass a resolution for independence. The first two paragraphs of the Declaration are approximately 275 words. The concluding paragraphs are about 265 words. The middle? About 770 words. The grievances are longer than the rest of the document combined. To boil down the list of grievances to only taxation without representation and the quartering of troops is a perversion of history in the highest order.

Before the Declaration lists the specific grievances, a short, two-sentence transitional introduction potently explains that the preconditions for a revolution are met. The first sentence reveals that "[t]he history of the present King of Great Britain is a history of repeated injuries and usurpations, all having in direct object the establishment of an absolute Tyranny over these States." This sentence moves from the theory of the First Principles into the reality of the moment. It explains that the conduct of King George III proves he has indeed engaged in that long train of abuses and usurpations justifying revolution. Although the language shifts from "absolute despotism" to "Tyranny," for Americans, there is no practical difference. The king is crushing the unalienable rights of the people, violating the Social Compact, subverting equality, exploding limited government, and undermining the rule of law—all in violation of the founding First Principles.

There is no shortage of absolute tyrannies over the ages—ancient Egypt and the pharaohs, absolutist kings, the Soviet Union, Communist China, North Korea, Revolutionary France, and so many others. However, there is another aspect of this sentence that deserves elaboration, and our modern eyes mostly gloss right over it. The sentence lays fault on the "King." Yet, as we will discover when we begin our review of the grievances, the colonists do not always direct their ire toward the monarch. British oppression against the colonists starts in the 1760s, and for many years, the colonists place the blame squarely at the feet of Parliament or the king's misguided and wicked ministers, but hardly ever at the feet of the king himself.

Somewhat like our presidential cabinet and administrative state today, the British Empire is administered through various functionaries, including the Privy Council, the Cabinet, the Admiralty Board, the Board of Trade, Parliament, generals, and admirals. For many years, most colonists agree that King George III is being misled by wicked and conniving ministers. If only he would perceive the reality of the situation and intervene, the colonies would be free of oppression.

When George III ascends to the throne in 1760, there is a series of short-tenured prime ministers who lead the Cabinet: Thomas Pelham-Holles, John Stuart, George Grenville, Charles Watson-Wentworth, William Pitt the Elder, and Augustus FitzRoy. Lord North (technically the Right Honorable Frederick North, second Earl of Guilford, KG [knight of the Most Noble Order of the Garter], PC [Privy Council]) serves as prime minister from 1770 to 1782. The colonists have many royal officials to blame before targeting the king.

George III rules throughout the entire critical period before, during, and after the American Revolution. His nearly sixty-year reign (1760–1820) is the longest at the time and the third longest to date. George III is the descendant of Germans and is the prince-elector of Hanover in the Holy Roman Empire; he even becomes king of Hanover in 1814. His great-grandfather, King George I, is born in Hanover, and George I's second cousin is Queen Anne of Great Britain. When Queen Anne dies, George I is her closest living Protestant relative, and he ascends to the throne of Great Britain. When George I dies, his son—also born and raised in Hanover—becomes king of Great Britain. George II focuses on his German properties and, for the most part, defers to Parliament and his ministers to govern Great Britain. The son of George II dies in 1751, so when George II passes away in 1760, his grandson becomes King George III and takes the throne. Unlike his predecessors, King George III is thoroughly British, dedicates himself to serving the British Empire, and makes Great Britain, not Hanover, the key focus of his reign. One of the reforms he implements is to establish the Office of the Prime Minister.

When troubles confront the colonists, they initially focus their ire on the ministry and Parliament. After all, many of the vexing issues with Great Britain stem from Parliament's infringement of the colonists' right to govern themselves. As but one example, the colonists argue that Parliament cannot legally impose a tax on the colonists because only the elected legislatures in the colonies have such authority. The king is not the problem; it is Parliament, led by or in league with the king's ministers. The colonists vigorously oppose Parliament and the wicked ministers. They have no desire to condemn or oppose the king.

However, that attitude slowly changes. Year after year, the colonists' concerns are rebuffed by the entire British government, including the king. The colonists slowly awaken to the reality that George III is a major source of the evils they suffer. As the years pass, the British become more oppressive, and he becomes more entrenched in his position. Soon, he will be an iron wall, unwilling to bend. The king becomes the rightful focus.

This transitional passage in the Declaration summarizes that the king is not stumbling into sporadic, oppressive acts but is purposefully imposing an absolute tyranny on the colonists. This is not the first time the colonists make this accusation. On October 26, 1774, the First Continental Congress adopts its Petition to the King in opposition to the Intolerable Acts. The over 2,100-word document describes a wide range of grievances, many of which are later recounted in the Declaration of Independence. The grievances in the Petition to the King include the danger of a standing army, the replacement of civil authorities with military commanders, the creation of various governmental officers who are overburdening the colonies (the

Declaration characterizes them as "swarms"), the operation and establishment of new admiralty and vice-admiralty courts that run roughshod over the unalienable rights of the colonists, the unwarranted dissolution of colonial assemblies, the illegal restrictions on trade, the dependency of judges' salaries on imperial authorities, the Murder Act, the Boston Port Act, and the Quebec Act of 1774. Congress details to King George III that since the conclusion of the French and Indian War, English policy relentlessly oppresses the colonists. Here, they hope that the king will see the error of the imperial policy and intervene to halt the oppression. Congress explains to the king that the colonists are not at fault for the "destructive system of colony administration."* The colonies are not provoking the affliction they suffer under. The affliction is coming from Great Britain.

The Petition to the King falls on deaf ears. As noted previously, as early as September 11, 1774, George III declares, "[T]he die is now cast, the colonies must either submit or triumph."* A few months later, he writes to Prime Minister Lord North that "the New England governments are in state of rebellion, blows must decide whether they are to be subject to this country or independent."* In early February 1775, Lord North addresses the House of Commons and the House of Lords in a joint session, announcing that Massachusetts is in rebellion and the king must subdue it. On February 9, the House of Lords and Commons jointly submit an address to King George III, proclaiming, "[W]e find that a part of your Majesty's subjects, in the province of Massachusetts Bay, have proceeded so far to resist the authority of the *Supreme Legislature* [Parliament], that a *rebellion* at this time actually exists within the said province [italics in original]."* Accordingly, Parliament authorizes troop shipments to Boston.

As colonial resistance stiffens and spreads throughout the colonies, on February 15, 1775, King George III writes to Lord North, "[O]nce vigorous measures appear to be the only means left of bringing the Americans to a due submission to the mother country, [...] the colonies will submit."* The king decides military power must be used. He puts it more forcefully on July 5, 1775, in yet another letter to Lord North, declaring that he is "duty bound" to put down the rebellion.*

Even when the colonists, at the bloody Battle of Bunker Hill (in which the British suffer appalling losses while achieving a minor technical victory), reveal their steely resolve to fight for their unalienable rights, the king remains firm. The consequences be damned. King George III believes he has a duty to crush the colonies.

On the other side of the Atlantic, the colonists still seek peace. After the fighting breaks out at Lexington and Concord on April 19, 1775, Congress determines to move forward with one final peace effort. In May 1775, the Second Continental Congress appoints a committee of John Dickinson, Benjamin Franklin, John Jay, John Rutledge, and Thomas Johnson to draft a peace overture. On June 17, 1775, the vicious Battle of Bunker Hill breaks out. Although the British dislodge American forces, they pay a terrible price in blood. Peace is slipping away, and Dickinson desperately desires to remain within the empire. He primarily drafts what history now dubs the "Olive Branch Petition" addressed to the king. Approved on July 5, 1775, and signed and engrossed on July 8, 1775, it "entreat[s] your majesty's gracious attention to this our humble petition."* The Olive Branch Petition recounts how the colonists helped defeat the French in the French and Indian War in an unprecedented victory, yet Parliament institutes

> a new system of statutes and regulations adopted for the administration of the colonies, that filled their [the colonists'] minds with the most painful fears and jealousies; and, to their inexpressible astonishment, perceived the dangers of a foreign quarrel quickly succeeded by domestic danger, in their judgment, of a more dreadful kind.*

The petition then recounts how the colonists desire only peace, yet are now compelled to protect their unalienable rights through force of arms. Hoping His Majesty will kindly view their peace overtures, the petitioners flatter the king and blame those who abuse his trust. The petition joyously observes that if George III reconciles the two sides, he will enjoy glory throughout the ages. It all but begs the king to take control of the situation and bring a just peace between the colonies and the empire by repealing the oppressive acts of Parliament. The petition recognizes the colonies' traditional ties to Great Britain, professes their desire to remain loyal, lays the blame on the king's ministers, and pleads with him to look favorably on the colonies and personally intervene to achieve peace with the empire. It is the rational and emotional supplication of a grateful child to a loving father.

Despite suing for peace, Congress also determines to justify violence to defend the unalienable rights of the people. As noted earlier, the very next day after approving the Olive Branch Petition, the Second Continental Congress in its Declaration of the Causes and Necessity of Taking Up Arms approves military action in defense of the unalienable rights of the people. This declaration proclaims that Parliament, having "attempted to effect their cruel and impolitic purpose of enslaving these colonies by violence [...] rendered it necessary for us to close with their last appeal from reason to arms."* It explains that Americans are unwilling to be enslaved without a fight:

> We have counted the cost of this contest, and find nothing so dreadful as voluntary slavery.—Honor, justice, and humanity,

> forbid us tamely to surrender that freedom which we received from our gallant ancestors, and which our innocent posterity have a right to receive from us. We cannot endure the infamy and guilt of resigning succeeding generations to that wretchedness which inevitably awaits them, if we basely entail hereditary bondage upon them. [...]
>
> In our own native land, in defense of the freedom that is our birthright, and which we ever enjoyed till the late violations of it—for the protection of our property, acquired, solely by the honest industry of our forefathers and ourselves, against violence actually offered, we have taken up arms.*

Although they make quite clear their position to defend their rights, the colonists still seek reconciliation with the Crown. They hope that although they have a right to fight to protect liberty—and are committed to doing so if necessary—the Olive Branch Petition will avoid further bloodshed. The colonists determine to deliver the petition directly to the king. They entrust it to Richard Penn, the grandson of William Penn (the Quaker founder of Pennsylvania) and former lieutenant governor of Pennsylvania. Penn quickly sets sail across the Atlantic Ocean to personally convey the petition to American envoy Arthur Lee, who is stationed in London. So vital is this mission that Penn is barred from breaking the petition's seal and reading it. On August 13, Penn finally lands at the British port of Bristol. He is unable to meet with Lee in London until August 21. When Lee is given the petition, it comes with a personal letter from Dickinson that explains that its rejection will lead to war.*

In the interim, the king learns of the Battle of Bunker Hill. On August 23, two days before a copy of the Olive Branch Petition is given to Lord Dartmouth (the king's secretary of state for the colonies), the king issues his Proclamation for Suppressing Rebellion and Sedition. Any doubts about King George III's perspective are wiped out; he considers the colonies in a hopeless state of rebellion that must be crushed by military action. The king could not be clearer. In his proclamation, he refers to the Patriot leaders as "dangerous and ill-designing men," "traitorous," and "wicked and desperate persons," and charges all his subjects to disclose any traitorous activities and persons to the English authorities.*

When Penn and Lee deliver to Lord Dartmouth an original signed Olive Branch Petition on September 1, the king has already proclaimed the Americans wicked traitors. Lee and Penn press Dartmouth about the king's reception of the petition; Dartmouth curtly responds, "as His Majesty did not receive it on the throne, no answer would be given."* The king cannot be bothered to read it. Instead, the real answer is delivered the day after the petition is received—the lord commissioners of the admiralty order the Royal Navy to seize nearly all American ships and vessels on the high seas.

On October 26, 1775, the king delivers his annual address to Parliament, which is entirely dedicated to America. He expresses his disdain for the colonists, asserting that they have gained "great advantage from the difference of our intention and theirs. They meant only to amuse by vague expressions of attachment to the parent state, and the strongest protestations of loyalty to me, while they were preparing for a general revolt." Although subjects of Great Britain are "the freest member[s] of any civil society in the known world," the colonists are misled by the "trait[o]rous views of their leaders." As the colonists' resistance is "manifestly carried on for the purpose of establishing an independent empire," it will not be allowed to happen. In fact, "wisdom" requires that the empire "put a speedy end to these disorders by the most decisive exertions." The king explains that in reaction to the colonists, he has increased the navy, greatly expanded the army, redeployed troops, and is receiving "friendly offers of foreign assistance." He notes that he intends to empower the granting of pardons and the readmittance of colonies that turn back their independence-seeking ambitions. He also proposes a military budget to the House of Commons to fund the war.* The king presses forward with an absolute tyranny over the colonies.

The Olive Branch Petition, however, has another potential audience: Parliament. Approximately two weeks after the king's speech, on November 9, 1775, a debate in the House of Commons erupts about whether to even receive (in other words, consider) the petition. American envoy Richard Penn is summoned and assures Parliament that the colonies do not want independence and wish to reconcile with the empire. The Duke of Richmond speaks in favor of receiving the petition. Lord Dartmouth scoffs at these overtures. He declares that Parliament cannot accept the petition

> without at the same instant relinquishing the sovereignty of the British parliament. It was no longer a question about taxation, about the quantum to be raised, or the mode of raising it; it was not the conquest, but the allegiance of the colonies, which administration were desirous of obtaining. [...] The petition [...] was unexceptionable, but there was every reason to believe that the softness of the language was purposely adopted to conceal the most traitorous designs.*

Following the king's and Lord Dartmouth's expressions of disdain, the House of Commons votes overwhelmingly to reject the petition.

This result is all but determined well before the Olive Branch Petition or the Declaration of Causes and Necessity of Taking up Arms arrive in England. The king intransigently opposes compromise. He writes Lord North on July 26, 1775, "[W]e must persist. [...] I know I am doing my duty and therefore can never wish to retract."* On the same day, Lord North writes to the king, "[T]he war is now grown to such a height, that it must be treated as a foreign war, and that every expedient which would be used in the latter case should be applied in the former."* This view takes the conflict to an entirely different magnitude. To put down a protest, a boycott, smuggling, rabble rousing, riot, or civil outbreak is one thing; to conquer a foreign enemy is an entirely different matter.

On November 10, Lord Dartmouth resigns after he fruitlessly expends significant effort to reconcile with the colonists. His replacement, Lord George Germain, harbors no ideas of reconciliation. Joining with the king and crushing the colonists is his only aim. By overwhelming margins, in December, Parliament passes the Prohibitory Act, which cuts off all trade with the colonies, authorizes the seizure of American vessels, orders a blockade of the colonies, and even orders that any foreign ships trading with the colonies be seized. Vanquishing any doubts, the British Empire all but declares war against the colonies. After all, a blockade is only the act of a belligerent nation. Seizing vessels of those trading with an adversary is an act of war.

Fittingly enough, on the first anniversary of Patrick Henry's "Give Me Liberty or Give Me Death!" speech (March 23, 1775), John Adams writes to Massachusetts General Horatio Gates:

> I know not whether you have seen the act of parliament called the restraining act, or piratical act, or plundering act, or act of independency, for by all these titles is it called. I think the most apposite is, the act of independency, for king, lords, and commons have united in sundering this country from that, I think, forever. It is a complete dismemberment of the British empire. It throws thirteen colonies out of the royal protection, levels all distinctions and makes us independent in spite of all our supplications and entreaties.*

Adams also expresses befuddlement to Gates. Adams knows that the British have just declared the colonies independent States and that the empire has declared war against the colonies, but the colonists seem to refuse that reality: "It may be fortunate that the act of independency should come from the British parliament, rather than the American congress; but it is very odd that Americans should hesitate at accepting such a gift from them."*

Adams's bewilderment will soon pass. To counter—or perhaps complement—these salvos from the king himself, the Americans have their own thunder: Thomas Paine. For being such a pivotal figure in American history, many overlook the fact that Paine is an Englishman, living in England until he sets sail for the colonies in 1774. Through his unparalleled, powerful pamphlets, *Common Sense* and *The American Crisis,* he plays a critical role in sparking and supporting the American Revolution.

Born in Thetford, England, on January 29, 1737, Paine's eclectic background before the American Revolution includes careers as (among other things) corset maker, merchant seaman, supernumerary officer, excise officer, stay-maker, schoolteacher, and inventor. In other words, he seems incapable of maintaining steady employment. Nevertheless, he writes some fabulously persuasive pamphlets. However, they are in favor of increasing the pay of his then-current profession: tax collector. This is not a particularly effective way to endear oneself to the public. He almost certainly fails to consummate his marriage. Despite his many shortcomings, he impresses Benjamin Franklin with his writing, and Franklin indulges this talent with a letter of recommendation. His wife gifts Paine some money to depart England and leave her. He barely survives the transatlantic voyage and arrives in Philadelphia bedridden, near death on the ship. However, Franklin's letter of recommendation comes to the attention of the city's most famous physician, Founding Father Dr. Benjamin Rush, who personally nurses Paine back to health.

At the urging of Rush, who even supplies the title, Paine pens *Common Sense* at the beginning of 1776. More than any other tract, it gives voice to the reasons why the time has come for America to declare independence from the British Empire. *Common Sense* is a masterstroke. It obliterates the strongest arguments about why the colonists should remain loyal to the king—or any king.

First, Paine explains that if the king has begun a war and the colonists are now forced to take up arms to defend their rights, simply attempting to change policies or ministers is too little, too late:

> The object, contended for, ought always to bear some just proportion to the expense. The removal of [Lord] North, or the whole detestable junto [the Cabinet], is a matter unworthy the millions [of pounds] we have expended. A temporary stoppage of trade, was an inconvenience, which would have sufficiently balanced the repeal of all the acts complained of, had such repeals

> been obtained; but if the whole continent must take up arms, if every man must be a soldier, it is scarcely worth our while to fight against a contemptible ministry only. Dearly, dearly, do we pay for the repeal of the acts, if that is all we fight for; for in a just estimation, it is as great a folly to pay a Bunker-hill price for law, as for land.*

No—now is the time for independence.

Second, Paine takes deadly aim at the entire idea of monarchy. Although the prevailing view is that, to ensure peace, monarchs arise with God's blessing, Paine argues quite the opposite: "In the early ages of the world, according to the scripture chronology, there were no kings; the consequence of which was there were no wars; it is the pride of kings which throw mankind into confusion."* Scripture reveals that monarchy is not only destructive but the wicked product of Satan himself: "Government by kings was first introduced into the world by the heathens, from whom the children of Israel copied the custom. It was the most prosperous invention the devil ever set on foot for the promotion of idolatry."*

Drawing upon scripture's famous story (1 Samuel 8:4–22) in which Israel establishes a monarchy only after the Israelites repeatedly cry out for a king, Paine explains that contrary to the doctrine of Divine Right and similar beliefs, God is quite against the establishment of kings over men. Following God's instructions, the prophets Gideon and Samuel repeatedly resist the Israelites' demands for a king. The prophets relent only after warning that disaster will eventually befall Israel; still, the people of Israel compel the anointing of a king.

This is not all. Monarchy is made even worse by *hereditary* kingship. Although the prevailing view in the modern age is that monarchies are passed down through bloodlines, this is not always the case. Paine eloquently condemns hereditary kingships as an especially corrupt and evil practice and "[o]ne of the strongest *natural* proofs of the folly of hereditary right in kings, is, that nature disapproves it, otherwise she would not so frequently turn it to ridicule by giving mankind an *ass for a lion.* [Italics are in the original.]"* This comedic observation is well grounded in history. As *Common Sense* observes, many hereditary kings are ignorant, disinterested, self-indulgent, abusive, and tyrannical.

Paine also dismantles the fanciful belief that kings are honorable, noble, servant-leaders who seek justice and protect the rights of their subjects. Instead,

> could we take off the dark covering of antiquity, and trace them to their first rise, [...] we should find the first of them nothing better than the principal ruffian of some restless gang, whose

> savage manners or pre-eminence in subtlety obtained him the title of chief among plunderers; and who by increasing in power, and extending his depredations, over-awed the quiet and defenseless to purchase their safety by frequent contributions.*

Paine's position is not a flight of fancy. He exhaustively reviews history to prove the point. The history of England is chock-full of kingships and nobility. If hereditary kingships forge peace and happiness, those beneficial consequences should easily be discernable in England's history. Paine snickers that an honest accounting of the past proves quite the opposite, including its most prominent hero king:

> England, since the conquest [of William the Conqueror], has known some few good monarchs, but groaned beneath a much larger number of bad ones; yet no man in his senses can say that their claim under William the Conqueror is a very honorable one. A French bastard landing with an armed banditti, and establishing himself king of England against the consent of the natives, is in plain terms a very paltry rascally original.—It certainly has no divinity in it. However, it is needless to spend much time in exposing the folly of hereditary right, if there are any so weak as to believe it, let them promiscuously worship the ass and lion, and welcome. I neither copy their humility, nor disturb their devotion.*

Paine's insight cuts to the bone. The celebrated William the Conqueror, from whom flows the modern monarchy, is a Frenchman (the product of an unmarried relationship) who invades England, takes power in 1066, and imposes his rule with an iron fist. Since then, hereditary succession even results in minors (sometimes babies) ascending the throne.

Paine observes that the best justification for a hereditary kingship is that a line of succession determined by bloodlines keeps the peace because everyone knows who the next monarch will be. There will be no civil wars of succession. Paine then demolishes this argument:

> The whole history of England disowns the fact. Thirty kings and two minors have reigned in that distracted kingdom since the conquest [of William the Conqueror], in which time there have been (including the [Glorious] Revolution) no less than eight civil wars and nineteen rebellions. Wherefore instead of making

> for peace, it makes against it, and destroys the very foundation it seems to stand on.*

He concisely delivers the argument in three compelling short sentences:

> In short, monarchy and success have laid (not this or that kingdom only) but the world in blood and ashes. 'Tis a form of government which the word of God bears testimony against, and blood will attend it. [...] Of more worth is one honest man to society and in the sight of God, than all the crowned ruffians that ever lived.*

Paine's closing argument prevails. As circumstances change, so do the perspectives of the Founders. Any reluctance against declaring the king as the enemy disappears on July 2, 1776. As revealed by the list of twenty-eight grievances in the Declaration, Congress realizes that the whole of the British Empire is engaging in a long series of tyrannical actions, rejecting all peace overtures, and planning to crush the colonies. The king, too, is the enemy. There is no turning back.

Article I, Section 9 of the Constitution goes so far as to declare that "No Title of Nobility shall be granted by the United States: And no Person holding any Office of Profit or Trust under them, shall, without the Consent of the Congress, accept of any present, Emolument, Office, or Title, of any kind whatever, from any King, Prince, or foreign State." There is no royalty in America. As evidenced by the Revolutionary State governments, the Articles of Confederation, and the Constitution, no king shall ever again rule America.*

*To prove, this let facts be submitted to a candid world for the truth of which we pledge a faith yet unsullied by falsehood.**

Thomas Jefferson (1776)

# 22

## "To prove this, let Facts be submitted to a candid world."

***How will the colonies prove to the world that revolution is justified?***

- ☆ To justify the American Revolution, the revolutionaries rely on an honest recounting of the history of English oppression.

- ☆ The Founders lay out these facts before the entire world.

This seemingly minor sentence is of monumental importance. The Founding Fathers do not rely upon opinion, supposition, rhetoric, or feelings. They are not suffering from a form of mass paranoid personality disorder. They justify the Revolution based on *facts*. Samuel Johnson's 1768 *A Dictionary of the English Language* defines *fact* as, "1. A thing done; an effect produced. [...] 2. Reality; not supposition. [...] 3. Action; deed." Noah Webster's 1828 *An American Dictionary of the English Language's* definition is very similar:

> 1. Any thing done, or that comes to pass; an act; a deed; an effect produced or achieved; an event. Witnesses are introduced into court to prove a *fact. Facts* are stubborn things. To deny a *fact* knowingly is to lie. 2. Reality; truth; as, in *fact.* So we say, *indeed.* [Italics are in the original.]

The initial definition from both sources is "an event or thing that has come to pass." This is exactly what the Founders mean. They list a whole host of past events proving that the king and Parliament are attempting to tyrannize the colonies. This is no mere perfunctory exercise—it is indispensable to the justness of the Founders' actions. The colonists do not just make a bald assertion; they prove it through specific historical actions undertaken by the British Empire. Otherwise, the Founders might be deluded, acting out of self-interest, or grounding their resort to violence on fantasy or illusions. By basing the Revolution on facts, the justness of their cause cannot be genuinely questioned.

Furthermore, the revolutionaries are not reviewing the facts solely for their edification. The audience is far beyond their fellow Americans and the British. Perhaps for the first time in history, revolutionaries are justifying before the entire *world* the basis for their Revolution. Such a move is both audacious and humbling.

Congress also adds the essential qualifier that the facts are being proven to a "candid" world. Johnson's 1768 dictionary definition of "candid" is "2. Fair; open; ingenuous." Webster's 1828 dictionary (second and third definitions) even better captures the essence of the Founders' meaning:

> 2. Fair; open; frank; ingenuous; free from undue bias; disposed to think and judge according to truth and justice, or without partiality or prejudice; *applied to persons.* 3. Fair; just; impartial; *applied to things;* as a *candid* view or construction. [Italics are in the original.]

In other words, the Founders are appealing to those who think and judge according to truth and justice. If the people of the world review the Declaration's list of grievances with impartiality and honesty, they will conclude that the king and British Empire are working to impose an absolute despotism on the colonists. The Declaration is not based on lies, misperception, illusions, deceit, misrepresentations, paranoia, or deflections. To the contrary—the Declaration truthfully lays out for all to see the tyrannical actions of the British.

*For the most trifling reasons, and sometimes for no conceivable reason at all, his majesty has rejected laws of the most salutary tendency.* [...]

*With equal inattention to the necessities of his people here has his majesty permitted our laws to lie neglected in England for years, neither confirming them by his assent, nor annulling them by his negative.**

Thomas Jefferson (1774)

# 23

# "He has refused his Assent to Laws, the most wholesome and necessary for the public good."

☆ For his own purposes (or no purpose at all), the king refuses to approve vital laws passed by the colonial legislatures, thereby gravely subverting self-rule and the common good.

To understand this first grievance, a reference to the current United States Constitution is most helpful. Under the Constitution, a proposed law generally only becomes effective if each chamber of Congress passes the same bill and the president approves it. If the president vetoes a bill passed by both chambers of Congress, it can become law only if two-thirds of each chamber overrides the veto. A similar concept applies in colonial America. Although colonial legislatures are authorized to pass bills, both the respective colonial governor and the king must approve any bills before they become law. Unlike the Constitution, colonial legislatures have no authority to override the king's refusal to assent. If the king refuses his assent, the bill simply dies. The king can refuse to assent for any reason (or no reason) whatsoever.

As demonstrated by being listed as the first grievance, King George III's refusal to approve colonial legislation is a very critical complaint. Although George III possesses this prerogative, for generations, the monarchy has relinquished the practice in connection with legislation passed by Parliament. However, George III continues to exercise the prerogative robustly in connection with legislation passed by colonial legislatures.

Considerations other than justice now direct the king's actions. George III fails to approve colonial legislation, which desperately requires approval. Sometimes the failure is not an outright refusal but rather neglect. The king just does not bother to address the proposed law. Yet, neglect is just as devastating as an outright refusal, because it allows pressing issues to fester and colonists to suffer while awaiting a decision.

Neglect is hardly the colonists' sole complaint. Indeed, George III outright refuses his assent in connection with many vital issues. This pernicious practice eviscerates the Social Compact, self-rule, and the public good. Thomas Jefferson rails that the king engages in "the wanton exercise of this power [...]. For the most trifling reasons, and sometimes for no conceivable reason at all, his majesty has rejected laws of the most salutary tendency."* In other words, the colonists have good reason to pass legislation, and the king disregards those concerns for his own selfish reasons—or for no reason at all.

Considering his modern, infamous reputation as a slaveholder, one of the specifics of Jefferson's umbrage is surely surprising to nearly all modern readers: Several of the colonies have come to understand that the slave trade is a damnable practice and enact laws to squelch it. Yet George III stands alone and prevents the slave trade from being abolished. In particular, Pennsylvania's General Assembly in 1712 and 1773, South Carolina in 1760, New Jersey in 1763, and Virginia in 1772 all pass acts severely taxing the slave trade (which likely would have ended the damnable trade in those colonies), but the monarch withholds his assent. King George III orders the governor of New Hampshire to reject all acts restricting the importation of slaves. Likewise, the king orders the governor of Massachusetts to reject two bills passed by the Massachusetts legislature to tax the slave trade.

Jefferson observes that ending the slave trade is the first step to emancipation. His analysis is prophetic. Both in the United States and the United Kingdom, the slave trade must end before slavery is abolished. Fittingly, then-President Jefferson himself signs the federal law banning the slave trade on January 1, 1808 (the first date legally permissible under the federal Constitution). Well before this, many North American colonies, as well as other New World British colonies like Jamaica, attempt to impose prohibitive duties and other restrictions on the importation of enslaved peoples. Yet, the king refuses to assent to those laws.* In truth, the king's refusal to assent here is a "shameful [...] abuse of a power trusted with his majesty for other purposes."*

When they are free of the grip of the empire, even before formal independence, some of the States act. "In January 1775, one of the first acts of Pennsylvania's Provincial Convention was to reject British oversight, and prohibit the importation of slaves."* In 1780, before the American Revolution is complete, Pennsylvania passes An Act for the Gradual Abolition of Slavery, which (as the name states) gradually abolishes slavery.* Even Virginia passes An Act to Authorize the Manumission of Slaves in 1782, permitting for the first time the emancipation of slaves without government approval by enslavers—leading to many individual acts of emancipation.* However, later legislative efforts for statewide involuntary manumission are defeated in Virginia.*

The king also refuses his approval of laws addressing the naturalization of aliens,* issuance of bills of credit,* compensation of victims of the Stamp Act riots,* methods of taxation,* payment of salaries of government officials,* emission of colonial paper currency,* immigration of convicts to the colonies,* colonial representatives to Parliament,* and even divorce.*

Moreover, the Declaration's phrase "wholesome and necessary" is carefully chosen by Jefferson. It originates from a bill passed by the Massachusetts legislature (the General Court) in the wake of the Stamp Act crisis. The enactment of the Stamp Act generates a huge and vigorous resistance movement in the colonies—some of it resulting in property destruction. Under enormous pressure, the empire reluctantly repeals the Stamp Act. However, that hardly ends the matter. When the act is rescinded, Henry Seymour Conway, secretary of state for the Southern Department (who has authority over the American colonies), explains that the colonies will be required to pay damages for the destruction of property that occur during the colonies' resistance to the Stamp Act. Massachusetts concedes to this instruction and passes a law providing for such indemnification. Massachusetts includes pardons in the law for anyone involved in such property destruction. The Massachusetts legislature determines that the pardons are wholesome and necessary for the public good. The king refuses to assent, and Massachusetts's phrase is directly incorporated into the Declaration.

Thomas Paine's *Common Sense* summarizes the great issue: Who will rule? Will the people rule themselves? Or will King George III? Paine elaborates:

> The powers of governing still remaining in the hands of the king, he will have a negative over the whole legislation of this continent. And he has shown himself such an inveterate enemy to liberty, and discovered such a thirst for arbitrary power; is he, or is he not, a proper man to say to these colonies, "*You shall make no laws but what I please.*" [...] [I]s there any man so unwise, as not to see, that (considering what has happened) he will suffer no law to be made here, but such as suit *his* purpose. [Italics are in the original.]*

To allow the English monarch to control colonial legislation is slavery. The form of tyranny is not important; the Crown's power of assent will be abused to ensure that the colonies are laid low and unceasingly cower beneath his tyrannical heel.

Paine recognizes that because the monarch has such authority in England (although unused for generations), some argue he should have the same authority in America. Paine eviscerates this argument by ridiculing the notion that the small island nation across the ocean should govern America. Such a proposition is a preposterous affront to the laws of Nature because

> there is something very absurd, in supposing a continent to be perpetually governed by an island. In no instance has nature made the satellite larger than its primary planet, and as England and America, with respect to each other, reverses the common order of nature, it is evident that they belong to different systems: England to Europe, America to itself.*

More importantly, even if the monarch should have a veto over legislation in Great Britain, no such veto should exist over the colonies—because any king's interests diverge with those of Americans. The monarch lives in England, and England is his primary concern, not the colonies. Any king views proposed colonial legislation only through the lens of whether it best serves the monarchy and England, not America.

The refusal to provide assent is common. The monarchy refuses to assent to laws across all the colonies. One study reveals that in eighty-three years, the monarchs refuse their assent to fifty-nine Massachusetts laws alone—which is the *smallest* number of all the colonies.*

This grievance is directly remedied by the United States Constitution. There is no hereditary king, only an elected president under Article II. Article I, Section 1 specifically vests the lawmaking power in the elected Congress. Article I, Section 7 provides that once both houses of Congress pass a bill, it is presented to the president for consideration. If the president approves the bill, the president is to sign the bill and it becomes law. If the president does not approve it, the president has the prerogative to veto the bill and return it to Congress. Upon return to Congress, the veto can be overridden by a two-thirds vote of each of the House of Representatives and Senate. In the end, legislation can be enacted over the president's disapproval. If the president takes no action for ten days, the bill becomes law (unless Congress recesses before the ten-day period expires). Bills can no longer languish for years with no action. The opposite occurs under the Constitution—inaction results in the automatic approval of the law in just days. Executive assent is no longer necessary.*

As we have previously addressed, the First Principle of a just and free Social Compact requires that the people consent to their laws. This is what is at stake in this first grievance. The will of the people is crushed single-handedly by the king. This subversion of the Social Compact means that the people are not governing their lives—King George III is. Coupled with Paine's devastating critique of the rule of the monarchy, the foundation for the Revolution is laid.

*Whereas* [King George III] [...] *entrusted with the exercise of the kingly office in this government has endeavored to pervert the same into a detestable and insupportable tyranny* [...] *by denying to his governors permission to pass laws of immediate and pressing importance, unless suspended in their operations for his assent, and, when so suspended, neglecting to attend to them for many years.**

Thomas Jefferson (June 1776)

# 24

## "He has forbidden his Governors to pass Laws of immediate and pressing importance, unless suspended in their operation till his Assent should be obtained; and when so suspended, he has utterly neglected to attend to them."

☆ The king instructs colonial governors to withhold assent to many critical colonial laws until and unless the king approves them, thereby severely subverting self-government and neglecting the needs of colonists.

The second grievance complements the first and harkens back to the English Bill of Rights 1689.* Recall that it is adopted in the wake of the Glorious Revolution, in which the English Parliament overthrows King James II for several abuses. In the preamble, Parliament declares that King James II, with the assistance of "evil counsellors, judges and ministers employed by him, did endeavor to subvert and extirpate the Protestant religion and the laws and liberties of this kingdom" by engaging in fourteen grievances.* The first grievance of the 1689 document identifies King James II as "assuming and exercising a power of dispensing with and suspending of laws and the execution of laws without consent of Parliament."* Parliament declares that "the pretended power of suspending the laws or the execution of laws by regal authority without consent of Parliament is illegal."* And yet, this is exactly what King George III is doing to the colonies.

The Declaration's second grievance again attacks the king's obstruction of the will of the people by preventing colonial legislation from taking effect. The monarch simply uses an indirect means to achieve his devious end. Instead of directly refusing to assent to a bill becoming law, he uses the subterfuge of instructing colonial governors to suspend approval of critical colonial laws until and unless George III approves. Often, this subterfuge results in lengthy delays in considering the bills, and at times prevents them from being considered at all.

George III's tactics have a devastating effect. Laws addressing urgent needs just languish in legal limbo, neither approved nor rejected. In some instances, the very circumstances that necessitate the law come and go before any assent is acted upon. At times circumstances change so dramatically that the proposed laws become irrelevant or worse.

In 1759, the New York General Assembly passes a bill allowing justices of the peace to try minor cases, and King George II orders the governor not to assent. He refuses to allow the local elected assembly thousands of miles away to tweak the administration of justice. The king's inaction ravages the Social Compact and rule of law.

A striking abuse occurs under King George III in 1764 when the New York General Assembly passes a bill to establish a beneficial alliance with the powerful Native American Six Nations. Colonial New York Governor Cadwallader Colden wishes to assent the bill, but the king instructs him—and all colonial governors—to halt any attempts to ally with Native Americans until the king decides whether any particular alliance is warranted. New Yorkers never receive an assent or rejection. A dozen years pass, and George III still takes no action. Hence the observation in the Declaration's grievance that the king "utterly neglected to attend to them."

Governors are ordered by George III to withhold their assent to lotteries because the higher classes in England consider them immoral. Then (as now) lotteries are a key means of raising desperately needed revenue. More importantly, the colonists believe they are more than capable of regulating their own moral conduct, and the king's directives strike at the heart of self-government.

Likewise, in 1770, the Massachusetts General Court passes a bill taxing British government officials in the colonies. The colonists believe that the governor has a duty under the Massachusetts charter to approve the law. Nevertheless, the king orders the governor not to approve the law, and it is never approved or disapproved. Instead, it is utterly neglected. The king protects his officials from the taxes rendered on everyone else in the colony.

Similarly, Virginia passes four laws in 1770. It takes three years before the bureaucracy of the empire even bothers to look at them. Eventually, three of the laws are approved. However, the last bill just languishes until the colonies revolt.

The king is so petty that even divorces come to a standstill in 1773. The king now stands in the bedrooms and homes of the colonists.

The empire's overbearing control of even the most minute issues is on display. The colonists are subject to the whims and fancies of an arbitrary monarch thousands of miles across the ocean. This grievance is felt throughout the colonies as a "monstrous wrong, an outrageous and unbearable tyranny."* That this heavily weighed on the minds of colonists is evidenced by listing this grievance second in Jefferson's draft of the Virginia Constitution of 1776 as well as the Declaration.

Again, this grievance is cured by the United States Constitution. There is no intermediary between Congress and the president to circumvent Congress's lawmaking authority. Congress need not obtain the permission of State governors to pass legislation. In a parallel fashion, State legislatures need not obtain permission from Congress to enact laws. As exemplified in the structure of the Constitution, the doctrine of enumerated powers (in other words, Congress only has the specific powers expressed in the Constitution), and federalism as protected in the Tenth Amendment (all powers not specifically reserved to the federal government are reserved to the States), Congress is supreme in exercising federal authority, and the States are supreme in exercising their authority. The lawmaking process set forth in Article I, Section 7 assures that presidential inaction only results in the enactment of the law after ten days.

The first two grievances regarding King George III's refusal to assent or even consider colonial laws are not trivial matters. They strike at the core of liberty, self-government, equality, and unalienable rights. The king repeatedly violates the Social Compact in grave and unforgivable ways. Only by revolution can Americans reclaim self-government.*

*Whereas* [King George III] [...] *entrusted with the exercise of the kingly office in this government has endeavored to pervert the same into a detestable and insupportable tyranny* [...] *by refusing to pass certain other laws, unless the person to be benefited by them would relinquish the inestimable right of representation in the legislature.**

Thomas Jefferson (June 1776)

# 25

## "He has refused to pass other Laws for the accommodation of large districts of people, unless those people would relinquish the right of Representation in the Legislature, a right inestimable to them and formidable to tyrants only."

☆ King George III refuses to create new counties in the West unless the people surrender their right to representation in the legislature, thereby violating the Social Compact, eviscerating equality, undermining the rule of law, and infringing on the unalienable rights of the people.

The theme of subverting the Social Compact, equality, unalienable rights, and self-government continues in the next set of grievances.* As Virginia expands westward, it needs to incorporate new counties. They are required because the western boundaries of Virginia are not yet fixed like they are today. It is difficult to imagine today, but for the colonists (not Native Americans), the westward boundaries of Virginia are mostly unexplored territory—a vast wilderness reaching thousands of miles. The westernmost counties encompass all this uncharted territory. Much of the population of the thirteen colonies is still packed within just a few miles of the Atlantic Ocean. A feverish desire to settle westward drives expansion toward the interior. With more land comes additional opportunities and the ability to create a new, independent life for the colonists.* As the colonial population shifts, the need for representative government comes with it. Law enforcement, courts, roads, mail, military defense, customs, and similar matters all need attention. The colonists envision wonderful opportunities in this vast region and move there in droves. They expect a government to protect their interests and counties to be formed sequentially along with the western expansion.

Before the end of the French and Indian War, the monarch regularly allows the expansion of colonies to the west, and the colonists are represented in their respective colonial legislatures. After the war, the dangers of westward expansion diminish substantially. The French and their Native American allies have been defeated, and the frontier is nearly wide open. In the eyes of the colonists, their sacrifices in blood, toil, and treasure in the recent war are rewarded with a greater opportunity to settle westward. Many American settlers are gripped with wanderlust.

However, after the war, the English hold exactly the opposite perspective. The British Empire flips positions and wishes to halt westward migration. Parliament passes the Proclamation of 1763, which bans expansion west of the Allegheny Mountains. The British look upon the western counties with heightened suspicion. Their populations are considered to be patriotic—that is, patriotic to their home colonies—and aggressive in protecting their unalienable rights against the Crown. One way to slow down (or at least seriously mitigate) westward expansion is to prevent western settlers from establishing counties.

The colonists are taken aback by the empire's newfound resolve to halt westward expansion. Even if they reluctantly agree to the westward boundary of the Proclamation of 1763, there is still vast territory to settle. George III, however, refuses to allow new counties to be established unless the settlers there give up the right to vote for members in Virginia's elected assembly (the House of Burgesses). With whatever limited expansion is permitted, the additional settlers will be disenfranchised.

The colonists vigorously object to the notion of not allowing new counties with voting rights to be carved out of the enormous existing jurisdictions. One specific protest is practical but with ramifications that affect a foundational purpose of government: the establishment of justice. Remember: There are no emails, no phones, no cars, no trucks, no trains, and no canals. There is only a scant dirt road system—you go as far as your horse can take you (if you have one) on any given day. Travel is physically challenging and often dangerous. George III's refusal to allow new counties to be organized presents serious real-world obstacles to obtaining justice. People on the western edge of Virginia must travel to the nearest courthouse, likely weeks if not months away, to obtain redress of their grievances. This not only undermines justice, but it also tamps down on Virginians' desire to move west. Justice delayed is justice denied.

Thomas Jefferson comments that the king's tactic of only allowing new counties at the cost of losing their right to vote in the House of Burgesses is motivated by the worst possible sentiments: Either George III desires to deprive his subjects of the English right to self-government, or he seeks to more easily control the House of Burgesses. The king's motives are obvious—the imposition of tyranny and corruption of the House of Burgesses.

This oppression is not limited to Virginia. The king takes the same stand in Massachusetts, New York, New Jersey, and New Hampshire. For example, New York tries to provide representation to the new counties of Cumberland in 1766 and Albany in 1768, only to be foiled by the empire. Likewise, New Hampshire valiantly struggles to obtain new county representation.

To the British, this third grievance of the Declaration seems rather petty. In their view, upstart colonials who are pushing the boundaries of the empire simply have no right to representation in the colonial legislatures. To the contrary, this is a vitally important grievance.

> In the wake of the Revolution, the federal Constitution facilitates westward expansion and protects the unalienable rights of the settlers. Article IV, Section 3 provides that new States may be created in new territories, and Article IV, Section 4 guarantees "every State in this Union a Republican Form of Government." Citizens of each new State have the right to vote.

This grievance is yet another example of the huge chasm that has opened between the Americans and the British. Americans understand that for a government to be just, the people must be part of the Social Compact, and the government's actions must be based on the consent of the people. By forcing the colonists who wish to move westward to give up their right to representation, the empire is violating the Social Compact, infringing on the unalienable rights of the people, undermining the rule of law, and subverting equality. As Jefferson explains, the only reason to fear recognizing the rights of all colonists equally is the unjustified fear that the king holds for those bound west. George III is forcing the people to forfeit their fundamental rights. He is a despotic tyrant.

[Massachusetts], *and his Majesty's other colonies in North America, have long been struggling under the heavy hand of power, and our dutiful petitions for the redress of our intolerable grievances, have not only been disregarded and frowned upon, but the design totally to alter the free constitution of civil government in British America, and establish arbitrary governments, and reduce the inhabitants to slavery, appears more and more to be fixed and determined.**

Massachusetts House of Representatives (June 17, 1774)

# 26

## "He has called together legislative bodies at places unusual, uncomfortable, and distant from the depository of their public Records, for the sole purpose of fatiguing them into compliance with his measures."

- ☆ Governors force colonial legislatures to meet away from their traditional capitols, without access to key official documents, in attempts to intimidate and grind them down into submission.
- ☆ This oppressive tactic subverts self-government, the Social Compact, and the unalienable rights of the people.

The fourth grievance continues the theme of subverting the colonial legislatures chosen by the people. This particular one involves not undermining representation *per se* but instead intimidating and making the lives of the legislators so miserable that the king will overpower them.

To properly understand this grievance, we need to appreciate that in the colonial era, although the capitol building of each colony is generally fixed in one city, the monarch and each colonial governor possesses the absolute authority to move the meeting location of the legislature to any place within the colony. Also, the king or governor may call the legislature into session whenever he wants. Recall, traveling within even a single colony can be quite a lengthy and arduous journey. Furthermore, the records of official business are housed and remain in the traditional capital city. When the legislature moves, the records stay put, and the legislature is deprived of the voluminous official records critical to conducting official business.

Although the first instance of this grievance occurs in South Carolina, the controversy stems from England. Radical member of the British House of Commons John Wilkes is charged with the crime of seditious libel, and an organization is formed to raise money in his defense. In support of the cause, the South Carolina Commons House of Assembly (informally known as "the Commons") appropriates £10,500 (a very large sum at the time—call it the equivalent of over £2.4 million or about $3 million today*).

The empire's reaction is as expected: fierce opposition. Governor Lord Charles Greville Montagu refuses to assent to the bill. A standoff ensues, and government operations grind to a halt. The assembly refuses to approve any additional funds unless the Wilkes appropriation passes. The governor tries to cow the assembly into compliance by dissolving it and calling for new elections. The elections do not change the attitude of the newly elected assembly, only stiffen its resolve. On August 28, 1772, the governor dissolves the assembly yet again, orders a new election, and deploys his trump card by ordering the newly elected legislature to meet in Beaufort—about seventy miles away. He hopes this tactic will break the deadlock and sway the new assembly to his will. This trek to Beaufort is most uncomfortable and fatiguing, and it separates the legislators from the public records stored in Charleston. The governor expects that a more favorable assembly will be elected and that the Patriots concentrated in Charleston will forgo the arduous trip. Alas, the gambit backfires. The newly elected assembly is filled with the governor's opponents and supporters of the appropriation for Wilkes.

The governor's scheme fails spectacularly. Montagu relents and orders the assembly to reconvene in Charleston in a few weeks. When they meet in late October and early November 1772, the assembly passes resolutions condemning the governor for, among other things, forcing the assembly to meet in Beaufort.

The other key demonstration of this grievance flows from Parliament's enactment of a whole new set of taxes, commonly known as the Townshend Acts. As we will explore later in great detail, after Parliament repeals the Stamp Act, it passes the Townshend Acts in 1767 to replace the stamp taxes. It was named after Charles Townshend, the British chancellor of the Exchequer (our equivalent to the secretary of the Treasury) and, like the Stamp Act, these taxes are unsuccessful in raising revenue and instead spark outrage in the colonies. By adding duties to the importation of glass, lead, paints, and tea, they trigger protests and boycotts of British goods. The protests in Boston are so intense that four regiments of British troops are sent to tamp down opposition to the unjust taxes. In turn, the Boston-based Massachusetts legislature (the General Court) protests that it is surrounded by British troops—a most intimidating circumstance. In 1769, Governor Francis Bernard reacts—not by pulling out the troops, but by ordering the Massachusetts legislature to move to Cambridge, several miles away. The legislators trudge over to Cambridge, suffer fatigue and coercion, and are separated from the indispensable public records maintained in Boston. Thankfully, the legislature returns to Boston in 1772. The next year, the General Court is subjected to more severe treatment. After the Boston Tea Party in 1773, King George III determines that Massachusetts deserves military leadership and appoints General Thomas Gage to impose imperial control. Gage permanently moves the capital to Salem, about twenty-five miles away from Boston. Of course, the key public records still remain in Boston—guarded by two regiments of soldiers.

A third, nearly comical incident occurs in Virginia on the cusp of the Revolution. By June 1775, Royal Governor Lord Dunmore loses control of the colony. He flees his home and takes up residence on the British warship HMS *Fowey*, anchored in the York River. The House of Burgesses and the governor become hostile pen pals, exchanging a series of provocative letters and resolutions. The house comments that official business needs to be conducted and complains that it cannot occur while Dunmore is residing in the middle of the river. Dunmore calls their bluff by reminding them that "[t]he Constitution vests me with an undoubted power to call the assembly for the business of, to any place in the colony exigency may require."* The House of Burgesses responds by officially chiding Dunmore for failing to conduct official business on the mainland. Dunmore cheekily replies that he is "ready to receive the house on Monday, at twelve of the clock, at my present residence, for the purpose of giving my assent to such acts as I shall approve."* The house takes umbrage at this disingenuous invitation to convene on the warship and passes a resolution condemning Dunmore's command "requiring this house to attend him on board one of his majesty's ships of war," as "a high breach of the rights and privileges of this house."* This standstill is only resolved by the American Revolution. Dunmore eventually vacates Virginia.

The federal Constitution ensures that this oppression will never happen again. Article I, Section 5 provides that "[n]either House, during the Session of Congress, shall, without the Consent of the other, adjourn for more than three days, nor to any other Place than that in which the two Houses shall be sitting." In other words, Congress determines when and where it will meet. The same provision ensures that each House creates its own rules of governance and is responsible for creating and publishing its own journals. Article I, Section 8 authorizes Congress to locate, create, and govern the federal capital. The president has nothing to do with any of it.

Because of our current extensive interstate highway, train, and air travel systems, as well as the internet and mass communication, justifying a revolution on changing the location of the capital is difficult to imagine in today's society. Forcing the California legislature to move from Sacramento to San Diego—which is still hundreds of miles—might be inconvenient, but it will not cripple or paralyze the legislature. The legislators could easily travel there, stay in hotels, and access their documents by computer. Perhaps a better example is compelling the Alaskan legislature based in Juneau to meet in Lusaka, Zambia, prohibiting the legislators from taking their official records, and preventing the legislators from using the internet or engaging in other electronic communications once they arrive. Add to this scenario that the entire purpose of the move is to intimidate and wear down the legitimate representatives of the people. This is no trivial matter. This oppressive tactic subverts self-government, the Social Compact, and the unalienable rights of the people. Another brick in the wall of British tyranny.*

*With a good deal of surprise I have observed, that little notice has been taken of an act of parliament, as injurious in its principle to the liberties of these colonies, as the Stamp Act was: I mean the act for suspending the legislature of New York.* [...]

*If they may be legally deprived, in such a case, of the privilege of legislation, why may they not, with equal reason, be deprived of every other privilege? Or why may not every colony be treated in the same manner, when any of them shall dare to deny their assent to any impositions, that shall be directed?**

John Dickinson (December 2, 1767)

# 27

## "He has dissolved Representative Houses repeatedly, for opposing with manly firmness his invasions on the rights of the people."

☆ To force his arbitrary will on the people, King George III and his governors shut down colonial legislatures that courageously resist his repression, thereby subverting the Social Compact, violating unalienable rights, destroying equality, and exercising absolute power over the colonists.

The fifth grievance, although in the same vein as the fourth grievance, cuts even deeper. The monarch and each colonial governor not only possess the authority to force a colonial legislature to relocate, but they also have the power to shut it down. When this happens, the terms of the legislators end, and the legislature can only reconvene when it is called back into session by the king or the respective governor. This grievance again echoes Thomas Jefferson's commentary in *A Summary View of the Rights of British America*. Jefferson notes that since the Glorious Revolution of 1688, the monarch and his ministers disavow any authority to dissolve Parliament. But that is not the case with the colonies. The king and governors retain full authority to dissolve colonial legislatures at any time for any (or no) reason at all. Yet again, the colonists are denied basic constitutional protections afforded to their brethren in the British Isles. George III and his governors crush colonial opposition to unjust and unconstitutional British rule by abusing their authority to dissolve the colonial legislatures.

One prominent example of the basis for this grievance involves New York's refusal to abide by the Mutiny Act passed on May 15, 1765.* The act requires that New York pay upfront for the food, drink (including liquor), provisions, and public quartering of thousands of troops that are proposed to be stationed in New York. (The most objectionable provision, which would have required the quartering of troops in private occupied homes, is removed before passage.) Led by Judge Robert R. Livingston (whose son later serves on the Declaration's drafting Committee of Five), New York's legislature balks at this blank check for English troops. Instead, it agrees to pay only for limited expenses incurred by soldiers who are actually stationed in New York. The general assembly also squawks over where the troops are to be stationed.

In the eyes of the imperial authorities, this will not do. New York Governor Sir Henry Moore directs troops to New York City, reasoning that a show of force will intimidate the general assembly into complying with the Mutiny Act (otherwise known as the Quartering Act). In truth, the legislators are totally unpersuaded by the troops. The Mutiny Act demands that the New York General Assembly pay for the very troops suppressing those leading the struggle for their freedoms.

Completely unrelated to challenging British oppression, riots erupt outside of New York City. The legislature now accepts that some troops are needed to keep the peace. On July 2, 1766, it passes the New York Barracks Act, compromising legislation that maintains local colonial control of the expenditures, cuts back on the allowable expenses, refuses to pay for liquor (a prominent expense for the soldiers), and pays for expenses through a prior "loan" on behalf of troops that has been previously approved but never spent years before.*

The imperial authorities will have none of it. The governor writes to London, suggesting that only force will make New York's General Assembly comply. The empire's patience with New York is exhausted. Parliament declines the use of force but takes nearly as strong an action. On March 12, 1767, the King's Cabinet determines to ask Parliament to suspend New York's General Assembly. Running nearly simultaneously (and perhaps in conjunction), the empire is also preparing to enact the Townshend Acts. Charles Townshend proposes to Parliament the New York Restraining Act, which effectuates the suspension of the New York General Assembly for so long as it fails to comply with the Mutiny Act. A year to the date that the New York Barracks Act is enacted, George III assents to the New York Restraining Act.* New York's General Assembly responds by passing condemnatory resolutions. The result is predictably outrageous: the governor dissolves the general assembly.

New York's injury is opposed across the continent. Leading the charge is Pennsylvanian John Dickinson in his famous series of pamphlets, *Letters from a Farmer in Pennsylvania, to the Inhabitants of the British Colonies.* Dickinson writes that the New York Restraining Act is "injurious in its principle to the liberties of these colonies."* He concludes that the New York legislators "have been punished in a manner pernicious to *American* [italics in original] freedom, and justly alarming to all the colonies."* At its bottom, Great Britain is claiming the authority to legislate *anything* for the colonies, including taxation, in violation of the Social Compact, representative government, and limited government:

> If the *British* Parliament has a legal authority to issue an order, that we shall furnish a single article for the troops here, and to compel obedience to *that* order, they have the same right to issue an order for us to supply those troops with arms, clothes, and every necessary; and to compel obedience to *that* order also; in short, to lay *any burdens* they please upon us. What is this but *taxing* us at a *certain sum*, and leaving to us only the *manner* of raising it? [Italics are in the original.]*

Since Parliament does not have the authority to pass such a mandate, it also does not have the authority to punish New York for refusing to comply. Parliament's assertion of unyielding supremacy is tyrannical.

The New York Restraining Act will take effect in three months if New York does not relent. Under the impending threat of legislative suspension, a few days before the July 2 effective date, New York passes another law giving the English all they want. Or do they? The colonial assembly enacts the Three Thousand Pound Act, which appropriates this lump sum for several purposes, including quartering troops.* Cleverly, it does not actually authorize such quartering, nor does it expressly include payment for liquor rations. Nevertheless, upon reflection, the imperial authorities decide to let the controversy rest, and the general assembly is considered to have complied. In the end, the New York Restraining Act becomes moot even before it takes effect. Important for this grievance, during the controversy, the governor dissolves the legislature for its impetuosity, and London's aggression exposes for all to see that the British are intent on dominating the colonies. In essence, Parliament, with the full backing of the king, coerces the New Yorkers into submission by threatening to disembowel their legislature.

Another prominent example of this suppression of the right of self-government arises in 1765 in Virginia. When the Stamp Act is enacted, resistance in the colony is initially uncertain and hesitant. But twenty-nine-year-old Patrick Henry, a freshman legislator, rails against taxation without representation. With mesmerizing speeches and cold logic, he inspires the initially sleepy and complacent House of

Burgesses to implement the most aggressive legislative reaction to the Stamp Act to date. Virginia adopts a set of resolutions (dubbed the Virginia Resolves), in the most vociferous of terms, condemning the act. The governor responds by dissolving the House of Burgesses. No matter. The Virginia Resolves are the match that sets ablaze a massive resistance fire across the continent.

Similar politically motivated dissolutions in several other legislative assemblies occur just a few years later. What kicks off this new round of dissolutions is the "Massachusetts Circular Letter," drafted by Samuel Adams and James Otis. The Massachusetts legislature adopts the "Circular Letter" on February 11, 1768. It robustly denounces the Townshend Acts for levying taxes without representation. The "Circular Letter" declares that any attempt to tax the colonists without their consent violates their natural rights as men and their constitutional rights as Englishmen. The "Circular Letter" is distributed to the legislatures of all the colonies. Proclaiming that the "Circular Letter" is seditious, Massachusetts Governor Francis Bernard demands that the legislature rescind it. When the measure to rescind is put to the vote, the Massachusetts legislature defiantly refuses by a tally of 92 to 17.

At the direction of London, Governor Bernard dissolves the General Court in 1768 and dispatches troops to Boston. On September 14, 1768, the selectmen (members of the city council) of Boston respond by distributing their own circular letter to the towns of Massachusetts. Among other things, the Boston circular alerts the other towns to the "melancholy and very alarming circumstances to which this province, as well as *America* in general, is now reduced," observes that the people of Massachusetts are "deprived of the councils of a general assembly in this dark and difficult season," and calls for a convention to meet on September 22 at Boston.* A groundswell against Great Britain surges in Massachusetts. Ninety-six towns and eight districts attend the convention. It passes resolutions demanding satisfaction of their grievances and then peacefully retires.

In 1769, the Virginia House of Burgesses passes resolutions denouncing the dissolution of the Massachusetts General Court and the stationing of troops in Boston, and it sends a formal letter of protest to George III. The king's answer? Naturally, he dissolves the Virginia House of Burgesses, too. The Earl of Hillsborough, in essence the new secretary of state for the American colonies, instructs the remaining colonial governors to prevent other assemblies from following Virginia's lead. The colonial legislatures ignore him. Because South Carolina and Georgia refuse to follow the Earl of Hillsborough's directive that the "Circular Letter" should be met with the "contempt it deserves," those governors shut down their legislative assemblies.*

As we learned in connection with the last grievance, South Carolina's assembly is dissolved (again) in 1769, when it appropriates the payment of £10,500 to support John Wilkes. The truth is that South Carolina's assembly is ungovernable. With (perhaps) the exception of Massachusetts, it resists British rule with more vigor than any other colony. Within eighteen months, Governor Charles Montagu dissolves the South Carolina Assembly four times. South Carolinians respond by demanding that the governor be recalled. In essence, royal government in South Carolina dies in 1771—five years ahead of the rest of America.

Virginia's legislative assembly is dissolved yet again in May 1769, when it passes a set of resolves condemning the revival of a law allowing persons accused of treason to be shipped across the sea for trial in England. In reaction, the burgesses immediately reconvene as a convention (in a private home or perhaps the Raleigh Tavern). Led by Peyton Randolph, the convention passes new resolutions sharply criticizing Parliament and creates an association of nonimport, which sparks a new round of boycotts against British goods.

The North Carolina legislature also challenges those acts of Parliament and suffers the same fate when Governor William Tryon dissolves it. Like Virginia, the members of the now-dissolved North Carolina legislature convene in a private meeting and establish a nonimport association.

In 1773, the Virginia House of Burgesses establishes an official committee of correspondence to communicate with its sister colonies—and it is sent home once more. The next year, the House of Burgesses issues a call to convene the First Continental Congress and support Boston when Great Britain cracks down after the Boston Tea Party. In particular, the burgesses issue a resolution of support of Massachusetts and declare June 1, 1774, as a day of public fasting, humiliation (i.e., confessing sins and seeking divine mercy), and prayer in favor of Boston. The legislature is only in session three weeks—exactly three weeks too long for Governor Lord Dunmore. In May 1774, he dissolves the House of Burgesses. The now-private citizens of the house tromp over to Raleigh Tavern that very day, approve another boycott association, and call for a convention to be held at Williamsburg that summer to choose delegates for the First Continental Congress.

With each passing year, the colonial legislatures more boldly challenge—in the words of the Declaration, with "manly firmness"—the despotic attacks of the king and Parliament. And with each passing year, the governors grow more desperate to beat them down by repeatedly dissolving them. The pattern is widespread and rampant. When the First Continental Congress meets in 1774, ten of the thirteen colonial legislatures are already dissolved.

This subversion of the Social Compact is directly remedied by the federal Constitution. Article I, Section 4 provides, "The Congress shall assemble at least once in every Year, and such Meeting shall be on the first Monday in December, unless they shall by Law appoint a different Day." Under Article I, Section 2, Congress—not the president—determines when to recess. Congress never dissolves; it only takes temporary recesses. However, under Article II, Section 3, the president "may, on extraordinary Occasions, convene both Houses, or either of them, and in Case of Disagreement between them, with Respect to the Time of Adjournment, he may adjourn them to such Time as he shall think proper." In other words, he may require Congress to meet (not dissolve), and if the two chambers disagree, he can determine when they should adjourn. Nevertheless, Congress is a permanent institution that the president has no power to dissolve.

This grievance is extraordinarily destructive of our First Principles. Suppose the legislature in Kansas has a dispute with its governor. Would the neighboring citizens of Iowa or Nebraska tolerate the governor's brazen dissolution of the Kansas legislature? Now, exponentially increase the injury by making the governor an appointee, serving at the pleasure of a president-for-life. This transcends any transient political issue; it strikes at the heart of self-government. The empire is violating the separation of powers as well as gagging the voice of the people by smothering their elected legislatures. The British policy is an imposition of absolute power over the colonies and a grave affront to the Social Compact and unalienable rights. The colonists uniformly and vigorously reject it. They are firmly determined to challenge and oppose this despotic policy.*

[King George III] [...] *heretofore entrusted with the exercise of the kingly office in this government has endeavored to pervert the same into a detestable and insupportable tyranny* [...] *by dissolving legislative assemblies* [...] *when dissolved, by refusing to call others for a long space of time, thereby leaving the political system without any legislative head.**

Thomas Jefferson (June 1776)

# 28

## "He has refused for a long time, after such dissolutions, to cause others to be elected; whereby the Legislative powers, incapable of Annihilation, have returned to the People at large for their exercise; the State remaining in the mean time exposed to all the dangers of invasion from without, and convulsions within."

☆ Some dissolutions of colonial legislatures last for years, depriving the colonists of any functioning representative government, returning lawmaking authority to the people, and exposing the colonists to invasion and civil disorder. This destroys the Social Compact, the rule of law and limited government, as well as endangers equality and unalienable rights.

☆ The king's insolence backfires because colonies begin to establish their own governments to fill in the gap in governance.

The sixth grievance disclaims the ensuing chaos following the long-standing dissolution of several colonial legislatures. As we reviewed, dissolved legislatures cannot reconvene until the governors call for new elections. One maddening tactic some governors exploit is simply to defer the calling of elections for so long that it endangers the colonists.

The dissolution of legislatures extends well beyond any proper time under tradition, custom, and law. What happens then? Representative government collapses. Without a legislature, the power to govern returns to the sovereign—that is, the people. But this returns us to the state of Nature we all are trying to avoid by consenting to live under a government in the first place. With no government, there is no overarching authority to guard the unalienable rights of the people. There is no rule of law, no equality, no due process, no security, no border protection, no peace, no justice. The people are exposed to convulsions from within and invasions from without. We devolve into the nightmare that English philosophers Thomas Hobbes and John Locke warned us about so long ago—the war of all against all.

Massachusetts falls prey to this chaos. As explained in the last grievance, in 1768, the Massachusetts General Court opposes the Townshend Acts with "manly firmness" by issuing the "Circular Letter"; in reaction, the Governor Thomas Hutchinson dissolves the assembly. Months pass. Boston requests that the governor convene a new legislature. He refuses. There is serious civil disorder in the intervening period. Although the Patriots try to establish a shadow (if not new) government, the governor deploys troops to halt those proceedings. Of course, from the Patriots' standpoint, any tumults, riots, and acts of violence are engendered by the governor's violation of the Social Compact by stripping the people of the right to representation. Nearly a year passes before the governor finally concedes to convening a new legislative assembly. When the new General Court finally meets, the capitol building is surrounded by a military guard and cannons are trained on the building. The legislature refuses to conduct sessions under such hostile conditions, their powers once again vanish, and the people soak them up.

The British also inflict these wounds on the people of Virginia. On May 25, 1774, the House of Burgesses declares support for Massachusetts in light of the recent enactment of the Boston Port Act and designates June 1 as a day of humiliation, fasting, and prayer. The next day, Governor Lord Dunmore appears before them and dissolves the house. Lord Dunmore also initially refuses his own executive council's recommendation to call for new elections. Eventually, the elections are held, but the new house is not convened for over a year. Too little, too late. Subsequent Virginia conventions (which, recall, form in the absence of the government) are meeting and displacing the old regime. When it finally meets, the

House of Burgesses adjourns itself until the Declaration is promulgated. Virginia is threatened by the dangers of all-out war.

South Carolina is the most stunning example of this grievance. As we detailed in connection with the last grievance, beginning with the controversy over the John Wilkes appropriation in 1769, the governor and legislature are constantly at odds. The governor retaliates by repeatedly dissolving the South Carolina Assembly. The legislature stops functioning in 1771.

In 1775, South Carolina, Virginia, and New Hampshire (which by this time joins their ranks), realize that they are sinking back into the state of Nature. Each separately seeks guidance from the First Continental Congress about what course it should take. Congress responds to each identically: Establish "a form of government" that will "best produce the happiness of the people," and "most effectually secure peace and good order" in the colony.* South Carolina establishes its own legislature in 1775 and never looks back. Other colonies follow suit. As we have also seen, well before the Declaration, all the colonial legislatures are dissolved at one time or another, and none are really functioning on Independence Day.

> As noted in the last grievance, this utter destruction of the Social Compact and representative government is impossible under Article I, Sections 2 and Section 4 of the United States Constitution. As such, the legislative power never needs to return to the people.

The cold reality is that the king and governors crush self-governance in the colonies, causing the legislative power to revert to the people. This places everyone in a precarious situation in which disorder and anarchy can easily spring. This destroys the Social Compact, the rule of law and limited government, and endangers equality and unalienable rights. The result is that many in the colonies convene conventions that eventually substitute for the closed legislatures. The king's insolence backfires. By quashing legislative resistance, George III plants seedbeds for new legislatures. When these legislatures flower, they are accountable —not to the empire—but to the people.*

*Whereas* [King George III] [...] *heretofore entrusted with the exercise of the kingly office in this government has endeavored to pervert the same into a detestable and insupportable tyranny* [...] *by endeavoring to prevent the population of our country, & for the purpose of obstructing the laws for the naturalization of foreigners & raising the condition [lacking appro]priations of land.**

Thomas Jefferson (June 1776, italicized brackets in original)

# 29

## "He has endeavoured to prevent the population of these States; for that purpose obstructing the Laws for Naturalization of Foreigners; refusing to pass others to encourage their migrations hither, and raising the conditions of new Appropriations of Lands."

☆ To preserve England's dominance within the empire, George III smothers immigration and stymies the growth of America.

☆ By cutting new immigration off at the knees and oppressing the rights of new immigrants, this grievance strikes at the heart of the Social Compact, denigrates the rule of law, subverts unalienable rights, and annihilates any pretense of limited government.

To modern ears, this grievance's language may be a bit awkward. An understanding of the background will make it crystal clear. The first phrase—"endeavour[ing] to prevent the population of these States"—refers to the king's motive for engaging in this seventh grievance. Specifically, the king desires to stop the growth of the population of the colonies. This seems entirely counterintuitive. After all, the British

Empire establishes (or otherwise takes control over) these colonies to extend the empire's reach, acquire territory, and reap new riches. As we will explore, some refer to it as the "promised land." The thirteen colonies are an irreplaceable asset for the empire. To control and fully exploit that asset, Great Britain desperately needs people to settle and administer it. Labor is indispensable for gathering the raw materials necessary for the empire's imperialist adventures, as well as to meet the insatiable hunger for such resources in the British Isles. Further, the populace of the colonies is a huge market for the finished and manufactured goods produced in the British Isles. Why then does George III desire to limit their population?

The king's perspective can only be fully comprehended in context. In 1700, the population of the thirteen colonies is approximately half a million. It explodes to nearly three million in 1775. Driving this tremendous population spike are many factors, including a high birth rate, waves of immigration from Britain and Europe (including indentured servants and convicts), and the steady forcible importation of enslaved Africans (and the continued enslavement of their descendants). In 1775, the colonies are more populous than Holland or Switzerland—and almost as large as Denmark or Portugal. Meanwhile, the imperial center is increasing at a much slower pace. England and Wales grow from approximately five million in 1700 to approximately eight million in 1775. With the doubling of the American population approximately every twenty-five years, and the slower increase in the British Isles, it will take perhaps two or three generations for the American population to eclipse that of Britain.

With this phenomenal rise in colonial population comes a dramatic cultural shift. We previously explored how the colonists originally view themselves as Englishmen, entitled to the rights and privileges of England's citizens. Still, much like the Scots and the Welsh view themselves as both subjects of the empire and culturally distinct from the English, many of the colonists in the thirteen colonies consider themselves culturally Americans well before 1776. As we previously learned, with population growth comes a conjoined development of a uniquely *American* character and culture embedded within the British Empire.

Moreover, there is a ubiquitous spirit of optimism and progress among the colonists, one that takes for granted that the population will continue to grow robustly and expand vigorously westward into the frontiers of the unexplored wilderness. This expectation becomes a flashpoint between the empire and the colonists. The old empire is gripped with serious doubt about the desirability of allowing the colonies to meet their fullest potential. George III and Parliament guardedly watch the expansion of the American frontier and an amazing population explosion. They are hardly interested in presiding over the shift of the population, culture, and political future of the empire to the American frontier. They are deeply concerned that a growing population will begin to establish their own manufacturing capacity, undermining the mercantilist system, which, until now, dictates that the colonies ship to the empire inexpensive raw materials and the home country ships back expensive finished goods. If the colonies develop their own factories and become self-sufficient, it will spell doom for the mercantilist regime. These and other concerns motivate the king and Parliament to purposefully hem in the colonists and curtail their growth. With this background, the seventh grievance comes into focus. It describes three specific ways that the king is strangling colonial population growth.

The first is straightforward: "obstructing the Laws for Naturalization of Foreigners." At its core, America is a nation of immigrants. With the exception of Native Americans, everyone here since Christopher Columbus arrives directly from overseas or is the descendant of someone who did—regardless of whether they come here joyfully, desperately, or in chains. As such, core to the American polity is the need to naturalize immigrants—that is, to enable immigrants to become fully integrated participants into the political society. Today, we refer to ourselves as "citizens." But until July 2, 1776, colonists are the "subjects" of the British Empire. Becoming officially recognized as full subjects of Great Britain is vitally important for immigrants to succeed.

Immigrants from the British Empire (England, Wales, Scotland, and colonial possessions) are already considered subjects of the empire, but huge swaths of the immigrant population come from other European countries, including the Netherlands, Germany, Sweden, and France. Immigrants also come from North and South America. We must not overlook that there is a sizable number of free African Americans. Naturalization is vital to non-British immigrants because only if they become subjects of the British Empire can they own property. Inexpensive land, open frontiers, and freedom draw in immigrants. In the words of Thomas Paine, the colonies are becoming an "asylum for mankind," and the British perceive that this status threatens their own control of this most valuable asset.*

In addition, following the end of the French and Indian War, a huge influx of immigrants arrives from the British Isles. The king is alarmed when the vital lifeblood of the empire bleeds out of the British Isles and strengthens the colonies. Some consider the colonies parasites, ungratefully leaching people from the homeland. Population growth, a large foreign population, and the talented British moving to America create a perfect storm for the king.

The empire first moves to squelch the problem by trying to stifle non-British immigration into the colonies. In 1699, the king requires colonial legislatures to approve the naturalization of individual persons specifically. This changes in December 1773, when he orders every colonial governor he appointed to refuse assent to acts naturalizing any foreigners or allowing nonnaturalized subjects to obtain new land. Because the king does not appoint the governors in all the colonies, the effect is limited. However, the king's order applies to major population centers, and where applied, the clampdown works extraordinarily well. The lockdown is so effective that New York Lieutenant Governor Cadwallader Colden reflects on the deleterious effect it is having in his colony—many settlers simply leave the colony for those not under the king's thumb.

The second complaint in this grievance explains that the king is "refusing to pass others to encourage their migrations." Following the end of the French and Indian War, the British Empire starts to withdraw incentives for immigration to its North American colonies. As early as 1767, the British refuse to assent to a Georgia law that offers free transportation to any Protestants who emigrate from Great Britain. The king also refuses to assent to a 1771 North Carolina law exempting all Europeans from taxation for four years. Likewise, he refuses to assent to a different North Carolina act of 1771 that incentivizes immigrant Scottish Highlanders from the Isle of Skye.

Great Britain is so committed to ending immigration to the colonies that, in 1776, it even prohibits the transportation of convicts to American shores. Some might expect that this measure would be warmly welcomed by the colonies—far from it. This directive is quite a sacrifice on both sides of the Atlantic. We must understand that Parliament enacts the Transportation Act of 1717, which provides a new form of punishment for felons: banishment and servitude in America. Before then, because long-term incarceration is not widely available, most convicts are whipped, branded, or hanged. The courts eagerly adopt the new punishment. One study reveals that between 1718 and 1775, approximately fifty thousand convicts are sentenced to North America from England, Scotland, and Ireland. In 1775, three colonies alone host up to thirty-five thousand to forty thousand convicts. This is a win-win-win scenario for the homeland (it disposes of its criminal trash), the colonies (which obtain desperately needed workers), and at least many of the convicts (who might otherwise face the gallows).

The third specific complaint in this grievance highlights that the empire is "raising the conditions of new Appropriations of Lands." It points out that the empire changes the rules by which immigrants can acquire new land. During the beginnings of the American colonies, the king and Parliament provide strong enticements for individuals and families to leave the Old World, take the perilous journey across the Atlantic, and undergo severe hardships to establish a new life. Many die during the passage on the Atlantic, while others die after arriving from disease, starvation, and conflict with Native Americans or other European settlers. In exchange for taking on this very risky adventure, immigrants usually obtain land (as well as religious and political freedom). In the eyes of the empire, land is plentiful and inexpensive, and Great Britain sells the immigrants land at very low prices to encourage them to depart for the New World.

In *A Summary View of the Rights of British America*, Thomas Jefferson argues that this entire paradigm is wrongheaded. George III does not even possess a legal basis for selling land to the pioneers. Although the king owns large estates in the British Isles, he owns no land in the colonies. The king is the descendant of William the Conqueror, who invades England and deposes King James II. William the Conqueror then personally takes for himself the spoils of war by confiscating the property of his enemies. But he never conquers America. As such, the monarchy does not have a legal title to the land that it is selling to the colonists; the sale of the land is a fraud. Still, no one bothers to complain because the monarchy hoodwinks the buyers into thinking it is legal, and the land is so cheap that challenging the legal title is not worth the hassle.

But on the cusp of the American Revolution, George III changes the terms of the exchange, including doubling the price of land. Jefferson argues that the people should no longer ignore the illegality of the king's position. The only authority to distribute the land is from the people directly or their representatives in their colonial legislatures, but certainly not George III. The settlers win the land for themselves—not by the grace of the monarch. Jefferson throws down the gauntlet.

Moreover, the king orders his governors to stop selling any land to foreigners, even those who are already naturalized. In 1773, the governors of royal colonies are ordered to halt any additional land grants to immigrants unless they are approved by the Commissioners of Trade and Plantations. In February 1774, with some narrow and immaterial exceptions, the temporary halt of land conveyances is made permanent. The empire throws down its own gauntlet—no more foreigners are going to build their homes in the colonies.

Meanwhile, the colonists have an entirely different worldview. They welcome new immigrants. The colonists see the colonies as a new asylum for religious and civil liberty, a palladium of virtue that is against corruption, which encourages a pioneering spirit where grueling work is rewarded with vastly improved living conditions. Most importantly, the New World is free of the corruption and tyranny of the Old World. This creed motivates many immigrants and takes deep root in the American psyche. In the words of Silas Downer, America is a "promised land" imbued with unparalleled natural resources.* However, none of it matters because without liberty, the people will not flourish but rot under the thumb of oppression.

Downer's characterization of America as the "promised land" echoes the Lord's promise to Moses and the Israelites that Israel's sojourn in the desert will end when they settle in a land flowing with milk and honey.* This New World of America protects liberty, ensures prosperity, avoids oppression, alleviates misery, and bolsters virtue. If there is any doubt whether the Founding Generation genuinely feels this way, it is swept away in just a few sentences in Thomas Paine's *Common Sense*:

> This new world has been the asylum for the persecuted lovers of civil and religious liberty from *every part* of Europe. Hither have they fled, not from the tender embraces of the mother, but from the cruelty of the monster; and it is so far true of England, that the same tyranny which drove the first emigrants from home, pursues their descendants still. [Italics are in the original.]

Paine powerfully continues that America offers the entire world a new chance for liberty and equality:

> O you that love mankind! You that dare opposed, not only the tyranny, but the tyrant, stand forth! Every spot of the old world is overrun with oppression. Freedom has been hunted round the globe. Asia, and Africa, have long expelled her.—Europe regards her like a stranger, and England has given her warning to depart. O! receive the fugitive, and prepare in time an asylum for mankind.*

By stopping the flow of new immigrants, the British are cutting off their own subjects and other Europeans from reaching the last best hope of a free and virtuous society. In addition, this policy puts up a hedge to protect their corruption, boxes in the colonists from further spreading liberty, and deprives the colonists of new allies from reaching our shores.

Reflect on more modern examples of the Soviet Union and the Eastern Bloc (most notably East Germany), Cuba, and North Korea. They all deprived their subjects of the right to freely leave their countries and find freedom in the United States and the West. They also cheat the free world of much-needed talent. That is what is happening with the British Empire and America.

Article I, Section 8 of the United States Constitution rectifies this grievance by vesting Congress with the enumerated authority to "establish an uniform Rule of Naturalization." The people's representatives shall determine naturalization policy, not an arbitrary king.

By cutting off new immigration and oppressing the rights of new immigrants, this grievance strikes at the heart of the Social Compact. The king is limiting who is eligible to become part of the Social Compact, overriding colonial sentiments. Likewise, by resting on a false premise of land ownership, George III is denigrating the rule of law and subverting unalienable rights. This aggressive anti-immigrant strategy stretches the tentacles of the empire to the core of the American experiment—annihilating any pretense of limited government.*

*[T]he House of Assembly presented to me a bill "to amend and continue an act passed in the year 1768, for establishing superior courts" etc,* [...] *which my duty obliged me to reject, as being repugnant to His Majesty's Royal Instructions, relating to the attachment of effects of persons who have never resided in the colony.* [...]

*I was yesterday informed, that there was a temperate but firm resolution in the majority of the house, rather to be without courts of justice, than conform to the direction of that instruction.**

North Carolina Governor Josiah Martin (February 24, 1773)

# 30

## "He has obstructed the Administration of Justice, by refusing his Assent to Laws for establishing Judiciary powers."

- ☆ To compel North Carolina to abide by his vision of justice, George III forces the closure of the courts and the North Carolina legislature.
- ☆ By closing courts, the king destroys the rule of law and the Social Compact—and threatens unalienable rights, equality, and limited government.

This eighth grievance returns to George III's undermining the colonists' right to self-govern. Again, the king refuses to approve necessary laws. This grievance focuses on the judiciary, condemning the king's refusal to approve laws establishing judicial powers.

This is nearly unfathomable for us in modern times, but not so for the Founding Generation. This controversy arises, out of all things, from how to enforce a money judgment. In broad strokes, in a civil case—meaning between private parties and not involving alleged crimes—the party bringing the suit (the plaintiff) claims that it has suffered injuries caused by the party being sued (the defendant). In most civil cases, the plaintiff argues that they have been harmed by the defendant and demands monetary compensation. When a plaintiff prevails, the plaintiff obtains a judgment for a certain amount of money. However, as any judge and prevailing plaintiff can attest, obtaining a judgment does not necessarily mean that the defendant promptly pays the money. The judgment only means that the defendant legally owes the plaintiff the money (in other words, the defendant becomes a judgment debtor). To collect the judgment, sometimes a plaintiff is forced to take specific legally authorized actions, such as garnishing wages or seizing the property of the defendant (cash, real property, cars, stocks and bonds, business assets, and so forth). The legal mechanism for seizing the assets is often called an "attachment."

In 1746, a North Carolina act provides for such attachments in the colony, even if the judgment debtor is never physically in the colony. For example, a defendant might own large landholdings or business interests in North Carolina but never visit the colony. The law authorizing these "foreign attachments" is patterned after the English practice in large commercial cities, most notably London. Putting aside this large-city exception, under English law, for a court to exercise jurisdiction over someone's property, the defendant must have some minimal physical contact in the court's jurisdiction. Nonetheless, beginning no later than 1746, provisions for foreign attachments are enacted continuously throughout the entire colony of North Carolina (not just its large commercial centers).

In 1772, the king instructs colonial governors to refuse to assent to any law authorizing foreign attachments without a special provision suspending the overall law until the king assents. In 1773, the law authorizing North Carolina's courts expires. Without a new law, the courts will close. The North Carolina legislature ignores the king's instructions and Governor Josiah Martin's objections and enacts a new superior court law, including foreign attachments. Governor Martin demands that the attachment provision be struck. The governor and legislature engage in a robust debate, exchanging a series of strongly worded petitions, protests, and letters. After much maneuvering, the legislature relents and passes the law with the suspension provision. However, the king refuses to assent to the law because of the foreign attachment provision. A stalemate ensues. North Carolina will not pass a new law without the attachment provision, and the king and governor will not assent. In 1773, the statutory authority for the court system vanishes. There are no courts.

As much as taxation without representation, this grievance fuels North Carolina's resistance to Great Britain. As but one example, future United States Supreme Court Justice James Iredell is a very young lawyer and comptroller of the customhouse at Edenton, North Carolina—and up until this point a loyal subject. Great Britain's intransigence on this issue turns him into a reluctant penman for the Revolution. He is flabbergasted by the empire's position. In particular, he excoriates the governor's command that the colony must follow the king's instructions.

The king cleverly determines to bypass the legislature. He instructs Governor Martin to commission royal criminal courts based on the king's prerogatives alone. Iredell eviscerates their legitimacy by explaining that the king's courts use jurors "whose qualifications are not consistent with the law of the land, but appointed at the discretion of judges acting under a commission of doubtful authority," and their decisions are "evidently illegal and void."*

Iredell's argument carries the day. The North Carolina House of Commons refuses to recognize these royal courts and declines to fund their judges. The legislature then reenacts the original superior court law without the suspension clause. Predictably, the governor dissolves the House of Commons. This is the end of the North Carolina colonial legislature for all time. There will be no courts in North Carolina from 1773 until the American Revolution—and no legislature after 1774!

The federal Constitution guards against the annihilation of the judicial power. Article III, Section 1 vests the judicial power in the Supreme Court and any "inferior Courts" as Congress creates. Article I, Section 8 specifically authorizes Congress "to constitute Tribunals inferior to the supreme Court." Once appointed, the president cannot remove a judge. Federal judges are the closest thing to a nobility in America—unless impeached and convicted, they hold their positions for life under Article III, Section 1. The judicial branch is a permanent, independent court system established as the third branch of the government. The judiciary is not at the mercy of an arbitrary or corrupt president.

Fair and just courts are vitally important to the rule of law, protecting unalienable rights, guaranteeing equality, ensuring a limited government, and maintaining the Social Compact—all of which are destroyed by the king's imperious actions.*

*At this period* [of the winter of 1773–1774], *the universal cry, among the friends of their country was "What shall we do to be saved?" It was by all agreed, as the governor was entirely dependent on the crown, and the council in danger of becoming so if the judges were made so too, the liberties of the country would be totally lost, and every man at the mercy of a few slaves of the governor.**

John Adams (1802–1807)

# 31

## "He has made Judges dependent on his Will alone, for the tenure of their offices, and the amount and payment of their salaries."

☆ By conspiring to make the judiciary completely dependent on him, George III seeks to corrupt these judges, violate the rule of law, and impose an unlimited tyranny on the people.

☆ The plot strives to destroy an independent judiciary, a necessary protection of truth, justice, and unalienable rights.

Understanding the role of courts in the colonies is essential to set the stage for this ninth grievance. Like today, key functions of the courts are the search for truth, obtaining justice, and the fair, peaceful resolution of disputes through an impartial application of the law to the facts. Court rulings are especially important in the colonies, which are on the edge of Western civilization. In addition, colonial courts play other critical roles, now played by municipal and county government. Of paramount concern, judicial independence is critical to protecting the unalienable rights of Englishmen.

In England, judges are independent of the king and serve during terms of good behavior—which basically means that unless a judge is corrupt or commits a crime or a dereliction of duty, he maintains his office for life. Thus, judges in the imperial seat serve for life unless they are ejected from office for misconduct in office. Such removal is difficult and very rare. It requires that the judge be impeached by the

House of Commons and convicted by the House of Lords.* (This procedure is nearly identical to the impeachment process today applicable to federal judges in the United States.*) These protections are afforded to judges in England beginning in 1701. From almost the beginning of his reign, King George III recognizes that this judicial independence is vitally important to the rights of Englishmen. He recommends to Parliament that judicial independence be secured by guaranteeing the pay of the judges so long as they serve.

However, in December 1761, the king changes the rules of the game. Judges in the colonies now serve solely at the pleasure of George III; he has full authority to remove a judge for any reason or no reason at all. King George III will not relinquish this power over colonial courts, even if it contradicts his public declaration to Parliament. The practical effect is that colonial judges are keenly aware of the reality that if they render decisions contrary to George III's wishes, the king may very well retaliate by dismissing them. This power lurks over the backs of the judges, ready to deprive them of their positions and livelihood. Other than for the most fortified, this enormous power threatens the impartial administration of justice.

This untenable situation is a long-standing irritant for the colonists. As early as the 1760s, a leading opponent of arbitrary English rule, Pennsylvanian John Dickinson, raises the alarm in his famous *Letters from a Farmer in Pennsylvania*. He decries the dependence of colonial judges on the king as a grave threat to liberty because they will bias their decisions toward their paymasters. Dickinson reflects that judicial independence is even more important in the colonies; in England, the people can hope that Parliament will rise up to oppose the king—but in the colonies, Parliament and the standing army are likely to support the king along with his courts.

At the same time, English law provides that customs officials armed with a writ issued by a court dependent on the monarch may search any home, business, store, warehouse, and other buildings. These writs are already a proven "engine of oppression" in Great Britain.* Dickinson notes that friends of liberty in England strongly oppose the use of writs there, and "[i]f such a power is in the least degree dangerous *there*, it must be utterly destructive to liberty *here* [italics in original].* At least in Great Britain, individuals aggrieved by the use of the writs can sue "and have it tried by independent judges, who are no parties in committing the injury. *Here* [italics in original] he must have it tried before dependent judges, being the men who granted the writ."* The judges' dependence on the king eviscerates justice in connection with invasions of sacred homes and businesses by imperial authorities.

The king further subverts liberty through another clever tactic: enforcing the trade laws in the admiralty courts. These courts have no juries, and like colonial judges, the admiralty judges serve at the pleasure of George III. Such courts are originally designed to address maritime issues, but their jurisdiction is now expanded to enforce the new taxes imposed by the empire. Worse, the judges receive a commission on the sale of any property they order seized. If colonists are found guilty of violating trade laws, their ships, cargo, and other goods are ordered sold, and the judges get a cut of the proceeds. Judges now have a financial incentive to rule against colonial defendants—a most corrupt system. John Adams rails against these courts during the Stamp Act crisis because

> the Stamp Act has opened a vast number of sources of new crimes which may be committed by any man, and cannot but be committed by multitudes, and prodigious penalties are annexed, and all these are to be tried by such a judge of such a court!—What can be wanting, after this, but a weak or wicked man for a judge, to render us [...] a slave of the servants of a minister of state?*

Strong language indeed. In fact, John Adams's interest in politics is greatly spurred by his dedication to judicial independence. He believes to his core that judicial independence is critical to liberty, freedom, and justice. He goes so far as to argue that the judges should hold office for life, subject to impeachment—just like we have in our federal system today, and they have in England at the time. Adams's recommendation will find life in the Massachusetts Constitution of 1780. But in 1776, it is but a dream—and a searing hot point of contention.

This philosophical difference flashes into a concrete point of controversy in New York and Massachusetts over the payment of judges and their tenures of office. London decides it will pay the judges in these colonies. That this proposal would erupt into an intense dispute might at first seem unlikely from our modern perspective. The crux of the issue is the colonies' passionate desire to pay their own judges—even when the empire wishes to assume that burden. You would think the colonies are delighted to remove this expense from their colonial budget. Quite the contrary.

Originally, colonial judges are paid by the colonies. As mentioned earlier, in 1761, the king determines that colonial judges should hold office only at his pleasure. A few years later, in 1767, as part of the several Townshend Acts, Parliament imposes new taxes. In particular, the Revenue Act of 1767 (sometimes referred to as simply the singular Townshend Act) imposes taxes on lead, glass, paper, painters' colors, and tea imported into the colony. Importantly for this ninth grievance, the preamble to the Revenue Act of 1767 explains that since it is a revenue-raising measure, the costs of the administration of justice enforcing the act should be defrayed by the empire; furthermore, the act specifically provides that all monies from the new taxes should first be used for the costs of the administration of justice "where it shall be found necessary."* This generates fiery opposition from many colonists. That the judges serve at the pleasure of the king is bad; that the Revenue Act of 1767 will tax the colonists without representation is worse; that the judges will now bend to enforce these unjust laws unjustly because they are dependent on the pay of the king is completely intolerable. The colonial legislatures refuse to allow the payment of their judges by the crown. After fierce widespread opposition to the Townshend Acts, in April 1770, Parliament repeals the Revenue Act of 1767. This clever ploy never becomes reality.

This crisis again comes to a head, like so many of the events leading up to the American Revolution, in Massachusetts. In 1772, Prime Minister Lord North announces court reforms and determines that their colonial judges should be paid by the Crown.

Adams attacks. He understands that any attempt at protecting the rule of law against the king will be all but demolished if the judges are appointed by George III, hold their terms at the pleasure of the king, and are paid by the Crown. In a series of seven weekly articles in *The Boston Gazette* in 1773, Adams demolishes the argument that colonial judges serve at anything but at the pleasure of the king. He also convincingly demonstrates that when the monarch previously possesses such authority in England, the judges are subservient to his will, producing injustice and oppression. Adams's recounting of English history proves that even a once-honorable character can be perverted when he is subject to the dependency of the king's pleasure—and if not perverted, the rare person of character will be subjected to cruelty for standing on principle. In his autobiography, he reflects what is at stake: The "liberties of the country would be totally lost, and every man at the mercy of a few slaves of the governor" if George III prevails.*

Adams's arguments are widely distributed and adopted by nearly all Patriots. Even the members of the Massachusetts Supreme Court appear ready to decline the Crown's pay. But then the unthinkable happens. Chief Justice Peter Oliver changes his mind and agrees to accept the king's money. The Patriots are dumbstruck and bewildered about how to react to Oliver's betrayal.

Adams acts. He understands that if no resistance is quickly offered, all the judges will follow Chief Justice Oliver and become utterly dependent on the king—and become the unjust instruments of a tyrant. He drops a bombshell. The chief justice must be impeached. This is an idea alien to the lawyers and members of the Massachusetts legislature. In fact, a judge has never been impeached in America, and it is beyond the contemplation of most everyone. Still, Adams educates his allies on the process and is most persuasive as to its necessity. The idea quickly becomes reality. Soon, Adams ghostwrites the unprecedented Articles of Impeachment. They begin by condemning the king's scheme to subvert justice by paying the judges. Then Adams trains his wrath on the chief justice himself, reasoning that by allowing the king to be his paymaster, he is a corrupt, base destroyer of impartial justice who violates the liberties of the people and supports tyranny.

Similar to impeachment in England, only the Massachusetts General Court (the elected legislature) is authorized to approve the impeachment. This is not an issue. On February 24, 1774, the Articles of Impeachment are adopted 92 to 8. The next step is a trial. If he is convicted, Oliver will be removed from office. However, because there is no Massachusetts House of Lords, his trial falls within the province of the governor and his ruling council. This poses an insurmountable obstacle. No trial is convened.

The impeachment and refusal to try the chief justice leads to immense strain across the colony. Tempers in the court system flare. Some jurors protest Oliver's appearance on the bench, and he is forced to avoid service on the bench more than once. There is no resolution in sight. However, the issue soon becomes moot. The people of Massachusetts close down the court system in August 1774 in protest of the Intolerable Acts, and their colonial courts close forever.

Article III, Section 1 of the United States Constitution hedges against any such oppression by providing judges lifetime appointments. In addition, the provision provides that they shall "receive for their Services a Compensation, which shall not be diminished during their Continuance in Office." In other words, neither Congress nor the president can slash the pay of judges with whom they disagree. The combination of lifetime tenure and a guaranteed salary insulates the judiciary from outside political pressure, making them truly independent arbitrators of justice.

By conspiring to make the judges completely dependent on himself, the king seeks to corrupt the judges, violate the rule of law, and impose an unlimited tyranny on the people. The plot strives to destroy an independent judiciary, a necessary protection of truth, justice, and unalienable rights. The colonists oppose this diabolical scheme with great vigor.*

*[H]e has erected a multitude of new offices by a self-assumed power & sent hither swarms of officers to harass our people & eat out their substance.**

Committee of Five (June 28, 1776)

# 32

## "He has erected a multitude of New Offices, and sent hither swarms of Officers to harrass our people, and eat out their substance."

- ☆ British efforts to enforce previously ignored trade restrictions and impose new taxes lead to the great proliferation of British trade and judicial officials in the colonies.
- ☆ The new officials consume American liberty and prosperity as well as explode the First Principle of limited government.

This tenth grievance sounds as if it is lifted out of the Old Testament. This is not accidental. Recall that many of the Founders are deeply religious, and even the irreligious are all well-versed in the Bible as a foundational text. Exodus 10:12–15 provides this grievance in its proper context. Before this verse, Moses demands that Pharaoh let the Israelite slaves go—and when Pharaoh refuses, God visits several plagues on Egypt. He turns the Nile into blood. There is a plague of boils, frogs swarm the kingdom, flaming hail falls from the sky, and livestock is annihilated. Yet none of this matters, for Pharaoh's heart is still hardened. Now comes the plague of locusts which

> covered the face of the whole earth, so that the land was darkened; and they did eat every herb of the land, and all the fruit of the trees which the hail had left: and there remained not any

> green thing in the trees, or in the herbs of the field, through all the land of Egypt.*

The analogy is apt. As the king and Parliament crack down on trade law violations and impose new taxes, hordes of new officials despoil the land and devour wealth.

As we have previously explored, before 1764, the empire follows a policy of salutary neglect. The colonists undertake robust and widespread smuggling operations to evade British taxes. The British mostly turn a blind eye. The colonists are almost entirely left to their own devices; so long as they generally follow the lead of the empire, they can trade as they please. Customs and trading laws are toothless.

But this policy is reversed in 1764 with Prime Minister George Grenville, who decides to vigorously enforce the trade restrictions constituting mercantilism, the regulatory scheme by which all colonial trade must occur within the empire. Under Grenville, the British Navy begins to vigorously enforce the trade laws. In essence, naval captains operate as customs officials and search and seize goods and ships with impunity. Grenville empowers the navy to function as a "revenue service," and the captain of each vessel patrolling North America is "instructed to take the customs house oath, and aid in the seizure of those engaged in the illicit trade which had been connived at for years."*

Trade violations and related criminal charges are enforced in the juryless admiralty courts that John Adams rails against in connection with the ninth grievance. Traditionally, these courts are located in England and are rarely used against colonists. To assist in stepping up enforcement, in 1764, the empire creates a vice-admiralty court in Halifax, Canada, which hears cases from across North America. In 1768, even more vice-admiralty courts are established in Boston, Charleston, and Philadelphia. Americans view these courts' sole purpose as one to eat away at colonial wealth and resources.

The locusts are not limited to the seas. As we will explore in greater detail in connection with the seventeenth grievance, the Stamp Act in 1765 imposes new taxes that are paid through the purchase of royal stamps from stamp officials posted throughout the colonies. At the time the Stamp Act is enacted, there is no administrative bureaucracy to enforce it. Mimicking Moses, Great Britain calls forth a continental-wide taxing administration in America; the winds bring in rolls of new officials to enforce tax laws by forcing the people to pay their stamps—and criminalizing those who avoid it.

This is no small burden. The British plan for stamp distributors to be housed in every port and nearly every town of any significant size. Sure enough, like locusts, many tax agents rapidly appear throughout the colonies. But a funny thing happens on the way to the stamp office. Most of the Stamp Act officials are quickly frightened away by massive and vigorous protests by the colonists. The empire loses control of the situation. The Stamp Act is soon repealed, and the locusts are held at bay.

Still, the die is cast: With new taxes come new British officials leeching off America. With the passage of the Townshend Acts, the pattern repeats. Learning absolutely nothing, London appoints new tax commissioners, who, in turn, possess the authority to appoint an infinite number of deputies to enforce the new tax regime. Although their salaries are paid out of the collections of the new taxes, this only creates the perverse incentive for tax officials to collect as much as humanly possible, regardless of their legality. These tax officials are imbued with broad authority to search and seize colonial ships and warehouses. Limited government is replaced with imperial tyranny.

The British counter that these complaints about the vice-admiralty courts, the crackdown on smuggling, and new tax collectors are petulant and exaggerated. Defending smuggling and tax evasion is hardly a crisis of biblical proportions. Loyalist Governor Thomas Hutchinson and other Loyalists scoff at the colonists, especially since most of the enforcement authorities are paid out of the funds they collect—or, if there is a shortfall—from London.

The British are unpersuasive. The Americans hold firm to a diametrically opposed perspective. In the end, British efforts to enforce previously defunct trade restrictions and impose new taxes leads to the great proliferation of British officials on the ground in North America—seen as the destroyers of American liberty and prosperity.

The federal Constitution provides strong protection against the locusts. Article I vests all legislative authority in Congress, meaning that it has the sole authority to establish federal offices not otherwise specified in the Constitution. Article I, Section 8 also strictly enumerates and limits the powers of the federal government. Under Article II, Section 2, the president has the authority to appoint "Ambassadors, other public Ministers and Consuls, Judges of the supreme Court, and all other Officers of the United States, whose Appointments are not herein otherwise provided for, and which shall be established by Law," but such appointments require approval of the Senate. Congress may also "by Law vest the Appointment of such inferior Officers, as they think proper, in the President alone, in the Courts of Law, or in the Heads of Departments." In short, the president's appointment power is entirely dependent on Congress. And Congress's authority is strongly prescribed by the Constitution. No locusts will eat out the substance of the people—at least not without congressional approval. Abuses can be rectified at the ballot box.

The massive expansion of the British government after 1763 obliterates the First Principle of limited government. Resistance is the only barrier between the colonies and biblical disaster.*

*That in order to enforce the arbitrary measures before complained of, his majesty has from time to time sent among us large bodies of armed forces, not made up of the people here, not raised by the authority of our laws: Did his majesty possess such a right as this, it might swallow up all our other rights whenever he should think proper. But his majesty has no right to land a single armed man on our shores, and those whom he sends here are liable to our laws made for the suppression and punishment of riots, routs, and unlawful assemblies; or are hostile bodies, invading us in defiance of law.**

Thomas Jefferson (1774)

# 33

## "He has kept among us, in times of peace, Standing Armies without the Consent of our legislatures."

☆ To enforce the empire's oppressive policies, the king and Parliament station troops in the colonies without the approval of the colonial legislatures.

☆ The deployment of these troops severs the Social Compact, subjects the colonists to repression, and eviscerates limited government.

Why this eleventh grievance is even an issue is difficult to fathom for most modern readers. Almost 250 years after the Declaration, a standing army is simply an accepted part of everyday life. As of the publication date of this work (2026), there are approximately two million active and reserve American military service personnel.* Since the Japanese sneak attack on Pearl Harbor on December 7, 1941, we are in an almost-constant state of war—punctuated with a few fleeting periods of peace. A belligerent Communist China, nuclear-armed North Korea, militant Russia,* and hostile Iran are all rising threats. Most Americans likely think we absolutely need a standing army. This grievance in the Declaration may seem irrelevant.

To really understand it, we must once again review English history. From 1642 to 1651, the realm is torn apart by the English Civil War, which pit the forces of the elected, representative Parliament (the "Parliamentarians") against the absolutist forces of the hereditary King Charles I (the "Royalists"). At the beginning, the battling armies are raised only temporarily. This is consistent with long-standing British practice—with the Royal Navy at the ready, standing armies are only raised temporarily in the face of invasion or civil war.

The Parliamentarian forces have an epiphany: with a professional, standing army, they will prevail. In 1645, at the urging of General Oliver Cromwell, the Parliamentarians create the New Model Army. Because it is a professional and permanent fighting force, this army will be much better trained and equipped than temporary forces. Plus, it will stand at the ready to fight anytime and anywhere, at Parliament's command. Led by Cromwell, the New Model Army defeats the Royalist forces and takes control. King Charles I is imprisoned and beheaded. Cromwell purges the Parliament of his enemies.

Unsatisfied, Cromwell militarily subdues all of England, Scotland, Ireland, Portugal, and the Netherlands. Flush with these successes, Parliament considers disbanding Cromwell's army. This is not warmly received and is successfully resisted. Cromwell is named "Lord Protector" and effectively rules Great Britain as a military dictator for several years. Meanwhile, Parliament is dissolved, purged, and reconstituted in various ways, but always subservient to Cromwell and his military forces. When Cromwell dies in office, the army attempts to perpetuate the dictatorship under Cromwell's son, Richard. The younger Cromwell convenes a new Parliament, but Parliament is disagreeable to the military. Predictably, Richard dissolves the body. But then, circumstances turn once again, and the military deposes Richard. After many more twists and turns, the son of the executed Charles I takes power and restores the monarchy. King Charles I is dead. Long live the king—Charles II.

Charles II knows that the key to defeating his enemies and ruling unencumbered is to gather a standing army loyal to him. He slowly builds his own standing army. Soon enough, Charles II becomes a tyrant. Worse, the people are complacent about the loss of their liberties. John Trenchard, an English journalist who is wildly popular with the Founding Generation, laments, "Towards the latter end of this king's reign, the nation had so entirely lost all sense of liberty, that they grew fond of their chains."*

A trick of fate comes to the rescue: Charles II dies. His Catholic brother, James II, ascends to the throne. As we have learned, this leads to the Glorious Revolution, by which the restored Parliament invites Prince William III of Orange and his wife Mary to invade England and depose King James II. William and Mary accept the offer and invade in 1688. King James II flees, tossing the great seal of England into the River Thames. William and Mary became joint rulers of England.

In exchange for their crowns, William and Mary pledge to several conditions, including agreeing to the Bill of Rights of 1689. It includes a provision "[t]hat the raising or keeping a standing army within the kingdom in time of peace, unless it be with consent of Parliament, is against law."* The English codify this policy in the Mutiny Act of 1689, so named because it is the first act to punish mutiny and desertions of military forces. Important for our purposes, the Mutiny Act also provides that no standing army can be approved for longer than a single year. Parliament must enact a new Mutiny Act every year to approve the number and types of military forces in the realm.

The Founding Fathers agree that this prohibition against standing armies without the consent of the legislature is an essential protection for unalienable rights, maintaining the Social Compact, and ensuring a limited government. It is a cornerstone of English liberty. James Madison, father of the United States Constitution, explains on the floor of the Constitutional Convention that

> [a] standing military force, with an overgrown executive will not long be safe companions to liberty. The means of defense against foreign danger, have been always the instruments of tyranny at home. Among the Romans it was a standing maxim to excite a war, whenever a revolt was apprehended. Throughout all Europe, the armies kept up under the pretext of defending, have enslaved the people.*

Elbridge Gerry is a signer of the Declaration of Independence, framer of the Bill of Rights, and vice president under James Madison. Gerry sums up the Founders' proposition exceedingly well: "[A] standing army, [is] the bane of liberty."*

This sentiment is widespread in the colonies. In 1772, Dr. Joseph Warren rages that a standing army is "ever to be dreaded as the ready engines of tyranny and oppression."* In 1776, leading Son of Liberty Samuel Adams writes to Massachusetts political leader James Warren that a standing army threatens liberty. Professional soldiers can easily be made into ready instruments of tyranny to crush the people. This is so because

> [s]oldiers are apt to consider themselves as a body distinct from the rest of the citizens. They have their arms always in their hands. Their rules and their discipline is severe. They soon become attached to their officers and disposed to yield implicit obedience to their commands. Such a power should be watched with a jealous eye.*

As Englishmen, the Founders believe that, in accordance with the Bill of Rights 1689 and the Mutiny Acts, no standing armies may lawfully be stationed on colonial soil without the annual approval of the colonial assemblies. Yet, following the conclusion of the French and Indian War in 1763, British troops remain deployed throughout North America. The empire's future undersecretary of the American Department, William Knox, admits as early as 1763 that stationing a large body of troops in America is "necessary for securing the dependence of the colonies on Great Britain."* There is no question about the loyalties of the British standing army: They are the enemy of the people and colonial liberties.

In 1765, English troops arrive in New York; the colony is most chagrined about this state of affairs. New York is intended to be the central command for British America's regular troops, and yet, the New Yorkers refuse to give them barracks. A confrontation between the colonial legislature and the empire ensues, but New York eventually relents.

The passage of the Townshend Acts in 1768 is the pivot point of the eleventh grievance. Boston becomes the center of robust protests, and the empire responds by landing two regiments of redcoats in Massachusetts. Four thousand imperial soldiers occupy Boston to suppress the rights of the Patriots. After this, a standing army, not approved by the colonies, is a fixture on the continent—and a hated symbol and instrumentality of British oppression.

Mercy Otis Warren writes the first real history of the American Revolution. She plumbs primary sources, including many firsthand accounts and eyewitness interviews. In her groundbreaking work, she explains the importance of this 1768 decision:

> [T]he troops arrived from Halifax. This was indeed a painful era. The American [Revolutionary] War may be dated from the hostile parade of this day; a day which marks with infamy the councils of Britain. At this period, the inhabitants of the colonies almost universally breathed an unshaken loyalty to the king of England, and the strongest attachment to a country whence they derived their origin. Thus was the astonishment of the whole province excited, when to the grief and consternation of the town of Boston several regiments were landed, and marched forward in hand through the principal streets of their city, then in profound peace.*

Before the French and Indian War, owing to the policy of salutary neglect, the colonists govern themselves with minimal intrusion from the British Isles. Once troops land in Boston, the ground rules are fundamentally altered. The British assert their rule by military force. Every other grievance the Founding Fathers detail in the Declaration is compounded by the threat of a standing army to enforce British oppression. They intend to stamp out American liberties with troops. The colonial legislatures are ignored—George III and Parliament sever the Social Compact. The First Principles of limited government and protecting unalienable rights are crushed underfoot of the standing army.

Thomas Jefferson writes that because George III has no authority to send standing armies to America, these troops are illegally stationed in the colonies and subject to colonial laws against unlawful assemblies—and should even be considered foreign invaders. To exacerbate this affront, George III later sends foreign troops from Hanover. As we have reviewed, the German province of Hanover is the birthplace of King George III's great-grandfather, King George I. Although King George I resorts to such troops, he must first obtain Parliament's permission. Jefferson explains that this precedent applies to the entire empire, even now. The British must ask the colonial legislatures to accept the foreign troops. Only if a colony agrees may a monarch station troops in the colony, and no colonies have given their assent. Quite the opposite—the foreign mercenaries coming to America are the king's troops alone, loyal to him and not the colonies. They are puppets of the king meant to crush American liberties.

At the conclusion of their meeting, the First Continental Congress issues the Declaration and Resolves, demanding that Great Britain retract its American oppressions. Much of the Declaration and Resolves echoes Jefferson's *A Summary View of the Rights of British America*. Issued on October 14, 1774, the Declaration and Resolves unequivocally declares "[t]hat the keeping a standing army in these colonies, in times of peace, without the consent of the legislature of that colony in which such army is kept, is against the law."* The British absolutely ignore it.

> Article I, Section 8 of the United States Constitution directly addresses the issue of standing armies by providing that "no Appropriation of Money" for establishing and maintaining an army "shall be for a longer Term than two Years." There will be no roaming, free standing permanent armies in America, at least not without the approval of Congress.

The colonies are united in opposing the standing armies authorized only by the king and Parliament. Without a colonial legislature's consent, the standing armies completely break the Social Compact. They are totally unaccountable to the elected representatives of the people. Furthermore, such standing armies subvert limited government and the unalienable rights of the people. Only revolution can save the people from military tyranny.*

*To render these proceedings still more criminal against our laws, instead of subjecting the military to the civil powers, his majesty has expressly made the civil subordinate to the military. But can his majesty thus put down all law under his feet? Can he erect a power superior to that which erected himself? He has done it indeed by force; but let him remember that force cannot give right.**

Thomas Jefferson (1774)

# 34

## "He has affected to render the Military independent of and superior to the Civil power."

- ☆ George III replaces the civilian governor of Massachusetts with an all-powerful military general intent on crushing colonial resistance.

- ☆ Toppling civilian control with martial law smashes the Social Compact, destroys unlimited government, and violates unalienable rights.

The twelfth grievance builds on the eleventh. It arises out of one of the several repressive acts that Parliament passes in reaction to the Boston Tea Party. On December 16, 1773, the Sons of Liberty lead Bostonians disguised as Mohawk Native Americans to board three cargo ships in the Boston Harbor and toss precious tea into its depths. They do so because the cargo has been taxed by Parliament without the representation of the colonists.

This protest enrages the British leadership, and it lowers the hammer on Boston through a set of new statutes passed by Parliament—which the colonists dub the Intolerable Acts, and the British label the Coercive Acts. One such act, the Massachusetts Government Act, is passed on May 20, 1774; it totally upends the government in Massachusetts. Perhaps its most egregious feature is that it revokes the existing 1691 colonial charter and empowers the king to appoint the governor.

While visiting with King George III in London, British General Thomas Gage, commander in chief of British troops in North America since 1763, reports that if things do not change, the colonies "will be lions, while we are lambs." But if the empire will "take the resolute part," the colonies "will undoubtedly prove meek."

He estimates that "four regiments [...] sent to Boston are sufficient to prevent any disturbance."* Convinced, the king appoints English-born General Gage to command the colony, deposing the civilian native Massachusetts Governor Thomas Hutchinson.

General Gage relishes the opportunity to put down the inklings of a revolt in Boston and eagerly deploys troops to suppress colonial dissent. Redcoats patrol Boston Common and aggressively crack down on Bostonian Patriots. As we just learned from the eleventh grievance, in great measure, the reality of liberty hinges on the practical fact that civilian authorities control the military. But here, the English military is now independent of and superior to civil Massachusetts authorities. In essence, General Gage is the supreme leader in Massachusetts, combining military command and civil government—the very subversion of freedom.

General Gage enacts a series of repressive actions, smothering freedom. He criminalizes with the most severe punishment the basic exercise of the rights of assembly and association, as well as runs roughshod over due process protections. The House of Burgesses forcefully concludes that Gage is acting as a "*despotic viceroy* [italics in original]" who considers himself "bound by *no law* [italics in original], nor regard the constitutional rights of his majesty's subjects, whenever they interfere with the plan he has formed for oppressing the good people of the Massachusetts-Bay." Gage's despotism justifies colonial "RESISTANCE and REPRISAL [emphasis in original]."*

The burgesses' reasoning is embraced by the First Continental Congress. Its Declaration and Resolves, adopted in 1774, specifically condemn the Massachusetts Government Act as an egregious infringement "of the rights of the colonists" and that its repeal "is essentially necessary, in order to restore harmony between Great-Britain and the American colonies."* In a parallel fashion, the list of grievances in the Second Continental Congress's Declaration of the Causes and Necessity of Taking Up Arms includes "altering fundamentally the form of government established by the charter, and secured by acts of its own legislature solemnly confirmed by the crown."*

After the First Continental Congress's Declaration and Resolves, but before the Second Continental Congress's Declaration of the Causes and Necessity of Taking Up Arms, on April 19, 1775, the first shots of the American Revolution are fired at Lexington and Concord. In reaction, on June 12, 1775, Governor Gage publishes a proclamation, offering a general amnesty to anyone who took up arms at Lexington and Concord, "excepting only from the benefit of such pardon, *Samuel Adams,* and *John Hancock* [italics in original], whose offenses are too flagitious a nature to admit of any consideration than that of condign [deserved] punishment." After all, the skirmishes at Lexington and Concord erupt because imperial redcoats are sent on a secret mission to arrest Hancock and Adams. Under no circumstances will Gage offer those treasonous vipers mercy. Gage also proclaims that anyone who does not take advantage of the amnesty and anyone who takes up arms against the British in the future will be unequivocally declared "rebels and traitors, and as such to be treated." This condemnation not only includes those who actually take up arms, but all their "adherents, associates, and abettors." Furthermore, he orders all persons to "resist, encounter and subdue the rebels and traitors." As if there was any doubt, the proclamation declares martial law throughout Massachusetts.*

The United States Constitution directly addresses this grievance in several ways. It provides for civilian control of the government elected by the people. The House of Representatives, Senate, president, and judges are independent of the military. The civilian government controls the military, not the other way around. Under Article II, Section 2, the elected president (as opposed to a hereditary monarch) is the commander in chief of the armed forces. Article I, Section 8 places the authority to establish, regulate, and organize the armed forces in Congress. The critical power to declare war is also vested solely in Congress. In addition, Congress possesses the authority "for calling forth the Militia to execute the Laws of the Union, suppress Insurrections and repel Invasions" and

> for organizing, arming, and disciplining, the Militia, and for governing such Part of them as may be employed in the Service of the United States, reserving to the States respectively, the Appointment of the Officers, and the Authority of training the Militia according to the discipline prescribed by Congress.

By placing the organization of the military and militia under the control of Congress and the president, the Constitution ensures civilian control of the armed forces, and the military serves the people.

In addition, as a keystone of federalism, federal authorities and State governmental authorities are completely independent. State governors, legislatures, and judiciaries may not be suspended, terminated, chosen, or replaced by the federal governement.

In contemporary terms, imagine that in reaction to riots in Phoenix, the president fires Arizona's governor and replaces her with a US Army general from

Washington, D.C., who then sends in an army corps to occupy the city and impose martial law. Imagine further that the general declares all rioters and their friends treasonous and orders the rest of the city to take them down. Unthinkable today. Great Britain's subordination of the civilian government to the military smashes the Social Compact, destroys unlimited government, and violates unalienable rights. The military is the servant of the people, not the other way around. Martial law is untenable and justifies revolution.*

*[T]hat fatal edict* [...] *proclaims a power to frame laws for us in all cases whatsoever, thereby entailing the endless and numberless curses of slavery upon us, our heirs and their heirs forever.**

Suffolk Resolves (September 9, 1774)

# 35

## "He has combined with others to subject us to a jurisdiction foreign to our constitution, and unacknowledged by our laws; giving his Assent to their Acts of pretended Legislation:"

☆ Because the Social Compact requires representation of the governed in the legislature, and the colonists do not vote for members of Parliament, it has no legal authority over the colonists.

☆ By pretending that Parliament legislates for the colonies, George III and Parliament violate the rule of law, ravage the Social Compact, destroy limited government, abolish equality, and infringe the unalienable rights of the people.

In contrast to previous grievances, the thirteenth may seem vague. It awkwardly refers to George III's working with "others" and an unnamed "jurisdiction." This critique is very sly—it never mentions those who conspire with the king. Yet even on cursory reflection, it clearly addresses Parliament and its lawmaking over the colonies.*

This grievance also reads like a prefatory or introductory phrase to another set of grievances. In truth, it is. But it is also much more. In fact, it is the key grievance in the entire Declaration. It addresses a fundamental question: *Who* will govern Americans—Parliament or the American People represented in their American legislatures? The grievance answers its own question: Parliament has no authority to legislate for the colonists. The Declaration, as a whole, addresses the consequence of the answer: independence.

As we have explored, decades-long salutary neglect by Parliament and the monarchy generally allows the colonies to govern themselves. If we put aside global wars and trade policy, the governance of each colony is based *in* the colonies. As such, each colony has an elected legislative assembly to enact laws appropriate for its circumstances. If the colonists are unsatisfied with their lawmakers, they can vote them out of office. The colonists become accustomed to and relish self-rule. For the colonists, this is not just tradition but a matter of constitutional law. The colonists draw on the Lockean idea of the Social Compact—and firmly believe that to be just, any legislation must be enacted by the elected representatives of the people. Not a single member of Parliament is elected from the colonies. As such, only the respective colonial legislature possesses the legitimate authority to enact legislation to govern its people.

The empire jeers. To make Parliament's position exceedingly clear, the same day Parliament rescinds the Stamp Act (March 18, 1766), it enacts the Declaratory Act. Many Americans perceive the Declaratory Act as a symbolic measure by the empire to save face and expect it will be insignificant.* However, the British are deadly serious. Parliament understands that with the repeal of the Stamp Act, the colonists will likely believe that they are free to disobey Parliament's laws. Parliament sets the record straight. With the Declaratory Act, it reestablishes the basic premise of its own unquestionable and intrinsic supremacy. The Declaratory Act provides that Parliament has full authority to "bind the colonies and people of *America* [italics in original], subjects of the crown of *Great Britain* [italics in original], in all cases whatsoever" and any contrary colonial enactments are "utterly null and void."* The Declaratory Act asserts parliamentary supremacy over the colonists "in all cases whatsoever." This is no longer about taxation. It is about *everything*. Self-government in the colonies is dead.

The British contest the baseline argument that the colonists must be represented in Parliament in order for legislation to be binding. Furthermore, the empire has no intention of adding legislators from the colonies. Instead, it claims that the colonists are *virtually* represented in Parliament. Parliament lectures that although none of the colonists actually vote for anyone who serves in Parliament, the colonies are represented in Parliament. The English highlight that important constituencies of the British Isles also have no elected representatives. Large cities like Manchester, Birmingham, and Sheffield have no members in Parliament. If such cities in the heart of England need no parliamentarians, neither do the colonies. Prime Minister George Grenville points out that "[n]ot a twentieth part of the people are actually represented."*

This is an impossible position for the colonists to accept. James Otis is a leading colonial opponent of British tyranny in the 1760s. As an excellent lawyer, he rallies opposition to repression, including the dreaded writs of assistance. After being struck in the head by a customs official, his already precarious mental health turns into insanity (with pockets of lucidness). His life ends when he is struck by lightning—which, remarkably enough, is exactly how he wishes to die. His sister is the renowned historian, Mercy Otis Warren. In 1765, James Otis brilliantly responds to the theory of virtual representation, explaining that

> [r]ight reason and the spirit of a free constitution require that the representation of the whole people should be as equal as possible. [...]
>
> No good reason however can be given in any country why every man of a sound mind should not have his vote in the election of a representative. If a man has but little property to protect and defend, yet his life and liberty are things of some importance.*

That Parliament excludes major English cities and large segments of the empire's population from actual representation does not justify virtual representation of the colonies. On the contrary, it only reveals that Parliament must be reformed. Otis vividly demonstrates that virtual representation is a farce:

> It may perhaps sound strange to some, but it is my most humble opinion as good *law* and as good *sense* too, to affirm that all the plebeians of Great-Britain are in fact or virtually represented in the assembly of the [Native American tribe of] Tuskarora's, as all the colonists are in fact or virtually represented in the honorable House of Commons of Great-Britain. [Italics are in the original.]*

Massachusetts colonial agent Arthur Lee cuts to the chase with a stinging rebuke: "Our *privileges* are all *virtual*, our sufferings are *real*. [Italics are in the original.]"* To illustrate the ridiculous nature of the British view, Lee offers an example of a member of the House of Commons in Greenwich, England, who is supposedly virtually representing those in America:

> When we are to be taxed, we are in *America* [...] but when we are *to choose our representatives*, our trustees, who are bound thereby in duty and interest to treat us with the same justice and

> tenderness, with which they would treat themselves, then, my countrymen, we are unhappily in the *manor* of Greenwich [Palace (a pleasure palace used by British Kings and Queens)]. Thus, I *John Thomas,* of the county of *Richmond,* in *Virginia,* freeholder [a property owner and voter], do vote without knowing it, for a burgess in the manor of *Greenwich,* in *England;* which manor I never saw, nor indeed ever hear of before, to lay a duty upon the glass I want to mend my windows in my tenement [my house], on my freehold [freely owned property], in *Richmond* county, *Virginia.* This my countrymen, would, in the days of superstition, have been called witchcraft. [Italics are in the original.]*

The preposterous nature of Parliament's position is self-evident. Virtual representation is a mockery of representative government.

In 1772, Dr. Joseph Warren explains that virtual representation destroys the keystone to British liberty:

> [I]t is undeniably true, that the greatest and most important right of a British subject is, that *he shall be governed by no laws but those to which he either in person or by his representative has given his consent:* And this I will venture to assert, is the grand basis of British freedom; it is interwoven with the constitution; and whenever this is lost, the constitution must be destroyed. [Italics in the original.]*

In 1774, Thomas Jefferson attacks virtual representation in *A Summary View of the Rights of British America*. He begins by condemning a series of acts passed by Parliament as null and void and implores the king to intervene to protect colonial rights. Jefferson writes this plea to George III in 1774; Congress has not yet taken the step to declare the king the enemy. Here, Jefferson is hoping that George III will intervene on behalf of the colonies and instruct Parliament that it has no power over the colonies and to cease its efforts to exercise such power.

Alas, this is a laughable proposition to George III. He and Parliament are working hand in glove to pass the very acts of pretended legislation that the colonies are chafing under. Former Governor Thomas Hutchinson explains that this argument flies in the face of the law and history. For a century, Parliament passes laws regulating the colonies, and now, all of a sudden, everything Parliament does is pretend legislation? Utter nonsense.

Virtual representation receives a full-throttled savaging in *A Summary View of the Rights of British America*. First, under the laws of Nature, when a people emigrate from a homeland and establish a new government, they are no longer beholden to their old homeland's government. The Saxons settle the British Isles, and their old rulers in Saxony no longer govern those who live in England. This is more so in America.

Second, although the British provide vital assistance during the French and Indian War, this is no different from helping other allies like Portugal. It does not alter the fundamental relationship between the colonies and Parliament any more than giving foreign assistance to Portugal converts that independent country into the vassals of the king of Great Britain.

Third, if Americans accept that Parliament rules over them, "[I]nstead of being a free people, as we have hitherto supposed, and mean to continue ourselves, we should suddenly be found the slaves, not of one, but of 160,000 tyrants," those being the voters of Great Britain.*

When the First Continental Congress passes its Declaration and Resolves, it deploys very blunt language to eliminate any doubt of Congress's position

> [t]hat the foundation of English liberty, and of all free government, is a right in the people to participate in their legislative council: and as the English colonists are not represented, and from their local and other circumstances, cannot properly be represented in the British parliament, they are entitled to a free and exclusive power of legislation in their several provincial legislatures, where their right of representation can alone be preserved, in all cases of taxation and internal polity.*

But the reality is that at times the colonies act as if they *are* subject to Parliament's authority—which is Hutchinson's point. Congress is not blind to history and tradition. But instead of bowing to it, Congress explains that prior colonial compliance with parliamentary acts is a matter of voluntary adherence, not a required constitutional mandate. The colonies are never required to abide by Parliament's mercantilism and the regulatory regime. Rather, colonists in the past do so because of the mutual advantages it affords everyone involved. This is akin to an arrangement of goodwill between trading partners. But that is quite a different proposition than Parliament's possessing unfettered power to impose its will on the colonists without their consent.

The colonists also draw upon rich English history in their phrasing of the grievance. The Bill of Rights 1689, enacted by Parliament in the wake of the Glorious Revolution, specifically condemns the deposed King James II for exercising "the *pretended power* of suspending of laws, or the execution of laws [...] without consent of Parliament" and declares that "the *pretended power* of dispensing with laws, or the execution of laws, by regal authority, as has been assumed and expertise of late, is illegal."* Of course, this phraseology is well known to the colonists, the king, Parliament, and the British People—it is a key part of their liberty and the freedoms enjoyed by British subjects.* The Declaration taps into this wellspring of constitutional law.

The Constitution dispels any pretended legislation by ensuring a representative form of government. All legislation, executive action, and judicial rulings flow from the duly authorized agents of the people. Under Article I, Section 1, all legislative power is vested in Congress. Congress is composed of two chambers—the House of Representatives and Senate. Article I, Section 2 provides that "The House of Representatives shall be composed of Members chosen every second Year by the People of the several States, and the Electors in each State shall have the Qualifications requisite for Electors of the most numerous Branch of the State Legislature." In other words, the people elect the members of the House of Representatives roughly based on population. Under the original Constitution, Article I, Section 3 provides that the Senate was composed of two members from each State, elected by the State legislatures (in other words, the duly elected representatives of the people). With the Seventeenth Amendment, Senators are directly elected by the people of each respective State. Pursuant to Article II, Section 1 (and many amendments thereto), the president and vice president are elected via electors in a manner chosen by each State legislature. Today, every State provides that the people directly vote for the electors. Although judges do not stand for election in the federal system, pursuant to Article II, Section II, they are nominated by the elected President and approved by the elected Senate. All major executive officers are appointed directly by the president with the consent of the Senate, and inferior officers are appointed by the president. As the Preamble reflects, the Constitution ensures that the federal government derives its authority from "We the People."

The thirteenth grievance is the crux of the American Revolution—all the dangers of infringing on the First Principles are present. There is no rule of law, just the raw rule of Parliament. There is no Social Compact, just the imposition of parliamentary authority devoid of any representation of the American People.

There are no unalienable rights, just Parliament's power to violate them. There is no equality, just the repression of Americans. There is no limited government, just the king's and Parliament's unfettered authority to lord over the colonists in all cases whatsoever.*

*The sun is not about to stand still or go out, nor the rivers to dry up because there was a mob in Boston on the 5th of March that attacked a party of soldiers* [provoking the Boston Massacre].—*Such things are not new in the world, nor in the British dominions, though they are comparatively, rarities and novelties in this town. [I]ndeed, from the nature of things, soldiers quartered in a populous town, will always occasion two mobs, where they prevent one.—They are wretched conservators of the peace!**

John Adams (December 4, 1770)

# 36

## "For Quartering large bodies of armed troops among us:"

- ☆ The forced quartering of troops leads to violent clashes between the people and redcoats, causing more mischief than it solves.
- ☆ Quartering troops without consent subverts the Social Compact, violates the unalienable rights of the people, and guts limited government.

The fourteenth grievance* addresses the housing, feeding, and other provisioning of British soldiers (called "quartering") in the colonies. This is perhaps the second-best-known grievance of the Declaration. Today, there seems to be a general belief among Americans that redcoats barged into people's homes, evicted elderly residents, forced their way into citizens' beds, and devoured the colonists' food like locusts. But like just about everything else you learned about the American Revolution, this is more myth than reality.

To understand why the quartering of troops is an affront to the colonists, we must delve into the history of the quartering of troops in England. As we explored in the eleventh grievance, under the English Bill of Rights 1689 and the various Mutiny Acts, there is no standing army in England unless Parliament approves one each year. In addition, the Bill of Rights 1689 protects the right of the British People to be free from the burden of quartering of troops without the consent of the homeowner.

Up until 1765, the colonies need not quarter troops. Under the circumstances, this makes perfect sense; the colonies raise their own militias to keep the peace and defend their people. The colonies are on the frontier of the empire, and the policy of salutary neglect generally leaves the colonies to their own devices.

But like so much more, this attitude changes with the end of the French and Indian War. The British are now enthusiastically behind basing a large corps of soldiers in the colonies. First, the British face a serious quandary: What to do with the thousands of troops presently stationed in North America now that they have won the French and Indian War? During the war, the colonies generally provided for the needs of the soldiers, including food and shelter. The British treasury is already saddled with an enormous war debt. The British prefer to avoid paying for transporting soldiers home, as well as their quartering.

Second, the British determine to halt the expansion of the colonies to the West. As addressed in connection with the third grievance (halting westward expansion of counties) as well as the seventh grievance (hindering immigration and migration westward), Parliament passes the Proclamation of 1763, barring the colonies from expanding beyond the Proclamation Line, roughly aligned with the eastern edge of the Appalachian Mountains. To enforce the Proclamation Line, the British begin to erect a series of forts along the border. These forts will be fed by an influx of troops who will need to pass back and forth through the colonies.

Third, the British Empire dramatically increases in size with the defeat of France in the Seven Years' War. It gains thousands of miles of new territory in Canada (Quebec and its environs) and the land between the Appalachian Mountains and the Mississippi River. New forces are required to maintain order and security from Native American and European powers.

Fourth, most cutting to the colonists, the British require troops to enforce their repression of the colonists. Imperial policies are increasingly deeply unpopular and meeting stiffening resistance. The British crackdown on the colonists will be greatly facilitated by redcoats on the ground.

In 1765, the British determine that thousands of imperial troops need to be stationed in the colonies—all of whom now must be housed and fed. The British commander in chief in North America, General Thomas Gage, urges Parliament to pass a law specifically requiring the colonies to quarter imperial troops. Parliament agrees, and on March 24, 1765, it enacts the Quartering Act of 1765. It provides that if public houses and barracks are unavailable, redcoats will be lodged in "uninhabited houses, outhouses, barns, or other buildings" as necessary.* Notice there is *no* authorization for soldiers to live in *occupied* homes. Colonial governments are required to pay for food, shelter, bedding, cooking utensils, firewood, salt, vinegar, beer, cider, and candles. Soldiers, however, may be punished if they attempt to live in places other than where authorized (such as a common occupied home).

Unsurprisingly, the colonists have a view diametrically opposed to that held by Parliament. The Americans view the Quartering Act of 1765 as an attempt to force the colonists to pay for a standing army that they reject. Furthermore,

Samuel Adams notes that the act is basically just as much a tax on the colonies as the Stamp Act. After all, it forces the colonists to absorb the cost of quartering the troops. Direct tax or not, it costs the colonists dearly. The Quartering Act of 1765 is intensely unpopular.

No matter. In 1766, the British sail 1,500 imperial troops to New York City, the British headquarters for the colonies. The New York General Assembly balks, and the redcoats are unable to disembark from their ships. A small riot breaks out on the streets of New York City. As we learned in connection with the fifth grievance (dissolution of legislative assemblies), enraged Parliament votes to close down the New York General Assembly to force New York to accept the quartering of the troops. The assembly reluctantly capitulates.

Boston now becomes a focus of quartering. As we discussed in connection with the eleventh grievance (standing armies), when Boston protests the Townshend Acts in 1767, the British deploy more than a thousand Irish troops to occupy the city. Most arrive in Boston Harbor on September 18, 1768. When the troops arrive, they have no living accommodations. Boston is not eager to lend a helping hand. The local government refuses to allow the troops to quarter in the major portions of Boston. They kindly suggest to the army that they quarter in Castle William—about three miles away from the population center of the city. This suggestion is not warmly received. The British commander plans for at least half of his troops to have an imposing presence in the city. When the local government refuses to allow the troops to be housed near the city center, the British commander orders one regiment to march through the city and camp on Boston Common. Another regiment occupies Faneuil Hall, a famous public meeting hall in the heart of Boston. Other redcoats take over the city's governmental offices. The Bostonians are unmoved—they continue to refuse quarters.

On October 27, 1768, redcoats occupy other commercial buildings that the military commander rents. The redcoats will not leave, and tensions only continue to increase between the soldiers and the common folks of Boston who, egged on by the Sons of Liberty, are increasingly hostile. This situation explodes on March 5, 1770, at the Boston Massacre, in which imperial soldiers shoot dead five colonists and injure several more. At the resulting murder trial of the British soldiers, John Adams poetically remarks for the defense that the quartering of troops causes at least twice as much mischief as the troops themselves prevent—such troops are "wretched conservators of the peace!"* Adams shifts at least some of the blame from the soldiers on the ground to London for ordering them to be quartered among a hostile population. Without quartered troops in Boston, there is no massacre. Apart from the trial, the city is seething with resentment over the massacre. John Adams's cousin, Samuel Adams, confronts Governor Thomas Hutchinson and demands that the troops evacuate the city. Intimidated, Hutchinson blinks, and the troops depart. The Quartering Act of 1765 is allowed to quietly expire later that year. The issue recedes into the background.

But not for long. One of the Intolerable Acts passed by Parliament in the aftermath of the Boston Tea Party is the Quartering Act of 1774, which applies to all the colonies. The act basically resurrects the Quartering Act of 1765, requiring troops be quartered in "uninhabited houses, out-houses, barns, or other buildings" if no barracks are available.* Although many history books and articles (including recently published works) report that this act changed prior law by allowing the quartering of troops in occupied homes, this is a myth.*

However, there is one major oppressive change from prior legislation. Historically, the local legislative assembly is directed to procure the various buildings used to quarter troops. The Quartering Act of 1774 circumvents the colonial legislatures and invests the colonial governors with the authority to secure quarters. If the colony does not secure lodging within twenty-four hours after the commander in chief of British forces in North America demands them, the governor has the absolute power to quarter the troops. With just a couple of exceptions, governors are loyal to the Crown, while the legislative assemblies are uniformly hostile to the empire. The oppressive nature of the act is self-evident. Additionally, in Massachusetts, the colonial assembly is abolished by another Intolerable Act, the Massachusetts Government Act. The governor (who, as we learned in the twelfth grievance, is also the general commanding the occupying troops) has the sole authority to assign quarters. Seven hundred redcoats occupy Boston, supported by a British fleet armed with cannons. Bostonians refuse to quarter the soldiers, and the events of 1768 start to repeat themselves.

Meanwhile, exacerbating the fears of a standing army, Parliament votes to raise another ten thousand men for the American theater, including Boston, New York, Philadelphia, Charleston, and other seaports.

Needless to say, supporting a standing army that is occupying their land to crush their liberties is too much for the Patriots. It is another vital grievance against the empire highlighted in the Declaration and Resolves of the First Continental Congress in 1774. John Adams captures the essence of the grievance quite succinctly: "the quartering troops [...] here has proved the occasion of many evils."*

The Third Amendment of the United States Constitution provides that "No Soldier shall, in time of peace be quartered in any house, without the consent of the Owner, nor in time of war, but in a manner to be prescribed by law." This provision is sacrosanct and has never been violated.

The forced quartering of troops causes bloody conflict between the people and imperial troops. By forcing quartering without the consent of colonial legislatures, Great Britain subverts the Social Compact. By forcibly quartering troops on private property without their consent, it violates the unalienable rights of the people. The quartering regime guts limited government. It is another grievance warranting revolution.*

*[A] murderous law is framed to shelter villains from the hands of justice.**

Suffolk Resolves (September 9, 1774)

# 37

## "For protecting them, by a mock Trial, from punishment for any Murders which they should commit on the Inhabitants of these States:"

- ☆ The Administration of Justice Act (otherwise known as the Murder Act) shelters British officials and soldiers who allegedly commit murder and other capital offenses in Massachusetts by permitting their trials to occur in England under biased conditions in favor of the perpetrators and onerous circumstances for witnesses.

- ☆ By hindering fair and impartial criminal trials, the Administration of Justice Act destroys the rule of law by subverting the system of justice, breaks the Social Compact by removing trials to England, infringes unalienable rights by depriving the right to a trial by a jury of one's peers, savages equality by treating crimes in the colonies completely differently than in England, and swallows up limited government by imposing the will of Great Britain on the colonists.

This fifteenth grievance takes clear aim at yet another Intolerable Act that Parliament adopts on May 20, 1774, in the wake of the Boston Tea Party.* The Administration of Justice Act (coined the Murder Act by some colonists) fundamentally switches the rules of justice by sheltering British officials and soldiers from trial in America.

This may be surprising considering the extraordinarily fair trial of the British soldiers involved in the Boston Massacre. The massacre occurs on March 5, 1770, when British soldiers gun down and kill five unarmed Bostonians. The town is livid, and the soldiers and officers involved are put on trial for murder. John Adams, an exemplary lawyer and a leading force against British oppression, is possessed by a zealous spirit to ensure that justice is achieved. As the lead attorney, Adams admirably defends the British soldiers. Although his cousin, Samuel Adams, is leading the Sons of Liberty on the streets, John Adams is dedicated to ensuring the pursuit of justice in the Massachusetts courts—the rule of law must prevail. Captain Thomas Preston is tried first and acquitted of murder. A second trial involves eight soldiers; all are acquitted of murder, and only two are convicted of the lesser charge of manslaughter. The convicted soldiers are branded with an *M* (for manslaughter) where the thumb meets the palm—much better than execution. Adams and the jury prove that even the hated "lobsterbacks" find justice in an American court of law.

Nevertheless, Boston's admirable administration of justice is ignored by the imperial authorities. After the Boston Tea Party in 1773, the British pound on Massachusetts. The dreaded Administration of Justice Act invests the military governor with unlimited power to remove to another colony—or even to England—trials involving murder or other capital offenses perpetrated in favor of Great Britain's oppressive policies. The statute specifically finds that Massachusetts courts are untrustworthy and that the laws of Parliament are not being enforced as circumstances demand. Accordingly, the act protects government officials who are executing their duties, working to suppress riots, or enforcing tax laws in Massachusetts.

The law also authorizes the governor to require witnesses to attend such trials and post bail to ensure their own appearance. Moreover, the statute allows the accused to post bond and not be held in custody pending trial—a highly unusual privilege at the time for a defendant accused of murder or other capital offenses.

Such provisions seem patently ridiculous to the colonists. The Murder Act is unnecessary. The trial of the soldiers complicit in the Boston Massacre (on the center stage of the resistance to British rule) clearly rebukes the reasoning of the act. Worse, moving the trial to England is not done to protect the unalienable rights of the people but to protect the soldiers and British officials enforcing martial law and oppressing the unalienable rights of the people. To protect British soldiers or officials who kill Americans and commit other capital crimes while enforcing unjust laws, the governor may move their trials to another colony or, better yet, to Great Britain before the king's bench—with a jury drawn from Middlesex, England. The right to be tried by a jury of peers in the venue (in other words, the court district or circuit) where a crime allegedly occurs is firmly embedded in English law. Should not the community where these evils are committed have a voice in ensuring justice is done? A defendant should be tried by a jury of his or her *peers*. Here, a special class of criminal defendants is set apart; they are elevated above everyone else, with special protections afforded to no one else. Why? The whole point of the act is to ensure a different verdict than would be obtained in Massachusetts—presumably one much more favorable to imperial repression. As Dr. Joseph Warren writes in the Suffolk Resolves, at bottom, the Murder Act is a blunt tool "to shelter villains" from just prosecution.* A leading Connecticut minister, Reverend Ebenezer Baldwin, preaches that this act "seems calculated with a most barefaced design to screen the soldiers and customhouse officers from punishment, when they should be guilty of any excesses."* Justice itself is yet another casualty of the Intolerable Acts.

Thomas Jefferson recoils at the idea of a trial held overseas by a jury of Englishmen. In *A Summary View of the Rights of British America*, he fatally assaults the idea of forcing witnesses to go across the ocean and post a bond to ensure their appearance—which in essence is another tax without representation, targeted at the special class of witnesses. Jefferson then flips the British argument on its head. If the accused is a resident of Massachusetts, the defendant loses his right to be tried by a jury of his peers. Under such circumstances, American defendants will certainly be convicted in England:

> And the wretched criminal, if he happen to have offended on the American side, stripped of his privilege of trial by his peers of his vicinage, removed from the place where alone full evidence could be obtained, without money, without counsel, without friends, without exculpatory proof, is tried before judges predetermined to condemn. The cowards who would suffer a countryman to be torn from the bowels of their society, in order to be thus offered a sacrifice to parliamentary tyranny, would merit that everlasting infamy now fixed on the authors of the act!*

This broadside is echoed in the Declaration and Resolves of the First Continental Congress.

Compounding its insidious nature, the Murder Act subverts self-representation and the Social Compact. The Virginia Instructions to the Continental Congress of August 1, 1774, explains that the act is yet another blow to "[t]he end of government" as Parliament would again be "exercising a power over the lives, the property, and the liberty of the American subjects; who are not, and from their circumstances cannot, be there represented."* Like the prior fourteen grievances, this Administration of Justice Act strikes at the heart of self-government.

The Sixth Amendment of the Constitution directly remedies this grievance. It provides that "[i]n all criminal prosecutions, the accused shall enjoy the right to a speedy and public trial, by an impartial jury of the State and district wherein the crime shall have been committed, which district shall have been previously ascertained by law." No one will be shipped overseas or to another hostile State for trial. Witnesses and evidence will be not overburdened or placed in jeopardy by attending a trial thousands of miles away. The affected community administers justice for wrongs committed in its jurisdiction. The Sixth Amendment ensures justice for the accused and the public.

The Murder Act epitomizes British arrogance and pretended supremacy, deserving of a grievance in the Declaration. By hindering upright prosecutions of murderers and other capital offenders, the Administration of Justice Act destroys the rule of law. By ripping trials away from local communities with a vested interest in murder trials, it breaks the Social Compact. Undermining fair trials and depriving the defendant of the right to be tried by a jury of peers infringes unalienable rights. By favoring a subset of British officials and soldiers differently than all other murder and capital defendants, it savages equality. By warping the due process of law and justice without the input of the colonial governments, it swallows up limited government. No wonder the Declaration of the Causes and Necessity of Taking Up Arms issued by the Second Continental Congress in 1775 lists "exempting the 'murderers' of colonists from legal trial, and in effect, from punishment" as one of the causes for taking up arms against Great Britain.*

*[T]he present unhappy situation of our affairs is occasioned by a ruinous system of colony administration, adopted by the British ministry about the year 1763, evidently calculated for enslaving these colonies, and, with them, the British Empire. In prosecution of which system, various acts of Parliament have been passed, for raising a revenue in America* [...] *And in prosecution of the same system, several late, cruel, and oppressive acts have been passed, respecting the town of Boston and Massachusetts-Bay.* [...]

*[T]hese grievances* [...] *threaten destruction to the lives, liberty, and property of his majesty's subjects in North America.**

First Continental Congress (October 20, 1774)

# 38

## "For cutting off our Trade with all parts of the world:"

- ☆ Before 1763, the British bind the colonies to a system of mercantilism, but it is lightly enforced through the doctrine of salutary neglect. After 1763, the British draconianly enforce trade restrictions through new laws and invigorated enforcement.
- ☆ By harshly enforcing the system of mercantilism, the British ruin American industry, infringe the unalienable rights of liberty and the pursuit of happiness, violate the Social Compact by imposing trade regulations without the consent of the governed, and eviscerate limited government by imposing unlimited British rule on the colonists.

The sixteenth grievance is one of the longest standing, but it takes generations to become a contentious issue with the empire. As we have previously explored, the American colonies are part of the system of mercantilism: Colonists gather and ship to the rest of the British Empire relatively inexpensive raw materials, and the British Isles and other parts of the empire ship back relatively expensive, manufactured goods. In the age of imperialism, this is standard operating procedure for all the great empires. England exploits her colonies for profit and power. It works exceedingly well for generations. Over time, the colonists became a huge new market for British manufacturers, merchants, insurance companies, and financiers. A contributor to *The London Magazine* in 1766 explains the practical reality that "[t]he American is apparelled from head to foot in our manufactures [...] he scarcely drinks, sits, moves, labours or recreates himself, without [...] contributing to the emolument of the mother country."*

This mercantile arrangement originally comes into form as a matter of practice and tradition. The tradition becomes written policy under the reign of King Charles I. The empire slowly institutes a set of laws to reinforce the overarching policy, ever expanding the list of raw resources and finished products legally subject to this web of trade restrictions. Through the Staple Act of 1663, unless specifically exempted, all exports to Europe must be sent to Great Britain. The Crown even holds the right to mark and harvest the king's trees—the tallest, straightest, and thickest northern pines in America, which serve as ship masts in the Royal Navy. The British greedily horde key natural resources from the colonies.

In tandem, the empire possesses a monopoly on many finished goods purchased by the colonists. Certain key finished goods industries in the colonies are tightly controlled to prevent competition with the homeland. Moreover, all shipping and trade must be conducted solely by English or colonial ships.

Yet salutary neglect means that enforcing colonial trade laws is among the lowest of British priorities, relegated to an ineffectual and listless bureaucracy. As historian Edmund S. Morgan recounts, the "government of Great Britain [...] regard[s] the problem of turnpikes in Yorkshire [an area of northern England] as vastly more important than the enforcement of the Navigation Acts in New York."*

Still, even if not legally compelled, practically, the system is broadly in effect. Mercantilism provides clear benefits for the colonies. However, this is not to deny the reality that there are significant downsides for the colonists. Mercantilism substantially stifles manufacturing. The colonists cannot produce finished goods for export, and often for home consumption.

Despite these issues, for decades, the bottom line is that the main colonial concern involving mercantilism is the Navigation Act of 1733 (also referred to as the Molasses Act). This act places an import duty of sixpence per gallon of molasses from sources other than within the empire. New England imports molasses and refines it into rum. Enforcement of the sixpenny tax would cripple New England's rum industry. The British West Indies, the only viable British source of molasses, cannot possibly produce the amount of molasses necessary to sustain New England's vibrant rum trade. Instead, the colonists engage in a robust illicit trade with the French West Indies—even *during* the French and Indian War.

Fortunately for the colonists, the British are much too concerned with "turnpikes in Yorkshire" to enforce the sixpenny duty in America. Bribes ensure that underpaid and underappreciated customs officials ignore the duty (and their own duty). In another violation of the Navigation Acts, New England traders ship surplus timber, fish, beans, shoes, and other resources to the French West Indies. This produces tension between the colonies and the imperial authorities, but it hardly amounts to a desire to declare independence by the colonies or impose despotism by London—that is, until the 1760s.

Even before the definitive conclusion of the French and Indian War, Prime Minister William Pitt, "the Elder," imposes a draconian crackdown to end the illicit trade with the West Indies. Pitt leaves office, but his successor, Prime Minister George Grenville, also enacts an oppressive policy. To stop bribery, the empire orders that customs officials live in America and directly enforce the laws. In 1761, Grenville orders the Royal Navy to suffocate the illicit colonial trade. He instructs colonial courts to issue general writs of assistance to search for customs violations. A writ of assistance is the worst version of a search warrant—it is a broad-ranging permission slip for imperial officials to search anyone and anywhere, without probable cause.

With the conclusion of the French and Indian War, the empire's focus moves from the vanquished French enemy to a new enemy: the Americans. Unless the empire springs into action now, it will never be able to control colonial trade. It enacts a whole series of new laws to expand the powers of the Royal Navy, customs officials, and courts to suffocate and destroy illicit trading. Great Britain passes over fifty acts attempting to control colonial trade from 1688 to 1765, but until 1764, they amount to next to nothing. Now they mean everything.

Smuggling, bribery, and evasion of trade laws are replaced with the iron rod of oppression. Parliament passes the Revenue Act of 1764, more commonly known as the Sugar Act of 1764. This act essentially resurrects the Molasses Act of 1733 by taxing sugar, wine, molasses, and similar products. If enforced, the Sugar Act of 1764 will wipe out New England's trading patterns, obliterating long-standing commerce and industry critical to the colonists.

Economics is just the beginning of the issues with this new crackdown. The Crown ruthlessly deploys the Royal Navy to enforce the Sugar Act of 1764 and mercantilism in general. The British are on a war footing with their own subjects, demolishing their constitutional legal protections. To add insult to injury, customs officials are paid half the proceeds arising from the sale of any confiscated smuggling ships or cargoes. The empire is all in.

With every passing year, the British twist the screws tighter. In 1768, Parliament establishes an American Board of Customs (based in Boston) to enforce the Townshend Acts. Foreshadowing the tenth grievance, one Virginian merchant writes that the board is "one of the plagues of Egypt. [...] Swarms of hungry locusts through all our coasts, to feed on the fat of the land, and annoy, impoverish and perplex us."* To prove the point, spying is encouraged, customs officials are immunized from lawsuits, the presumption of innocence is flipped to a presumption of guilt, cases are tried in admiralty or vice-admiralty courts with no juries, and judges receive their salary from the proceeds of captured customs funds.

The Crown expands the reach of the mercantilist system by banning colonial fishing off the coast of Newfoundland. They also add other key natural resources to the list that can only be exported to Great Britain. The empire increases bounty payments for privateers and others who capture colonial smugglers; it also prohibits colonial imports of various French and Asian goods and adds high duties to non-English imports.

The colonists are further harassed regarding perhaps their most lucrative crop: tobacco. The colonists ship it to England, and English merchants resell the crop to the rest of Europe at higher prices. This regulation steals away profits from colonists, having the effect of a hidden tax.

The increasing enforcement also deepens the debt of many colonists. By definition, selling less expensive raw materials and buying more expensive finished goods creates a trade deficit with the British Isles. Trade with other countries could mitigate this dilemma, but since surplus goods cannot be sold or traded with other buyers, the debt burden only compounds. Like the trade regulations, colonists' debt issues increase exponentially. Many of America's leading characters, such as George Washington and Thomas Jefferson, face perpetual debt.

As the oppression increases, many Americans realize that the disadvantages of the mercantilist system overshadow its benefits. As this awareness takes hold, the empire exacerbates the situation exactly where tax policy and trade policy come together. As noted earlier, in 1767, to replace the Stamp Act, Parliament enacts the Townshend Acts, which, among other things, place duties on paper, paint, glass, tea, and other imported products. Like the Stamp Act before them, the Townshend Acts are met with robust resistance in the colonies. The empire eventually backs down and repeals almost all those duties in 1770. But following the pattern of the despised Declaratory Act, the empire cannot help itself and must leave some vestige of supremacy by maintaining the tax on tea. Tea is an enormous commodity in the colonies; perhaps the equivalent in today's society is soft drinks, coffee, tea, and bottled water all rolled up into one. For many, the tea tax is viewed as a minor irritant, which is simply circumvented by purchasing duty-free, smuggled Dutch tea. Before 1773, many Americans buy Dutch tea because it is far less expensive than the duty-laden English tea and has the added benefit of avoiding unconstitutional English taxes—after all, the English duties are the epitome of taxation without representation. Because it is so easy to evade, before 1773, there is not much public agitation over it.

But Parliament inflames the situation with the passage of the Tea Act of 1773. Ironically, this act actually drops the price of the tea tax. But it strengthens England's grip on the tea industry by imposing a monopoly of production, supply, and transportation. The East India Company, a sprawling and vitally important company in control of the empire's tea trade, is on the verge of bankruptcy. It is, for all practical purposes, the embodiment of Great Britain's crown jewel of India. At one point, it is the second-most important business concern in Great Britain, only behind the Bank of England. To save it, Parliament enables the company to penetrate America and completely take over the tea trade in the colonies.

In one sense, the British plan is genuinely brilliant. We need not review the mechanics, but with the passage of the Tea Act of 1773, the legally imported English tea, even with the unconstitutional tax, suddenly becomes substantially less expensive than smuggled Dutch tea. The British government believes it has concocted a win-win-win scenario to entice the colonies into delighted acquiescence. The colonists will be most pleased to save money and can patriotically buy a less expensive product, the East India Company will be saved with new American revenue, and Great Britain will obtain desperately needed tax revenue while reasserting its legal authority to impose taxes in accordance with the Declaratory Act. The almighty pound will placate any American sensibilities regarding freedoms and liberties.

The English have another thing coming. Americans immediately reject the tax scheme. They understand that although the Tea Act of 1773 may save them money, it cannot stand. First, it will ruin American industry for the sake of salvaging the incompetent and corrupt East India Company. By establishing a monopoly, it wipes out American businesses tied to this key commodity. Second, and much more importantly, it is nothing but a thinly disguised attempt to bribe Americans into giving up their liberties. As we will learn in the next grievance, this is no small matter—it is fundamental.

Under the statute, tea laden with the new taxes is shipped by the East India Company from England to the colonies to be distributed to merchants for retail sale. This presents an opportunity for the colonies to resist. The Sons of Liberty organize throughout the colonies to prevent this damnable cargo from being unloaded at American ports. They direct an intricate set of oppositional and intimidating maneuvers, causing several ships to turn back to England before they can even dock. Others are stuck in harbors and cannot unload their tea.

But then there is Boston. On Sunday, November 28, 1773, HMS *Dartmouth*, holding 114 chests of tea laden with taxes, arrives in Boston Harbor. Samuel Adams, Dr. Benjamin Church, Dr. Joseph Warren, and other Sons of Liberty organize town meetings, anti-tea propaganda, and other resistance to stop the tea from being disembarked in Boston. They hope to force the *Dartmouth*—and two other later-arriving ships, the *Eleanor* and the *Beaver*—to return to England with the tea. This tactic previously succeeds with similar ships in other ports across America. But the *Dartmouth* and other ships remain docked in Boston Harbor. The town's agitation increases.

On the evening of December 16, 1773, there is a heated, seven-thousand-person-strong town meeting—the largest ever to gather in Boston. The town meeting resolves that the tea shall not be unloaded onto the docks. When pressed at the meeting, the ships' captains refuse to agree to return to England with their tea cargo. Samuel Adams announces before the faithfully assembled, "This meeting can do nothing more to save the country."* This is the signal. War whoops quickly follow his pronouncement. The overflowing crowd streams out toward the harbor, and approximately fifty men disguised as Native Americans board the offending ships and toss into the harbor about ninety thousand pounds of East Indian tea. A large fortune dissipates, "brewing" the tea in the saltwater of Boston Harbor.

The British react harshly by passing the Intolerable Acts—in other words, the Boston Port Act, Massachusetts Government Act, Administration of Justice Act, and Quartering Act. In connection with trade, the Boston Port Act completely shuts down Boston Harbor until full restitution is made for the Boston Tea Party. A pen stroke from Parliament wipes out the livelihoods of thousands. The British have hearts of stone.

American hearts, likewise, harden. Patriots begin to abandon any willingness to participate in the mercantilist system. In *A Summary View of the Rights of British America*, Jefferson expresses the new prevailing American sentiment that British oppression of the natural rights of the colonists in connection with free trade persists for generations. Americans have historically overlooked it, but there it is. Jefferson observes that mercantilism violates the natural unalienable rights of the colonists to trade freely. What is happening now is a well-designed, deliberate imperial conspiracy to crush the liberties of the Americans and make them slaves of the empire. The empire has engaged in "a series of oppressions, begun at a distinguished period, and pursued unalterably through every change of ministers, [which] too plainly prove a deliberate and systematical plan of reducing us to slavery."*

The Boston Port Act and imperial restraints on trade spark outrage across America. Concurring with Jefferson, the Declaration and Resolves of the First Continental Congress of October 14, 1774, specifically condemns the establishment of an American board of trade with unconstitutional powers to cut off trade with the rest of the world. A few days later, on October 20, 1774, primarily citing the Boston Port Act, the First Continental Congress agrees to the Continental Association—a nonimport, nonexport, and nonconsumption agreement among the colonists. When it takes full effect, it essentially prohibits the colonists from importing and consuming British, Irish, and British West Indian goods, and it prohibits the export of American goods to the same. This even includes the slave trade.

Simultaneously, the British are busy implementing the Restraining Acts, which prohibit the colonists from trading with anyone for anything—except the

British Empire. The Royal Navy is empowered to capture any vessels violating the acts. Originally, the acts only apply to New England, but soon enough, with some minor exceptions for protecting Loyalist areas, the Restraining Acts encompass all but four of the colonies—the British still hope these colonies will remain loyal. Like so much else, the colonial and British positions are diametrically opposed. On October 19, 1774, the king declares that Massachusetts is in a state of rebellion and prohibits the export of war supplies to the colonies. Without due process, the Restraining Acts unjustly punish all Americans for the sins of a few, and with no attempt to reconcile the parties. In other words, they are tyrannical.

Article I, Section 8 of the Constitution vests authority over legislating rules about international trade in Congress and enforcing those rules in the president. Because they are accountable to the people, they have strong incentives to ensure that any such trade regulations are fair and reflect public sentiment. If not, the people will make them pay at the ballot box.

Despite everything we have discussed in this grievance, serious historical scholars recognize that the mercantilist system is only one of many causes of the American Revolution. As we have noted, many other political grievances deeply overshadow economic concerns. Although cutting off trade with the rest of the world is a vital grievance, it is hardly the only one, and it alone almost certainly would not have led to the Declaration. Nevertheless, Great Britain cripples American industry and infringes the natural rights of the people. Like so much else, the king and Parliament impose their policies in violation of the Social Compact and eviscerate limited government. And the resistance to the tea tax goes well beyond monetary concerns. Viewed in this broader context, it is a vital reason why we declare independence.*

*2d. That his majesty's liege subjects in these colonies are entitled to all the inherent rights and privileges of his natural born subjects within the kingdom of Great Britain.*

*3d. That it is inseparably essential to the freedom of a people, and the undoubted right of Englishmen, that no taxes be imposed on them, but with their own consent, given personally, or by their representatives.*
*4th. That the people of these colonies are not, and from their local circumstances cannot be represented in the House of Commons in Great Britain.*
*5th. That the only representatives of the people of these colonies, are persons chosen therein, by themselves; and that no taxes ever have been, or can be constitutionally imposed on them, but by their respective legislatures.* [...]
*8th. That the late act of parliament* [Stamp Act] [...] *by imposing taxes on the inhabitants of these colonies* [...] *have a manifest tendency to subvert the rights and liberties of the colonists.**

Stamp Act Congress (October 19, 1765)

# 39

## "For imposing Taxes on us without our Consent:"

- ☆ The Sugar Act of 1764, the Stamp Act, the Revenue Act of 1767 (otherwise known as one of the Townshend Acts), and the tea tax all impose taxation without representation, and the Declaratory Act affirms that Great Britain is free to impose such taxes at will.

- ☆ By repeatedly imposing taxes without the consent of the colonists, Parliament and George III infringe the rule of law by violating the constitutional order, breach the Social Compact by imposing taxation without consent, subvert the unalienable rights of liberty and the pursuit of happiness, infringe equality by depriving colonists of their rights as English subjects, and demolish limited government by empowering the government to do whatever it wishes with the colonists' property.

This seventeenth grievance is the one anyone educated in America remembers. Yet it is far down the list of grievances and but one example of Parliament's pretended legislation. Nevertheless, there is no doubt that it is critically important to the course of the American Revolution.

As we have explored, the Founders believe they are entitled to the same rights as Englishmen. A bedrock right is that taxation may only be levied with the consent of the governed. Since the United Kingdom is not a direct democracy, such consent is obtained through a representative legislative assembly. For the British Isles, that elected representative body is Parliament, in particular the House of Commons.* In America, each colony has its own legislative assembly, each having at least one chamber equivalent to the British House of Commons. As we learned from the thirteenth grievance and the Declaratory Act, in the eyes of the colonists, Parliament has no legitimate authority to legislate on behalf of the colonies. The idea of virtual representation is a mere mockery of the principle of representation in legislation. Thus, only taxes approved by the elected chamber of a colony's legislature are legitimate.

For much of colonial history, other than the duties and customs on goods that we discussed in the last grievance, Parliament typically does not try to impose taxes within the colonies. This approach ends in 1763. Despite sharp tax increases, the French and Indian War causes the national debt to more than double to approximately £140 million—a crushing burden on the empire's finances. To put this amount in perspective, before the French and Indian War, the empire's annual budget is approximately £6.5 million; during the war, the annual budget balloons to £14.5 million a year. The debt is now twenty-one times larger than the prewar annual budget, and interest payments alone account for over half the annual budget. Even after the war, the empire must continue to defend against France and Spain in Europe, as well as the newly conquered North American territories. All along, taxpayers in the British Isles are paying oppressive taxes.

Something must be done to reduce the debt. The lightly taxed colonies are the natural target for increased revenue. During the French and Indian War, the empire directs each colony to contribute a certain amount of funds to pay for the war effort and leaves to each the decision of how to raise this sum. This requisitions (quota) system is difficult to enforce at any time and particularly unreliable in peacetime. There are always colonial legislatures reluctant to pay their full requisitions, and there definitely will be infighting about the amount any particular colony must contribute versus its siblings. After consulting with American agents in London, the ministry in London decides that the journey of taxation must take a different path—taxes must be laid on the colonists directly.

Sensing that the colonials will object to taxation without representation, there is debate under Prime Minister George Grenville about whether the colonies, through colonial assemblies, should elect members to the House of Commons. This idea is stillborn. The English think it has little merit. The sun literally never sets on the British Empire, which includes (among many other places) Canada, Jamaica, St. Vincent, Honduras, Barbados, Senegal, India, and Grenada. None of the colonies are directly represented in Parliament. The colonists believe this solution evades the real issue—they are already represented in their local colonial legislatures. Giving the colonists token representatives in Parliament will only place them in an untenable position in which they will be swamped by representatives from England, Wales, and Scotland. Furthermore, Parliament cannot possibly understand the facts and circumstances on the ground in America. The South Carolina House of Commons and the Virginia House of Burgesses both expressly reject this approach in 1764. Massachusetts joins the opposition in 1768. The scheme is repeatedly opposed by the Continental Congress and other official proclamations.

As we reviewed in connection with the last grievance, as an initial step, Parliament passes the Sugar Act of 1764, which enforces the taxation of imported molasses at an oppressive rate. Its technical title is the Revenue Act of 1764. This is not a misnomer. The act specifically provides that its purpose is all about raising taxes. The revenue raised is to be placed into a separate account in the Exchequer (the British Department of Treasury) for the sole purpose of defraying the expenses for defending, protecting, and securing the colonies.

The legislatures of New York and South Carolina smell a rat from across the Atlantic. On October 18, 1764, the New York General Assembly adopts a petition to the House of Commons condemning the taxation power grab as violating their rights as Englishmen to only be taxed with the consent of their representatives. This oppression comes after the unappreciative sacrifice and tremendous effort to settle the wilderness for the empire. New York understands what is at stake: If Parliament can legislate and tax the colonists, they are no longer free but are the vassals of the empire. Eight other colonies oppose the act, but only South Carolina agrees with New York that it violates the colonists' natural rights.

As noted in connection with the previous grievance, most of the resistance to the Sugar Act of 1764 is focused on trade regulations and the oppressive nature of enforcement. Many colonists at this point accept that Parliament has the legal authority to regulate and tax imported goods. This is viewed as *external* taxation or regulation of trade. Because the Sugar Act of 1764 taxes imports of molasses, most colonists concede that Parliament may levy the tax. This is despite Parliament's candor about using the act to raise revenue rather than to regulate trade.

However, the colonies will soon end this self-deception. Grenville develops a new tax to collect substantially more revenue from the colonies. He rises before Parliament on February 6, 1765, to propose the Stamp Act. He observes that the empire has incurred a huge debt and ongoing expenses for the protection of the colonies, with barely any contribution from the colonists. The Stamp Act "is founded on that great maxim, that protection is due from the governor, and support and obedience on the part of the governed."* Grenville is convincing. The Stamp Act passes in the House of Commons 250 to 50 and unanimously in the House of Lords. It becomes the law on March 22, 1765. The act is projected to raise £60,000, an amount Parliament and Grenville consider a light burden to the colonies.

Taxes are imposed on over fifty-five categories of goods and services, including legal pleadings, university degrees, bills of lading, certificates of appointment for public employment or office, liquor licenses, wills, guardianships, bonds, deeds, surveys, indentures, leases, contracts, bills of sale, mortgages, playing cards, dice, pamphlets, newspapers, almanacs, calendars, and apprenticeships. Like the Sugar Act of 1764, the Stamp Act establishes a separate account in the Exchequer to ensure the funds collected are directed to defend and secure the colonies. The taxes are enforceable in vice-admiralty courts—which means there is no jury, and the judge serves at the pleasure of the king. Every item subject to the tax must have a stamp placed on it to prove that the tax is paid. A set of commissioners is empowered to dole out the stamps and collect the taxes. There is no pretense that the Stamp Act is an external tax—it taxes within the colonies, completely divorced from imported goods and trade regulation.

When news of the Stamp Act's approval arrives in America, some minor signs of opposition arise, but elected colonial officials are initially hesitant to outwardly oppose the act. This all changes with Patrick Henry. On May 29, 1765, the Virginia House of Burgesses debates the issue. Henry is the newest member of the House, having just won his seat in a special election nine days before. Still, he is a famous lawyer who makes his name by litigating in favor of colonial rights. Henry thunders that the Stamp Act violates the ancient principle of no taxation without representation. He urges the house to adopt several resolves (commonly known as the Virginia Resolves) opposing the Stamp Act taxes.

There is controversy about exactly what transpires. Henry introduces seven resolves. Some newspapers report that only the first five are adopted. Others report the first six are adopted. Still others report all seven are ratified. The first resolve explains that Virginians are entitled to all the rights of Englishmen. The second elaborates that Virginia's royal charters grant Virginians the same rights as those who are born in England. The third declares that as "the distinguishing characteristic of British freedom," that taxation must be approved by the people or their representatives. The fourth explains that this right has never been relinquished by the colonists. The fifth resolve strikes at the heart of the matter, declaring that Parliament has no right to tax the colonists—such authority is reserved solely to the House of Burgesses "and that every attempt to vest such power in" anyone else "has a manifest tendency to destroy British as well as American freedom."* Remember, this is 1765—eleven years before the Declaration and nine years before the first meeting of the First Continental Congress. The gauntlet is thrown down. Great Britain will never recover its authority.

The sixth resolve flatly states that Virginians are not obligated to pay taxes imposed by Parliament. The seventh goes further, declaring anyone who, in speech or writing, claims Parliament has the authority to tax the colonists to be an enemy of Virginia.

Some historians contend that the sixth and seventh resolves are not adopted.

To add to the confusion, the day after the Virginia Resolves are adopted, a few lingering legislators convene a rump session and purport to repeal the fifth resolve (as well as the sixth and seventh if they are actually enacted). In this farcical maneuver, they follow Parliament's practice of *pretended* legislation.

Regardless of how many of the Virginia Resolves are officially ratified or rescinded, the effect is electrifying. Many newspapers across the continent report that all seven Virginia Resolves are adopted. With Virginia's shot across the bow, the colonies quickly unite against the Stamp Act. Protests, speeches, marches, petitions, intimidation, and even riots spread like wildfire. Stamp distributors are hanged in effigy and resign under intense pressure. Sons of Liberty across the colonies attack officials of the vice-admiralty courts. Nearly all stamp distributors refuse their commissions or resign.

Massachusetts Lieutenant Governor Thomas Hutchinson, who privately opposes the Stamp Act but is responsible for enforcing it, faces the wrath of Boston. On the glorious or nightmarish night (depending on your point of view) of August 30, 1765, he and his family narrowly escape from their home with their lives. The house is savagely sacked and gutted; all the family's possessions are destroyed or stolen. It is a barren husk. Boston resists in the most dramatic way possible, short of murdering its lieutenant governor.

Meanwhile, nonimportation associations begin to form. English goods are boycotted; businesses that require stamps grind to a halt. But then an easier solution arises—everyone just ignores the law. That no one enforces the Stamp Act requirements is hardly surprising since stamp officials resign or refuse appointment.

Massachusetts calls for a Stamp Act Congress, which meets in October 1765, in New York City Hall. Virginia, New Hampshire, North Carolina, and Georgia do not appear, but the other colonies participate. On October 19, 1765, twenty-eight representatives from the nine attending colonies approve the Declaration of Rights and Grievances, likely primarily drafted by Pennsylvanian John Dickinson. Echoing New York's petition to Parliament regarding the Sugar Act of 1764 and the Virginia Resolves, it proclaims that, as Englishmen, the colonists possess the right to be tried by juries and to be taxed only with representation. It reaffirms that the colonists are not, and could never be, represented in Parliament, and that the Stamp Act violates their constitutional rights. It prays that Parliament will repeal the Stamp Act. The American sentiment is articulated: Nearly no one in the colonies outwardly supports imperial authority.

Meanwhile, British merchants suffer huge losses from American boycotts. London merchants issue their own petition against the Stamp Act on January 17, 1766, explaining that the reaction of the colonists is disrupting trade, harassing the fair trader, causing confusion, and causing bankruptcies. A continued boycott threatens their utter ruin. Not only is the Stamp Act scheme dead, but it is wrecking England's economy. The new prime minister, William Pitt, concedes that the Stamp Act must go. Parliament retreats, repealing the Stamp Act in March 1766. This repeal is met with universal jubilation in the colonies. There are celebratory bonfires and public dinners, and some communities even erect commemorative statues of Prime Minister Pitt and the king.

But at the same time, on March 18, 1766, Parliament passes the Declaratory Act, asserting that Parliament has the authority to make all laws binding the colonies. The thirteenth grievance is born. In addition, a 1766 law replaces the three-pence-per-gallon molasses tax with a single penny per gallon tax. It is a tremendous reduction of the Sugar Act of 1764 duty, but it continues the policy of taxation without representation and stringent enforcement of the tax.

Although Pitt is sympathetic to the colonials, he is ailing. Nature abhors a vacuum, and Charles Townshend, chancellor of the Exchequer, fills it. Townshend is brilliant, a fabulous orator, and entirely committed to yanking the colonies back into the subservient orbit of the empire. Parliament agrees and soon passes his proposed legislation. As we previously discussed, the Revenue Act of 1767 levies taxes on key consumable goods. Although raising only two-thirds of the revenue of the Stamp Act, it strikes the colonists as a thinly veiled attempt to subvert the Social Compact and the colonists' unalienable rights.

Townshend passes away on September 4, 1767, well before his plans are realized. The Revenue Act of 1767 is met with some fleeting and hesitant opposition. Since its taxes take the form of import duties—as opposed to internal taxes like the Stamp Act—some colonials are unsure whether they are unconstitutional. Remember, only South Carolina and New York oppose the Sugar Act of 1764 on those grounds.

This hesitation vanishes with the publication of John Dickinson's *Letters from a Farmer in Pennsylvania*. Dickinson engages in a lucrative legal practice and buys a country estate in Delaware, giving him a very slight pretense of being considered a "farmer." He is elected to the assembly in Delaware and then in Pennsylvania. The *Letters from a Farmer in Pennsylvania* are extremely popular and widely published in multiple newspapers and printings as a stand-alone pamphlet. He advocates that Americans oppose the Townshend taxes through petitions, nonconsumption of imported goods, and home production. He blasts any attempt to tax without representation for revenue (as opposed to regulating trade) and asserts that the Townshend duties are clearly for revenue. After all, they fund imperial officers—that is the point. However, Dickinson's letters are not incendiary calls to arms, and although they resolve the constitutional issue in favor of the colonists, they provoke little action on the ground—that is, for a few weeks.

Then, Samuel Adams and James Otis in Massachusetts spring into action. On February 11, 1768, they prompt the Massachusetts General Court to approve a circular letter (a document to be sent to the other colonies) to create a united front of opposition to the Revenue Act of 1767. The "Massachusetts Circular Letter" explains that

> his majesty's American subjects [...] have an equitable claim to the full enjoyment of the fundamental rules of the British constitution; that it is an essential, unalterable right in nature, engrafted into the British constitution, as a fundamental law, and ever held sacred and irrevocable by the subjects within the realm, that what a man has honestly acquired is absolutely his own, which he may freely give, but cannot be taken from him without his consent; that the American subjects may, therefore, exclusive of any consideration of charter rights, with a decent firmness, adapted to the character of free men and subjects, assert this natural and constitutional right.*

The colonists are endowed with a fundamental, natural right to consent to any taxation. The colonists firmly reject the idea of virtual representation and unite in opposition to any taxation without representation—whether internal or external, and whether related to revenue or to trade. As Englishmen, Natural Law requires they be treated equally with their brethren in the British Isles.

Starting in Boston in the summer of 1768, nonimportation agreements sweep across the continent. The events surrounding the Stamp Act repeat. Colonial resolve once again prevails. It takes more time than with the Stamp Act, but on April 12, 1770, the Townshend duties are all repealed, except (as we learned in the last grievance) the tea tax.

We need not repeat grievance sixteen's review of the Boston Tea Party, but the colonists smell the stench of corruption. The New York Sons of Liberty pass resolutions on tea on November 29, 1773, explaining what is at stake, and agree to boycott English tea. Americans must win this battle "[t]o prevent a calamity which, of all others, is the most to be dreaded—slavery, and its terrible concomitants."*

This is not hyperbole. Simply because they live in America, the colonists are deprived of the rights granted to Englishmen on the British Isles. There is no equality. If, as the British claim, Parliament and the monarch can legislate for the colonies in all cases whatsoever (including taxation without representation), the colonists have no control over their lives, liberty, or property—the very definition of slavery. Silas Downer earlier exclaims that

> [t]he *common people of Great-Britain* very liberally give and grant away the property of the *Americans* without their consent, which if yielded to by us must fix us in the lowest bottom of slavery: For if they can take away one penny from us against our wills, they can take all. If they have such power over our properties they must have a proportionate power over our persons; and from hence it will follow, that they can demand and take away our lives, whenever it shall be agreeable to their sovereign wills and pleasure. [Italics are in the original.]*

The New York Sons of Liberty's resolutions on tea also echo Patrick Henry's seventh Virginia resolve: Anyone opposed to this viewpoint "shall be deemed an enemy to the liberties of America."* A few days after the resolutions pass, Bostonians demonstrate their agreement by hosting the Boston Tea Party.

When the First Continental Congress meets, it echoes and expands on the prior petition of the New York General Assembly, the Virginia Resolves, the "Massachusetts Circular Letter," and the New York Sons of Liberty. The Declaration and Resolves of the First Continental Congress proclaims that any taxation without representation is an egregious violation of natural rights:

> [T]he foundation of English liberty and of all free government, is a right in the people to participate in their legislative council; and the English colonists are not represented, and from their local and other circumstances cannot properly be represented by the British parliament, they are entitled to a free and exclusive power of legislation in their several provincial legislatures, where their right of representation can alone be preserved, in all cases of taxation and internal polity.*

There it is. All questions about taxation without representation are washed away.

> The federal Constitution addresses this affront by establishing an elected Congress with the power "To lay and collect Taxes, Duties, Imposts and Excises" as laid out in Article I, Section 8. Of course, the president must approve (or not disapprove) any tax as well. No other federal governmental authority can lay taxes. Because Congress and the president are elected by the people, any taxation is clearly made with their consent.

George III and Parliament unquestionably violate the principle of no taxation without representation through pretended legislation. The Declaration of the Causes and Necessity of Taking Up Arms issued July 6, 1775, explains that among other reasons, revolution against the British is justified because Parliament has "undertaken to give and grant our money without our consent, though we have ever exercised an exclusive right to dispose of our own property."* By repeatedly imposing taxes without the consent of the colonists, Parliament and the king violate the rule of law, sever the Social Compact, subvert unalienable rights, infringe equality, and demolish limited government. The time is now to fight to preserve our natural rights.*

*The several acts* [...] *which impose duties for the purpose of raising a revenue in America, extend the powers of the admiralty courts beyond their ancient limits, deprive the American subject of trial by jury* [...] *and are subversive of American rights.* [...] *To these grievous acts and measures Americans cannot submit.**

First Continental Congress (October 14, 1774)

# 40

## "For depriving us in many cases, of the benefits of Trial by Jury:"

- ☆ The Sugar Act of 1764, the Stamp Act, and the Vice Admiralty Court Act of 1768 deny colonists the sacred right of a trial by jury.
- ☆ The suppression of the right to a jury trial strikes at the rule of law by abolishing a sacred method of determining the truth and achieving justice, eviscerates unalienable rights by depriving colonists a fundamental protection from government tyranny, infringes equality by singling out the colonists from their English brethren, severs the Social Compact by eliminating trial by a jury of peers, and delimits government by expanding the reach and authority of imperial power.

The eighteenth grievance addresses the suppression of the right to trial by jury. This issue has been raised in connection with several prior grievances; however, a fuller exploration is warranted in light of the Declaration's emphasis on this wrong as an independent grievance. Considering how most modern Americans seem to view jury service as a dreaded inconvenience, a review of its vital importance is justified.*

The fundamental right of Americans to be tried by a jury of their peers has long-standing roots in British law. Although there are multiple sources of the right, the dominant one arises with the Norman invasion of England by King William the Conqueror in 1066.* He lives up to his moniker by fundamentally changing England in many important ways. Pertinent to the eighteenth grievance, one institution he establishes for the better is convening a group of inhabitants to resolve low-level disputes. This practice may have been borrowed from the Franks

(French), Romans, and/or Teutonic Germans. King William or his authorized representative places the convened group under oath. *Jurare* in Latin means "to swear"—hence the name "jurors." The questions put to the jurors are wide ranging, including the resolution of crimes, property disputes, and alleged misconduct of government officials.

Through a long and complicated process, William the Conqueror's successors begin to appoint officials who preside over the resolution of disputes with something akin to a jury. These juries are used in selective circumstances, such as disputes involving the king, nobility, military, or clergy—or if someone has enough money to pay for the honor. This takes on a more modern form under King Henry II. He revolutionizes justice by making the court system available to all his subjects—for just a small fee. Originally, this jury system is used only for civil disputes, but in 1166, Henry II extends it to criminal cases.

From our modern concept, these juries are nearly the opposite of what we expect. Today, juries must be fair and impartial; individual jurors should know nothing about the case and not be biased for or against a party, witness, or the issue at hand. But under Henry II, to be qualified as a juror, you must know about the controversy and be able to resolve it based on what you and the other jurors know. This is exactly the opposite of today's system.

Nevertheless, Henry II's courts are dramatically better than the prior methods of adjudicating justice. Before Henry II, crimes are addressed in ways that today we consider divorced from the pursuit of truth and justice. First, there is no government prosecutor. Fundamentally, justice is privately prosecuted and decided. Second, the methodology for reaching a verdict is downright outlandish and barbaric. One way of deciding guilt or innocence is the hue and cry. When someone is accused of a felony, the accuser yells the accusation and a crowd pours out and chases down the accused; once the accused is caught, right on the spot, she must convince the crowd of her innocence. If the accused fails, they lynch her. Then there is the "ordeal." The accused is tested by some sort of physically painful test. For example, an accused is burned on the arm with a hot poker—after three days, if the injury heals one way, the accused is innocent; if the burn heals another way, the accused is guilty. Of course, there is always "trial by combat." The accused and the accuser—or their champions—fight with preselected weapons in a field or an arena. Whoever wins the melee is vindicated, because God ensures that the just party prevails. Other even more bizarre methods exist.

King Henry II is a rational leader and a true humanitarian in the legal arena. He attempts to standardize the law for all of England and replace at least some of these superstitious, cruel ways of determining guilt with a trial by jury. Yet Henry's system is far from what we consider the fair and impartial adjudication of justice. Jurors are all knights drawn from across the realm. Only nobles can serve on the jury. They do not hear witnesses. They can rely on hearsay—when a person repeats what he or she heard someone else say outside of court. To be brought to trial, a large set of jurors must agree that there is enough information to bring the case forward. That is basically the equivalent of today's "grand jury." If the grand jury agrees, the charges are issued, and the accused must face trial. Then a smaller "petit jury," usually composed of twelve persons, sits in judgment of the case and renders a verdict.

In 1215, Pope Innocent III abandons the practice of ordeals, and England follows suit. The Magna Carta of 1215 specifically provides for the right to a jury. The Magna Carta of 1225* and the Magna Carta of 1297* both reaffirm this fundamental right to a jury. Over generations, the process gradually changes into the one we have today.

One key development in the right to a jury is the trial of William Penn and William Mead in 1670. As members of the Religious Society of Friends (i.e., Quakers), they are subject to severe restrictions on religious worship. They attempt to attend a large worship service at a London church, but the authorities—having caught wind of the plans—padlock the premises. Penn begins to address the locked-out crowd in front of the church, and he and Mead are arrested within minutes. The charge? They "unlawfully and tumultuously did assemble and congregate themselves together, to the disturbance of the peace of [...] the King."*

The trial is a farce in which the defendants' procedural due process rights are thoroughly violated. The judges blatantly favor the prosecution, and the witnesses are hardly compelling. When the jurors report back after about ninety minutes of deliberating, they announce that eight members are ready to convict but four are unconvinced. The two judges are enraged and order the jurors to renew deliberations. On several occasions, the jury renders a verdict to acquit Mead and finds Penn guilty of speaking to a crowd (in other words, a noncrime). The judges are exasperated and refuse to accept the verdicts; the jury is sent back to continue deliberations. The judges proclaim that the jury will not be free to leave until they find both defendants guilty. They are held overnight and deprived of food, drink, fire, and even a chamber pot. The next morning, the jurors report the same verdicts. Judge Samuel Starling is enraged and even declares he will cut the foreperson's throat. The jury is sent away yet again and later returns with the same verdicts. Another night in the same oppressive conditions, and the jury collapses. Instead of finding Penn guilty, they deliver a verdict of not guilty for both defendants.

The acquittals are accepted, but the jurors are fined (with no explanation) and sentenced to be jailed if they do not pay. Puritan foreperson Edward Bushel and three others resolve to be imprisoned. The prisoners petition for their release through the ancient writ of habeas corpus (Latin for "bring the body"), which allows judges to release wrongfully imprisoned persons. Lord Chief Justice John Vaughan releases the jurors after they spend ten weeks in a horrid prison. Never before has a judge reversed another judge's decision to imprison jurors.

Chief Justice Vaughn not only breaks that precedent, but he establishes a new rule that thunders throughout the ages—a jury's verdict will be sacrosanct and the jurors cannot be punished for concluding contrary to the view of the judges. A proper separation of powers between the jury, as fact finder, and the judge, as determining the law, is guaranteed. The independence of a jury and its rightful role as the arbitrator of the facts in an impartial manner is finally tested and won. As the Penn and Mead trial evinces, this is a critical bulwark of freedom against unjust and tyrannical government prosecutions and judges.*

Before the American Revolution, English law continues to solidify the right to a jury. For example, the Bill of Rights 1689 provides "[t]hat jurors ought to be duly impanelled and returned, and jurors which pass upon men in trials for high treason ought to be freeholders."* By the mid-1700s, criminal procedures evolve to be much more like the processes we expect today. These changes, along with the lore of the Penn and Mead trial, dramatically reinforce the fundamental, indispensable importance of the jury. Although colonial charters often generally refer to protecting the liberties of Englishmen, in 1641, Massachusetts is the first colony to expressly guarantee the right to a jury trial. Others follow suit.

In 1735, in the celebrated New York trial of printer John Peter Zenger, Americans distinguish themselves in the annals of momentous jury trials and the right to a free press. Two years before, New York's first independent newspaper, *The New-York Weekly Journal*, is established. Zenger is its printer. In a series of articles, the newspaper viciously attacks New York's colonial Governor William Cosby. By 1735, Cosby has had enough, and Zenger is arrested for seditious libel. The government has a strong case, but the jury acquits Zenger, "[u]pon which there were three huzza[h]s" in the courtroom.* Many First Amendment scholars point to the verdict as a turning point in protecting freedom of the press. The jury, using its authority to determine the facts, acquits Zenger to protect his (and their and our) unalienable rights. In connection with this eighteenth grievance, the verdict firmly roots in the rich soil of colonial liberty the idea that juries must be fiercely independent guardians of the rights of the people.

Another momentous trial, commonly dubbed the Parsons' Cause, begins as a simple collections case. In colonial Virginia, the Church of England is the established (official government-approved) church of Virginia, and its ministers are paid through government edict and tax revenue. Because Virginia is an overwhelmingly agricultural economy, the law provides that the ministers be paid in—of all things—tobacco, the main staple of the colony. In 1758, the value of the annual stipend skyrockets to £400, providing the clergy a major windfall. The House of Burgesses intervenes and passes what is commonly called the Two Penny Act, readjusting the clergy's pay to about £133.

Naturally, the ministers feel cheated. With some effort, they convince English authorities in London to disallow the Two Penny Act, yet another example of the very first grievance. The English even suggest to the clergy that they sue their vestries (local churches who are the clergy's paymasters) for lost compensation. Parson James Maury gladly embraces the suggestion and sues his vestry for the value of the payment lost while the Two Penny Act is in effect. He easily proves in court that he is entitled to compensation, and the only issue left for a jury trial is how much he should be paid.

A young Patrick Henry now ambles onto the stage, defending the vestry solely in connection with determining the amount of damages. On the day of the trial, Henry walks to court and spies his uncle, the Reverend Patrick Henry, also walking to the courthouse. Patrick convinces his uncle not to attend out of fear of embarrassment. But no matter what the young man's feelings, he is still unable to stop his father from attending—Colonel John Henry, after all, is the presiding judge.

As is the custom at the time, the Sheriff goes about town and wrestles in twelve jurors. Unable to cajole gentlemen to do their duty, Parson Maury complains that the Sheriff collects out of the "vulgar herd"*—men who are not of substance or loyal Anglicans. Patrick Henry responds that they are all "honest men," and they are sworn in at once.* Henry is no fool: Three of them are "New Lights"—that is, they are not members of the Anglican church and do not believe much in organized religion—and one is his cousin. Despite the apparent advantages to Henry, no one seems to think it will matter much. Liability is already determined. On hand to cheer on Parson Maury are up to twenty ministers. Also present is a large crowd of colonials, hoping that, by divine intervention, Henry will somehow minimize the damages.

Opposing counsel straightforwardly argues that, but for the Two Penny Act, Parson Maury should have received £450; he was only paid £150 and so is entitled to £300. He then heaps praise on the Anglican clergy.

William Wirt, the first major historian of Patrick Henry, explains what happens next, describing that Henry

> rose very awkwardly, and faltered much in his exordium. The people hung their heads at so unpromising a commencement; the clergy were observed to exchange sly looks with each other;

> and his father is described as having almost sunk with confusion from his seat. But these feelings were of short duration, and soon gave place to others, of a very different character. For now were those wonderful faculties which he possessed, for the first time developed; and now was first witnessed that mysterious and almost supernatural transformation of appearance, which the fire of his own eloquence never failed to work in him. For as his mind rolled along, and began to glow from its own action, all the *exuviae* of the clown, seemed to shed themselves spontaneously. His attitude, by degrees, became erect and lofty. The spirit of his genius awakened all his features. His countenance shone with a nobleness and grandeur which it had never before exhibited. There was a lightning in his eyes which seemed to rive the spectator. His action became graceful, bold, and commanding; and in the tones of his voice, but more especially in his emphasis, there was a peculiar charm, a magic, of which any one who ever heard him will speak as soon as he is named, but of which no one can give any adequate description. They can only say that it struck upon the ear and upon the heart, *in a manner which language cannot tell.* Add to all these, his wonder-working fancy, and the peculiar phraseology in which he clothed its images; for he painted to the heart with a force that almost petrified it. In the language of those who heard him on this occasion, "he made their blood run cold, and their hair to rise on end." [Italics are in the original.]*

Henry's argument is so convincing and eloquent that the audience is completely enraptured, the clergy panic and despair (some literally flee the courtroom), and his father loses his composure and cries tears of joy.* Henry suggests that the jurors need not award any damages, but if they decide to do so, let it be a farthing. The jury awards a judgment four times more than Henry suggests—a whole penny. The courtroom erupts into a frenzy of celebration; supporters grab Henry, hoist him on their shoulders, and carry him out of the courtroom in triumph.

Parson Maury is appalled. Thanks to his disgust, we have some sense of the argument. Henry declares that the "king, by disallowing" the Two Penny Act, "from being the father of his people, degenerated into a tyrant, and forfeits all right to his subjects' obedience."* At this point, court observer Peter Lyons rises from his chair and yells, "[T]he gentleman has spoken treason," and that he is astonished "that your worships can hear it without emotion, or any mark of dissatisfaction."* Henry, Judge Henry, and the crowd ignore the protest.

Henry then launches into a frontal assault on the established church and Parson Maury and urges the jury to make the verdict an example against tyranny,

> excepting they (the jury) were disposed to rivet the chains of bondage on their own necks, he hoped they would not let slip the opportunity which now offered, of making such an example of him as might, hereafter, be a warning to himself and his brethren, not to have the temerity, for the future, to dispute the validity of such laws, authenticated by the only authority, which, in his conception, could give force to laws for the government of this colony, the authority of a legal representative of a council, and of a kind and benevolent and patriot governor.*

Henry's amazing argument and the astonishing verdict have several long-lasting effects. They embolden Americans to directly oppose the king and Parliament and undermine royal rule. In effect, the verdict negates the empire's disallowance of the Two Penny Act and restores the Social Compact by defending representative government. None of this is possible without the independent jury. The verdict solidifies the reputation and legal effect of the independence of juries as a vital hedge against tyranny. This unalienable right must be protected at all costs.

Jurist and legal scholar Sir William Blackstone's *Commentaries on the Laws of England* are tremendously influential with the Founding Generation. Writing just a few years after the Parsons' Cause, he tellingly writes that trial by jury "is adapted and framed for the investigation of truth, beyond any other method of trial in the world."* Blackstone also recognizes that trial by jury is "the grand bulwark of his liberties."* This is so because "the truth of every accusation" by the prosecutor must be

> confirmed by the unanimous suffrage of twelve of his equals and neighbours, indifferently chosen, and superior to all suspicion. So that the liberties of England cannot but subsist, so long as this *palladium* remains sacred and inviolate, not only from all open attacks (which none will be so hardy as to make) but also from all sacred machinations, which may sap and undermine it. [Italics are in the original.]*

Providing for a trial before a jury of one's peers also reinforces the Social Compact. The jurors are, in essence, the duly appointed representatives of the people to determine the facts in any given case—a sort of mini-representative body. The colonists concur. Trial by jury certainly is a difficult, expensive, complicated, and lengthy process. But it is well worth the price. Indeed, it is the glory of English law.

This is why on October 26, 1774, the First Continental Congress's appeal to the inhabitants of Quebec expressly includes recognizing the right of a jury trial as a "great right."* The tremendous value of the jury is revealed for all to see when even the despised lobsterbacks that perpetrate the Boston Massacre are all acquitted of murder and all but two acquitted of all charges.

However, the British determine to carve up the right to jury and deprive the colonists of this vital institution when it conflicts with Britain's oppressive policies. This oppression begins almost immediately after the conclusion of the French and Indian War. As we learned in the last grievance, the Sugar Act of 1764 establishes a new vice-admiralty court in Halifax, Canada. Violations of customs laws are triable in this court, which has no jury. Moreover, the accused is presumed to be guilty—the reverse of a criminal jury trial. Perhaps worse, the judges have an incentive to find the defendants guilty. Confiscation and the sale of the ships and other property involved in smuggling is one of the punishments the judges can render under the act. The judges are paid out of those very proceeds in a commission-like fashion. The British impose a corrupt system with perverse incentives. With no jury, there is a strong temptation for the judges to cast aside the law, facts, and justice. This is a grievous violation of justice and unalienable rights.

In a parallel fashion, the short-lived Stamp Act is enforceable in any court of record—which includes the admiralty courts. This is unprecedented. The Stamp Act has absolutely nothing to do with trade laws, sea routes, or transportation. Stamp Act enforcement in admiralty courts is a complete affront to the unalienable right to a jury trial. It removes a substantial area of criminal law from the protection of the jury system. Although the Stamp Act is quickly repealed in 1766, the attempt to suppress the right to trial by jury leaves a deep scar in the American psyche. It might have healed in time, but the English reopen that wound in just two years by enacting the Vice Admiralty Court Act of 1768. The act establishes new vice-admiralty courts in the colonies—Boston, Philadelphia, and Charleston are saddled with more juryless courts, the presumption of guilt, and incentives for guilty verdicts. The Founding Generation despises it.

As we reviewed earlier, the admiralty courts are established in England for over a century. Yet, in light of the policy of salutary neglect (including the nearly nonexistent enforcement of the trade laws) as a practical matter, colonists are rarely tried in an admiralty court. Before the 1760s, any such trials must occur in England, and there is no appetite by the British to do so. In the colonies, jury trials are firmly rooted as the expected and revered method of adjudicated justice. The Zenger trial and Parsons' Cause bolster this sentiment. Trials in colonial courts of record are before colonial judges and juries. But beginning with the Sugar Act of 1764, the ground shifts completely—then the Stamp Act, then the Vice Admiralty Court Act of 1768.

Americans refuse to accept this serial violation of their sacred rights. This always remains a very serious grievance for the colonists. John Adams elaborates on October 14, 1765, among the despicable features of the Stamp Act,

> the most grievous innovation of all, is the alarming extension of the power of courts of admiralty. In these courts, one judge presides alone! No juries have any concern there! The law and the fact are both to be decided by the same single judge, whose commission is only during pleasure, and with whom, as we are told, the most mischievous of all customs has become established, that of taking commissions on all condemnations; so that he is under a pecuniary temptation always against the subject.... We have all along thought the acts of trade in this respect a grievance; but the Stamp Act has opened a vast number of sources of new crimes, which may be committed by any man, and cannot but be committed by multitudes, and prodigious penalties are annexed, and all these are to be tried by such a judge of such a court! ... We cannot help asserting, therefore, that this part of the act will make an essential change in the constitution of juries, and it is directly repugnant to the Great Charter [the Magna Carta] itself.*

Five days later, the Stamp Act Congress convenes, and it passes the following condemnation:

> That trial by jury is the inherent and invaluable right of every British subject in these colonies. [...]
>
> That the late act of parliament [Stamp Act] [...] and several other acts, by extending the jurisdiction of the courts of admiralty beyond its ancient limits, have a manifest tendency to subvert the rights and liberties of the colonists.*

Nearly a decade later, the First Continental Congress's Declaration and Resolves issued on October 14, 1774, attacks the admiralty courts as "subversive of American rights."* Likewise, when it determines it is time to fight, the Second Continental Congress's Declaration of the Causes and Necessity of Taking Up

Arms issued on July 6, 1775, highlights the violation of the right to a jury trial as part of a long-term conspiracy by the British to crush American liberties.

The Bill of Rights protects the right to trial by jury in two amendments. The Sixth Amendment provides that "[i]n all criminal prosecutions, the accused shall enjoy the right to a speedy and public trial, by an impartial jury of the State and district wherein the crime shall have been committed." The Seventh Amendment provides that in civil cases "where the value in controversy shall exceed twenty dollars, the right of trial by jury shall be preserved, and no fact tried by a jury, shall be otherwise re-examined in any Court of the United States, than according to the rules of the common law." These two amendments ensure this palladium of freedom is guaranteed for all in both criminal and civil cases.

The suppression of the right to trial by jury strikes at the heart of the rule of law by abolishing the sacred method for searching for the truth and achieving justice. It eviscerates unalienable rights by depriving colonists of a fundamental protection from government tyranny. It infringes on equality by singling out the colonists from their English brethren. It severs the Social Compact by eliminating trial by a jury of peers. Further, it delimits government by expanding the reach and authority of imperial power. This fundamental oppression warrants revolution.*

*The* [Dockyards, etc. Protection Act of 1772] *is, as we apprehended, a violent infringement of our rights. By this act, any one of us may be taken from his family, and carried to any part of Great-Britain, there to be tried.* [...] *Thus we are not only deprived of our grand right to trial by our peers in the vicinity, but any person suspected, or pretended to be suspected, may be hurried to Great-Britain, to take his trial in any county the king or his successors shall please to direct; where, innocent or guilty, he is in great danger of being condemned; and whether condemned or acquitted, he will probably be ruined by the expense attending the trial, and his long absence from his family and business; and we shall have the strongest reason to apprehend that we shall soon experience the fatal effects of this act.**

The Boston Pamphlet (November 2, 1772)*

# 41

## "For transporting us beyond Seas to be tried for pretended offences:"

- ☆ The Treason Act of 1543, the Vice Admiralty Court Act of 1764, the Dockyards, etc. Protection Act of 1772, the Murder Act, and similar measures violate the right to be tried by a jury of your peers by allowing trials to be conducted in England or elsewhere outside of the county in which the alleged crime occurred.

- ☆ By ripping colonists away from their homes to stand trial in England and elsewhere, the British subvert the rule of law, violate the unalienable right to be tried by a jury of one's peers, destroy the Social Compact by isolating the accused from their homes, mock equality by depriving the colonists of rights secured to their English brethren, and gut limited government.

The nineteenth grievance is tightly related to the eighteenth by opposing the empire's changing the location of trials. English law has long held that the jury must be drawn from members of the local community. Additionally, jury trials are to be held in the county (often referred to as a "shire") out of which the case arises. The jurisdiction in which a case is to be tried is its "venue," and the area from which the jury pool is selected is its "vicinage." For example, if a murder is allegedly committed today in Oakland County, Michigan, barring extraordinary circumstances, the case will be tried at the circuit court located in the Oakland County seat, Pontiac, Michigan, with jurors drawn from across Oakland County.* This ensures a criminal defendant is tried by a jury of peers.

The jurors are chosen from the accused's community so that the defendant will receive fair justice. People familiar with the circumstances of the community are best equipped to provide justice in any given case. It also ensures that witnesses and other evidence are readily available. Since most defendants are from the venue, conducting the trial in their home community protects defendants from being harassed by requiring them to travel far away. It also allows them to be with their family, continue work (if granted bond), and find a lawyer they trust. Plus, the community possesses a vested interest in ensuring that justice is achieved. The rule of law demands it. Not to be overlooked, a jury of your peers is a physical embodiment of the First Principle of the Social Compact—the people have a stake in ensuring that justice is done in connection with crimes that occur within their local jurisdiction. Prosecutors, law enforcement, witnesses, and judges are all held accountable for their actions by the family and friends of the victims and defendants, the local press, other government officials, and voters. All these purposes are furthered by having trials with juries composed of peers. This protection is embedded in the Magna Carta of 1215 in connection with trials of nobles and eventually expands to address all defendants.

But like so much else, when it comes to the colonies, the British toss away a deeply rooted tradition. The empire once again singles out the colonies for oppressive treatment. As we have learned, the original admiralty courts are in England, and with the Vice Admiralty Court Act of 1764, a new vice-admiralty court is established in Halifax, Canada. Colonists will be shipped to another colony to face trial.

Furthermore, a mostly neglected law is resurrected by the British Empire, which allows perhaps the gravest of all crimes—treason—to be tried overseas. The Treason Act of 1543 is passed during the reign of King Henry VIII and provides that treason committed outside of England may nevertheless be tried within England. Because the realm of England is the imperial seat of the vast British Empire, treason committed in any outpost of the British Empire is triable in England. After all, the crime is against the empire. Not to mention, a conviction is much more likely in the imperial seat. However, because of salutary neglect, before 1763, no American colonist faces such a trial overseas.

Still, the colonists have reason to be concerned that enforcement will spring to life. In 1769, the colonists robustly protest the Townshend Acts. Parliament questions whether some of these protests are treasonous. It instructs Massachusetts Governor Francis Bernard to investigate Bostonians for treason, which, if charged, will be tried in England. Fortunately for the colonists, Governor Bernard never finds enough evidence to levy charges, so the issue is rendered practically moot for a few years.

The issue soon enough raises its ugly head again. In the autumn of 1772, Parliament enacts the Dockyards, etc. Protection Act, which criminalizes arson or other destruction of the empire's ships, vessels of war, military stores, or ammunition while in a dockyard or warehouse. The act provides that the crime is punishable by death, and any person accused of such a crime, wherever committed, may be tried in England whenever the monarch chooses.

This law now comes to the forefront. On the night of June 9, 1772, in Narragansett Bay, Rhode Island, the *Gaspee*, a British schooner tasked with suppressing smuggling, chases a suspected smuggling colonial sloop, the *Hannah*, but runs aground during the chase. Eight smaller colonial whaleboats capture the helpless ship after midnight and burn it to the waterline. The empire is outraged. The imperial authorities direct that any accused perpetrators be transported to England to face trial. Unfortunately for the British, no witnesses meaningfully cooperate with the investigation. Although no one is accused, the very threat of exiling the accused across the sea riles the ire of Americans across the continent.

The issue cannot fade when the dreaded Murder Act (also known as the Administration of Justice Act of 1774) removes certain murder trials to England. One of the Intolerable Acts, this constitutes part of the fifteenth grievance. Although the Murder Act maintains the right to trial by jury, it authorizes murder trials—among the gravest of crimes—to be tried not by a jury of one's peers, but by Englishmen.

The colonists understand what these degradations are all about: making sure that colonists are uprooted from their communities and shipped overseas for show trials in front of authorities sympathetic to the empire's oppressive policies. The Virginia House of Burgesses initially condemns English attempts to undermine long-standing venue and vicinage protections in a set of resolves adopted on May 16, 1769, and drafted by George Mason (a leading Founding Father in Virginia who is later instrumental in ensuring that the United States Bill of Rights is adopted). The House of Burgesses strenuously objects to removing trials as violating the rights of the accused. The oppression is palpable. Due process and the rule of law are smashed. These violations of the right to be tried by a jury of peers are the epitome of British tyranny.

There is one noteworthy (and perhaps surprising) caveat to this grievance. Historians are unable to identify any colonists actually shipped to England for trial. The failure to prosecute is almost certainly because the American authorities and everyday colonists are not about to allow any of their brethren to be seized and sent overseas for trial. After all, they refuse to allow the Stamp Act to be administered and for taxed tea to even reach a dock to be unloaded. That they will willingly allow a Patriot to be tried in England is inconceivable.

As we have explored, the Sixth Amendment of the Constitution provides that "[i]n all criminal prosecutions, the accused shall enjoy the right to a speedy and public trial, by an impartial jury of the State and district wherein the crime shall have been committed, which district shall have been previously ascertained by law." No defendants will be shipped overseas or to other States to face trial. Witnesses and evidence will not be forced to undertake perilous journeys for trial. Justice will be rendered in open courtrooms, by a fair jury drawn from the locality that suffers the alleged harm. The Sixth Amendment ensures due process for the accused and justice for the public.

The British assault on the right to be tried by a jury of one's peers in their home venue and vicinage subverts the rule of law, violates a key unalienable right, annihilates the Social Compact, undermines equality, and explodes limited government. It can only stop with revolution.*

*[I]t behooves us to be upon our guard against the deceitful wiles of those who would persuade us, that we have nothing to fear from the operation of the Quebec Act* [of 1774]. *We should consider it as being replete with danger to ourselves, and as threatening ruin to our posterity. Let us not, therefore, suffer ourselves to be terrified at the prospect of an imaginary and fictitious Scylla* [a man-eating monster preying on one side of a narrow strait], *and, by that means, be led blindfold into a real and destructive Charybdis* [a man-eating whirlpool monster waiting on the other side of the strait].*

Alexander Hamilton (June 22, 1775)

# 42

## "For abolishing the free System of English Laws in a neighbouring Province, establishing therein an Arbitrary government, and enlarging its Boundaries so as to render it at once an example and fit instrument for introducing the same absolute rule into these Colonies:"

☆ The Quebec Act of 1774 establishes the rules for governing the newly conquered territory of the French province of Quebec. It vastly increases the size and population of the province, all but makes Catholicism the official religion, enforces tithes to the Catholic church, abolishes English common law as well as rights (including the sacred right of trial by jury), and eliminates a representative form of government.

☆ The Quebec Act of 1774 threatens colonial independence and freedom by encircling the colonies with historic enemies accountable solely to the king. The colonists also fear that with the bald abolition of representative government and English law and rights in Canada, the British are plotting to do the same in the colonies.

☆ This conspiracy violates the rule of law by supplanting English law with the French Civil Code, abolishes the Social Compact by annihilating any form of representative government, imposes inequality by treating the colonists entirely differently than their brethren in England, threatens their long-standing unalienable rights, and destroys any pretense of limited government by implementing complete authority to remake colonial governments.

The twentieth grievance proceeds to Canada. When the British Empire defeats the French Empire in the Seven Years' War, the French are forced to cede Canada to the British. The British create the province of Quebec from their newly won territory.

But the handoff is a tricky matter. Nearly all the colonial inhabitants of Canada are of Catholic French origin, with a different culture and expectations. Once British King Henry VIII cuts ties to Rome and declares himself the head of the Church of England, the majority of British are decidedly Protestant. There are successive religious persecutions during waves of bloody infighting among Christian denominations in the British Isles. Well before the 1760s, the Protestant church of England prevails and dominates the British government and culture. Catholics are treated as second-class subjects and are severely repressed. In Great Britain, the Catholic threat to the English monarchy is crushed.

Then in 1763, the Protestant English take control of a firmly Catholic Canada. The province poses a vastly more difficult challenge than the Catholic minority in England. Canadian Catholics outnumber Canadian Protestants by approximately four hundred to one. They have no allegiance to the British. A policy of reconciliation is easily the most efficacious method of placating Canadians and avoiding a Catholic French revolt in Quebec. Fortunately for the British, the Canadians are not particularly opposed to English rule if they can maintain their way of life. In the end, to ingratiate the British Empire with the Canadians, Parliament enacts the Quebec Act of 1774. The act provides vital concessions to the French Catholics to allow them to maintain their culture and customs within the loving embrace and protection of the British Empire.

The colonists view the act with deep suspicion and alarm. Even if none of the other grievances existed, it is a dire development. Although the British ministry designs the act well before the Boston Tea Party and Britain's subsequent response, that is immaterial. The timing of its passage is disastrous—it comes right along with the Intolerable Acts, and the colonists naturally treat it as such. When viewed in light of the other twenty-seven grievances, the colonists cannot help but view the twentieth as part of an imperial plot to violate the liberties and destroy self-rule of the colonists. The act has five major features that prove the point.

First, surprisingly, the act massively expands Quebec's territory. It more than quadruples the size of the French-speaking province, expanding into modern-day Ontario, Michigan, Ohio, Wisconsin, Illinois, and Minnesota. Yet, as we explored earlier, some colonies claim lands far to the West—they assert that their western borders reach across to the end of the continent. Many colonists believe they were indispensable to winning the French and Indian War and are entitled to settle the western frontier. In one fell swoop, the Quebec Act of 1774 quashes colonial claims for western lands previously made by Virginia, Pennsylvania, Connecticut, and Massachusetts. England betrays the colonists by giving the land to, of all people, the French Catholics—the very enemy whom the colonists sacrificed and risked their lives and treasure to defeat. Because the act is enacted to bottle up the colonies on the East Coast and prevent western expansion, Richard Henry Lee, the influential Virginian Patriot who moves for independence at the Second Continental Congress, denounces the act as "the worst grievance" against the empire.*

Second, this geographic expansion sweeps another eighty thousand French settlers into the colony. The French population of the province substantially expands. Most colonists continue to consider the recently defeated French Catholic colonists as a threat. Compounding this understandable animosity is the reality that more than a few Founding Fathers are religious bigots and despise Catholics—or at least oppose the growth of Catholicism in the colonies. New England, in particular, harbors deep-seated animosity against the French Canadians. Bitter, violent clashes plague their relations for over a century before the French and Indian War. Wretched stereotypes are strongly held by both sides. Now the colonists must face down a tightly organized province under British rule populated by their historical enemies. Some even perceive Canada as becoming a new arsenal that Great Britain is building up to invade the colonies if necessary. Connecticut religious leader Ebenezer Baldwin preaches that the real reason for the act is to encircle the colonists and coerce them into submission:

> When this vast extent of territory comes to be filled up with inhabitants, near half America will be under this arbitrary *French* government. So that upon the whole the Quebec act [of 1774] doubtless wears as threatening an aspect upon Americans as any act that has been passed by the British parliament. [Italics are in the original.]*

The British establish a vast province, full of well-armed, hated enemies to intimidate and threaten the colonists.

Third, as long as local priests recognize King George III as their sovereign, the practice of Catholicism is protected and promoted. A Catholic bishop settles in Canada, extending the pope's reach into North America under British protection. Moreover, tithes in support of the Catholic church are collected and enforced by the authorities. Only a handful of the leading Founding Fathers are Catholics. For the most part, the Founding Generation is composed of Protestants and deists who firmly reject Catholicism in general and more robustly oppose any kind of tax or other support for the universal church. The Quebec Act of 1774, however, journeys in the opposite direction. Meanwhile, the rights of Protestants and other religious minorities in Quebec are oppressed. This completely bewilders the colonists. After all, did not the English win the war? Why should the French Catholics flourish in the newly conquered territory of Canada to the great detriment of English Protestants?

Fourth, the Quebec Act of 1774 ends the British military rule that had been in place since the end of the French and Indian War and establishes a centralized civilian government. Unlike in England, Catholics are eligible to serve as government officials. Much more crucial is the noticeable absence of an elected legislative assembly. In theory, the act allows for an elected assembly, but none is ever convened before the American Revolution. George III's appointed governor and his council rule the province without check. The act creates an arbitrary government solely accountable to the monarch in London—and perhaps also the pope in Rome—*not* the people. A diabolical combination.

John Adams observes that, along with the Massachusetts Government Act, the Quebec Act of 1774 is a direct threat to representative self-government. George III and Parliament are revealing that they will not hesitate to abolish the existing forms of elected representative government in the colonies and replace them with authoritarian regimes if it serves their interests: "The question we insist on most is not whether the alteration is for the better or not, but whether parliament has any right to make any alteration at all. And it is the universal sense of America, that it has none."*

The government established in Canada is a grave omen of what will happen in the thirteen colonies. Leading South Carolinian Patriot William Henry Drayton explains that, combined with the Massachusetts Government Act, the Quebec Act of 1774 is an illustration and model for what the British truly have in store for the rest of the colonies. Since the empire argues that the American colonies and Canada are subject to the same authority of the king and Parliament, "[W]hat fiction of argument shall prevent the same power being exercised over the other, and in short over all the colonies in America, since the law considers them all but in one and the same light?"* The empire shows that it will uproot and annihilate any government opposed to it and replace it with a government wholly beholden to the king and Parliament.

Fifth, the act preserves the French Civil Code, effectively wiping out English common law. For centuries, the common law is the prevailing method of resolving civil and criminal disputes in Great Britain. Common law is made by judges who reason through cases based on prior legal precedents as applied to the specific facts in any given case. Over the centuries, judicial innovations in common law expand the people's liberties and privileges. Combined with the right to a jury trial, common law is seen as the great guardian of liberty and justice. On the other hand, the French Civil Code is a written statutory text adopted by French legislative authorities, which is hardly concerned with the liberties of the people. The code is literally a foreign method of governing civil relations. Worse, there is no jury trial in the French Civil Code. Parliament snuffs out this palladium of freedom.

The overall situation in Canada poses a grave threat to individual liberty and self-government. This is particularly distressing considering that the colonists who ventured past the Proclamation Line are now swept into Canada and lose all their English rights. Dr. Joseph Warren's Suffolk Resolves expresses the widely held view

> [t]hat the late act of Parliament for establishing the Roman Catholic religion and the French laws in that extensive country, now called Canada, is dangerous in an extreme degree to the Protestant religion and to the civil rights and liberties of all America.*

John Adams similarly reflects that the Quebec Act of 1774 is simply another manifestation of the Declaratory Act. The king and Parliament believe they can pass pretended legislation about anything—including the unalienable right to the free exercise of religion. Taxation without representation is already threatening to make the colonists slaves, and now they will lose their souls: "Have not the ministry shown by the Quebec bill, that we have no security against them for our religion any more than our property, if we once submit to the unlimited claims of parliament?"*

The Continental Congress takes an emphatic stand against this menace. On October 21, 1774, it issues the "Address to the People of Great Britain" written by John Jay, Richard Henry Lee, and William Livingston. It is a plea to the British People to wake up and support the colonists in their resistance to imperial tyranny. A large portion of the letter is dedicated to the danger posed by the Quebec Act of 1774. It specifically declares

> the legislature of Great Britain is not authorized [...] to establish a religion, fraught with sanguinary and impious tenets, or, to erect an arbitrary form of government in any quarter of the globe. These rights we, as well as you, deem sacred. And yet sacred as they are, they have, with many others, been repeatedly and flagrantly violated.*

The Quebec Act of 1774 is beyond the powers of Parliament and violates the sacred rights of Englishmen. The empire intends "to reduce the ancient free Protestant colonies to the same state of slavery with themselves."* The British purpose is obvious: Imperial authorities are clearly pursuing a policy to enslave the colonists under the boots of Catholic Canada. There can be no other explanation. "Admit that the ministry, by the powers of Britain, and the aid of our Roman Catholic neighbours, should be able to carry the point of taxation, and reduce us to a state of perfect humiliation and slavery."* It warns that after the colonists lose their freedoms, the people in the British Isles are next.

The First Continental Congress expresses similar alarm in its Declaration and Resolves, in which it names the Quebec Act of 1774 (along with the rest of the Intolerable Acts) as "impolitic, unjust, and cruel, as well as unconstitutional, and most dangerous and destructive of American rights."* The Declaration of the Causes and Necessity of Taking Up Arms, issued July 6, 1775, lists among the reasons justifying violent resistance to British oppression the "erecting in a neighboring province, acquired by the joint arms of Great Britain and America, a despotism dangerous to our very existence."*

The United States Constitution counters the dangers of the Quebec Act of 1774 in many ways. First, Article IV, Section 3 vests Congress with the "[p]ower to dispose of and make all needful Rules and Regulations respecting the Territory or other Property belonging to the United States." In other words, Congress dictates what laws govern any territory, all but barring any Quebec Act–type governance. The Northwest Ordinance is but the first of many such acts—and it bans slavery as well as guarantees religious and political liberty. Second, through the same mechanism, Congress can prevent any massive "super" state like Quebec from being formed. Instead, Congress will appropriately divide the western lands into several territories and eventual States. This also comes to fruition in the Northwest Ordinance and its successors. Third, Article IV, Section 4 provides that "[t]he United States shall guarantee to every State in this Union a Republican Form of Government."

Royal governors will not become dictators in America. Every State must have an elected legislature and executive branch. Fourth, the same section provides that the federal government "shall protect each" State "against Invasion." Foreign enemies will be kept at bay by the federal government, countering the specter of invasion by an encircling enemy. Fifth, the right to a jury trial is guaranteed by the Sixth and Seventh Amendments—no French Civil Code abolishing the right to a jury will prevail here. Sixth, the First Amendment to the Constitution provides "Congress shall make no law respecting an establishment of religion, or prohibiting the free exercise thereof." No church or State will coerce our citizens to pay tithes or taxes to support a religious sect, and no citizens will face discrimination because of their religion. Seventh, Article VI provides that "no religious Test shall ever be required as a Qualification to any Office or public Trust under the United States." A person of any faith can serve in any office.

The Quebec Act of 1774 proves true all the colonists' worst fears. It threatens colonial independence by encircling the colonies with historic enemies accountable solely to the king. The empire abolishes representative government and English law and rights in Canada; this foreshadows what will inevitably occur in the colonies. The British conspiracy violates the rule of law by supplanting English law with the French Civil Code, abolishes the Social Compact by annihilating any form of representative government, imposes inequality by treating the colonists completely differently than their Protestant brethren in England, infringes their long-standing unalienable rights (especially the right to a jury trial), and destroys any pretense of limited government. Only revolution will defeat this diabolical plot.*

[The Massachusetts Government Act of 1774 is a] *gross infraction* [...] *of those rights to which we are justly entitled by the laws of the British Constitution, and the charter of the province.**

Suffolk Resolves (September 9, 1774)

# 43

## "For taking away our Charters, abolishing our most valuable Laws, and altering fundamentally the Forms of our Governments:"

☆ The Massachusetts Government Act of 1774 abolishes the Massachusetts legislature and makes the governor a dictator solely accountable to the king.

☆ The Massachusetts Government Act of 1774 upends the rule of law by critically changing the governing charter of Massachusetts, destroys the Social Compact by decimating any form of representative government, imposes inequality by treating the Massachusetts colonists entirely differently than their brethren in the British Isles, violates colonists' unalienable rights, and ravages any pretense of limited government.

The twenty-first grievance is composed of three subparts, relating to a single overarching complaint. The first phase is "taking away our charters." To understand this, we need to remember that the king permits colonists to establish new colonies under his authority. Typically, the monarch authorizes such colonization in one of three forms: proprietary, charter, and royal. Regardless of the form, all the colonies have some form of legal authorization from the Crown to colonize North America, which is codified in a document commonly referred to as a "charter."

Proprietary colonies are literally owned by a single person or group of people.

Maryland ("Mary-Land") is the first proprietary colony given to the second Baron Baltimore, Cecil Calvert, in 1632 as a haven for Catholics. Soon, the area is colonized directly under Lord Baltimore's control. Still, he quickly cedes to the demands of the settlers and establishes a representative general assembly. Pennsylvania is granted to William Penn as a haven for Quakers. Although Penn has unlimited authority to govern the colony, he believes in a republican form of government and creates the Frame of Government with an elected legislature. New York, New Jersey, North Carolina, and South Carolina all begin as proprietary colonies, but, for various reasons, they become royal colonies over time. By the time of the American Revolution, only Pennsylvania, Maryland, and Delaware remain proprietary.

A charter colony is governed by a joint-stock company (comparable to a modern-day corporation). Investors pool money into the stock company, each investor is issued a certain amount of stock, and when they raise sufficient funds to underwrite a colonial venture, they apply to the monarch to colonize a part of the New World. If the Crown agrees, a charter is issued establishing the parameters of how the colony is to be explored, colonized, and governed. The charter is akin to a contract between the Crown and the investors about the rights and responsibilities of each party involving the colony. A few years before the American Revolution, Rhode Island and Connecticut are the only true charter colonies.

Royal colonies (also known as "crown colonies" and "provincial colonies") are governed by royal governors and a council, whom the king appoints. At the start of the American Revolution, more than half of the colonies are royal colonies. There is no intermediary—no proprietor or stock company. The colonial government works directly for the Crown through its appointees. Still, they all have representative assemblies elected by the people.

At the time of Revolution, Massachusetts is unique. Under the Massachusetts Charter of 1691, the monarch appoints the governor and deputy governor, and the governor has a legislative veto. The people of the towns elect the General Court, the lower legislative assembly. The equivalent to the House of Representatives, the General Court appoints the governor's council (the equivalent of a cabinet). The governor's council also serves as the upper house, the equivalent to the House of Lords or the State senate. Under the Massachusetts Charter of 1691, many government officials are only appointed with the approval of the governor's council. Practically, because the General Court appoints the governor's council, the General Court retains a great deal of (at least indirect) influence on such appointments. Jurors are selected by the residents of local towns. The heart of self-government in Massachusetts is the town meeting, in which all voters can attend and vote on the issues of the day.

Everything changes with the empire's reaction to the Boston Tea Party. The

Intolerable Acts include the Massachusetts Government Act of 1774. This act revokes and amends vital portions of the charter of 1691. Although some historians write that it revokes the whole charter, it is more accurately characterized as a fundamental amendment. Regardless of the characterization, it guts the key components of self-government that are guaranteed by the charter of 1691.

The second and third portions of this twenty-first grievance refer to "abolishing our most valuable laws, and altering fundamentally the forms of our governments." Under the act, Parliament closes the General Court as a bastion of opposition to British oppression. The governor's council is now appointed directly by the king and serves at his pleasure. They must do what George III wants, or they will be terminated. All significant government officials are discharged from office effective on August 1, 1774. The governor is now vested with total control of the appointment and the removal of all judges, the attorney general, justices of the peace, sheriffs, and similar judicial and law enforcement officers. Judges receive their pay directly from the king instead of the legislature. The governor, in essence, becomes the dictator of Massachusetts. Since the governor does the king's bidding, George III is now the indirect dictator of Massachusetts. Jurors are no longer selected by local residents, but by the sheriffs, who are now under the total control of the governor. Town meetings—the heart of the Massachusetts democratic process under the charter of 1691—are abolished unless approved by the governor. The only exception is an annual meeting at which local officials are elected. As we learned in the twelfth grievance, the king replaces the civilian governor with General Thomas Gage. Massachusetts is now a military dictatorship. The act even moves the colonial capital out of Boston and to Salem (of earlier witch trials infamy).

If such tyranny was attempted in the British Isles, George III would be condemned as a dictator of the first order, and a civil war would likely ignite. After all, its provocations are substantially less than what triggers the Glorious Revolution.

Some apologists for the Crown argue that George III is exercising his authority in accord with historical practice. By their very nature, royal charters can be altered by the king. In practice, charters are altered many times, including even the form of charter. The colonists universally reject this explanation as a thinly veiled attempt to hide what is really happening. Historically, charter reforms are undertaken to address changing circumstances and effectuated with the consent of the governed. No such necessity or consent is involved with the Massachusetts Government Act of 1774. The only thing that changes in the last eighty-five years is that the British Empire is now oppressive, and Massachusetts is resisting. Overnight, Massachusetts is transformed from perhaps the most democratic form of government in the British Empire (and likely the world) to a mere instrumentality of George III. The replacement of the Social Compact embodied in the charter of

1691 with the top-down, royal absolutism of the Massachusetts Government Act of 1774 is devastating.

The twenty-first grievance provokes a colonial backlash the likes of which the colonies have not witnessed since the opposition to the Stamp Act. The Massachusetts colonists will not accept these affronts to self-rule. Although George III and Parliament are attempting to lord over the people as puppet masters, in reality, those government officials lose nearly all control over the colony. Writing to the Committee of Correspondence of Marblehead, Samuel Adams declares that so long as "the sister colonies" continue to assist Boston, "we shall not disgrace the common cause of America, by any submissions to the barbarous edict."* This is no mere bluster. When Governor Gage attempts to appoint a new governor's council, enraged patriotic mobs intimidate most appointees to refuse or resign their offices, and the rest flee Boston. Governor Gage writes to Lord Dartmouth on September 2, 1774, that the colonial government is collapsing and only military occupation can prop up the regime:

> Things are worse here than I expected. Six [gubernatorial] councillors have had to fly to protection of troops and others have been intimidated. Andrew Oliver, Isaac Winslow, Thomas Harrison, Lee of Cambridge, Danforth and Watson have resigned. [The Massachusetts Government] Act [of 1774] is evaded and town-meetings continue. Court did not meet at Worcester or here [in Boston]. [...] The whole is now at stake and the only step to take is to secure friends of government in Boston and reinforce troops here. I propose to order troops at New York and Philadelphia to come here, possibly also 10th and 52nd regiments at Quebec. Civil government is near its end. I mean to avoid any bloody crisis as long as possible. To stem the torrent respectable force including irregulars will be necessary. The people are not a Boston rabble but the freeholders and farmers of the country. First stroke will decide a great deal. Vast concourse assembled this day eight miles from here: Lieut.-Governor Oliver begged I would not send troops there as it would be fatal to him.*

The colonists shut down the county courts in the summer of 1774, and some will not reopen until 1781. Towns and counties ignore the dictates of the Massachusetts Government Act of 1774. They simply continue to perform their duties in defiance of the law. Where courts are still operating, juries are selected on a local level as before. County and town meetings continue to meet. Samuel Adams and the other Sons of Liberty methodically take control of local militia. Meanwhile, massive protests throughout the colony result in many royalist government officials tendering their resignations. As Governor Gage relates to Lord Dartmouth, he is concerned that showing force will provoke the colonials into drawing blood. Gage's letter also reveals that he is exploring receiving troops from Quebec to occupy Boston—the exact fear dreaded by the colonists in connection with the Quebec Act of 1774.

The Suffolk Resolves call the Massachusetts Government Act of 1774 and other recent British oppressions "gross infractions of those rights to which we are justly entitled by the laws of nature, the British Constitution, and the charter of the province."* It demands that all officials who take office under the act resign or be deemed the worst enemies of the people.

In May 1775, after it becomes apparent that the overtures of the First Continental Congress are failing to reverse British policy, the Massachusetts Provincial Congress (the revolutionary governing body that replaces the General Court) seeks advice from the Second Continental Congress. Congress responds that it should act as if the charter of 1691 remains in full force, conducting new elections and proceeding as if there is no governor or governor's council.

Opposition is hardly confined to Massachusetts. Colonists across America know full well that the act is a dangerous precedent to undermine the rule of law, devastate the Social Compact, and destroy the unalienable rights of the colonists in all the colonies. The empire abolishes the form of the Massachusetts government in one masterstroke. Although the Massachusetts Government Act of 1774 is the most glaring apostasy, as we previously explored in the eighth grievance, in North Carolina, there is a royal attempt to so gravely interfere with the administration of justice that the courts shut down permanently. Add the Quebec Act of 1774, and every colony is at risk of being the next victim of absolute tyranny. The colonists fear that what happens in North Carolina, Quebec, and Massachusetts are just the first stage of oppression, a dreadful preview of British overarching repression that will violate the First Principles of a free and just government and make all the colonists slaves to the empire.

No surprise then that the First Continental Congress's Declaration and Resolves finds that the Massachusetts Government Act of 1774 violates "the rights of the colonists."* This is so because Parliament is fundamentally "altering the charter and government of the Massachusetts-Bay."*

This is worth drawing blood. Congress details as a key grievance that justifies violent defense the Massachusetts Government Act of 1774's "altering fundamentally the form of government established by charter, and secured by acts of its own legislature solemnly confirmed by the Crown."*

The federal Constitution counters this grievance in Article IV, Section 4 by providing that "[t]he United States shall guarantee to every State in this Union a Republican Form of Government." Every State must have an elected legislature and executive. In addition, Congress only has the powers enumerated to it in the Constitution. The Tenth Amendment provides that "[t]he powers not delegated to the United States by the Constitution, nor prohibited by it to the States, are reserved to the States respectively, or to the people." The federal government has no authority to change, revoke, suspend, or alter the government of any State. That is reserved for the people of each State. The federal government is powerless to disrupt the Social Compact of any State.

The twenty-first grievance is extraordinarily serious, destroying all American rights and the First Principles of a free and just government. It all but abolishes the representative charter of 1691 and creates an arbitrary, dictatorial government. The independence of the legislative and judicial branches is smashed. The Social Compact is torn asunder, the rule of law is ripped to shreds, the unalienable rights of the people are trampled underfoot, equality is mocked, and limited government is trounced. The same fate awaits the rest of the colonists unless they resist.*

*[T]his government has endeavored to pervert the same* [the exercises of the kingly office] *into a detestable and insupportable tyranny* [...] *by suspending our own legislatures & declaring themselves invested with power to legislate for us in all cases whatsoever.**

Thomas Jefferson (June 1776)

# 44

## "For Suspending Our Own Legislatures, and Declaring Themselves Invested with Power to Legislate for Us in All Cases Whatsoever."

- ☆ To coerce the quartering of troops, the empire enacts a law suspending the New York General Assembly.
- ☆ In the Declaratory Act, Parliament announces that it wields unlimited authority to legislate in all cases whatsoever on behalf of the colonies.
- ☆ By overriding colonial legislative authority, Great Britain subverts the rule of law by gutting colonial lawmaking, violates the Social Compact by destroying representative government, threatens unalienable rights by authorizing their destruction, imposes inequality by treating the colonists as completely different from other British subjects, and destroys limited government by fully vesting in Parliament unlimited power over the colonies.

The twenty-second grievance has two components. The first involves "suspending our own legislatures." This continues the themes of previous grievances involving British interference with the colonial assemblies. In addition, the twenty-second grievance partially overlaps with what we learned in connection with the fourteenth grievance involving the quartering of troops. Parliament enacts a law to suspend the

New York General Assembly over its refusal to support the quartering of troops in the colony. Thomas Hutchinson, former Massachusetts governor and Loyalist, thinks this grievance is hardly worth addressing. In his critique of the Declaration, he downplays the grievance by noting that

> [t]he only instance of the suspension of any legislative power is that of the province of New York, for refusing to comply with an act of Parliament for quartering the king's troops posted there for its protection and defense against the French and Indian enemies.*

Reflecting the rest of the empire's sentiments, Parliament's suspending a legislature to coerce it to do the Crown's bidding is trivial. Ex-Governor Hutchinson might believe it is of little concern, but in reality, it is fundamental to the relationship of the colonists to the empire: Colonists must bend the knee and submit to arbitrary rule whenever the empire decides it should be so. This threat subverts the First Principles of a free and just government.

The second part of the grievance is a definitive legal declaration by Parliament that it is "invested with power to legislate for us in all cases whatsoever." This is an elaboration of the thirteenth grievance involving the Declaratory Act. As we explored, Parliament passes the act on the same day Parliament rescinds the Stamp Act (March 18, 1766). The act is very similar to the Irish Declaratory Act of 1719. To shorten a complicated and long story, England invades Ireland, colonizes the kingdom, and suppresses the Catholic majority. After decades of conflict, Parliament passes the Declaratory Act of 1719, which proclaims that it has the authority to pass all laws for the Kingdom of Ireland and that the British House of Lords is the final court of any appeals from Irish courts.

Like with Ireland, Parliament conceives that it has the unfettered authority to legislate for the American colonies. The fact that no colonists serve in Parliament, that each colony has its own elected legislature authorized by their governing charters, and that England has not vanquished the colonies like it has Ireland, is of no importance. Section I of the Declaratory Act announces that

> the [...] colonies [...] in America have been, are, and of right ought to be, subordinate unto, and dependent upon the imperial crown and parliament of Great Britain; and that the king's majesty, by and with the advice and consent of the lords spiritual and temporal, and commons of Great Britain, in parliament assembled, had, has, and of right ought to have, full power and

> authority to make laws and statutes of sufficient force and validity to bind the colonies and the people of America, subjects of the crown of Great Britain, in all cases whatsoever.*

Parliament and the king rule over the colonies "in all cases whatsoever." No exceptions. Never mind the colonial legislatures, charters, and laws. In that vein, Section II of the act continues:

> [A]ll resolutions, votes, orders, and proceedings in any of the [...] colonies [...] whereby the power and authority of the parliament of Great Britain, to make laws and statues as aforesaid, is denied, or drawn into question, are, and are hereby declared to be, utterly null and void to all intents and purposes whatsoever. [Italics are in the original.]*

Parliament is deadly serious. All actions taken by the colonial authorities asserting that Parliament does not have the authority to legislate in the colonies are utterly null and void.

Despite its words, some colonists reason that the Declaratory Act is simply a token measure undertaken by Parliament in light of its humiliating repeal of the Stamp Act. In particular, some colonists argue that Parliament has the constitutional authority to pass legislation regulating the external trade of the colonies. Such regulations could even take the form of taxes, so long as they were directed at external trade. For example, tariffs on trade between the colonies and France would be considered valid external regulations. This external vs. internal taxation debate was addressed earlier in the seventeenth grievance regarding taxation without representation. These colonists hold on to the phantom hope that this is all the Declaratory Act effectuates.

Even a few members of Parliament question whether the proposed Declaratory Act justifies internal taxation, such as the Stamp Act. Prime Minister Charles Watson-Wentworth, Lord Rockingham, wishes to leave out of the bill any specific mention of taxation, hoping its omission will pacify the colonists and their sympathizers. At the time, many colonists believe that they owe no allegiance to Parliament, only to the king. Different propositions are bandied about on determining how the colonials will be properly loyal to the king and subject to his rule within the umbrella of the empire.

Parliament considers all these intellectual exercises and theoretical flights of fancy to be absolutely ridiculous. Parliament has been fighting against the authority of the monarchy for centuries and finally reduces it to an acceptable level following the Glorious Revolution of 1688. Legislative supremacy over the entire empire rests in Parliament; the colonies have nothing to do with it. Parliamentarian opposition leader and colonial sympathizer William Pitt refuses to support the Declaratory Act because he knows those supporting it assume all taxation is included in the act, even without express mention.

The Declaratory Act makes no pretense of even trying to justify the awesome, absolute power that Parliament claims over the colonists. There is no reference to representation and no acknowledgement of colonial representative legislative assemblies; it does not even rely on the old mystifying explanation of virtual representation. The colonists merely need to accept it.

Over and over again in history, optimists—or perhaps people blinded by hope—are surprised when those in power act on their promises. There should be no surprise here. The colonists who believe the act is harmless bewitch themselves into utter self-delusion. Parliament promulgates the act as a declaration of *principle* from which it will never retreat. Regardless of hopes and fanciful thoughts, the text is clear—it applies to all acts, including internal taxes among them. The act gains overwhelming majorities in the House of Commons and the House of Lords. The votes of each chamber are so lopsided that they do not bother to record the votes of individual members.

Soon enough, the colonists realize that the Declaratory Act is the lynchpin of the entire dispute with the empire. In full accord with the act, Pitt is vindicated in his fears with the passage of new internal taxes on the colonists through the Townshend Acts. The same pretense is used with the Intolerable Acts and the other statutory enactments that the grievances expose. As we explored in the thirteenth grievance, virtual representation is preposterous. Parliament cannot and should not represent the people of the colonies, and it should not pretend that it has such authority. This idea is repeatedly addressed in various pamphlets, petitions, resolutions, and proclamations from 1766 until 1776. One of the more striking examples is by James Wilson in a pamphlet published in August 1774, in which he asks searing rhetorical questions about Parliament's supposed unlimited authority over the colonies:

> But from what sources does this mighty, this uncontrolled authority of the house of commons flow? From the collective body of the commons [that is, the People] of Great Britain. This authority, must, therefore, originally reside in them: for whatever they convey to their representatives must ultimately be in themselves. And have those, whom we have hitherto been accustomed to consider as our fellow-subjects, an absolute and unlimited power

> over us? Have they a natural right to make laws, by which we may be deprived of our properties, of our liberties, of our lives? By what title do they claim to be our masters? What act of ours has rendered us subject to those, to whom we were formerly equal? Is British freedom denominated from the soil or from the *people* of Britain? If from the latter, do they lose it by quitting the soil? Do those who disembark freemen in Great Britain, disembark slaves in America? [Italics are in the original.]*

How exactly the representatives of the people of England conclude that they are now the masters of unrepresented Americans is a bewildering mystery. It is never satisfactorily answered. Wilson guts the pretense of the Declaratory Act.

Opposition to the Declaratory Act becomes an organizing force for resisting the empire. As but one illustration, another powerful denunciation of this theory comes from the hotbed of American resistance, Boston. In November 1772, a committee of correspondence is organized by Samuel Adams, James Otis, John Hancock, Dr. Joseph Warren, and others. The result is the *Boston Pamphlet*, which is widely distributed in Massachusetts and asks other towns to join the resistance. Soon, over one hundred towns answer the call to action. The *Boston Pamphlet* rebukes the Declaratory Act in the strongest of terms. Liberty will be annihilated if Parliament imposes its will on the colonists:

> Can it be said with any color of truth and justice, that this continent of three thousand miles in length, and of a breadth as yet unexplored, in which, however, it is supposed, there are five millions of people, has the least voice, vote, or influence in the decisions of the British Parliament? Have they all together, any more right or power to return a single member to that House of Commons who have, not inadvertently, but deliberately, assumed a power to dispose of their lives, liberties, and properties, than to choose an emperor of China!*

On behalf of the United Colonies, the Second Continental Congress eloquently joins the fray in the Declaration of the Causes and Necessity of Taking Up Arms issued on July 6, 1775. Foreshadowing the Declaration of Independence, it begins to list a set of important grievances against the empire. But it stops well short of the full list of grievances set forth in the Declaration of Independence. Why? Because no such list is necessary. The Declaratory Act—alone—is enough:

> But why should we enumerate our injuries in detail? By one statute it is declared, that Parliament can "of right make laws to bind us in all cases whatsoever." What is to defend us against so enormous, so unlimited a power? Not a single man of those who assume it, is chosen by us; or is subject to our control or influence; but on the contrary they are all of them exempt from the operation of such laws. [...] We saw the mystery to which such despotism would reduce us.*

Indeed, they do. Hence the Declaration of Independence.

> Like the last grievance, Article IV, Section 4 of the Constitution hedges against this grievance by providing that each State is guaranteed a republican form of government. Again, every State must have an elected legislature and executive. In addition, the doctrine of enumerated powers ensures that the federal government has very limited authority, and all remaining authority rests with the States. The Tenth Amendment prevents any abuse of the States because Congress has no authority to change, revoke, suspend, or alter the government of any State. Only the people of each respective State can make such fundamental alterations.

The empire overrides colonial legislative authority through legislative suspension and the Declaratory Act. Great Britain subverts the rule of law by destroying colonial lawmaking, cripples the Social Compact by disavowing representative government, threatens unalienable rights by authorizing their destruction, imposes inequality by treating the colonists completely different than other British subjects, and destroys limited government by fully vesting in Parliament unlimited power over the colonies.*

*If there is any man so base or so weak, as to prefer a dependence on Great Britain to the dignity and happiness of living a member of a free and independent nation—let me tell him, that* necessity *now demands, what the generous principles of patriotism should have dictated.*

*We have now no other alternative than independence or the most ignominious and galling servitude. The legions of our enemies thicken on our plains.—Desolation and death mark their bloody career; while the mangled corpses of our countrymen seem to cry out to us as a voice from Heaven— "will you permit our posterity to groan under the galling chains of our murderers—has our blood been expended in vain?"—Is the only reward which our constancy, 'till death, has obtained for our country, that it should be sunk into a deeper and more ignominious vassalage?—Recollect who are the men that demand your submission; to whose decrees you are invited to pay obedience!—Men, who, unmindful of their relation to you as brethren, of your long implicit submission to their laws; of the sacrifice which you and your forefathers made of your natural advantages for commerce to their avarice,—formed a deliberate plan to wrest from you the small pittance of property which they had permitted you to acquire.—Remember that the men, who wish to rule over you, are they who in pursuit of this plan of despotism annulled the sacred contracts which had been made with your ancestors; conveyed into your cities a mercenary soldiery to compel you to submission by insult and murder—who called your patience, cowardice; your piety, hypocrisy."***

Samuel Adams (August 1, 1776)

# 45

## "He has abdicated Government here, by declaring us out of his Protection and waging War against us."

- ☆ The king and Parliament resolve to treat the colonists as foreign enemies who must be conquered into submission.
- ☆ By waging war against the colonists, Great Britain annihilates the rule of law by ignoring peace overtures, tears apart the Social Compact by targeting colonists as enemies, violates the unalienable rights of life and liberty, destroys equality by treating Americans as foreign enemies, and runs roughshod over limited government.

The twenty-third grievance brings the urgency of the Declaration into sharp focus. To best understand it, we should recall the founding First Principles of a free and just government. The whole purpose of government is to secure your unalienable rights. But what happens when the government—instead of protecting you—makes you the target of its military might? That is the very position the colonists find themselves in 1776.

Tensions between the colonists and the empire are boiling over after the passage of the Intolerable Acts in 1774. The king all but abandons reconciling with the colonists. The empire enacts the Boston Port Act, Massachusetts Government Act, Quartering Act of 1774, and Administration of Justice Act. The Quebec Act of 1774 pours salt into the fresh wounds. The empire intends to break the spirit of the colonists, but the reaction is exactly the opposite. Those opposed to English oppression only stiffen their resolve to resist. Active opposition is widespread throughout Massachusetts and spreads throughout the other colonies. General Thomas Gage, military dictator of Massachusetts, repeatedly writes to the imperial authorities that the situation is completely out of hand, and that the only way to enforce the empire's edicts is massive military force, requiring tens of thousands of troops and foreign mercenaries. He is not wrong.

On August 26, 1774, Suffolk County in Massachusetts convenes a convention in which Boston Son of Liberty Dr. Joseph Warren introduces a set of resolves calling for open defiance of the Intolerable Acts. These Suffolk Resolves also declare a boycott of British goods and the raising of local militias. On September 17 (Constitution Day, the future anniversary of the signing of the Constitution), the Continental Congress adopts the Suffolk Resolves as their own. William Legge, second Earl of Dartmouth (most commonly referred to as Lord Dartmouth), is the secretary of state for the American colonies under his stepbrother, Lord North. When Lord Dartmouth learns that the Suffolk Resolves are adopted by the First Continental Congress, he writes on November 1 that the colonies have declared war against Great Britain.

Lord Dartmouth is premature. His analysis is also backward. Although the colonists substantially increase the vigor of their opposition, it clearly falls short of revolution; it is the British who are on a war footing. Just a few weeks later, King George III privately writes to Lord North that this contest will be decided by force of arms. Approximately six months later, this private conclusion is revealed to the public. In February 1775, Lord North addresses the House of Commons, declaring that New England is in a state of rebellion, and the king should subdue it. The House of Commons approves the address by a margin of two to one.

The outbreak of armed conflict occurs about two months later, on April 19, 1775, at Lexington and Concord. As related another two months later by the Second Continental Congress, British General William Howe,

> further emulating his ministerial masters, by a proclamation bearing date on the 12th day of June, after venting the grossest falsehoods and calumnies against the good people of these colonies, proceeds to "declare them all, either by name or description, to be rebels and traitors." [...] [A]nd he is exerting his utmost power to spread destruction and devastation around him.*

Yet the colonists are still seeking peace. As we have learned, the Second Continental Congress forwards to the king the Olive Branch Petition. The petition recognizes the traditional ties of the colonies, professes the colonies' desire to remain loyal, lays the blame of British oppression on George III's ministers (not the king himself), asks the king to look favorably on the colonies, and begs George III personally intervene to garner peace within the empire.

Despite this dramatic overture, the colonists are not servile. Only one day after approving the Olive Branch Petition, the Second Continental Congress approves military action to defend their unalienable rights in its Declaration of the Causes and Necessity of Taking Up Arms. The colonists stand on the razor's edge. On one foot, they plead for peace; on the other, they prepare for war. They are hoping this two-pronged approach will result in both reconciliation and the protection of their unalienable rights.

They need not have bothered. The Olive Branch Petition is the first and only document physically signed by the Second Continental Congress until the Declaration. Its tone is one of reconciliation. It recites no grievances against the empire; it seeks accommodation. The result? The petition is met with contempt, oppression, and injury.

But this should be no surprise. Between the time Richard Penn arrives in early August and Lord Dartmouth receives the petition on September 1, George III makes his position clear: war. On August 23, 1775, King George III issues the Proclamation of Rebellion. In substance, it proclaims that the colonists have forgotten their allegiance to the empire and are obstructing the law and commerce, acting in a hostile manner, and levying a war against the empire. The king then announces

> not only all our officers, civil and military, are obliged to exert their utmost endeavors to suppress such rebellion, and to bring the traitors to justice, but that all our subjects of this realm, and the dominions [...] are bound by law to be aiding and assisting in the suppression of such rebellion, and to disclose and make known all traitorous conspiracies and attempts against us, our crown and dignity; and we do accordingly strictly charge and command all our officers, as well civil as military, and all others our obedient and loyal subjects, to use their utmost endeavours to withstand and suppress such rebellion, and to disclose and make known all treasons and traitorous conspiracies which they shall know to be against us, our crown and dignity.*

The entire British Empire must unite to crush the colonists. The king is simply revealing the course of action that he plots well before the Olive Branch Petition or the Declaration of Causes and Necessities of Taking Up Arms arrive in England. Americans are now foreign enemies. This language parallels the text used by King

Charles Edward Stuart in 1745 to declare parts of Scotland in rebellion. The American colonists are condemned, not as subjects or even cousins, but as members of an enemy nation. This will take the conflict to an entirely different magnitude. To put down a protest and a boycott and confront smugglers, rabble rousers, and tax evaders is basically law enforcement. To conquer a foreign enemy in an overseas war is an entirely different matter. The scope of military violence and barbarism unleashed and justified is exponentially increased.

George III demolishes any remnants of doubt in his annual address to both houses of Parliament, delivered on October 26, 1775:

> The rebellious war now levied is become more general, and is manifestly carried on for the purpose of establishing an independent empire. I need not dwell upon the fatal effects of the success of such a plan. [...] It is now become the part of wisdom, and (in its effects) of clemency, to put a speedy end to these disorders by the most decisive exertions. For this purpose I have increased my naval establishment, and greatly augmented my land forces.*

The king will broker no mercy—the colonies will be crushed. By proclaiming the colonies outside his protection and ordering the military to strike, the king continues waging war. Parliament follows the king's lead by passing the Prohibitory Act by an overwhelming vote in the House of Commons, 112 to 16, and by the House of Lords, 48 to 12. The king gives his royal assent the day after its approval by the lords, making it law on December 21, 1775. It provides that all American vessels and their cargoes may be confiscated—treating Americans as foreign enemies.

This law provokes a strong reaction of condemnation in America. Although John Adams believes the Prohibitory Act spells doom for any allegiance to the Empire and that, in effect, American colonies are independent, his sentiment is not widely shared in the colonies—yet. In the end, Adams is proven 100 percent right. The *Instructions from the Town of Boston to their Representatives,* issued May 23, 1776, recognize the cold reality less than two months before the Declaration of Independence:

> We have seen the humble petitions of these colonies to the king of Great Britain repeatedly rejected with disdain. For the prayer of peace, he has tendered the sword; for liberty, chains; and for safety, death. He has licensed the instruments of his hostile oppressions to rob us of our property, to burn our houses, and to spill our blood.*

The United States Constitution is the antithesis of the king's war against the colonists. The Preamble explains the purpose of the Constitution: "We the People of the United States, in Order to form a more perfect Union, establish Justice, insure domestic Tranquility, provide for the common defense, promote the general Welfare, and secure the Blessings of Liberty to ourselves and our Posterity, do ordain and establish this Constitution for the United States of America." Through the rule of law, the Constitution forges the Social Compact to protect the equality and unalienable rights of the people, by which every government official is the public servant of the people—not their sworn enemy.

By waging war against the colonists, Great Britain annihilates the rule of law by ignoring peace overtures, tears apart the Social Compact by targeting colonists as enemies, violates the unalienable rights of life and liberty, destroys equality by treating Americans as foreign enemies, and runs roughshod over limited government.*

*The manner in which the war has been prosecuted has confirmed us in these sentiments; piracy and murder, robbery and breach of faith, have been conspicuous in the conduct of the king's troops; defenseless towns have been attacked and destroyed, the ruins of Charlestown, which are daily in our view, daily remind of this: the cries of the widow and the orphan demand our attention; they demand that the hand of pity should wipe the tear from their eye, and that the sword of their country should avenge their wrongs.**

Town of Malden (May 27, 1776)

# 46

## "He has plundered our seas, ravaged our Coasts, burnt our towns, and destroyed the lives of our people."

- ☆ The Royal Navy bombs and burns down coastal cities as well as attacks colonial shipping.
- ☆ The Royal Navy tears apart the Social Compact by targeting colonists as enemies, annihilates the unalienable rights of life and liberty, destroys equality by treating Americans as foreign enemies, and obliterates limited government.

This twenty-fourth grievance elaborates on the prior one. Although George III does not officially expel the colonies from the protection of the British Empire until August 1775, the imperial military is engaging in combat for months. Well before Lexington and Concord in April, the English military is pressing for a military solution to the troubles. British Vice Admiral Samuel Graves suggests torching Boston as early as February 8, 1775. He is hardly alone. For example, on March 4, 1775, British Marine Major John Pitcairn, stationed in Boston, writes to Lord John Montagu, fourth Earl of Sandwich (credited for inventing the sandwich) and the first lord of the Admiralty, in which he expresses much of the military's sentiment:

> Orders are anxiously expected from England to chastise those very bad people. The general had some of the Great Wigs [Patriots] [...] with him two days ago, when he took that opportunity of telling them, and swore to it by the living God, that if there was a single

> man of the king's troops killed in any of their towns he would burn it to the ground. What fools you are, said he, to pretend to resist the power of Great Britain; she maintained [the] last war [with] three hundred thousand men, and will do the same now rather than suffer the ungrateful people of this country to continue in their rebellion. This behavior of the general's gives great satisfaction to the friends of government. I am satisfied that one active campaign, a smart action, and burning two or three of their towns, will set everything to rights. Nothing now, I am afraid, but this will ever convince those foolish bad people that England is in earnest.*

Before any shots are ever fired, leading British officers are anxiously advocating burning down a few towns to intimidate the colonists into submission.

As soon as the fighting finally breaks out, the military seriously considers moving forward with such a brutal stratagem. On the day of the Battles of Lexington and Concord, Vice Admiral Graves advises General Thomas Gage to undertake "the burning of Charles town [*sic*] and Roxbury."* Instead, British ships merely attempt to coerce supplies from American colonies by threatening to bomb and burn down seaports. Captain James Wallace uses this tactic against Newport and Marblehead in Portsmouth (now New Hampshire). Meanwhile, commanded by Captain Thomas Bishop, HMS *Lively* trains its cannons on the towns of Marblehead and Salem, Massachusetts. Bishop not only demands that they not help the Patriots of Boston, but he also extorts supplies for the Royal Navy by threatening to destroy the towns. Many residents simply flee. In May 1775, the sixty-four-gun *Asia* pulls into New York City's harbor, intimidating the city.

On June 12, 1775, the Battle of Machias erupts, otherwise known as the "Lexington of the Sea." To abbreviate a lengthy tale, American colonists resist attempts by the British military to garner supplies from the port at Machias, Massachusetts. A small naval battle breaks out. The British Navy—the pride of the empire—is repelled, and HMS *Margaretta* is lost. Undeterred, in the same month, British coercion of seaports for supplies devolves into outright raiding.

Likewise, intimidation breaks out into bombardment when Charlestown, Massachusetts, just across the Mystic River from Boston, is ignited on June 17, 1775, by a cannon barrage. This bombardment occurs as part of the British army's lead-up to the Battle of Bunker Hill. Patriot sharpshooters are picking off British soldiers from empty houses in Charlestown, so Charlestown is considered a fair military target.

On the other hand, a nonmilitary target is chosen when a fleet of sixteen armed vessels under the command of British Captain James Wallace sails to Bristol, Rhode Island, on August 7, 1775, and demands provisions. When an hour passes without their delivery, "the whole fleet began a most heavy cannonading [...] and heave shells and carcasses into the town; which continued without intermission, an hour and an half."* The town coughs up forty sheep. Satiated for the time being, Wallace's flotilla departs. The next day, HMS *Falcon,* a sloop, bombards Gloucester, Massachusetts. Later that month, Wallace's marauding navy becomes hungry again. The Wallace flotilla raids several locations in Connecticut. Meanwhile, HMS *Otter,* a naval sloop, begins raiding plantations in Virginia. In New York City, on August 23, 1775, HMS *Asia,* still anchored off Wall Street, unleashes a thirty-two-gun broadside at New York City's Fort George in a futile attempt to stop the Patriots' retrieval of cannons from the Battery. Miraculously, the barrage is entirely ineffective—no one is killed, and property damage is minimal. The British are actually the worse for wear as a cannon is successfully removed, and Patriots slay British crew members with musket fire. Nevertheless, the *Asia*'s barbaric broadside provokes a mass exodus, emptying large portions of the city.

As we learned in the last grievance, in August 1775, King George III proclaims the colonies to be in a state of rebellion. Any pretense of restraint is obliterated in September when Vice Admiral Graves receives instructions from England to unleash the dogs of war. Graves orders his fleet to "proceed along the coast, and lay waste, burn and destroy such seaport towns as are accessible to his majesty's ships."* Just to reinforce the point, he orders that "you are to burn, destroy, and lay waste the said town[s] together with all vessels and craft in the harbour[s] that cannot with ease be brought away."*

The British take these orders to heart. In September, Captain Wallace's fleet bombards the minor seaport of Stonington, Connecticut. The soon-to-be-famous American Revolutionary War artist John Trumbull writes to George Washington, "Stonington had been attacked, and severely cannonaded and by divine Providence marvellously protected."* On October 7, 1775, British warships return to Bristol. This time, the town will not even give them a single sheep. The warships open fire.

To avenge the Battle of Machias, Lieutenant Henry Mowat is ordered "to execute a just punishment on the town of Falmouth."* On October 17, 1775, Lieutenant Mowat's small fleet pulls up to Falmouth (now Portland, Maine) and demands that its residents give up all weapons and take oaths of allegiance to the British Empire. The price of noncompliance is that the fleet will open fire. The townspeople refuse these demands, and most flee. As promised, Mowat lets rain down a massive bombardment lasting from 9:30 a.m. to 6:00 p.m. A landing party torches several buildings. The fires and bombardment wreck the courthouse, fire station, public library, and 130 homes. When reporting to Congress on this savage attack, George Washington remarks it is "an outrage exceeding in barbarity and cruelty every hostile act practiced among civilized nations."*

Eight days later, on October 25, British Captain Matthew Squire leads the first attack outside of New England and New York by striving to burn down Hampton, Virginia. Virginians brilliantly foil the flotilla's attack by sinking vessels in the channel, which the Royal Navy must navigate to approach the town. The British overcome the sunken vessels the next day. However, they are then met with fierce resistance, led by accurate Patriot riflemen who terrorize the British crews and drive off the fleet.

The British, however, are just beginning to spread their brutality. The next month, British Captain George Montagu bombards Jamestown, Virginia. In December, they occupy the port of Norfolk, Virginia (which ironically is a hotbed of Loyalists). Still, the Patriots repel British forces composed of redcoats, Loyalists, and freed enslaved at what has been dubbed the Battle of the Great Bridge on December 9, 1775. On New Year's Day, the British bombard Norfolk with their fleet, and the city erupts in flames. A British sailor who personally views the attack celebrates that "[t]he detested town of Norfolk is no more!"* As historians later learn, the British Navy is not alone in detesting Norfolk. The Patriots feed the fires to assist burning it down—to eradicate that hub of Loyalist villainy and scum in their midst.

The British continue on the warpath. Newport, Rhode Island, is periodically harassed, threatened, and fired upon for months. By the time Norfolk burns, Newport, which before the American Revolution is the fifth largest city in America, is largely destroyed and vacant. Other cities that come under attack include Gloucester, Massachusetts and Jamestown, Rhode Island. Historian Kevin Phillips summarizes the breadth of British military attacks:

> Between April 18, 1775, and New Year's Day 1776, British warships bombarded, torched, or attempted to burn over a dozen American cities and towns from Falmouth (now Portland), in the Maine district of Massachusetts, to Norfolk, Virginia, 700 miles south. Another dozen were openly threatened. For some months, this represented a deliberate policy, spelled out by Admiral Graves and reiterated by Lord George Germain.*

The Admiralty firmly believes that this show of force and cruelty will result in the utter collapse of American resistance. Instead, the violence only stiffens the resolve of the Patriots and pushes many previously unengaged and loyal subjects into the arms of the resistance. This should not be unexpected. Indeed, member of Parliament David Hartley announces to the august body, "I must ask whether you are to expect that while you burn their towns, take or destroy their ships and property they will sit with their arms folded, or whether they will not be driving to repel injury by injury."* The Americans certainly do not fold their arms.

The Second Continental Congress refers to this savagery in its Declaration of the Causes and Necessity of Taking Up Arms as one of the reasons why violent resistance against British oppression is justified. It explains that General Gage's troops have

> wantonly burnt Charles-Town, besides a considerable number of houses in other places; our ships and vessels are seized; the necessary supplies of provisions are intercepted, and he is exerting his utmost power to spread destruction and devastation around him.*

In accord with the Prohibitory Act, the empire plunders American ships at sea. Also highlighted in the Declaration of Causes and Necessities of Taking Up Arms is Parliament's enactment of a law banning colonists from fishing in traditional areas off the coasts of the colonies. The empire steals and hoards the seas for itself.

The Preamble of the Constitution explains that one of the purposes of the federal government is to "provide for the common defense." As such, the Constitution authorizes Congress in Article I, Section 8 to create a navy and army to protect the people. The president is the commander in chief of those forces and the militia under Article II, Section 2. Article VI, Section 4 provides that the United States "shall protect each of [the States] against Invasion." Instead of using the military as an engine of oppression, the Constitution creates these forces to protect the lives, liberties, and pursuit of happiness of the people.

This grievance unquestionably strengthens the necessity and urgency for independence. Bombarding and setting cities on fire, as well as harassing shipping and fishing, reveals that Great Britain is intent on imposing its tyranny on America. Instead of protecting Americans' unalienable rights, the empire destroys the colonists' lives, liberties, and pursuit of happiness. The Royal Navy tears apart the Social Compact by targeting colonists as enemies, destroys equality by treating Americans as foreign enemies, and obliterates limited government. It is another example by which London annihilates the First Principles of a free and just government.*

*[H]is Britannic Majesty, in order to destroy our freedom and happiness, has commenced against us a cruel and unprovoked war; and, unable to engage Britons sufficient to execute his sanguinary measures, has applied for aid to certain foreign princes, who are in the habit of selling the blood of their people for money, and from them has procured and transported here considerable numbers of such foreigners.**

Second Continental Congress (August 14, 1776)

# 47

## “He is at this time transporting large Armies of foreign Mercenaries to compleat the works of death, desolation and tyranny, already begun with circumstances of Cruelty & perfidy scarcely paralleled in the most barbarous ages, and totally unworthy the Head of a civilized nation.”

- ☆ The British Empire hires brutal and barbaric German mercenaries to conquer the Americans.
- ☆ By deploying foreign mercenaries to crush the colonists, the British violate the First Principle of the Social Compact.

This twenty-fifth grievance is damning. Of course, the English hold a different perspective. They are merely following their long-standing historical practice of hiring foreign mercenaries to fight their overseas wars. Recall that the English possess a deeply rooted aversion to standing armies. As an island empire, Britain focuses its military might on the Royal Navy. Considering these circumstances, hiring troops to fight the empire's land battles is the easiest path to mobilizing an army. The British hire mercenaries to put down rebellions in Ireland and Scotland, as well as during the French and Indian War against the French in Canada.

On the other hand, only with great reluctance does the government deploy such mercenaries within the British Isles. Prior to 1776, foreign troops are only posted in England twice: once to fight against Scottish rebels and again to guard against a possible French invasion. The English public are unconcerned about these exceptional events because the troops are not turned against Englishmen. Before 1776 (and even now), Scotland is a different kingdom, and the Scots are considered a different people, albeit within the British Empire. For centuries, the kingdoms of Scotland and England wage war. Of course, the French are mortal enemies.

The bottom line is that, at the time, suppressing colonial resistance becomes bloody; the British Army is tiny. Despite a population of approximately seven million people in England and Wales, the standing army only has about thirty-five thousand troops, with many coming from Ireland and Scotland. Recruiting Englishmen into the army is always difficult. To persuade them to fight their English cousins overseas is nearly impossible. If the British Empire is going to fight a land war in the vast colonial frontier, foreign troops are indispensable.

King George III engages in earnest, lengthy negotiations with Russia to hire twenty thousand soldiers, but eventually Empress Catherine the Great turns down the deal. With Russia providing no assistance, George III turns to more reliable, traditional sources of soldiers. Because the monarchy is from the German House of Hanover, British monarchs naturally draw on their deep Germanic ties and hire troops from northern Germany. In May 1776, the colonists learn that the empire is waging its war with forty thousand fresh troops who will soon be landing on the American homeland. Over seventeen thousand of these soldiers are Germanic mercenaries from various principalities and duchies. These Germanic soldiers are commonly referred to collectively as "Hessians." They are joined by thousands of Scottish Hollanders and Scottish Highlanders.

The news in May 1776 that those soldiers are coming to America is no surprise, but it still sparks an overwhelming chorus of opposition from the colonists. Mercy Otis Warren reports that, combined with the king's refusal to accept the Olive Branch Petition and other related obstinacy, deploying the Hessian forces compels many potentially neutral Americans to join the Patriots' cause:

> On this information, the indignation of all ranks can scarcely be described. The king's speech was condemned, and ordered to be burnt in the center of the camp at Cambridge. The wavering were resolved, the timid grew bold, the placid and philosophic lovers

> of peace left the retired haunts of literary felicity, and beneath the helmet and the buckler, courted the post of danger:—vigorous action was now the only line of conduct to be observed through every department.*

The king's move alienates a large swath of the American population and dramatically increases support for independence. It is a thunderous shot across the bow that unites American opposition to British oppression. Renowned British Historian William Edward Hartpole Lecky, who writes the monumental eight-volume *A History of England in the Eighteenth Century*, draws the point even more sharply by observing that "[t]he conduct [...] of England in hiring German mercenaries to subdue the essentially English population beyond the Atlantic, made reconciliation hopeless and the Declaration of Independence inevitable."*

Mercy Otis Warren refers to the Hessians as "barbarous strangers" who are "to assist in the entire subjugation of the colonies, if not otherwise reduced to unworthy submission."* The Hessians have a reputation for brutality and savagery. The English understand that hiring these mercenaries will absolutely be viewed as lowering down a hammer of barbarism on the American People. It also destroys any pretense that this is a battle within the Social Compact. Loosing bloodthirsty foreign mercenaries on Americans is beyond the pale of civilized behavior. The king's move is an existential threat that rips apart the Social Compact.

However, there is one upside to England's cruelty. By depending so heavily on foreign mercenaries, the British Empire's strategy embeds within itself the seeds of its own destruction. This twenty-fifth grievance is electrifying and raises the stakes for not just the colonists, but for the world. Because the British hire foreign mercenaries to battle and murder Americans, completely eviscerating the Social Compact, the Americans feel no hesitation about soliciting and accepting foreign assistance. It paves the way for France to aid America after the rebels are victorious at the Battles of Saratoga in September and October 1777. The British Empire is no longer at war just with the rabble in the colonies; the conflict draws the most powerful imperial powers into the American tinderbox. The American Revolutionary War is transformed from a civil uprising into a global conflagration. Spain allies with France against Great Britain (but not directly with the colonists). Battles erupt across the world, crippling Great Britain's ability to focus on battling the Americans. French assistance and the spreading of the war is critical to America's ultimate victory.

In addition, soldiers from across Europe are now free to join the American cause. Unlike the bloody thugs hired by the British, these volunteer soldiers are freedom fighters. Some, such as General Friedrich Wilhelm August Heinrich

Ferdinand von Steuben, the Marquis de Lafayette, Thaddeus Kosciuszko, and Kazimierz Pulaski, are indispensable to America's eventual victory. The hiring of Hessians is a major cause of sparking the American Revolution and of aiding America's eventual victory.*

Again, the Preamble of the Constitution explains that one of the purposes of the federal government is to "provide for the common defense." Article I, Section 8 authorizes Congress to create a navy and army, and the president is the commander in chief of those forces and the militia under Article II, Section 2. Article VI, Section 4 provides that the United States "shall protect each of [the States] against Invasion." The federal government will deploy America's homegrown military forces to defend against foreign enemies, not hire foreign forces to oppress the people.

*If impressing seamen is of right by common law, in Britain, slavery is then of right by common law; there being no slavery worse than that sailors are subjected to.**

Benjamin Franklin (sometime before Constitution Day, September 17,* 1781)

# 48

## "He has constrained our fellow Citizens taken Captive on the high Seas to bear Arms against their Country, to become the executioners of their friends and Brethren, or to fall themselves by their Hands."

- ☆ The British Empire impresses (kidnaps) colonial sailors to serve in the Royal Navy against their fellow Americans.
- ☆ By forcing Americans to become instruments for war against the colonists, impressment violates the rule of law by circumventing English law, erodes the Social Compact and unalienable rights by making slaves of the colonists, and destroys limited government by arbitrarily enforcing British tyranny by enslaving the colonists to fight their own people.

For your everyday sailor, serving in the Royal Navy is a grueling and often fatal affair. Because of attrition, poor living conditions, low pay, and losses to injury, illness, and war, the Royal Navy is chronically short of manpower. A simple, terrible remedy to fill the gap is colloquially called "impressment." Put simply, the British Navy abducts civilian sailors and coerces them into service. Royal Navy press-gangs round up sailors in coastal cities and ports and force them into service. The Royal Navy also boards ships at sea and seizes seamen—often fabricating excuses on the spot to do so. In addition to sailors, the press-gangs also swoop up the homeless, convicts, and men who just happen to be in the wrong place at the wrong time. In short, impressment is government-sanctioned kidnapping and forced labor.

Impressment begins as early as the thirteenth century and is explicitly legalized in 1563 by Queen Elizabeth when she approves An Act touching Politick Constitutions for the Maintenance of the Navy. This act is limited to impressing civilian sailors. The vagrancy act in 1597 expands press-gangs' targets to include men of disrepute. Many colonists are subject to this brutal treatment, a direct affront to their unalienable rights of liberty and the pursuit of happiness.

Impressment is a terrible fate. British Governor William Shirley of Massachusetts calls for legislation to prohibit impressment in the colony, observing that it is an "evil practice" and a "great grievance" to the people of Massachusetts.* Historian Kevin Phillips relates that "[t]o describe impressment into the Royal Navy as carrying a fate of death or slavery was only a slight exaggeration. Three out of four men who were pressed died within two years, with only one in five killed in battle."*

The devastating consequences of impressment are not isolated to the hapless sailors. It causes serious collateral effects. Families, homes, friendships, and communities are torn apart. By ripping sailors out of their communities, the British also rob the colonies of much-needed labor, driving down production and exports as well as driving up prices. The economy is blistered by impressment.

Impressment breeds deep resentment, and colonists strongly condemn the practice of having their scarce men being swallowed up by the Royal Navy. Under Queen Anne, Parliament finally enacts the Sixth of Anne Act of 1708, exempting the colonies from impressment. However, the act is only a temporary respite. In 1723, the Royal Navy implements a policy of impressment in the Americas despite the Sixth of Anne Act. Eviscerating the rule of law, this practice sparks colonial protests, which, in turn, leads to another impressment act in 1746. But unlike the Sixth of Anne Act, this latter act only bans impressment in the West Indies. The British Navy interprets Parliament's failure to officially reenact the protections of the Sixth of Anne Act as a free license to begin anew a robust campaign of impressment in the colonies.

The Americans are unwilling to placidly accept this campaign of impressment. Governor Shirley specifically explains that if the practice is not outlawed, it will be the source of great "trouble" to the government of Massachusetts.* True to Shirley's insight, colonists vigorously undertake two different forms of resistance. First, they relentlessly sue to protect their rights under the Sixth of Anne Act of 1708. Calling upon their rights under the rule of law, they seek succor in the courts. Second, completely disregarding the law, they violently resist. Press-gangs often trigger individual acts of physical self-defense and assault. In addition, personal resistance can quickly explode into mass riots.

The largest and most famous such uprising is dubbed the "Knowles Riot" in tribute to Sir Charles Knowles, first baronet, the commanding officer whose impressment orders in Boston spark the riot. Under Knowles's instructions, press-gangs hunt on the docks of Boston and impress forty-six men. On November 17, 1747, this blood sport unleashes a massive riot throughout Boston, paralyzing the town and British authority. Mobs surround and intimidate government officials, and the rioters capture Royal Navy officers and a deputy sheriff. They even burn a barge on Boston Common and smash the windows of the old courthouse where the General Court convenes. The governor calls upon the local militia to protect royal officials and government property, but the militia fails to muster. This should come as no surprise, as most of the militia are joyously partaking in the riot. After three days, the riot defuses when Knowles's fleet departs after the impressed men are exchanged for the hostages. This is the colonies' largest single incident of resistance against the empire until the Stamp Act. A similar riot breaks out in Newport, Rhode Island in 1765, resulting in the burning of the British ship *Maidstone*. Impressment engenders long-simmering disputes ready to explode at a moment's notice.

While the British, of course, are appalled by the lawsuits and riots, Americans believe these actions are completely justified to defend the unalienable rights of life and liberty. As early as 1720, the Massachusetts General Court condemns impressment as violating the "common liberty" of its victims.* In 1747, foreshadowing his career as the lynchpin of the Sons of Liberty in Boston, Samuel Adams vociferously condemns impressment. In the wake of the Knowles Riot, Adams articulates many of the arguments that will appear in the Declaration. The press-gangs, he observes, "are tools of arbitrary Power," and "lawless invaders of our liberty."* He asks, What shall the people do? He answers, Exercise their right to revolution by "running together for their mutual Defense [...] [f]or when they are suddenly attacked," the colonists return to "a state of Nature, and have a natural Right," to resist "their Oppressors, as under such Circumstances."*

In the aftermath of the Boston Tea Party, with resistance to the Intolerable Acts, Lexington and Concord, and other military skirmishes, the king declares the colonies to be in rebellion and out of his protection. As we have learned, on December 21, 1775, Parliament passes the Prohibitory Act, which authorizes and encourages the seizing of all American vessels and the impressment of entire crews. Before this act, impressment is limited to selected unfortunates; now, anyone on an American ship is fair game. Those impressed are not treated as civilians or even prisoners of war but essentially become the slaves of the Royal Navy.

In his seminal work *Common Sense,* Thomas Paine reflects that impressment is the modern-day parallel of the Prophet Samuel's warning to the people of Israel who are clamoring for a king. Despite Samuel's pleas to resist calling for a king, his kinsmen demand and achieve the establishment of a monarchy. Samuel prophecies that the king "will take your sons and appoint them for himself, for his chariots, and to be his horsemen, and some shall run before his chariots."* Samuel's prophecy comes to fruition. King George III is the new pharaoh, taking America's sons for himself and forcing them to man his Royal Navy.

Perhaps worst of all, the impressed are forced to fight against their fellow Americans or be imprisoned or executed for insubordination. If they do fight, they might be slain in battle at the hands of their fellow Americans. This dilemma is an outrage of the highest order, unbefitting a civilized nation.

North Carolina merchant and member of the Second Continental Congress, Joseph Hewes, previously a Loyalist, explains in early 1776 that the Prohibitory Act inevitably leads to war:

> The act of Parliament prohibiting all trade & commerce between Great Britain and the colonies [...] makes all American property found on the sea liable to seizure & confiscation and I fear it will make the breach between the two countries so wide as never more to be reconciled. [...] I see no prospect of a reconciliation, nothing is left now but to fight it out.*

Despite this prophecy, Hewes originally votes against independence. Still, he cannot escape destiny. John Adams remarks to Thomas Jefferson that the "unanimity of the states finally depended on the vote of Joseph Hewes, and was finally determined by him."* Adams describes the mesmerizing scene in the Second Continental Congress when debating independence:

> For many days the majority depended on Mr. Hewes of North Carolina. While a member, one day was speaking, and reading documents from all the colonies, to prove that the public opinion, the general sense of all, was in favor of the measure [the resolution for independence], when he came to North Carolina, and produced letters and public proceedings which demonstrated that the majority of that colony were in favor of it, Mr. Hewes who had hitherto constantly voted against it, started suddenly upright, and lifting up both of his hands to Heaven, as if he had been in a trance, cried out, "It is done! and I will abide by it."*

In the end, Hewes fulfills his prophecy.

The Reconstruction Amendments of the Constitution counter this grievance by protecting the liberty of our citizens. In particular, the Thirteenth Amendment prohibits involuntary servitude and the Fourteenth Amendment provides that "[n]o State shall make or enforce any law which shall abridge the privileges or immunities of citizens of the United States; nor shall any State deprive any person of life, liberty, or property, without due process of law." The purpose of government is to protect the unalienable rights of the people, not repress them.

This twenty-sixth grievance not only ushers in the American Revolution, but it also foreshadows the War of 1812. In both of these conflicts, a major cause of the movement to all-out war includes the unjust impressment of Americans. The practice infringes on nearly all the First Principles of a free and just government. It violates the rule of law by circumventing the Sixth of Anne Act of 1708, dissolves the Social Compact and unalienable rights by making slaves of the colonists, and destroys limited government by arbitrarily enforcing British tyranny by enslaving the colonists to fight their own people. Impressment warrants revolution.*

*Countrymen! the men, who now invite you to surrender your rights into their hands are the men who have let loose the merciless savages to riot in the blood of their brethren—*[...] *who have taught treachery to your slaves, and courted them to assassinate your wives and children.**

Samuel Adams (August 1, 1776)

# 49

## "He has excited domestic insurrections amongst us, and has endeavoured to bring on the inhabitants of our frontiers, the merciless Indian Savages, whose known rule of warfare, is an undistinguished destruction of all ages, sexes and conditions."*

☆ The British Empire taps into Americans' fears and perceived weaknesses by encouraging convicts, indentured servants, Native Americans, and slaves to engage in rebellions with British troops against the Patriot cause.

☆ The empire's tactics rip apart the Social Compact and threaten the lives, liberties, and happiness of the colonists.

The British are not satisfied with hiring German soldiers and impressing American sailors to fight against their own countrymen. The British survey North America and realize that there are other, perhaps eager, potential allies here to help crush the nascent rebellion. Convicts, indentured servants, Native Americans, and slaves make up huge portions of the American population. A rough estimate reveals that in 1776, about twenty-one million free people of European descent live in the colonies. At the same time, there are up to five hundred thousand enslaved African American persons, two hundred thousand Native Americans (east of the Mississippi River), and up to seventy-five thousand current or former convicts and indentured servants. The British eagerly view these populations as fifth columns to employ against the colonials. The penultimate grievance addresses this powder keg.

We all understand slavery is a despicable stain on American colonial life, and that many people arrive in America as indentured servants. That many come to America as convicts is mostly forgotten. We might have a vague notion that Australia began as a penal colony, but America? In truth, many Americans are the descendants of English, Scottish, and Irish criminals. Under the British Transportation Act of 1717, some convicts are sentenced to spend seven or fourteen years of indentured servitude in America. That appears harsh, but the sentence is often in lieu of execution. If a convict completes his term, he is freed and, in effect, pardoned. If he avoids his service or returns to the British Isles before he completes his term of servitude, he is executed. From the passage of the Transportation Act of 1717 until the American Revolution, approximately thirty thousand to fifty thousand convicts reach America's shores.

Convicts face brutality as soon as they are sentenced, on the passage to the New World, and then through years of toil in the colonies. They are sold and traded away, just like any other property. Similar to slaves, they can even be inherited. The convicts are forced to work for those who pay for their servitude, which usually means grueling and unrelenting labor. The result? Crippled bodies and often death. Many are treated no differently than chattel slaves. But in an unexpected twist, slaves are often treated better than convicts. Slaves are lifetime investments, so enslavers have an incentive to let them live a long life (at least until they can no longer work) and produce children who, in turn, become valuable enslaved assets. Masters possess an entirely different incentive for convicts; they want to squeeze every ounce of work out of the hapless charges before the end of their service. If the convict happens to drop dead the day after his release, the master loses nothing. Most convicts live a wretched life during their servitude.

Historians estimate that in 1776, roughly fifteen thousand convicts serving a term of involuntary servitude reside in the colonies. These miserable convicts are a potentially large fighting force against the colonies that the British Empire attempts to exploit.

Nonconvict indentured servants are a similar source of potential rebellion. Unlike convicts, traditional indentured servants willingly undertake their servitude. There are easily twice as many indentured servants in America as convicts. Remarkably, over half of the total nonslave immigrants to America in the colonial period are either convicts or indentured servants. However, because they are freed at the end of their terms of servitude, and their children are never born into servitude, their overall numbers at any given time are relatively low.

Although it varies, a typical indentured servant has a seven-year term of servitude. These indentured servants gain free passage to America in exchange for their term of labor. They may come to regret that trade. The condition of involuntary servitude is often just as brutal as with convicts. Perversely, the voluntary indentured servants with shorter seven-year terms are often treated much harsher than convicts with fourteen-year terms or chattel slaves. Just like convicts and slaves, the indentured servants are treated as property—traded and sold at will.

For reasons similar to convicts, the British Empire views indentured servants as ripe pickings to become allies. Certainly, the convicts and indentured servants hold lower social status than their free European-descended counterparts, and in the land of opportunity, the threat of a concerted uprising by them provokes intense fear in the hearts of colonists. That indentured servants could rally against their colonial overlords is not idle speculation. In September 1663, armed indentured servants band together in Gloucester, Virginia, to extort their freedom after only a year of service. This Gloucester County Conspiracy (otherwise known as the Birkenhead's Rebellion) is defeated when one of the conspirators reveals the plot. The turncoat (Birkenhead) gains his freedom and £200.

A few months before the Declaration, these fears manifest again when John Murray, Lord Dunmore and Virginia's royal governor, issues a Proclamation on November 7, 1775, imposing martial law and offering to free all indentured servants who join his majesty's troops against the rebels.* Dunmore is desperate. As we learned earlier, he has no position at all in Virginia, having been driven from the mainland and residing on a British warship near the Virginian coast.

Despite the benefits offered by Dunmore and the empire, only a small number of indentured servants take advantage of the offer. Several factors undermine Dunmore's gambit, including the voluntary and temporary status of indentured service—they can see light at the end of their servitude. In any event, the indentured are admittedly a tiny part of the population when compared to free European descendants in the colonies.

But the empire is hardly content with just targeting convicts and indentured servants. Indeed, the British eye additional potential allies—those who do not have a temporary status. Those other potential allies provoke true terror in the eyes of the colonists.

We all know that when the English and other European settlers arrive in America, the continent is populated by Native Americans. The intersection of European settlers and indigenous Native Americans is a fascinating, complicated, lengthy, and often very sad story about the destruction of lives and cultures. In connection with exploring the Declaration, high-level, broad-brushed strokes will need to suffice. At the time of the American Revolution, approximately two hundred thousand Native Americans live east of the Mississippi River. Many are allied with English forces, and many are not.

Before the American Revolution, tensions among Native Americans and colonists often run high. Skirmishes, raids, and outright massacres are not uncommon. As but one serious example, the Yamasee War of 1715–1717 between South Carolinian settlers and various Native American nations kills about 7 percent of South Carolina's colonial population. The colonists living closest to the western frontier are under a constant threat of confrontation with Native Americans. As a result of the French and Indian War, the English take control (from a European standpoint) of an enormous swath of the frontier west of the Allegheny Mountains. In a move that enrages many colonists, the empire determines to tamp down on the collisions between the colonists and Native Americans by enacting the Proclamation Act on October 7, 1763. As previously explored, the Proclamation of 1763 draws a westward colonial boundary roughly along the Allegheny Mountains. The colonists are barred from settling west of the mountains, which (in theory) should dramatically decrease violent and other risky conflicts between Native Americans and colonists. This is a vain hope. The colonists easily evade the Proclamation Line, and tensions and clashes between colonists and Native Americans mount.

One monumental explosion arising from these tensions occurs as colonists flood into the Ohio Valley—much of today's Midwest. Ottawa Nation Chief Pontiac ignites Pontiac's War (otherwise known as Pontiac's Rebellion) when he leads an assault on Fort Detroit on May 7, 1763. After the Native Americans achieve some initial success, the British prevail in a protracted military campaign and force Chief Pontiac to sign a peace treaty in 1766. Tensions between the colonists and Native Americans remain high.

The British determine to exploit this tension by recruiting Native Americans to assist in crushing the colonists. Englishman John Lind, a barrister who writes an enthralling pamphlet in opposition to the Declaration, cuts to the quick when justifying recruitment of Native American allies:

> [S]ince force is become *necessary* to support the authority of Parliament, that force which is most *easily* to be procured and most likely to be *effective*, is the force *which ought to be employed.* I should be bold enough to avow, that to me it would make little difference, whether the instrument be a German or a Calmack [Scot], a Russian or a Mohawk. [Italics are in the original.]*

Lind may be crass, but he speaks the truth. To win, the British will use whatever means and deploy whatever allies they need.

As early as 1774, Virginia Royal Governor Lord Dunmore recruits Native American allies. Massachusetts Governor Thomas Gage also solicits many Native American nations. In addition, Gage orders Canada's governor, Guy Carleton, to raise Native American troops, and overtures to the Native American Six Nations are largely successful. The British superintendent recruits Creeks and Chickasaws in South Carolina. The governor of North Carolina also follows Gage's lead. Meanwhile, imperial diplomats venture into the Ohio Valley, encouraging Native Americans to attack colonial settlers.

To be fair, the colonists also recruit Native Americans to the Patriot cause. Just like the British, Americans take whatever allies they can find. They seek assistance from their old nemesis France and other European nations, as well as local Native American nations and individuals. On balance, the British gain many more Native American allies than the colonists.

Great Britain's success in recruiting Native American allies engenders a deep psychological effect on the colonials. Many colonists possess a mixed view of Native Americans. In part, they admire Native Americans as (forgive the phrase) "noble savages." They are courageous, bold, enterprising, honest, honorable, handsome and beautiful, and fabulous storytellers—all while living in harmony with nature. On the other hand, they are considered (again, forgive the characterization) uncivilized, fearless, maniacal killers who mercilessly kidnap, massacre, and scalp men, women, and children.

The fear of being overrun by bloodthirsty Native Americans rivets colonists and begins to find a voice in many American protests against British tyranny. For example, on July 6, 1775, the Second Continental Congress reports in the Declaration of the Causes and Necessity of Taking Up Arms that

> [w]e have received certain intelligence that General Carleton, the Governor of Canada, is instigating the people of that province and the Indians to fall upon us; and we have but too much reason to apprehend, that schemes have been formed to excite domestic enemies against us.*

These fears are vindicated. Frontier attacks by Native Americans are encouraged by the British. For example, in December 1775, South Carolinian Patriots engage in a heated battle with hundreds of Loyalists and Native Americans. Although the Patriots prevail, the fear of Native American forces collaborating with the British Empire is being realized. In early 1776, in *Common Sense*, Thomas Paine condemns

British efforts to turn Native Americans against the colonists, referring to the empire as a "barbarous and hellish power" for unleashing a treacherous threat.* Several bloody episodes erupt. Native Americans engage in massacres of colonial settlements on the frontiers of various colonies.

On April 23, 1776, South Carolina Supreme Court Justice William Henry Drayton addresses this looming threat when he opens the Court of General Sessions of the Peace, Oyer and Terminer, Assize and General Gaol (Jail) Delivery. He reviews many of the grievances of South Carolina against the British Empire and gives particular emphasis to British officials having "made every attempt to instigate the savage nations to war upon the southern colonies, indiscriminately to massacre man, woman, and child."*

Just a month before the Declaration, Native Americans battle against American troops in Canada, including at the Battle of Trois-Rivières on June 8, 1776. This stinging defeat of American forces dashes any hope that Americans will conquer Canada. Perhaps heady with their recent victory, on the very eve of American independence (July 1, 1776), English troops join the Cherokee Nation, the Shawnee Tribe, and other Native Americans and unleash a multicolony, multipronged onslaught. Attacks are launched in Virginia, North Carolina, South Carolina, and Georgia. In the end, this turns out to be a great tactical error. General Charles Lee, the commander of the Southern Department of the Continental forces, quickly launches a counterattack, dubbed the Cherokee Campaign of 1776. The campaign devastates Native American forces, and more than fifty Cherokee settlements are utterly destroyed.

Throughout the American Revolution, the colonists and British-allied Native Americans repeatedly clash. In the end, the Native American allies do not have the pivotal military impact that the Americans fear. Nevertheless, that Native Americans engage in joint military operations with the English becomes a standard rallying cry for the Patriot cause. In his *The American Crisis* essays released throughout the American Revolutionary War, Thomas Paine repeatedly denounces this alliance as barbaric. This series of pamphlets strengthens the resolve and bolsters the morale of the American Patriots.

Although the British call upon convicts, indentured servants, and Native Americans to join their efforts, when they look across the chessboard of war against the Americans, the most powerful piece with the largest potential payoff by far is the nearly five hundred thousand slaves in the colonies. To explore the full dynamics of slavery in the pre-colonial era is well beyond the scope of this work. Infamously, the first African American slaves arrive in Jamestown, Virginia, in 1619. The key to this last grievance is that by the 1770s, there are hundreds of thousands of slaves, especially in the Southern colonies, and the free American population dreads that this sleeping giant will awaken and overwhelm the colonists in a violent uprising. Groundbreaking historian Herbert Aptheker recounts that

> sources yield enough evidence to demonstrate conclusively that the fear of slave revolts and the panic that ensued upon the discovery, or supposed discovery, of plots, or the suppression of revolts, were factors of prime importance in the social, political and economic life of the United States. This panic was no rare phenomenon. Indeed it was occasioned at least one hundred thirty times between 1670 and 1865.
>
> An examination of the laws and customs regulating slavery [...] substantiate this fear of revolt. [...] Laws or customs provided abysmal ignorance, patrols, passes, no arms to slaves, no resistance to whites, no anti-slavery agitation, and a policy of divide and rule: division between poor whites and slaves, domestic and field slaves and the drivers and the mass of negro slaves. Spying and the "Christian doctrine of resignation" reinforced these instruments of class rule in America's slave system.*

This panic over slave revolts grows in an evolving environment in the colonies. Three distinct mounting pressures begin to smash together before the American Revolution: demographics, attitudes, and revolts.

Demographically, the number of slaves in the colonies explodes from 1750 to 1776. For example, the number of slaves in Virginia doubles to three hundred thousand, and in South Carolina the number triples. Meanwhile, Georgia, which originally refuses to permit slavery within its borders, legalizes the institution in 1750; Georgia quickly becomes one of the staunchest supporters of the infernal institution. Corresponding with the growing enslaved population is the growing fear of revolt.

At the same time, in connection with the second factor, suspicion and disdain for slavery is increasing. The first known antislavery petition in the colonies is issued by the Quakers in 1688 in the Germantown Quaker Petition Against Slavery. It is authored by Francis Daniel Pastorius of Germantown, Pennsylvania. In the 1750s, the Quakers, who until then are dominated by slaveholders, finally live up to their faith and prohibit slavery. On a different front, Boston lawyer Benjamin Kent takes the fight against slavery to the courts. He successfully represents seventeen slaves who file suit for their freedom between 1764 and 1774. In 1775, the first American abolitionist society (the Society for the Relief of Free Negroes Unlawfully Held in Bondage, later known as the Pennsylvania Society for Promoting the Abolition of

Slavery) is formed by Quakers in Philadelphia. As we have explored, many colonies attempt to suppress the slave trade, but the British Empire rejects those efforts.

Despite the empire's protection of the slave trade, some cracks in the edifice of slavery are becoming visible. In a groundbreaking opinion in 1772, *Somerset v. Stewart*, Lord Mansfield, Lord Chief Justice of the King's Bench in England, rules that an escaped slave is liberated on English soil and that slavery is an affront to Natural Law. As such, slavery can only continue on British soil if there is a law expressly authorizing its existence. Because there is no such law, no one can be enslaved there. This does not mean that all slaves in the empire are now free, and it does not end the slave trade, but it is a serious beachhead of emancipation in the British Isles.

The third mounting pressure comes in the form of actual slave revolts. Although some scholars claim the Gloucester County Conspiracy of 1663 is the first slave uprising, they miss the mark. That revolt involves indentured servants of both European and African origin. The first serious, documented widespread slave plot to engage in rebellion is launched in Virginia's Northern Neck region in 1687. The conspirators intend to slaughter their enslavers, but the plot is uncovered, and the ringleaders are executed. Similar plots and uprisings continue all the way until the American Revolution. Defining a slave revolt or conspiracy as involving at least ten slaves, Aptheker counts approximately 250 incidents; more recent scholars count even more.

The Stono Rebellion (otherwise known as Cato's Conspiracy and Cato's Rebellion) is the largest slave revolt before the American Revolution. This riveting and gruesome episode is crisply explained by noted historian Henry Louis Gates, Jr.:

> On Sunday, Sept. 9, 1739, a day free of labor, about 20 slaves under the leadership of a man named Jemmy provided whites with a painful lesson on the African desire for liberty. Many members of the group were seasoned soldiers, either from the Yamasee War or from their experience in their homes in Angola, where they were captured and sold, and had been trained in the use of weapons.
>
> They gathered at the Stono River and raided a warehouse-like store, Hutchenson's, executing the white owners and placing their victims' heads on the store's front steps for all to see. They moved on to other houses in the area, killing the occupants and burning the structures, marching through the colony toward St. Augustine, Fla., where under Spanish law, they would be free.*

The uprising is quickly crushed by the South Carolina militia. But that does not break the spirit of the colony's slaves. Several uprisings occur the very next year, leading to the execution of fifty additional slaves. South Carolina is the scene of increased slave resistance from 1737 to 1740.

Just as South Carolina's uprisings are abating, hundreds of miles away, in 1741, a series of fires break out in New York City, culminating in the burning down of Fort George, the governor's residence. After an intense investigation, many accusations are made that the fires were part of a slave uprising. Reminiscent of the Salem witch trials, one historian summarizes the awful harvest as

> [a] series of mass arrests, mass accusations, and an extended period of trials and punishments followed. During these proceedings, which dragged out for over a year, the magistrates imprisoned 150 slaves and 25 whites; hanged 18 slaves and 4 whites; burned 13 slaves, and transported over 70 to the West Indies. All of this was carried out entirely within the law.*

Whether there was actually such a plot will likely never be satisfactorily answered. Renowned historians arrive at opposite conclusions. Regardless of the truth, what is important for our purpose is that many of the colonists believe such a conspiracy exists and are petrified it will happen again. They have good reason to believe it. In 1712, New York is the scene of an undoubtedly genuine slave rebellion involving twenty-four slaves, culminating in the death of at least five whites.

Fears of slave uprisings similarly grip Wilmington, North Carolina, in 1775, South Carolina in 1775, and Georgia in 1776. Whether there is any truth to these plots is impossible to discern, but again, their truth is irrelevant—they heighten colonial fears of slave revolts just the same.

One particularly heinous incident occurs in South Carolina in the summer of 1775. Thomas Jeremiah of Charleston is accused of plotting an insurrection and encouraging slaves to flee to the British to gain their freedom. Jeremiah is a wealthy harbor pilot. As a free African American, he actually enslaves others. No matter; the authorities quickly bring him to trial, and he is sentenced to be executed in a week. The royal governor, Lord William Campbell, along with judges and attorneys uninvolved in the case, and two prominent Anglican ministers—Robert Cooper and Robert Smith—all protest. They accurately claim that Jeremiah did not receive due process and the evidence is too weak to support the conviction. No matter. On August 18, 1775, Jeremiah is hanged, and his body burned to a crisp. A historical consensus finds that Jeremiah was unjustly convicted in a show trial with the thinly veiled purpose of keeping African Americans in their place. Although a terrible miscarriage of justice, it feeds colonial fears of slave insurrection.

Colonial fears are further aroused by global events. Ferocious and long-lasting slave revolts rock Surinam (Dutch Guiana) in South America in 1757 and 1772, Tacky's Rebellion in Jamaica bursts out in 1760, and the South American Dutch colony of Berbice is gripped with a slave rebellion from 1763 to 1764. They are widely publicized and seared into the consciousness of American slaveholders.

As we have reviewed, some colonists desire to end slavery, while others diabolically defend it. Some, not necessarily caring much one way or the other, are simply terrified of a slave uprising. James Madison writes on June 19, 1775, that such rebellions can doom Americans' bid for independence:

> It is imagined our governor has been tampering with the slaves & that he has it in contemplation to make great use of them in case of a civil war in this province. To say the truth, this is the only part in which this colony is vulnerable; & if we should be subdued, we shall fall like [Greek hero] Achilles by the hand of one that knows that secret.*

Madison's concerns are well grounded. As early as 1774, the British in London begin discussing emancipating slaves and enlisting African Americans in the armed forces. In 1775, Massachusetts Military Governor Thomas Gage writes to the secretary at war, Lord William Barrington, that "we must avail ourselves of every resource, even to raise negroes in our cause."* This advice is carefully considered. On October 26, 1775, William Henry Lyttelton, former royal governor of South Carolina, moves in the House of Commons that imperial policy should be to encourage slaves to rise up against their masters with the support of British troops. However, the measure fails 278 to 108.

Despite the failure of the motion (and the vote was almost certainly not yet known in the colonies), Virginia's Governor Lord Dunmore acts to gain African American allies. Recall that he is stewing onboard the *Fowey* off the coast of Norfolk, desperate to win back some toehold in Virginia. On November 7, 1775, in the same proclamation that offers indentured servants freedom, Lord Dunmore declares martial law and orders

> every person capable of bearing arms, to resort to his majesty's standard or be looked upon as traitors to his majesty's crown and government, and thereby become liable to the penalty the law inflicts upon such offenses; such as forfeiture of life, confiscation

> of lands, etc, etc. And I do hereby further declare all indented servants, negroes, or others, (appertaining to rebels,) free that are able and willing to bear arms, they joining his majesty's troops, as soon as may be, for the more speedily reducing this colony to a proper sense of their duty, to his majesty's crown and dignity.*

The colonists' worst fears are realized. Dunmore declares martial law, finds anyone not joining the British cause to be traitors, and then outright proclaims that slaves will be free—so long as they take up arms against the Patriots. As word of Lord Dunmore's proclamation spreads, as well as gossip and whispers of other British plans to free and enlist slaves, many slaves flee their bondage for asylum in British military posts and ships. Yet, despite colonists' fears, no slave uprisings are prompted by Dunmore.

But what about the other threat involving slaves—turning the newly freed slaves into soldiers against the colonies? This is not an empty threat. Dunmore organizes about eight hundred freedmen into what is dubbed the "Ethiopian Regiment." But they never see battle. Instead, smallpox takes a hideous toll. Dunmore leaves for England in August 1776, and only three hundred of the 800 Ethiopian Regiment's soldiers accompany him.

To put down the colonists, the British Empire pulls at every string it can, including exploiting the internal weaknesses of convicts, indentured servants, Native Americans, and slaves. In fact, although Dunmore's proclamation is intended to shock and awe the colonists into submission, it has the opposite result. It drives colonists who are otherwise neutral or even favorably disposed to the British into the arms of revolution. Chief Justice Drayton's April 23, 1776, charge to the grand jury vividly exemplifies how the empire's strategy galvanizes the colonists:

> The governours in general have demonstrated that truth is not in them; they have inveigled negroes from, and have armed them against their masters; they have armed brother against brother, son against father. Oh! Almighty Director of the universe! what confidence can be put in a government ruling by such engines, and upon such principles of unnatural destruction.*

This grievance is so palpable that it was the only one Congress adds to Thomas Jefferson's comprehensive draft. In the end, the king's cruel tactics backfire by uniting Americans against the empire. The empire's tactics rip apart the Social Compact and threaten the lives, liberties, and happiness of the colonists.

Based on the foregoing, one might naturally believe that the colonists are deeply suspicious of slaves and free African Americans and consider them either overt or covert enemies. To the contrary, their aid is welcomed. Some slaves and many free African Americans enlist in the Patriot cause. As we explored earlier, African Americans serve bravely at Bunker Hill and in many battles throughout the war. Although there were some racially segregated units, for the most part, Blacks serve in integrated corps distributed throughout various regiments. These troops perform valiantly. Indeed, Baron Ludwig von Closen, an aide to General Jean-Baptiste-Donatien de Vimeur, comte de Rochambeau, the commander of French forces at Yorktown, remarks that "three-quarters of the Rhode Island regiment consists of negroes, and that regiment is the most neatly dressed, the best under arms, and the most precise in its maneuvers."* Unfortunately, as the history of our nation unfolds past the Founding Generation, the bright glimpses of the full promise of American freedom and equality in the Revolutionary era are quashed for generations.*

Over time, the Constitution defuses the social fractionation and oppression exploited by the British in this grievance. Under the Constitution, we are all one people. As the preamble explains,

> We the People of the United States, in Order to form a more perfect Union, establish Justice, insure domestic Tranquility, provide for the common defense, promote the general Welfare, and secure the Blessings of Liberty to ourselves and our Posterity, do ordain and establish this Constitution for the United States of America.

The Constitution is a grand effort to unite all in society, ensuring everyone liberty, peace, and justice. Domestic insurrections, riots, murderous plots, and similar schisms are prevented by eliminating the underlying divisions that motivate many of them. If necessary, the federal government provides the means to defeat and heal such disruptions to the social fabric.

Of course, as the grievance illustrates, this was more aspirational than reality in 1776 for indentured servants, convicts, slaves, racial and religious minorities, and women. However, over too much time and with tremendous struggle and sacrifice, the First Amendment guarantees religious liberty; the Thirteenth Amendment abolishes involuntary servitude and slavery; the Fourteenth Amendment provides all citizenship, ensures equal protection of the laws, guarantees due process, and secures the privileges and immunities of all;

the Fifteenth Amendment grants emancipated men the right to vote; and the Nineteenth Amendment guarantees women the franchise. Enabled by those amendments, Congress enacts landmark civil rights legislation and the Supreme Court issues groundbreaking decisions protecting our unalienable rights and equality. The Social Compact is expanded to include all Americans, who enjoy their liberties equally in accordance with the rule of law.

*That some desperate wretches should be willing to steal and enslave men by violence and murder for gain, is rather lamentable than strange. But that many civilized, nay, [C]hristianized people should approve, and be concerned in the savage practice, is surprising; and still persist, though it has been so often proved contrary to the light of nature, to every principle of justice and humanity, and even good policy, by a succession of eminent men, and several late publications.*

*Our traders in men (an unnatural commodity!) must know the wickedness of that SLAVE-TRADE, if they attend to reasoning, or the dictates of their own hearts; and such as shun and stifle all these, willfully sacrifice conscience, and the character of integrity to that golden idol.**

Thomas Paine (March 8, 1775)

# 50

~~"He has waged cruel war against human nature itself, violating its most sacred rights of life & liberty in the persons of a distant people who never offended him, captivating and carrying them into slavery in another hemisphere, or to incur miserable death in their transportation thither. This piratical warfare, the opprobrium of infidel powers, is the warfare of the CHRISTIAN king of Great Britain. Determined to keep open a market where MEN should be bought & sold, he has prostituted his negative for suppressing every legislative attempt to prohibit or to~~

~~RESTRAIN THIS EXECRABLE COMMERCE. AND THAT THIS ASSEMBLAGE OF HORRORS MIGHT WANT NO FACT OF DISTINGUISHED DIE, HE IS NOW EXCITING THOSE VERY PEOPLE TO RISE IN ARMS AMONG US, AND TO PURCHASE THAT LIBERTY OF WHICH HE HAS DEPRIVED THEM, BY MURDERING THE PEOPLE UPON WHOM HE ALSO OBTRUDED THEM; THUS PAYING OFF FORMER CRIMES COMMITTED AGAINST THE LIBERTIES OF ONE PEOPLE, WITH CRIMES WHICH HE URGES THEM TO COMMIT AGAINST THE LIVES OF ANOTHER.~~"*

☆ Jefferson's draft condemns the slave trade as a barbaric violation of Natural Law, violating all the First Principles of a free and just government, as well as devastating its victims.

☆ Jefferson's draft also denounces George III's refusal to assent to several colonies' attempts to end the slave trade and his effort to use the enslaved against the colonists.

☆ Because success hinges on unity, the Second Continental Congress abides by the demands of South Carolina and Georgia and

> deletes this grievance. Instead, it adds the current twenty-seventh grievance. Unforgiveable.

Although this work has otherwise addressed only the final text of the Declaration, we shortly pause for an exception. We have just reviewed the twenty-seventh grievance of the final text, but the twenty-seventh grievance of Thomas Jefferson's original draft instead strongly condemns the king for enabling the barbaric slave trade and turning the enslaved against the colonists.

Jefferson's draft grievance begins by denouncing the slave trade as a war against human nature itself. As we have learned, men and women are born free and inherently possess the unalienable rights to life, liberty, and the pursuit of happiness. Slavery is the antithesis of this Natural Law and utterly shatters every First Principle. The enslaved live underneath the law and are afforded none of the protections of the rule of law. They are outside of the Social Compact and are treated absolutely unequally. All of their unalienable rights are annihilated. The master has absolute control of their lives; there is no pretense of limited government. Slaves have no ability to effectuate change. One cannot overstate the devastation of the slave trade.

Most of the enslaved begin as prisoners of war, victims of kidnapping by hostile tribes and villages, or captives of slave traders. This work makes no pretense of adequately describing the centuries-long barbarism and tragedy that affects the victims and their descendants. But two examples provide a meager glimpse. Olaudah Equiano (also later known as Gustavus Vassa) is one of the few slaves who describes in writing what happens in the colonial era. Born in approximately 1745 in Nigeria, his life changes at about the age of eleven or twelve:

> One day [...] only I and my dear sister were left to mind the house, two men and a woman got over our walls, and in a moment seized us both, and, without giving us time to cry out, or make resistance, they stopped our mouths, and ran off with us into the nearest wood.*

As shocking and evil as is Equiano's and his sister's abduction, it pales when compared to Broteer Furro, the son of a prince of the tribe of Dukandarra in Guinea. When he is about six years old, an enemy nation invades his homeland, and Broteer witnesses enemy soldiers torture and murder his father. They then take Broteer hostage. This is only the start of the terror.

Equiano recounts his dreadful journey to the African coast:

> We were then unbound, but were unable to take any food; and,

> being quite overpowered by fatigue and grief, our only relief was some sleep. [...] The next morning we left the house, and continued traveling all the day. [...] [M]y cries had no other effect than to make them tie me faster and stop my mouth, and then they put me into a large sack. [...] When we went to rest the following night they offered us some victuals; but we refused it; and the only comfort we had was in being in one another's arms all that night, and bathing each other with our tears. But alas! we were soon deprived of even the small comfort of weeping together. The next day proved a day of greater sorrow than I had yet experienced; for my sister and I were then separated, while we lay clasped in each other's arms. [...] I cried and grieved continually; and for several days I did not eat anything but what they forced into my mouth.*

The unfortunates are forced to march or are carried across the land to a port city. Equiano's trek takes approximately six to seven months. During the painful journey, he is sold several times and actually learns several languages. Broteer's journey is faster, and he is sold to Rhode Island slavers "for four gallons of rum, and piece of calico [cotton cloth]."* The slavers give him the new name of "Venture."

Traveling to the coast is frequently dangerous and miserable. Alexander Falconbridge, a British surgeon who serves on four different slave ship missions (and later converts to an abolitionist), writes a searing indictment of his former trade:

> And there is not the least room to doubt, but that even before they can reach the fairs [where slaves are sold], great numbers perish from cruel usage, want of food, traveling through inhospitable deserts, etc. They are brought from the places where they are purchased [...] in canoes; at the bottom of which they lie, having their hands tied with a kind of willow twigs, and a strict watch is kept over them. Their usage in other respects, during the time of the passage, which generally lasts several days, is equally cruel. Their allowance of food is so scanty, that it is barely sufficient to support nature. They are, besides, much exposed to the violent rains [...] as there is usually water at the bottom of the canoes, from their leaking, they are scarcely ever dry.*

African middlemen (who then trade to the Europeans) buy slaves at fairs or other exchanges. Falconbridge reveals that the middlemen subject their new subjects to abject cruelty. "As soon as the wretched Africans, purchased at the fairs, fall into the hands of the black traders, they experience an earnest of those dreadful sufferings which they are doomed in future to undergo."*

Upon arrival at the harbor, the captives are inspected by the European slave traders. Whether accepted or rejected, the prisoners face a terrible fate:

> The traders frequently beat those negroes which are objected to by the captains, and use them with great severity. [...] At New Calabar, in particular, the traders have frequently been known to put them to death. Instances have happened at that place, that the traders, when any of their negroes have been objected to, have dropped their canoes under the stern of the vessel, and instantly beheaded them, in sight of the captain.*

The captives accepted by the slavers are crammed into barbaric slave ships. An abstract of Equiano's description captures only some of the horror:

> I was soon put down under the decks [...] with the loathsomeness of the stench, and crying together, I became so sick and low that I was not able to eat, nor had I the least desire to taste any thing. I now wished for the last friend, death, to relieve me; but soon, to my grief, two of the white men offered me eatables; and, on my refusing to eat, one of them held me fast by the hands, and laid me across I think the windlass, and tied my feet, while the other flogged me severely. [...] One white man [...] flogged so unmercifully with a large rope near the foremast, that he [the captive] died in consequence of it; and they tossed him over the side as they would have done a brute. [...] The stench of the hold [...] was so intolerably loathsome, that it was dangerous to remain there for any time [...] now that the whole ship's cargo were confined together, it became absolutely pestilential. [...] [T]he air soon became unfit for respiration, from a variety of loathsome smells, and brought on a sickness among the slaves, of which many died, thus falling victims to the improvident avarice, as I may call it, of their purchasers. This wretched situation was again aggravated by the galling of the chains, now become insupportable; and the filth of the necessary tubs [buckets holding human waste], into which the children often fell, and were almost suffocated. The shrieks of the women, and the groans of the dying, rendered

> the whole a scene of horror almost inconceivable. [...] One day, when we had a smooth sea and moderate wind, two of my wearied countrymen who were chained together (I was near them at the time), preferring death to such a life of misery, somehow made through the nettings and jumped into the sea: immediately another quite dejected fellow, who, on account of his illness, was suffered to be out of irons, also followed their example.*

The Middle Passage is Hell. Equiano's experience is emblematic of this savagery. Floggings, beatings, rape, burning from hot coals (by which prisoners are forced to eat), and pouring of molten lead on bodies (as punishment for refusing to eat) are common. Falconbridge insightfully reflects on "one instance, as it serves to convey some idea, though a very faint one, of the sufferings of those unhappy beings":*

> [T]he excessive heat was not the only thing that rendered their situation intolerable. The deck, that is, the floor of their rooms, was so covered with the blood and mucus which had proceeded from them in consequence of the flux, that it resembled a slaughter-house. It is not in the power of the human imagination, to picture to itself a situation more dreadful or disgusting. Numbers of the slaves having fainted, they were carried upon deck, where several of them died.

Falconbridge observes that this is just a "middling" episode, and he experiences much worse. Even Venture's relatively smooth passage still results in the death of at least sixty out of a company of 260.

Jefferson also condemns the next stage of the enslavement—the slave market where slaves are bought and sold after the Middle Passage ends. Equiano enlightens us (in Barbados, although he is eventually sold again in Virginia):

> On a signal given, (as the beat of a drum) the buyers rush at once into the yard where the slaves are confined, and make choice of that parcel they like best. [...] In this manner, without scruple, are relations and friends separated, most of them never to see each other again.*

The brutality continues as men and women are sold like commodities.

Jefferson's denunciation that this all violates Christian principles is also testified to by Equiano:

> O, you nominal Christians! might not an African ask you, learned you this from your God, who says unto you, Do unto all men as you would men should do unto you? Is it not enough that we are torn from our country and friends to toil for your luxury and lust of gain? Must every tender feeling be likewise sacrificed to your avarice? [...] Why are parents to lose their children, brothers their sisters, or husbands their wives? Surely this is a new refinement in cruelty, which, while it has no advantage to atone for it, thus aggravates distress, and adds fresh horrors even to the wretchedness of slavery.*

In 1774, Thomas Paine also denounces the hypocrisy of Christians undertaking the slave trade:

> Most shocking of all is alleging [that] the sacred scriptures [...] favor this wicked practice. One would have thought none but infidel cavilers would endeavor to make them appear contrary to the plain dictates of natural light, and conscience, in a matter of common justice and humanity. [...] Mr. [Ames] Baxter declared, *the slave-traders should be called devils, rather than Christians; and that it is a heinous crime to buy them.* [Italics in original.]*

Modern scholars estimate that approximately eleven to twelve million captive men, women, and children were shipped from Africa across the Atlantic. Between 1.5 million and two million die on the Middle Voyage to North America, South America, and Central America. So take Equiano's narrative and multiply it by eleven to twelve million!* The agony and suffering are unfathomable. America is but one destination, as fewer than five hundred thousand slaves land on American shores before the abolition of the slave trade in 1808, approximately 4–4.5 percent of the transatlantic slave trade.

In addition to criticizing George III for blocking colonial attempts to end the slave trade, Jefferson's draft accuses the king of encouraging enslaved people to wage war against the colonists in exchange for freedom. Jefferson poignantly surmises that emancipating slaves is the equivalent of "paying off former crimes committed against the liberties of one people, with crimes which he urges them to commit against the lives of another." The essence of this charge finds its way into the current twenty-seventh grievance.

Appallingly, Georgia and South Carolina will not abide by Jefferson's bold condemnation of the slave trade. Without a union of all the States, the American

Revolutionary War will almost certainly fail. As a review of the course of the American Revolution reveals, if the British had been able to peacefully use Georgia and South Carolina as a base of operations, there is a high possibility that the Revolution would have been squashed. For the sake of unity and success, the Second Continental Congress determines to excise Jefferson's condemnation of the slave trade and replace it with this final version of the twenty-seventh grievance. The king's blocking colonial efforts to end the slave trade is also addressed the early grievances, but not so clearly and boldly. In the end, the Declaration references the slave trade, but not in the manner Jefferson suggests. Unforgivable.*

The original Constitution belatedly addresses the slave trade. Article I, Section 9 provides: "The Migration or Importation of such Persons as any of the States now existing shall think proper to admit, shall not be prohibited by Congress prior to the Year one thousand eight hundred and eight, but a Tax or duty may be imposed on such Importation, not exceeding ten dollars for each Person." Deploying coded language, the provision enables Congress to ban the slave trade, but not until 1808. Fittingly, on March 2, 1807, Thomas Jefferson signs the legislation prohibiting the pernicious practice.

*We saw the misery to which such despotism would reduce us. We for ten years incessantly and ineffectually besieged the throne as supplicants; we reasoned, we remonstrated with parliament, in the most mild and decent language. But* [the] *administration, sensible that we should regard these oppressive measures as freemen ought to do, sent over fleets and armies to enforce them.* [...] *A congress of delegates from the United Colonies was assembled at Philadelphia.* [...] *We resolved again to offer an humble and dutiful petition to the king.* [...] *We have pursued every temperate, every respectful measure.* [...] *But subsequent events have shown, how vain this hope of finding moderation in our enemies.*

*[O]ur petition, though we were told it was a decent one, and that his majesty had been pleased to receive it graciously, and to promise laying it before his Parliament, was huddled into both houses amongst a bundle of American papers, and there neglected.**

Second Continental Congress (July 8, 1775)

# 51

## "In every stage of these Oppressions We have Petitioned for Redress in the most humble terms: Our repeated Petitions have been answered only by repeated injury."

☆ Following English tradition, at every turn, the colonists petition the empire to remediate their oppression. But the imperial authorities rebuff all those entreaties for a peaceful resolution of the crisis, only increasing and widening royal oppression.

☆ This final grievance turns to the cruel reality that the colonists' repeated petitions to the British Empire to cease the other twenty-seven grievances are ignored.* This observation draws upon a wellspring of English history in which petitioning plays a critical part in checking governmental repression.

In England, the first solid codification of a petition is set forth in the Magna Carta of 1215. Recall that this is the binding written agreement between "Bad" King John and English nobles, by which the monarchy recognizes certain rights and privileges, mostly in favor of the nobles. It has sixty-three chapters establishing various rights of the king's subjects. Chapter 61 creates a clear method for enforcing the document. In essence, it establishes a council of twenty-five nobles who can be petitioned by individuals seeking to enforce the guarantees provided in the Magna

Carta. Although extremely limited, it is really the first time in Western civilization that a monarch, in a written document, guarantees rights to some of his subjects and establishes a legal mechanism by which to enforce those rights. This makes into reality the idea of the First Principle of the rule of law, by which the government, as well as the governed, must follow the law.

Beginning no later than the thirteenth century, individual members of Parliament and the entire House of Commons petition the king for the redress of grievances or other relief. After all, the king is considered the "fountain of justice" and possesses the "royal prerogative of mercy"* (such as issuing pardons) since at least the reign of King Edward the Confessor (1042–1066). These petitions often result in the requested relief.

Fast forward several centuries. In 1628, Parliament confronts King Charles I with the Petition of Right. It claims that he has violated the law and makes several key demands for reining him in: no taxation without the consent of Parliament, no imprisonment without due process of law through lawful judgment of an accused's peers, no quartering of troops without permission of Parliament, and no martial law in peacetime. The king accepts the Petition of Right, and ever since, it is considered binding constitutional law in Britain.

In the wake of the Glorious Revolution of 1688, Parliament enacts—and newly installed monarchs William and Mary accept—the Bill of Rights 1689. It specifically recognizes the right of British subjects to petition the monarch and that no subject can be punished for doing so. Thus, the legal right to petition is broadened to include any subject asking the government for relief. Often, such petitions have legal justification or arguments, but this is not always the case.

Today, most likely envision a petition as a piece of paper, an email, or a posting with some kind of call for action at the top, with signatures of support at the bottom. The Founding Generation issues its petitions in much more formal and grand terms. They are not circulated by individual persons for signature, but promulgated by business associations, towns, colonial legislatures, and the Continental Congress. In accord with the Petition of Right of 1628, the Founders, through various governments and organizations, make formal written demands to Parliament, the king, and the British People. They typically are not signed by a long list of people but are issued under the authority of the sponsoring organization or governmental unit—oftentimes signed by its president or clerk. These are not dashed off at a moment's notice, but are the result of careful drafting, contentious debates, deliberative compromises, and solemn approval. The period leading up to the American Revolution is marked by many vital and compelling petitions.

The first vital petition comes from the New York General Assembly, addressed to the House of Commons in 1764, challenging the Sugar Act of 1764. However, the passage of the Stamp Act in 1765 sparks this movement with deadly seriousness. While Patrick Henry leads the opposition in Virginia with the Virginia Resolves, James Otis of Massachusetts leads resistance to the Stamp Act in a different manner. A brilliant, influential lawyer and political leader in the Massachusetts legislature, on June 8, 1765, Otis moves that a "circular letter" be sent to all the colonial governments requesting that the colonies convene a congress to address how to combat this affront to English liberty. Nine colonies agree, and their delegates meet in New York City in October 1765, in what is now dubbed the Stamp Act Congress. It approves the Declaration of Rights and Grievances to be sent to London. The Stamp Act Congress's declaration and petition set the tenor of American resistance for the next eleven years.

The Stamp Act Congress's declaration of rights is very respectful ("humble" in terms of the Declaration), but also very demanding. It is a powerful signal about how the colonists recognize the gravity of petitioning the Crown:

> The members of this congress, sincerely devoted, with the warmest sentiments of affection and duty to his majesty's person and government, inviolably attached to the present happy establishment of the [P]rotestant succession, and with minds deeply impressed by a sense of the present and impending misfortunes of the British colonies on this continent; having considered as maturely as time would permit, the circumstances of said colonies, esteem it our indispensable duty to make the following declarations, of our humble opinions, respecting the most essential rights and liberties of the colonists, and of the grievances under which they labor, by reason of several late acts of [P]arliament.*

It lists thirteen independent arguments that attack the Stamp Act and justify the colonies' resistance to the act. The last argument provides "[t]hat it is the right of the British subjects in these colonies, to petition the king or either house of [P]arliament."* As we have learned, this petition is not for naught. Due to massive colonial resistance, the Stamp Act is dead on arrival. The empire backs down and repeals it.

But as we have also learned, Parliament does not take to heart any lessons learned. Soon it passes the Townshend Acts, which trigger another round of petitions. For example, in January 1768, the Massachusetts General Court issues a series of letters to various officials in London. The letters are drafted by future Son of Liberty Samuel Adams, and he argues that the Constitution is fixed and that the Townshend Acts violate its fixed principles. Massachusetts, again with Samuel

Adams's leadership, also directly petitions George III on January 20, 1768. The Massachusetts Townshend Acts petition is very respectful, humble, and nearly apologetic in tone:

> Your Majesty's faithful subjects the representatives of your Province of the Massachusetts Bay, with the warmest intentions of loyalty, duty, & affection, beg leave to approach the Throne; & to lay at your majesty's feet their humble supplications in behalf of your [...] subjects the People of the Province [...].*

Unsurprisingly, this petition never receives a direct response. Nevertheless, the Townshend Acts are repealed because of widespread resistance to their enforcement.

When the British enact the Intolerable Acts in the wake of the Boston Tea Party, the colonists react by convening the First Continental Congress. As we have reviewed, because Thomas Jefferson is unable to attend Congress, he drafts a groundbreaking set of instructions for the Virginia delegation's consideration. They are later printed as *A Summary View of the Rights of British America*, with which we have become well acquainted. The document is phrased as a resolution directing the First Continental Congress to issue a petition to the king to hear the grievances of Congress. *A Summary View of the Rights of British America* also highlights that several individual colonies previously petition the king for relief in vain. Thus, it is time for the colonies to petition in union.

Although Jefferson's lengthy draft is not adopted, on October 14, 1774, the First Continental Congress promulgates the Declaration and Resolves of the First Continental Congress. It rails against the Intolerable Acts and includes the following resolution of action for the colonists:

> 1st. To enter into a non-importation, non-consumption, and non-exportation agreement or association. 2. To prepare an address to the people of Great-Britain, and a memorial to the inhabitants of British America, And 3. To prepare a loyal address to his majesty, agreeable to the resolutions already entered into.*

Exactly two weeks later, on October 26, 1774, the First Continental Congress adopts its Petition to the King in opposition to the Intolerable Acts. The over-2,100-word petition enumerates a wide range of grievances in exceedingly respectful language, as is revealed by its introductory passage:

> To the King's Most Excellent Majesty:

> Most Gracious Sovereign: We, your majesty's faithful subjects [...] by this our humble petition, beg leave to lay our grievances before the throne.*

The leading lights of the colonies present a gracious, polite request that literally begs the King to receive their concerns. The petition then makes a brilliant argument: British subjects are freemen, Divine Providence has placed King George III on the throne to preserve their liberty, and as a wise ruler appointed by the Divine, George III must recognize that the rights of freemen are being violated—he must be compelled to act. The petition also explains to George III that because he is undoubtedly a lover of liberty, his subjects have a duty to inform him of the injustices being inflicted by his cruel ministers. Naturally, he will turn his wrath on these freedom-destroying ministers. George III is unmoved by the Petition to the King. He utterly ignores it. By the time it arrives in Great Britain, he has already determined that the problem of America will only be solved by war.

Still, the colonists are nothing but tenacious. Even after the "Shot Heard 'Round the World" is fired at Lexington and Concord on April 19, 1775, as we have previously explored, the Second Continental Congress decides to send the Olive Branch Petition, adopted on July 8, 1775. It also begins with a most gracious greeting to George III and entreats his attention to their humble petition. It then implores the king to give them succor. As we have explored, the king will not even read it.

Not surprisingly, Congress now abandons petitions. It now emphasizes the reality that the petitions and addresses go unheeded, which in turn justifies radical changes on the ground. The refusal of the British to even acknowledge these petitions outrages many colonists and is the basis of repeated critiques.

In his amazingly influential *Common Sense,* Thomas Paine begins with a different approach altogether. Instead of raging against the lack of a response, he simply observes as a matter of fact that petitions are useless because of the complexity of governance in the colonies and the lengthy delays between a petition, a response, a counterpetition, and so forth:

> As to government matters, it is not in the power of Britain to do this continent justice: The business of it will soon be too weighty, and intricate, to be managed, with any tolerable degree of convenience, by a power, so distant from us, and so very ignorant of us; for if they cannot conquer us, they cannot govern us. To be always running three or four thousand miles with a tale or a petition, waiting four or five months for an answer, which when obtained requires five or six more to explain it in, will in a few

> years be looked upon as folly and childishness—There was a time when it was proper, and there is a proper time for it to cease.*

Paine moves on. Americans should no longer debase themselves with petitions of peace and reconciliation but instead wage war for their liberty and independence: "[F]or God's sake, let us come to a final separation, and not leave the next generation to be cutting throats, under the violated unmeaning names of parent and child."*

Recognizing this reality, Congress determines it too must move on. On May 15, 1776, the Second Continental Congress takes a momentous step by authorizing the colonies to abolish their prior colonial governments and adopt new American governments. John Adams's preamble to the resolution notes it is necessary because

> no answer, whatever, to the humble petitions of the colonies for redress of grievances and reconciliation with Great Britain, has been or is likely to be given; but, the whole force of that kingdom, aided by foreign mercenaries, is to be exerted for the destruction of the good people of these colonies.*

New York delegate James Duane rises to oppose the preamble, arguing for patience:

> How does it appear that no favorable answer is likely to be given to our petitions? Every account of foreign aid, is accompanied with an account of commissioners. Why all this haste? Why this urging? Why this driving?—Disputes about independence are in all the colonies. What is this owing to, but our indiscretion?*

Leader of the Boston Sons of Liberty, Samuel Adams, who rarely speaks in public, rises to the challenge and convincingly answers:

> Our petitions have not been heard—yet answered with fleets and armies and are to be answered with Myrmidons [soldiers]* from abroad. [...] We can't go upon stronger reasons, than that the King has thrown us out of his protection. Why should we support governments under his authority?*

The double-barreled gun of Adams and Adams is most convincing. Congress passes the preamble and resolution.

As evidenced by this grievance, the right to petition the government is critical to freedom. The Founders ensure that this unalienable right is guaranteed in the First Amendment to the Constitution when it provides that "Congress shall make no law [...] abridging the freedom [...] to petition the Government for a redress of grievances." As evidenced by the abolitionist, suffragette, temperance, persons with disabilities, and civil rights movements (among many others), this right has led to miraculous changes in our government and society over the generations.

The colonies' sad history witnesses the Declaration's observation that "[i]n every stage of" British oppression, the colonists petition in "the most humble terms," and that "[o]ur repeated Petitions have been answered only by repeated injury." The jig is up. King George III, Parliament, and the British People are not going to assist their brethren overseas. For now, they are enemies. The empire will not bend; it is utterly confident it will prevail. Petitions to imperial authorities will only lead to tyranny and doom.*

*Single acts of tyranny may be ascribed to the accidental opinion of a day; but a series of oppressions, begun at a distinguished period, and pursued unalterably through every change of ministers, too plainly prove a deliberate and systematical plan of reducing us to slavery.**

Thomas Jefferson (1774)

# 52

## "A PRINCE, WHOSE CHARACTER IS THUS MARKED BY EVERY ACT WHICH MAY DEFINE A TYRANT, IS UNFIT TO BE THE RULER OF A FREE PEOPLE."

***Based on his long history of actions toward the colonies, is King George III fit to rule Americans?***

☆ For over a decade, George III's repression proves him to be a tyrant who forfeits his authority to rule over Americans.

Samuel Johnson's 1768 *A Dictionary of the English Language* defines "tyrant" as "1. An absolute monarch governing imperiously. 2. A cruel[,] despotic and severe master."

The twenty-eight grievances since 1763 remove all doubt that King George III is a tyrant to Americans. Despite their traditional, great deference to the monarch, early on, some leading colonists condemn George III's actions as tyrannical. Like so much else, Patrick Henry leads the way. On May 30, 1765, Henry's twenty-ninth birthday and the day after he introduces the Virginia Resolves attacking the Stamp Act, a vigorous debate is unleashed on the floor of the House of Burgesses. Henry rises and achieves immortal fame by strongly condemning the king. To fully grasp this remarkable condemnation, we must understand that the colonists consider (Gaius) Julius Caesar as the archetype of a tyrant. This brilliant, charismatic, daring, and amazingly successful Roman general becomes dictator for life in 49 BC, after he occupies Rome by crossing the Rubicon River with his army (in defiance of centuries of Roman law and the tradition that the army never enters Rome) and eviscerating his political enemies. He so fatally wounds the Roman Republic that he is assassinated by a group of liberty defending senators (led by Marcus Junius Brutus and Gaius Cassius Longinus) on the Ides of March (March 15) 44 BC.

The assassination triggers an epic civil war in which the freedom-loving Brutus and Cassius lose their lives in the cause of liberty. The end result? The birth of the Roman Empire under a new tyrant, Emperor Augustus Caesar.*

The Founding Generation is also very well acquainted with two much more recent infamous English tyrants: King Charles I and the man who deposes him, Lord Protector Oliver Cromwell. King Charles I fervently defends Divine Right, imposes taxation without representation, repeatedly dissolves Parliament, governs without Parliament for eleven years, illegally seizes silver and spices, raises an army without Parliament's approval, personally attempts to arrest members of Parliament (who flee before he appears before Parliament to arrest them), and raises and leads an army to wage war against Parliament in the English Civil War. As we learned in connection with the eleventh grievance (standing armies), the Parliamentary forces challenging King Charles I are led by Oliver Cromwell. Charles I loses the English Civil War and is beheaded after a show trial. As we explored, Cromwell soon becomes Lord Protector—a tyrant of a different kind. Well steeped in this history, the Founding Fathers are on heightened alert for signs of English tyranny. Roman and English tyrants serve as twin warnings to the Americans.

With this context in mind, we can better understand the gravity of Patrick Henry and his 1765 condemnation of King George III in his remarks about the evils of the Stamp Act. His leading biographer describes the uncanny scene based on eyewitness accounts (including by Thomas Jefferson):

> It was in the midst of this magnificent debate, while he [Henry] was descanting on the tyranny of the obnoxious [Stamp Act], that he exclaimed, in a voice of thunder, and with the look of a god, "Caesar had his Brutus—Charles the First, his Cromwell—and George the Third—("Treason" cried the speaker [of the House of Burgesses]—"Treason, treason!" echoed from every part of the house. It was one of those trying moments which is decisive of character. Henry faltered not for an instant; but rising to a loftier attitude, and fixing on the speaker an eye of the most determined fire, he finished his sentence with the firmest emphasis) *may profit by their example.* If *this* be treason make the most of it. [Italics are in the original]."*

Henry boldly equates George III with the infamous tyrants Caesar and Charles I. Henry is an oracle. It only takes eleven years for the rest of America to catch up.

Paralleling the Caesars, Charles I, and Cromwell, King George III may be maintaining the pretenses of colonial liberty, but in reality, he is annihilating freedom. The twenty-eight grievances laid out in the Declaration unequivocally reveal that George III is the newest manifestation of a tyrant. Like prior tyrants, King George III is possessed with an unbending spirit of repression against the colonists. At every stage, the Americans ask for redress, and at every stage, he continues his oppression unabated.

As we have learned, tyranny and oppression are the default way of life for most of human civilization. Americans understand the precious and unique blessings of liberty and have no intention of losing them. Americans are a free people, and in accord with the First Principle of revolution, they need not continue to submit under George III's tyranny. Simply put, King George III forfeits his authority to rule Americans. As James Otis reflects, "The people will bear a great deal, before they will even murmur against their rulers: but when once they are thoroughly roused, and in earnest, against those who would be glad to enslave them, their power is *irresistible* [italics in original]."* America becomes King George III's Brutus. The king is king no more.*

As noted earlier, Article I, Section 9 of the Constitution prohibits nobility in the United States. As evidenced by the Revolutionary State governments, the Articles of Confederation, and the federal Constitution, no king shall ever again rule America. The entire Constitution is established to prevent a tyrant. Separation of powers, checks and balances, enumerated powers, federalism, the Bill of Rights, elections, judicial review, and other provisions are all designed to prevent despotism.

*We* [...] *addressed our fellow-subjects of Great Britain. We have pursued every temperate, every respectful measure.* [...] *But subsequent events have shown, how vain this hope of finding moderation in our enemies.**

Second Continental Congress (July 8, 1775)

# 53

"Nor have We been wanting in attentions to our Brittish brethren. We have warned them from time to time of attempts by their legislature to extend an unwarrantable jurisdiction over us. We have reminded them of the circumstances of our emigration and settlement here. We have appealed to their native justice and magnanimity, and we have conjured them by the ties of our common kindred to disavow these usurpations, which, would inevitably interrupt our connections and correspondence. They too have been deaf to the voice of justice and of consanguinity. We must, therefore, acquiesce

# In the necessity, which denounces our Separation, and hold them, as we hold the rest of mankind, Enemies in War, in Peace Friends."

***What is the role of the colonies' fellow citizens in Britain?***

> ☆ The colonists' reoccurring entreaties to the people of Great Britain and Canada for assistance prove fruitless. Their former British brethren are their enemies until a peace is reached.

In addition to petitioning Parliament and George III, Congress addresses petitions directly to the people of England. Although the king is not particularly influenced by public sentiment, the members of the House of Commons are elected, and they, at times, move with public opinion.

In fact, British merchants have great influence in convincing Parliament to repeal the Stamp Act. The shockwave of losing the lucrative and growing colonial markets through colonial boycotts sparks British merchants, especially those in London, to petition Parliament to reverse course.

As we explored earlier, in the wake of the Intolerable Acts, the First Continental Congress passes three resolutions, one of which is to appeal to the people of Great Britain to assist in repealing the acts. On October 21, 1774, this petition is approved. Addressed to the people of Great Britain, it refers to them as "Friends and Fellow-Subjects."* This tract parallels many of the arguments made by the Second Continental Congress in its Petition to the King, but it is even longer—over 3,500 words. The "Address to the People of Great Britain" posits that the colonists and English are brethren, descend from common ancestors, and united in blood and rights. Echoing their appeals to the king, it expresses the idea that the colonists have a duty to inform their fellow subjects of their oppression. It also explains that the colonists have the rights of Englishmen—just like the people they are addressing—and the fact that an ocean separates them cannot be a pretense to deprive the colonists of their unalienable rights. It enumerates many of the grievances also outlined in the Petition to the King. It then takes a different tack that is unavailable with the king: It warns their English Brethren that they, too, will suffer negative consequences at home if a war breaks out, and may even lose their liberty. After all, if Parliament and the king can tyrannize the colonies, "May not a ministry with the same armies enslave you. [...] Do not treat this as chimerical. [...] [I]n a word, take care that you do not fall into the pit that is preparing for us."* The petition also boldly calls upon the British public to elect a new Parliament with members who will respect the rights of the colonists and return amity to the empire.

This is all wishful thinking. The parliamentary elections in 1774 result in a Parliament supportive of the king's aggressive policy against the colonies. Only the smallest minority of the people of the United Kingdom and Parliament support the colonists' position. True enough, there are British supporters of America and critics of English policy beginning from 1763. However, they are mostly impotent when it comes to what matters—reversing British oppression. The most potent allies the colonists secure in Great Britain are London merchants, who send another petition to Parliament on January 23, 1775. It describes the crushing effect of the renewed American import-export boycott of British goods. Unlike the petition addressing the Stamp Act, this petition falls on deaf ears.

Congress is not alone in its efforts to reach the British People. On April 26, 1775, the Massachusetts Provincial Congress issues the Massachusetts address to the inhabitants of Great Britain. Under the leadership of its president and Son of Liberty, Dr. Joseph Warren, the Provincial Congress explains to the British People how Lexington and Concord began and firmly places blame at the feet of British royal troops. Warren and Congress believe it is extraordinarily important to ignore the British ministry and to directly address the people of Great Britain. The petition majestically urges the British public to change the course of affairs to avoid tyranny. Despite Dr. Warren's eloquence, the petition has no discernible effect in England.

The colonists also turn their sights on Canada. As close British neighbors, they could be invaluable allies. However, as we have explored, the residents are overwhelmingly French (or their descendants) who want nothing to do with their so-called British brethren in the lower colonies. They possess a different worldview and do not share the colonists' perspective regarding the First Principles of equality, unalienable rights, limited government, the Social Compact, and the right to revolution. The Quebec Act of 1774 works to accommodate the French perspective in governance and religion, thereby calming many of the new English colonists' concerns.

Still, the Second Continental Congress optimistically views an opening and issues a letter to the inhabitants of Canada on May 29, 1775. They surmise that the Quebec Act of 1774 creates a despotic form of government in Canada and that Canadians might be willing to break from Great Britain. Saluting the Canadians as "Friends and Countrymen," leading statesman and future chief justice of the United States Supreme Court John Jay drafts the appeal. The "Letter to the Inhabitants of Canada" explains that the Canadians and the thirteen colonies face a common foe, plotting to crush the unalienable rights of everyone in North America. It pleads for the Canadians to join the colonists in fighting against the empire. The Americans declare that, like them, the Canadians are already living under tyranny. The Canadians must act to save their freedom. It proclaims point-blank the colonists' decision: "We, for our parts, are determined to live free, or not at all; and are resolved, that posterity shall never reproach us with having brought slaves into the world."* Despite its enthusiasm, majesty, and logic, the letter fails to sway the Canadians.

That none of the petitions and addresses to the British People work is disheartening. Still, in a fashion parallel to the Olive Branch Petition, the Second Continental Congress issues a final address to the inhabitants of Great Britain, addressed to their "Friends, Countrymen, and Brethren." Released on July 8, 1775, this last-ditch effort notes the rejected petition from the year before, reiterates and elaborates on the grievances and other remarks, and comments on new troubling events. Drafted by Richard Henry Lee, it registers at approximately four thousand words. (It could be examined at length, but nearly all the arguments are redundant with what has been previously issued to George III, Parliament, and the British People. There is little new for us or the British to consider.) It lands with an unremarkable thud—dead on arrival.

Blood will not be squeezed from this stone. The British People are unmoved by the repeated petitions, their ancestral ties to their American brethren, and shared history and culture. For the most part, they are unwilling or unable to effect any meaningful change to the aggressive and oppressive policies of Parliament and the king. America has no choice but to bid goodbye to the British People. As the Declaration recounts, they will be friends in peace and enemies in war. For the time being, they are enemies.*

*[I]t* [is] *evident that George the Third, King of* Great Britain, *has endeavored to subvert the Constitution of this country, by breaking the original contract between king and people;* [...][he] *has violated the fundamental laws, and has withdrawn himself, by withdrawing the constitutional benefits of the kingly office and his protection out of this country,—from such a result of injuries, from such a conjuncture of circumstances, the law of the land authorizes me to declare, and it is my duty boldly to declare the law, that George the Third, King of Great Britain, has abdicated the government, and that the throne is thereby vacant;* [...] *he has no authority over us, and we owe no obedience to him.**

Chief Justice William Henry Drayton (April 23, 1776)

# 54

"We, therefore, the Representatives of the united States of America, in General Congress, Assembled, appealing to the Supreme Judge of the world for the rectitude of our intentions, do, in the Name, and by Authority of the good People of these Colonies, solemnly publish and declare, That these United Colonies are, and of Right ought to be Free and Independent States; that they are Absolved from all Allegiance to the British Crown, and that all political connection between them and the State of Great Britain, is and ought to be totally dissolved; and that as Free

**AND INDEPENDENT STATES, THEY HAVE FULL POWER TO LEVY WAR, CONCLUDE PEACE, CONTRACT ALLIANCES, ESTABLISH COMMERCE, AND TO DO ALL OTHER ACTS AND THINGS WHICH INDEPENDENT STATES MAY OF RIGHT DO."**

***Why are the United States justified in becoming an independent nation on the earth? What privileges and responsibilities do these new States now possess?***

- ☆ As representatives of the people of America and appealing to the Creator, the Second Continental Congress solemnly severs all legal ties to the British Empire and explains the reasons for independence to the world.

- ☆ The colonies are transformed into free and independent States, possessing all the powers and prerogatives of independent countries under international law—including the authority to engage in war, peace, and trade.

This passage reminds us who is issuing the Declaration: "We, therefore, the Representatives of the united States of America, in General Congress, Assembled." Thus, the Second Continental Congress accepts responsibility for promulgating the Declaration to the world.

The passage continues by "appealing to the Supreme Judge of the world." This is yet another reference to the Creator and Nature's God from the first few lines of the document. This particular reference to the "Supreme Judge of the world" is added by the Second Continental Congress to ensure that all Americans and the world know that Congress intends to please God.

The phrase continues, asking the Creator "for the rectitude of our intentions."

According to Samuel Johnson's 1768 *A Dictionary of the English Language*, "rectitude" means "[r]ightness; uprightness; freedom from moral curvity [crookedness] or obliquity." In other words, the Founders are asking God to judge that they are acting rightfully, morally, and ethically—that Congress is on the right path.

This invoking of the judgment of the "Supreme Judge of the world" echoes similar remarks by South Carolina Chief Justice William Henry Drayton a few months earlier. Chief Justice Drayton's April 23, 1776, charge to the grand jury makes a stirring call to the Divine at the conclusion of his charge:

> The Almighty created *America* to be independent of *Britain*. [...] In a word, our piety and political safety are so blended, that to refuse our labours in this Divine work, is to refuse to be a great, a free, a pious, and a happy people.
>
> And now, having left the important alternative, (political happiness or wretchedness) under *God*, in a great degree in your own hands, I pray the Supreme Arbiter of the affairs of men so to direct your judgment as that you may act agreeable to what seems to be His will, revealed in His miraculous works in behalf of *America*, bleeding at the altar of liberty! [Italics are in the original.]*

This theme flows throughout the entire Revolutionary era. Less than a month after the Declaration is approved, leading Son of Liberty and Congressman Samuel Adams prophesies that America must either continue on its righteous path or court doom:

> The head of heaven appears to have led us on to be perhaps humble instruments, and means in the great providential dispensation which is completing.—We have fled from the political Sodom; let us not look back lest we perish and become a monument of infamy and derision to the world.*

Although George Washington's first inaugural address is not delivered until April 30, 1789, there is little doubt that it reflects sentiments long held by him and many others of the Founding Generation during the American Revolution. America's journey, including the Declaration and success in the Revolutionary War, are all part of the Creator's plan:

> No people can be bound to acknowledge and adore the invisible

> hand which conducts the affairs of men more than those of the United States. Every step by which they have advanced to the character of an independent nation seems to have been distinguished by some token of providential agency.*

The next phrase of the Declaration is "do, in the Name, and by Authority of the good People of these Colonies." This again evokes the reality that Congress is composed of the representatives of the people. Recall the phrase "We hold these truths"—Congress is not acting on its own authority like aristocrats, dictators, nobles, or a monarchy, but on behalf of the people of America.

Congress then proclaims it does "solemnly publish and declare." Johnson's 1768 dictionary defines "solemn" as "3. Awful, striking with seriousness. [...] 4. Grave, affectedly serious." The Declaration is not being issued flippantly or with little consideration. As we explored earlier, the right to revolution should only be invoked when there is a long train of abuses and usurpations invariably evincing a design for oppression. As we have witnessed, approving the Declaration is a very careful and deliberative undertaking. Still, "solemn" may not have the same connotation today as in 1776. Johnson's definition also includes "religiously grave." Considering that Congress invokes the Supreme Judge of the world in the same sentence, we are safe to conclude that the meaning of "religiously grave" is at least part of the intention.

In addition, the men of Congress "publish and declare" this independence. As we explored earlier, the Declaration is novel in world history because it is written and announces to all mankind as to why independence is being undertaken.

The passage continues:

> [T]hat these United Colonies are, and of Right ought to be Free and Independent States; that they are Absolved from all Allegiance to the British Crown, and that all political connection between them and the State of Great Britain, is and ought to be totally dissolved.

This is the key transformative legal phrase of the Declaration: It both announces and legally effectuates that the United Colonies are now the United *States*. As we have explored, in accordance with the State of Virginia's instructions, and urged on by John Adams on June 7, 1776, Richard Henry Lee of Virginia moves that the Second Continental Congress adopt the following resolution of independence:

> That these United Colonies are, and of right ought to be, free

> and independent states; that they are absolved from all allegiance to the British Crown; and that all political connection between them and the state of Great Britain is, and ought to be, totally dissolved.*

This passage of the Declaration incorporates Richard Henry Lee's resolution. However, Lee's resolution is not original. The phrase "are, and of right ought to be, free and independent states" is the mirror image of the Declaratory Act's assertion that the colonies "have been, are, and of right ought to be, subordinate unto, and dependent upon the imperial crown and parliament of *Great Britain* [italics in original]."* Using its own language, Lee rejects Parliament's position of imperial supremacy. The Declaration is the "Anti-Declaratory Act." Great Britain no longer has any authority to govern America in any case whatsoever.

However, the movement for independence is already happening in some colonies well before July 2. In November 1775, New Hampshire is conducting elections for representatives to their Revolutionary provincial congress. At that time, the New Hampshire Congress passes a resolution that authorizes the creation of a new, independent house of representatives if Congress recommends it. Right on cue, on November 3, 1775, the Second Continental Congress passes a resolution recommending that the Provincial Congress of New Hampshire establish a new government to "effectually secure peace and good order in the province, during the continuance of the present dispute between G[reat] Britain and the colonies [brackets in original]."* In response, New Hampshire's Provincial Congress morphs into a house of representatives and adopts a constitution on January 5, 1776. The New Hampshire Constitution establishes a basic framework for government, intended to be a temporary measure. Accordingly, it is not submitted to the people or a separate constitutional convention for ratification. It is so basic that it does not even include a legislative branch or a bill of rights. Despite its shortcomings, it is monumental. It is the first constitution adopted in the United Colonies, completely independent of Great Britain. However, it does not expressly declare independence.

South Carolina is the second colony to make such a move. The legislature stops meeting in 1771 and the rest of the royal government grinds to a halt in 1775. In the Second Continental Congress, John Adams is advocating for Congress to authorize colonies to establish new governments separate from the king. Congressional Delegate John Rutledge from South Carolina agrees and diligently works to make Adams's idea come to life. On November 4, 1775, the day after Congress passes a resolution authorizing New Hampshire to create a new government, Congress passes a resolution recommending that South Carolina establish an independent government. Following the tradition set by several proclamations and resolutions before it—including the First Continental Congress's October 14, 1774, Declaration and Resolves and the Second Continental Congress's July 6, 1776, Declaration of the Causes and Necessity of Taking Up Arms—the constitution the State of South Carolina adopts on March 26, 1776, begins with a long list of grievances against the British Empire. It then establishes a new framework for government in South Carolina. Although it is completely independent from the British Empire, it too falls short of a true declaration of independence. One of the South Carolina delegates from the Second Continental Congress, Christopher Gadsden (who returns from Philadelphia and helps craft the new South Carolina government) urges that the constitution explicitly declare independence, but that proposition is defeated. The constitution is soon approved by the South Carolina Provincial Congress without such a declaration. Like New Hampshire, it is not submitted to the people or a specially convened ratifying convention.

Although the South Carolina Constitution does not expressly state that South Carolina declares independence, the people of South Carolina are no fools. They know what this means. Less than a month later, the leading legal figure in South Carolina, Chief Justice William Henry Drayton, charges the grand jury in Charlestown. He begins by noting that the courts had been silent for far too long—because they are closed by the imperial authorities for years. He proceeds to instruct as to the new legal status of South Carolina:

> [Y]ou are now met to regulate your verdicts, under a new [South Carolina] Constitution of government, independent of royal authority—a Constitution which arose according to the great law of Nature and of nations, and which was established in the late Congress [of South Carolina], on the 26th of *March* last [...]. [Italics are in the original.]*

Chief Justice Drayton continues by reviewing the history of the Hanoverian kings' rule over the colony, the recent collection of grievances, colonial resistance, the outbreak of violent resistance in the colonies, and the repeated failure of petitions to Great Britain—all foreshadowing the yet-to-be-drafted Declaration. Drayton also recounts the Glorious Revolution and how the English People are justified in deposing King James II because he tears asunder the Social Compact. Drayton then compares King George III's behavior with King James II's apostasy, reasoning that just as the English are justified in revolting against King James II, so the colonists are justified in revolting against King George III. Drayton draws the inevitable conclusion that just as King James II forfeits his crown in England by oppressing the People and trampling on the Constitution, King George III "has abdicated the government, and that the throne is thereby vacant [... H]e has no authority over us, and we owe no obedience to him."*

The next month, the ball of revolution continues rolling. On April 12, 1776, the Fourth Provincial Congress of North Carolina joins the independence movement with the unanimous passage of the Halifax Resolves. This document does not create an independent North Carolina; instead, it authorizes North Carolina's delegates to the Second Continental Congress to vote for the independence of all the colonies. However, the Halifax Resolves do not permit the North Carolinian delegates to initially move for independence, only to support a motion for independence if one is made by another colony.

In April, several Virginia counties also instruct their delegates to the colony-wide Virginia Convention to authorize their delegates to the Second Continental Congress to declare independence if necessary. The Charlotte County, Virginia, instructions are emblematic of such resolutions. Like the New Hampshire and South Carolina Constitutions, they explain that England is engaged in a conspiracy to crush colonial liberties, lists a set of grievances, announces the futility of petitions, and concludes that not only independence is likely necessary, but so is an offensive war against England.

As this is all happening, John Adams is bursting to finish off the debate and embrace independence. From Philadelphia, Adams writes on April 16, 1776, to the president of the Massachusetts Provincial Congress, James Warren:

> I perfectly agree [...] of the necessity proclaiming independency. The salvation of this country depends upon its being done speedily. [...]
>
> Reconciliation upon reasonable terms is no part of their [Great Britain's] plan: the only alternative is independence or slavery. Their designs still are as they ever have been to subjugate us. Our unalterable resolution should be to be free. They have attempted to subdue us by force, but God be praised! in vain. [...]
>
> The child of independence is now struggling for birth. I trust that in a short time it will be brought forth and in spite of Pharaoh.*

Adams's diagnosis is correct. The child of independence is near birth.

The next month adds Rhode Island to the roster of colonies severing their ties with England. On May 4, 1776, it passes the Act of Renunciation, renouncing all allegiance and ties to Great Britain. It specifically repeals the law that ensures allegiance to the Crown and replaces several English legal and governmental mechanisms with colonial processes and procedures, including oaths and even the dating of official documents. Following a short summary of grievances, including the open warfare Great Britain is waging, the Act of Renunciation finds that Rhode Island has a duty to oppose the tyranny of England.

Sensing that momentum is building, Adams and his allies at the Second Continental Congress vigorously work to support these moves for independence in the colonies, which they believe will ultimately lead to a resolution of independence for all thirteen colonies. On May 10, that work culminates in the adoption of the Resolution for the Formation of Local Governments, which authorizes all colonies to establish their own revolutionary governments separate from the British Empire. On May 15, Virginia's Fifth Convention adopts instructions for independence, authorizing its delegates in Congress to move for a resolution of independence. As noted, North Carolina previously instructs its delegates to agree to a resolution if any other colony first moves for independence, and now, Virginia takes the next vital step. Virginia's instructions for independence follow the common pattern. The first half of the document is a preamble forcefully outlining the grievances of the colonies, and it concludes by instructing its delegates to move for independence. Adams is elated when he learns of Virginia's actions. Although he is the pivotal figure for moving toward independence in the Second Continental Congress, he is still in awe of what is transpiring. He writes to his beloved wife Abigail on May 17, 1776:

> When I consider the great events which are passed, and those greater which are rapidly advancing, and that I may have been instrumental in touching some springs, and turning some small wheels, which have had and will have such effects, I feel an awe upon my mind, which is not easily described. Great Britain has at last driven America to the last step, a complete separation from her; a total absolute independence, not only of her parliament, but of her crown, for such is the amount of the resolve of the 15th [of May 1776]. Confederation among ourselves, or alliances with foreign nations, are not necessary, to a perfect separation from Britain. That is effected by extinguishing all authority, under the Crown, Parliament and nation as the resolution for instituting governments, has done, to all intents and purposes.*

The spirit of independence is also percolating up from local governments. On May 9, the Massachusetts House of Representatives passes a daring and bold resolution to conjure up local support by asking each town to determine whether

Congress "should, for the safety of the said colonies declare them independent of the Kingdom of Great Britain[;] [...] the said inhabitants will solemnly engage with their lives and fortunes to support the Congress in the measure."*

Less than three weeks later, the town of Malden unanimously approves instructions to its representative Ezra Sargeant. It begins calmly and then bursts forth into a thunderbolt:

> The time was, sir, when we loved the king and the people of Great Britain with an affection truly filial; we felt ourselves interested in their glory; we shared in their joys and sorrows; we cheerfully poured the fruit of all our labours into the lap of our mother country, and without reluctance expended our blood and our treasure in their cause.
>
> These were our sentiments toward Great Britain while she continued to act the part of a parent state; we felt ourselves happy in our connection with her, nor wished it to be dissolved; but our sentiments are altered, it is now the ardent wish of our soul that America may become a free and independent state.*

The Malden instructions then describe a series of grievances with which we have become most familiar. But being in same colony as the Battles of Lexington and Concord on April 19, 1775, it offers a uniquely powerful impression:

> This plan [to erect despotism] was brought to a crisis upon the ever memorable nineteenth of April. We remember the fatal day! the expiring groans of our countrymen yet vibrate on our ears! and we now behold the flames of their peaceful dwellings ascending to Heaven! we hear their blood crying to us from the ground for vengeance! charging us, as we value the peace of their names, to have no further connection with,—who can unfeelingly hear of the slaughter of—, and composedly sleep with their blood upon his soul. The manner in which the war has been prosecuted has confirmed us in these sentiments. [...] [W]e therefore renounce with disdain our connection with a kingdom of slaves; we bid a final adieu to Britain. [...]
>
> [A]nd we now instruct you, sir, to give them the strongest assurance, that, if they should declare America to be a free and

> independent republic, your constituents will support and defend the measure, to the last drop of their blood, and the last farthing of their treasure.*

The people of Malden are willing to defend American liberty with their last penny and drop of blood. Malden's instructions are representative of many such resolutions and instructions passed by fellow Massachusetts towns.

Likewise, in North Carolina, on the last day of May 1776, resolutions are adopted in Charlotte Town (now known as just "Charlotte") in Mecklenburg County. The Charlotte Town Resolves, also known as the Mechlenburg Resolves, declare all British authority null and void. They resolve that local governments should act to establish new laws, create a method for implementing a new government, and call for the activation and arming of the local militia.

The movement toward independence becomes red hot in June. On June 14, 1776, joining Virginia, the Connecticut Assembly unanimously adopts a resolution instructing its delegates to move that the Second Continental Congress declare independence from Great Britain. On June 24, 1776, Pennsylvania also instructs its congressional delegates to vote for independence, subject to the caveat that the internal affairs of Pennsylvania will be governed by the newly established government of Pennsylvania (which, after all, Pennsylvania creates at the request of Congress just the month before).

Meanwhile, in Virginia, they are debating a new constitution. Thomas Jefferson is tending to his duties in Philadelphia with the Second Continental Congress and desperately wishes he were in Virginia. After all, Virginia is following the directive by the Second Continental Congress for the colonies to begin creating their own systems of government independent of the empire. This once-in-a-lifetime opportunity is evading Jefferson. However, his absence will not steal his voice. Similar to when he drafts *A Summary View of the Rights of British America,* Jefferson writes a proposed Virginia Constitution while in Philadelphia. He entrusts George Wythe, his fellow congressional delegate and former teacher, to deliver it to the Virginia Convention. By the time Wythe arrives in Virginia, the Virginia Constitution is nearly finished. Still, Jefferson's genius will find expression in the preamble to the Virginia Constitution. As we have discerned, it is a remarkable dress rehearsal of the list of grievances in the Declaration. Although this is his second draft written on the eve of the Declaration, Jefferson lists only eighteen specific grievances along with a catchall grievance, as opposed to the twenty-eight specific grievances in the final version of the Declaration. After the grievances, Jefferson explains that Great Britain has forfeited any right to govern Virginia: "By which [these] several acts of misrule, the government of this country, as formerly exercised under the

Crown of Great Britain, is TOTALLY DISSOLVED [emphasis in the original]."* The Virginia Constitution, complete with a slightly revised version of Jefferson's preamble, is adopted on June 29, 1776—a testament to Jefferson's amazing skills as his draft arrives after the Virginia Constitution was all but complete and just five days before its adoption.

Historian Pauline Maier counts at least ninety documents that could be characterized as declarations of independence adopted between April and July 1776.* As we have reviewed, some are colonies declaring independence from England; others are instructions to delegates to the Second Continental Congress to propose or concur in independence; some are local resolutions embodying the sentiments of the local populace, and some are issued by associations such as mechanics or militia units. And then there are South Carolina's Chief Justice Drayton's two brilliant charges to the grand jury.

What is wrought by independence and the dissolution of all allegiance and bonds with the British Empire? The last phrase of the penultimate sentence of the Declaration answers in part that compelling question: "[A]nd that as Free and Independent States, they have full Power to levy War, conclude Peace, contract Alliances, establish Commerce, and to do all other Acts and Things which Independent States may of right do."

The ex-colonies transform from subsidiary units under the realm and control of Great Britain to independent actors on the world stage. Although the parameters are often debated, independent states (in other words, countries) generally are considered to possess certain defining characteristics. An independent state has territory over which it governs the inhabitants and resources, with a government that is acknowledged by other independent states. The government controls and defends its territory, population, and resources; issues and regulates currency; governs internal and international trade and commerce; provides for and controls lawful domestic and international security, including military forces; and engages in international relations with other independent states (such as treaties, war, and peace). Each state is considered legally equal.

Although often used interchangeably, a "nation" and a "state" are not identical. A "nation" is generally considered as a people sharing a common language, heritage, religion, and culture. Some nations have no state. The largest example today is likely the Kurds, who are dispersed among Turkey, Iran, Iraq, and Syria. A "nation-state" is basically a state composed of and governed by a particular nation, such as Japan, France, Denmark, and Germany. States also include empires or similar amalgamations in which many nations are governed by a single overarching government. For example, the Roman Empire, Persian Empire, Holy Roman

Empire, Austro-Hungarian Empire, Ottoman Empire, and Soviet Union are all states consisting of many nations.

The United States of America, in 1776, join* the international stage as independent states. They share the common heritage of British colonies and create the Continental Congress for a united, albeit weak, central government. Being considered independent states is absolutely essential to protecting Americans' unalienable rights and freedoms. Samuel Adams reflects that the time has come for independence:

> The hearts of your soldiers beat high with the spirit of freedom—they are animated with the justice of their cause, and while they grasp their swords, can look up to heaven for assistance.—Your adversaries are composed of wretches who laugh at the rights of humanity, who turn religion into derision, and would, for higher wages, direct their swords against their leaders or their country.—Go on then in your generous enterprise, with gratitude to heaven for past success, and confidence of it in the future.—For my own part, I ask no greater blessing than to share with you the common danger, and common glory:— If I have a wish dearer to my soul, than that my ashes may be mingled with those of a Warren and Montgomery*—it is—That these *American States* may never cease to be *free* and *independent.* [Italics are in the original.]*

This is why the Second Continental Congress directly specifies in the Declaration several attributes of independent states, including engaging in war, peace, alliances, and commerce. The United States will not be subservient to any other power. The United States stands equal to other nations. The Declaration births new independent States on the international stage.*

Soon enough the States formally unite under the Articles of Confederation, with very limited powers vested in the federal government. It resembles more of a loose coalition of independent nations than the singular nation-state with which we are familiar. With the Constitution's ratification in 1788, the United States of America is finally forged into the most unique—and revolutionary—federal form of government in human history.

*With a humble confidence in the mercies of the supreme and impartial Judge and Ruler of the universe, we most devoutly implore his divine goodness to protect us happily through this great conflict.**

Second Continental Congress (July 6, 1775)

# 55

## "And for the support of this Declaration, with a firm reliance on the protection of divine Providence, we mutually pledge to each other our Lives, our Fortunes and our sacred Honor."

***What solemn, dangerous, and irrevocable step is now taken by the signers of the Declaration?***

- ☆ The Second Continental Congress recognizes that Divine Providence moves affairs on earth and relies on Divine Providence to protect Congress.

- ☆ To fulfill the First Principles of a free and just government and achieve independence, the signers of the Declaration mutually pledge to each other and the new country their lives, fortunes, and sacred honor. Since they are engaging in treason, their lives and property are truly at risk. By pledging their solemn honor, they make an eternal promise of fidelity to the Revolution.

The beginning of this sentence forthrightly announces the self-evident truth that the signers of the Declaration support it. Despite its simplicity, it is very important. After all, the signers are the leading lights of the American Revolution. If they refuse to support the Declaration, there will be no new nation.

Then Congress makes an overture all but unheard of today—and one that we might not expect from the upper-class, white, privileged male elite of society of their time—an acknowledgment of humility. In particular, the delegates confess they require the assistance of a higher power to succeed. Like the reference to the "Supreme Judge of the world" in the preceding sentence, this phrase of humility is added by the Second Continental Congress. The delegates unequivocally rely on the protection of "divine Providence."

What exactly do the Founding Fathers mean when they refer to this "divine Providence"? In the earlier words of the Declaration, we know that "divine" references the Creator, Nature and Nature's God, and the Supreme Judge of the world. But what of this divine *Providence*? Although General George Washington is not at the Second Continental Congress because he is in the field commanding the Continental Army, his insight is most illuminating. Decades before, on July 18, 1755, Washington writes a letter to his brother John. At this point, Washington should be dead, slain in battle the day before. He improbably survives a vicious firefight with French and Native American forces. That he still breathes to write the letter is understood by Washington as the will of Divine Providence. He reports to his brother that the Hand of God literally protects him:

> [B]y the all-powerful dispensations of Providence, I have been protected beyond all human probability or expectation; for I had four bullets through my coat, and two horses shot under me; yet escaped unhurt, altho[ugh] death was leveling my companions on every side of me. [Brackets are in the original.]*

His survival is miraculous. No wonder he firmly believes that the Creator preserves his life in this harrowing experience. As expressed in his first inaugural address, the notion that God will intervene in the affairs of men, especially in favoring American independence and holding together the young republic after the American Revolution, becomes an unshakeable tenet of Washington for the remainder of his life.

Washington is not alone. Amazingly, the Native Americans who ambush his military expedition in 1755 have a similar explanation for his survival. Fifteen years later, the chief who commands the ambush undertakes an arduous, long journey to meet Washington. Reflecting on the bloody clash, he announces to his fellow warriors and Washington a most remarkable faith in Divine Providence and a conjoined prophecy about Washington:

> I have travelled a long and weary path, that I might see the young warrior of the great battle. [...] I called to my young men and

> said, mark yon tall and daring warrior? He is not of the red-coat [English] tribe—he has an Indian's wisdom, and his warriors fight as we do—himself is alone exposed. Quick, let your aim be certain, and he dies. Our rifles were leveled, rifles which, but for him, knew not how to miss—'twas all in vain, a power mightier far than we, shielded him from harm. He can not die in battle. [...] [T]here is a something, bids me speak, in the voice of prophecy. Listen! *The Great Spirit protects that man, and guides his destinies. He will become the chief of nations, and a people yet unborn, will hail him as the founder of a mighty empire!* [Italics are in the original.]*

The chief's prophecy is fulfilled. That Divine Providence protects Washington's life from certain death is embraced by friend and foe alike, well before the outbreak of the American Revolution. That the destiny of the nation he will lead is so profoundly protected, likewise, becomes an article of faith.

Washington is emblematic of several generations of colonials who embrace the reality of Divine Providence. On March 16, 1776, Robert Livingston (who serves on the Committee of Five that drafts the Declaration) authors a resolution that the Second Continental Congress adopts, which acknowledges and prays for favor from Divine Providence:

> In times of impending calamity and distress; when the liberties of America are imminently endangered by the secret machinations and open assaults of an insidious and vindictive administration, it becomes the indispensable duty of these hitherto free and happy colonies, with true penitence of heart, and the most reverent devotion, publicly to acknowledge the over ruling providence of God; to confess and deplore our offenses against him; and to supplicate his interposition for averting the threatened danger, and prospering our strenuous efforts in the cause of freedom, virtue, and posterity.*

Congress also prays

> that it may please the Lord of Hosts, the God of Armies, to animate our officers and soldiers with invincible fortitude, to guard and protect them in the day of battle, and to crown the continental arms by sea and land, with victory and success.*

As evidenced by this powerful resolution and the Declaration, the delegates of the Second Continental Congress unite in the belief that Divine Providence is real and that there is a sacred obligation to petition this Divine Providence to assist the American cause. Their faith is wide and deep. Among the signers of the Declaration, four are current or prior ministers, and a number (including John Adams) are sons of ministers. At least half of them study divinity while attending higher education. The Second Continental Congress includes Episcopalians, Anglicans, Congregationalists, Presbyterians, Quakers, Unitarians, and a single Catholic. Sprinkled among them are deists and others who clearly do not agree with or follow all the doctrines of their faiths. Still, there is no doubt that the delegates are unified in their belief that there is a Supreme Judge of the world—a creator, Nature's God, who intervenes in world affairs.

John Witherspoon is an oft-overlooked delegate to the Second Continental Congress and signer of the Declaration. Yet, his influence cannot be overstated. One scholar explains,

> Witherspoon taught one president (James Madison, B.A. 1771) and one vice president (Aaron Burr, B.A. 1772), forty-nine U.S. representatives, 28 U.S. senators, three Supreme Court justices, one secretary of state, three attorneys general, and two foreign ministers. More than 11 percent of his graduates became college presidents, in eight different American States.*

He is by far the most articulate delegate in explaining Divine Providence. In 1776, he is elected to represent New Jersey in Congress. He favors independence and is the only active man of the cloth to sign the Declaration. He delivers a rousing sermon in Princeton on May 17, 1776, entitled the Dominion of Providence Over the Passions of Men. The sermon is quickly published in Philadelphia a few weeks before the Declaration is debated and approved. True to the title, the sermon begins by embracing Divine Providence:

> There is not a greater evidence either of the reality or the power of religion, than a firm belief of God's universal presence, and a constant attention to the influence and operation of his providence. It is by this means that the Christian may be said, in the emphatic scripture language, "to walk with God, and to endure as seeing Him who is invisible."*

God is always present on the earth. He is no mere watchmaker who creates the world and then walks away. The Supreme Judge of the world is actively involved in the affairs of men. Witherspoon explains:

> The doctrine of Divine Providence [...] extends not only to things which we may think of great moment, and therefore worthy of notice, but to things the most indifferent and inconsiderable: *Are not two sparrows sold for a farthing,* says our Lord? *and one of them falls not on the ground without your heavenly Father; no, the very hairs of your head are all numbered.* It extends not only to things beneficial and salutary, or to the direction and assistance of those who are the servants of the living God; but to things seemingly most hurtful and destructive and to persons the most refractory and disobedient. He over-rules all his creatures, and all their actions. Thus we are told, that *fire, hail, snow, vapor, and stormy wind, fulfill his word,* in the course of nature; and even so the most impetuous and disorderly passions of men, that are under no restraint from themselves, are yet perfectly subject to the dominion of Jehovah. They carry his commission, they obey his orders, they are limited and restrained by his authority, and they conspire with everything else in promoting his glory. [Italics are in the original.]*

Calling upon the Gospels, Witherspoon explains that to the Supreme Judge of the world, nothing is beneath notice, and divine intervention may happen at any time.

Witherspoon declares that Divine Providence is already directing the course of the conflict with England and will continue to do so. He preaches that the previous success of American resistance and the collapse of British military operations far exceed the expectations of all involved. Lexington, Concord, and Bunker Hill are just the most notable examples. He proclaims that only God's intervention accounts for this remarkable turn of events. Still, he warns, Americans must not become prideful, as this is the original and gravest sin. Pride, the desire to exalt man above God, leads to the original fall of Adam and Eve and the casting down of Lucifer to Hell. And precisely because of their successes, the Americans must ever be vigilant against this deadliest of sins. Still, so long as the cause is just and their conduct prudent, Americans will succeed with God's Divine Providence:

> [I]f your cause is just,—if your principles are pure,—and if your conduct is prudent, you need not fear the multitude of opposing hosts.

> If your cause is just—you may look with confidence to the Lord and entreat him to plead it as his own.*

Witherspoon preaches that God is active in man's affairs, and that so long as the colonists avoid sins and are true to their principles, Divine Providence will ensure an American victory. Witherspoon's message spreads like wildfire and is by far the most influential sermon in the Revolutionary War era. Petitions for help from the Almighty and heartfelt gratitude for Divine Providence are ubiquitous throughout the entire Revolutionary period, as reflected in personal correspondence, speeches, pamphlets, and government resolutions.

That Divine Providence assists the revolutionaries in winning their independence is a widespread sentiment often commented on by the Founding Generation. In his audacious "Give Me Liberty or Give Me Death!" speech, Patrick Henry assures his colleagues that they will prevail against Great Britain because "we shall not fight our battles alone. There is a just God who presides over the destinies of nations, and who will raise up friends to fight our battles for us."*

When reflecting back on the Revolution, James Madison concurs with Washington, Witherspoon, and Henry:

> The real wonder is that so many difficulties should have been surmounted, and surmounted with a unanimity almost as unprecedented as it must have been unexpected. [...] It is impossible for the man of pious reflection not to perceive in it a finger of that Almighty hand which has been so frequently and signally extended to our relief in the critical stages of the revolution.*

Madison's speaking voice is famously weak, but his insight booms.

The end of the final sentence of the Declaration attests, "we mutually pledge to each other our Lives, our Fortunes and our sacred Honor." At first glance, "pledge" may be thought of as a promise, usually formal or ritualized, such as the Pledge of Allegiance. But Samuel Johnson's 1768 *A Dictionary of the English Language* and Noah Webster's 1833 *A Dictionary for Primary Schools* both define "pledge" as a "pawn" and "deposit." "Pawn," of course, means to leave something of value as security for a debt. Johnson's dictionary elaborates that it also means to give something as a warrant or security, to secure by a pledge. This is more than just a normal promise. Instead, this is the delegates mutually agreeing to support the Declaration—and they post their lives, fortunes, and sacred honor as security for that pledge. If they fail to support the Declaration, then their lives, fortunes, and sacred honor are forfeit.

We all have at least an intellectual appreciation of what it means to lay your life on the line for something. Our military personnel, first responders, and similarly situated courageous men and women literally do that every day. We also know that some people lose their lives as sacrifices while fighting evil. Unfortunately, there is a tremendously long list of such martyrs and victims.

What may be lost today is the seriousness of this pledge in the context of the American Revolution. With hindsight, we know that the Founding Generation is victorious. If we are attentive, we remember Lexington and Concord, Bunker Hill, Saratoga, and Yorktown. But we overlook how many American Continental soldiers and militia, as well as civilians, die of battlefield wounds, disease, exposure, and hunger.

Furthermore, we have little appreciation for the very real risks facing the members of the Second Continental Congress. On first blush, the common impression that the signers are safe from British retribution appears reasonable. After all, they are not on a battlefield, but ensconced in Philadelphia, and they generally live in the upper crust of society. Even so, North Carolina delegate Joseph Hewes (the key vote for independence) is believed to have worked himself to death in the Continental Congress. He more than fulfills his pledge in the end.

By declaring independence, the signers of the Declaration instantly become the highest profile, unequivocal traitors to Great Britain—which just happens to possess an amazingly powerful navy and army that is already waging war against the colonists on American soil. In fact, the British Army actually sparks the first shots of the American Revolution at Lexington when they attempt to arrest congressional delegates Samuel Adams and John Hancock for treason.

In one sense, because most of the delegates are at the top of society, they have the most to lose. Why jeopardize your life, health, comfortable lifestyle, riches, family's future, and good name to rebel against the greatest empire on earth? It is not to perpetuate racism or for a land grab. They have plenty of money, and many of the Founders are appalled by slavery. As this work reveals, it is because there are twenty-eight grievances against the empire that are destroying the First Principles of a free and just government. This is why they pledge their lives to the cause of the American Revolution.

Many signers of the Declaration do literally take up arms in the Revolution, usually in a local militia. Thomas Lynch, Jr., Arthur Middleton, George Walton, Edward Rutledge, Thomas Heyward, Jr., William Whipple, Oliver Wolcott, James Smith, George Taylor, George Ross, William Paca, and Thomas Nelson, Jr., all do so. Dr. Benjamin Rush serves as the surgeon general for the Middle Department of the Continental Army. Several signers engage in battle. Arthur Middleton, Thomas Heyward, Jr., and Edward Rutledge are all taken prisoner after the British capture

Charleston, South Carolina. Richard Stockton is also imprisoned by British forces. Abraham Clark's sons are captured, George Clymer's son is killed in action, and Francis Lewis's wife is taken prisoner. Her health is so compromised that she dies shortly after she is released. To survive, several of the signers and their families are forced to flee their homes for many years.

A signer need not engage in combat to be at risk. In an 1811 letter to John Adams, fellow signer of the Declaration, Benjamin Rush reflects on the various Independence Day celebrations. He poignantly recounts the dread experience of signing the Declaration:

> Do you recollect your memorable speech upon the day on which the vote was taken? Do you recollect the pensive and awful silence which pervaded the house when we were called up, one after another, to the table of the president of Congress, to subscribe what was believed by many at that time to be our own death warrants? The silence & the gloom of the morning were interrupted I well recollect only for a moment by Col[onel Benjamin] Harrison of Virginia who said to Mr. [Elbridge] Gerry at the table, "I shall have a great advantage over you Mr. Gerry when we are all hung for what we are now doing. From the size and weight of my body I shall die in a few minutes, but from the lightness of your body you will dance in the air an hour or two before you are dead." This speech procured a transient smile, but it was soon succeeded by the solemnity with which the whole business was conducted.*

The Founders have good reason to be gravely concerned. Treason is a capital offense. If John Hancock and Samuel Adams were arrested instead of escaping the night before Lexington and Concord, they would have almost certainly faced the executioner. But death might be the least punishment. Sir William Blackstone is perhaps the most revered English jurist during the Founding era. His *Commentaries on the Laws of England* have an unparalleled influence in America. He describes the punishment of those found guilty of treason:

> The punishment of high treason in general is very solemn and terrible. 1. That the offender be drawn to the gallows [...]. 2. That he be hanged by the neck, and then cut down alive. 3. That his entrails be taken out, and burned, while he is yet alive. 4. That his head be cut off. 5. That his body be divided into four parts. 6. That his head and quarters be at the king's disposal.*

This is the brutal treatment awaiting the treasonous Founding Fathers. Under normal circumstances, this is a more-than-sufficient deterrent—especially if you are rich, safe, and among the elite of society. Yet, this is exactly what the Founding Fathers face when they sign the Declaration.

The Founders also place their funds, homes, and other property as security for independence. This is no idle pledge or risk; it is not mere poetry. With a treason conviction comes the ancient punishment of "attainder." Attainder has two consequences: forfeiture and corruption of blood. "Forfeiture" means that the accused loses all property rights. Everything the condemned owns becomes the property of the Crown, retroactively to the time when the treason is committed. "Corruption of blood" basically bans the descendants of a traitor from being able to inherit the property of the condemned and prohibits the condemned from transferring his property or obtaining new property via an inheritance. Attainder and corruption of blood alone risk the fortunes of the delegates.

Furthermore, we must not forget that the British troops relish nothing more than ransacking and burning down the homes and estates of revolutionaries. The homes, properties, and businesses of many delegates are demolished or severely damaged, including those of Richard Stockton, George Clymer, Arthur Middleton, Lyman Hall, William Hooper, William Ellery, Lewis Morris, Francis Lewis, Phillip Livingston, William Floyd, John Hart, and Carter Braxton.

Robert Morris puts up his massive fortune as collateral for financing the American Revolution. He eventually serves in debtors' prison and dies a pauper. Other signers also provide substantial financial support for the war effort, often outfitting troops and facilitating financing.

The lives, homes, families, and fortunes of quite a few of the signers of the Declaration are ruined or seriously jeopardized because they sign the document. Although the details are well beyond the scope of this work, as illustrated above, many of the signers and their families pay a very dear price indeed.

The last phrase of the last sentence of the Declaration is very peculiar to our modern ears—they pledge "our sacred honor." The most fitting definitions for "honor" in Johnson's 1768 dictionary and Webster's 1828 dictionary include "dignity," "reverance [*sic*]," "veneration," "true nobleness of mind," "reputation," "good name," and "true nobleness of mind." Today, "honor" for most appears to be an old-fashioned, antiquated notion from a more primitive age that we have gratefully discarded. Some even assert that honor is nothing more than an instrument of social and economic oppression conjured by dead, white, European, cisgender, heterosexual men to lord over the rest of society and the world. It causes needless duels, suffering, repression, and wars. As proof of this perspective, a cynic could very well quote Prussian King Frederick the Great's observation that "the one thing that can make men march into the muzzles of the cannon which are trained at them is honor."*

Yet, there are at least two ways to view Frederick the Great's proclamation. One is impugning honor—that is, men marching to their deaths for honor is preposterous. The other is praising it—that is, only honor makes men willing to die for a higher cause. To die for a cause, even inevitably, is better than to live with dishonor. Martyrdom for a greater purpose is the noblest and highest calling an individual can undertake. As Jesus reflects, "Greater love hath no man than this, that a man lay down his life for his friends."* This is the meaning clearly intended by the signers of the Declaration.

In any event, the cynic's view clearly glosses over the deeper meaning of the idea and how honor, in many senses, still undergirds our entire society, even if it is mostly implicit and hidden. If people do not act with higher purpose, respect, and integrity—if they only act out of self-interest and selfishness—civilization is doomed; recall Thomas Hobbes and the war of all against all.

Most importantly, we must not overlook that the Declaration's reference to honor is qualified by the most vital word "sacred." This is Thomas Jefferson's construction. Congress did not need to add this reference to the Almighty. Johnson's 1768 dictionary defines sacred as "1. Devoted to religious uses; holy. [...] 2. Dedicated; consecrate, consecrated. [...] 3. Inviolable." "Sacred" includes yet another overt devotion to God, laid over the idea of honor, almost certainly the most powerful combination of human duty. Extrapolating this to the signers of the Declaration, they declare that they embrace the First Principles of the rule of law, unalienable rights, limited government, the Social Compact, equality, and the right to alter or abolish oppressive government. They commit themselves to invoking that right of revolution by proclaiming independence from Great Britain. To maintain their sacred honor, they must meet those First Principles. The substance of sacred honor is more important than lives and fortunes. If the signers and the people do not act to protect the Declaration and the new, revolutionary nation it births, dishonor will fall upon them and us.

This pledge lasts well beyond 1776. Property, fortunes, and lives are all transitory. But sacred honor is forever. It transcends place and time. For the Founding Generation, who believe an afterlife is certain, a pledge of sacred honor invokes eternity. That the Declaration ends with a mutual pledge to maintain the sacred honor of the signers and America as a whole is most fitting. The Founders not only look to Divine Providence to assist them; in a very real sense, they create their own Divine Providence by mutually pledging their lives, fortunes, and sacred honor for the success of the new republic that is born in 1776.

The future of the world depends on it.*

# EPILOGUE

## *250 Years Later*

*At what point then is the approach of danger to be expected? I answer, if it ever reach us, it must spring up amongst us. It cannot come from abroad. If destruction be our lot, we must ourselves be its author and finisher. As a nation of freemen, we must live through all time, or die by suicide.**

Abraham Lincoln (January 27, 1838)

# 250 YEARS LATER

- ☆ The flaws of the men of the Second Continental Congress do not detract from the beauty and truth the Declaration reveals.
- ☆ The Declaration is indispensable to America's quest to become a more equal, free, and just society.
- ☆ We can revive the Declaration through education reform in K–12 schools, higher education, law school, nonacademic institutions, and the military.
- ☆ We can also revive the Declaration by commemorating traditional and new civic holidays, such as Patriot Week.
- ☆ Dedicated to the Declaration, we can continue to strengthen our fulfillment of the First Principles to achieve a more equal, just, and free society. Without it, we are doomed.

## The Declaration Still Matters and Is an Indispensable Force for Good

This book should be unnecessary. The fact that the foundational and definitive document of America requires a new, comprehensive review on its 250th anniversary is a calamity.

Or is it? A skeptic might crassly ask, "Who cares? Why does the Declaration matter today? How can it provide us any guidance in how we conduct our affairs now or in the future?" Vast changes have swept across society: technology, natural science (biology, astronomy, physics, earth science, and chemistry), healthcare, manufacturing, energy, entertainment, commerce, communication, transportation, agriculture, finance, law, war, religion, voting, and other arenas of life are radically different than in 1776. The Declaration cannot possibly provide us with insight.

Wrong. The age of the document does not render it superseded, irrelevant, or meaningless. Many things in this world are timeless. The world's greatest religious leaders promulgated truth centuries, if not millennia, before today. The teachings of Abraham, Moses, the Buddha, Confucius, Jesus Christ, the Prophet Muhammad, and similar seminal figures do not lose their validity and vitality simply from the passage of time. Scripture may need to be interpreted in light of new developments, but it still resounds with faith. The insights of philosophers Socrates, Plato, Aristotle, Thomas Aquinas, Thomas Hobbes, John Locke, and others are also ageless. The popularity of various philosophies and political theories may ebb and flow, but they still possess potency across the centuries. Literature, poetry, music, architecture, film, and so much more maintain their power and effect even with the passing of eras. A bouquet of flowers and a sunset are beautiful in any age. The Declaration is of a piece.

A harder-hitting critique is that the Declaration must be rejected as the product of white, racist, privileged, landowning, elite, educated, religiously bigoted, colonial, misogynistic cisgender men. All they cared about was power, oppressing the masses, and exploiting others. As one who believes in self-evident, timeless truths, I will not lamely wish away the accuracy of some of this critique. This work unflinchingly acknowledges that many delegates of the Second Continental Congress were racists, religious bigots, and misogynistic. As far as we know, they were all heterosexual men. They were all white colonists who owned land that Native Americans once occupied. A high percentage were very privileged, and almost all were Protestants. Like just about everyone alive before the Declaration, their views on many social and cultural topics strongly conflict with many of our modern sensibilities.

Certainly, the men who drafted and adopted the Declaration were far from perfect, and many held downright despicable opinions and led less-than-saintly lives. Like us, the delegates of the Second Continental Congress were composed of flesh and blood, living in a fixed historical epoch; they were not timeless spiritual angels. We should be less quick to condemn them with our 250 years of experience and more open to celebrating the miraculous good they forged. We all have clay feet, especially with hindsight.* Scribes and Pharisees, who were ready to stone a woman caught in the very act of adultery, taunted and attempted to accuse Jesus with the question, "Now Moses in the law commanded us, that such should be stoned: but what sayest thou?" Jesus "lifted up himself, and said unto them, 'He that is without sin among you, let him first cast a stone at her.'" This silenced and disarmed the supposedly morally superior accusers:

> And they which heard it, being convicted by their own conscience, went out one by one, beginning at the eldest, even unto the last: and Jesus was left alone, and the woman standing in the midst. When Jesus had lifted up himself, and saw none but the woman, he said unto her, Woman, where are those thine accusers? hath no man condemned thee? She said, No man, Lord. And Jesus said unto her, Neither do I condemn thee: go, and sin no more.*

This is what we *should* and *must* ask of America: to sin no more. We need not stone the Founding Generation.

That the drafters of the Declaration were flawed does not in any fashion undermine the brilliance of their work. Actually, it accentuates just what a miracle it is that racist, privileged, religiously bigoted, colonial, landowning, misogynistic, cisgender men declared for the world to see that all are created equal, possess unalienable rights, belong in the Social Compact, deserve a limited government, should be governed by the rule of law, and have the right to alter or abolish an oppressive government.

Thomas Edison invented the lightbulb in 1879. This old invention (as improved by countless others) is probably assisting you in some form or fashion in reading this book. The light bulb and electrification have exponentially improved, but not the illumination. Edison was hardly filled with all the virtues that we hope for in a great man. He was a racist and anti-Semitic. But we would be fools to smash every electrical light and go back to the Dark Ages. Likewise, we should not shred the Declaration—it still brilliantly illuminates all of mankind. Such a critique is a distraction. There is no constructive need to fixate on the flaws of the Founders.

Instead, we must remember that it is the Declaration which sparks a revolution that continues to this day. As this work reveals, it established the first and only nation on earth founded on our First Principles, which enable us today to live as free and equal individuals. Of course, we have not yet totally fulfilled our aspirations. We know too well that the Founding Fathers enforced slavery; discriminated against women, racial minorities, and religious minorities; and denied the vote to all but propertied white men. Each successive generation also fell short. Indeed, the true implications of fully realizing our First Principles often remained hidden or unacknowledged for decades or even generations. Yet when we understand and embrace those implications, they inspire wondrous changes in our society—and in Western civilization. It was the aspiration to meet the promise of our First Principles that drove successive waves of religious toleration, enfranchisement of the landless, abolitionists, suffragettes, civil rights activists, champions of the disabled, and LGBTQ+ advocates.

President Barack Obama captures this spirit in his remarks on the golden (fiftieth) anniversary of the seminal Selma to Montgomery civil rights marches:

> What greater expression of faith in the American experiment than this, what greater form of patriotism is there than the belief that America is not yet finished, that we are strong enough to be self-critical, that each successive generation can look upon our imperfections and decide that it is in our power to remake this nation to more closely align with our highest ideals? (Applause.)
>
> That's why Selma is not some outlier in the American experience. That's why it's not a museum or a static monument to behold from a distance. It is instead the manifestation of a creed written into our founding documents: "We the People...in order to form a more perfect union." "We hold these truths to be self-evident, that all men are created equal." (Applause.)
>
> These are not just words. They're a living thing, a call to action, a roadmap for citizenship and an insistence in the capacity of free men and women to shape our own destiny. For founders like Franklin and Jefferson, for leaders like Lincoln and FDR, the success of our experiment in self-government rested on engaging all of our citizens in this work.*

Whether America will continue its long march of freedom and equality or retreat is the critical question facing our generation. In 1992, Francis Fukuyama predicted in *The End of History and the Last Man* that with the collapse of the Soviet Empire, Western civilization would quickly and inevitably triumph against all other forms of government.* He was dead wrong. Samuel P. Huntington's 1996 insight in *The Clash of Civilizations and the Remaking of World Order,* that the end of the Cold War would instead usher in monumental clashes among the West and several alternative civilizations, was prescient.* As 9/11 and its horrible aftermath proved, many fanatics, totalitarians, and dictators are still trying to destroy America.

Yet the most dangerous of America's threats is internal. For much of our history, Americans who opposed our First Principles were confined to the all-but-lunatic fringes of royalists, communists, fascists, anarchists, and similar ilk. That is changing. Pernicious attacks on the Founding Generation and America itself are seeping out of the ivory tower of academia and into mainstream K–12 education, media, law, and political dialogue. Critical race theory* and the 1619 Project* unabashedly attack and denigrate America's founding and the Declaration as driven by racism and perpetuating slavery. With the lack of understanding of what undergirds America, there is no defense against these critics.

The Declaration, in particular the second sentence, expresses universal principles, or rather principles that should be embraced universally. We are in an age fraught with ignorance and disdain for these principles. Perversely, as America becomes more successful in recognizing greater equality and liberty than ever before (witness the more recent strides for the disabled and the LGBTQ+ community), the hyperbolic attacks on our First Principles and Constitution as systematically rooted in inequality and oppression only increase. Seeping with resentment, critics are apparently incapable of acknowledging the vast achievements undertaken to fulfill the First Principles: the end of slavery; enfranchisement of women and the landless; embedding in our constitutions and law monumental civil rights protections for all races, genders, ethnic groups, religions, sexual orientations, and the disabled; and the success, influence, wealth, and prominence of many women and minority (racial, ethnic, and religious) political figures, scientists, physicians, media personalities, military officers, cultural icons, and others. A biracial president served two terms, and a biracial woman vice president nearly succeeded in winning the election to the presidency. Obama inspiringly makes the point:

> [O]ur march is not yet finished, but we're getting closer. Two hundred and thirty-nine years after this nation's founding our union is not yet perfect, but we are getting closer. Our job's easier because somebody already got us through that first mile. Somebody already got us over that bridge. When it feels the road is too hard, when the torch we've been passed feels too heavy, we will remember these early travelers, and draw strength from their example, and hold firmly the words of the prophet Isaiah: "Those who hope in the Lord will renew their strength. They will soar on [the] [brackets in original] wings like eagles. They will run and not grow weary. They will walk and not be faint." (Applause.)
>
> We honor those who walked so we could run. We must run so our children soar. And we will not grow weary. For we believe in the power of an awesome God, and we believe in this country's sacred promise.*

Of course, we must continue to strive to do better, but denigrating our society as having achieved almost nothing and being hopelessly bigoted is specious.

Resentment and perpetuating a sense of permanent victimhood are not a strategy for progress. Our pernicious domestic critics and those who refuse to teach honest and balanced American history, the Declaration, and the Constitution are responsible for undermining our precious liberty and equality. We must remember why America is worth defending, and the Declaration is the keystone to that understanding.

**The Path Forward**

What can we do?

Let us rephrase that compelling question: What can *you* do? Although many volumes reviewing hundreds of proposals could be offered, there are two major practical recommendations that can have a renewing effect on the spirit of America: reforming education and reviving our civic calendar.

<u>Education Shortfalls</u>

We must make the Declaration a priority again at all levels of education. Although there are many noble and excellent efforts to provide American history and civics education, the reality is that current educational efforts are too weak, dispersed, and diluted to implement the dramatic changes we need. Current studies and surveys reveal that K–12 students are shockingly ignorant about American history and civics. The most recent test scores (in 2022) on the National Assessment of Educational Progress (also known as the Nation's Report Card) reveal that 79 percent of eighth-grade students fall below the proficiency standard for civics.* Although the scores rose slightly for a few years, they are back to the 1998 levels, the first year civics was tested.* The same pattern exists for eighth-grade United States history—the results in 2022 were all but the same as 1994, the initial year of testing.* Test results in American history can only be described as abysmal—86 percent are below proficient.*

Why we are failing is no mystery. Think tank RAND concludes that

> [s]tate-level infrastructure (such as academic standards, accountability politics, and assessment programs) to support elementary social studies instruction are largely missing in many states in the 2021–2022 school year. Where such infrastructure is in place, its quality varies widely.*

School district support for social studies is weak, haphazard, and generally an incoherent mess.* A recent national study concludes that

> [o]ver the last three decades, governments at all levels—from

> federal to local—have provided scant support for curriculum development, teacher professional development, assessment, and research and development in civic and history education. Nevertheless, state legislatures and departments of education often pass mandates to teach specific topics in these disciplines. This dynamic often results in incoherent standards at once lengthy and superficial, and too extensive to be taught in the limited time and with the scant resources allocated for social studies.
>
> In an era of high-stakes accountability, social studies—commonly the home of much civic education—has often gone untested. This drives declining investment of time and other resources in these disciplines. Students and educators are left to confront often fraught and controversial topics without adequate intellectual support, instructional time, and guidance.
>
> Curricula and instructional practices alike reflect this neglect.*

In short, "[g]enerations of students have not received the high-quality education in history and civics that they need, and deserve, to prepare them for informed and engaged citizenship."* To top it all off, the Declaration is usually reduced to a few paragraphs in textbooks and a lesson plan or two. As noted earlier, a leading review book for the Advanced Placement examination for US Government and Politics dedicates but a single three-sentence paragraph to the Declaration.* We are now unanchored from the Declaration—both historically and philosophically.

No wonder the Institute for Citizens & Scholars found that only a third of United States citizens can pass the US citizenship test (which naturalized citizens are required to pass to become citizens).* The bar is not high: 60 percent. The equivalent of a D minus. A D-minus grade earns a person citizenship in America! The study also notes that "[s]urprisingly, the poll found stark gaps in knowledge depending on age. Those 65 years and older scored the best, with 74 percent answering at least six in ten questions correctly. For those under the age of 45, only 19 percent passed with the exam, with 81 percent scoring a 59 percent or lower."*

Although the study suggests this generational gap is a "surprise," it is no such thing. In prior generations, social studies were taught with more rigor, priority, and attention. This poll simply confirms the effect of unraveling rigorous and focused civics and history education. The National Survey of Science and Mathematics Education concludes that K–3 teachers only spend sixteen minutes a day on social studies instruction, and fourth to sixth grade teachers only spend twenty-one minutes.* Because social studies also include world history, geography, and economics, American history and civics receive precious little time in our schools.

A policy brief by the Sandra Day O'Connor Institute for American Democracy summarizes the sad state of affairs:

> [W]hereas until the 1960s American public high-school students were typically required to take three courses in civics—Civics, Problems of Democracy, and US Government—today most get by with a single semester-long class. Even when civics is taught, many teachers avoid teaching it robustly.*

Even in the top-scoring State of Vermont, only 53 percent of those surveyed earn a "passing grade for U.S. history. People in every other state failed; in the lowest-performing state, only 27 percent were able to pass."* "Even more disturbing, nationally, only 27 percent of those under the age of forty-five were able to demonstrate a basic understanding of American history. Nationally, only four in ten Americans passed the exam."* A 2024 study revealed that 75 percent of the undergraduate college students surveyed correctly identified Jay-Z's spouse and 89 percent knew that Amazon is owned by Jeff Bezos, yet less than a third could correctly identify James Madison as the "Father of the Constitution" or knew that the legislative branch possessed the power to declare war, the Thirteenth Amendment abolished slavery, the Gettysburg Address was the source of the phrase "government of the people, by the people, for the people," or republicanism is a core principle of America.* Another 2024 study revealed that 15 percent of respondents were unable to name a single branch of government.* Less than 40 percent were able to name any right protected by the First Amendment, other than the freedom of speech.* The free exercise of religion, the prohibition against established churches, the freedom of press, the right to assemble, and the right to petition are apparently not particularly memorable. Only 7 percent could name five rights protected by the First Amendment.*

Meanwhile, over the last several decades, millions of legal and illegal immigrants have arrived in America. Whether one supports or opposes such generous immigration, we can safely assume that these millions are not well-grounded in the Declaration and Constitution. If these new immigrants are to become valued and informed participants in our political process, they must be well-educated in American history and civics. If we hope to hold the country together with our First Principles, it is absolutely essential.

I am hardly immune to these shortfalls. In the course of researching and writing this work—even after writing and producing the *Patriot Lessons: American History*

*& Civics* podcast series, including an extensive line by line review of the Declaration that composes the rough draft of this book—I uncovered many myths, hidden facts, and brilliant gems.* Pride is the first sin, and this book is certainly humbling. That it takes years of dedicated research by a judge with an honors history major and a juris doctorate from an elite law school to learn about our keystone document reveals just how far we have descended. What is taught in this book should be second nature for our historians and citizens, not requiring several years of detective work. What was once taken for granted and obvious is now rejected and obscure.

The reason these issues are so grave is that the key to maintaining our liberty is an educated citizenry. Our system of self-government and how our liberty and equality are preserved should be of the utmost importance in education. Anyone who believes we can survive as a free and equal people without understanding the roots of our freedom and equality is deluded. Noah Webster, the famous publisher of *An American Dictionary of the English Language*, fittingly observes, in an article advocating for the adoption of the Constitution, that in no other country than America

> ha[s] the body of the people such a knowledge of the rights of men and the principles of government. This knowledge, joined with a keen sense of liberty and a watchful jealousy, will guard our constitutions, and awaken the people to an instantaneous resistance of encroachments.*

As the Constitution is being debated, the Founding Generation is well aware that such principled comprehension would need to be fostered and expanded if the republic is to remain free. At his State's ratifying Constitutional Convention, Governor Samuel Huntington of Connecticut reflects the prevailing sentiment:

> [T]he people themselves must be the chief support of liberty. While the great body of freeholders are acquainted with the duties which they owe to their God, to themselves, and to men, they will remain free. But if ignorance and depravity should prevail, they will inevitably lead to slavery and ruin.*

Concurring with Huntington, Thomas Jefferson, an education visionary in the truest sense of the word, strongly advocates for the establishment of public education by law and State constitutional amendment. Although he proposes such schools for many reasons, Jefferson explains in his highly influential *A Summary View of the Rights of British America* that the most important and legitimate reason is "that of rendering the people the safe, as they are the ultimate, guardians of their own liberty."* He proposes that reading be learned through "chiefly historical" texts because understanding history is the key to protecting liberty:

> History by apprising them of the past will enable them to judge of the future; it will avail them of the experience of other times and other nations; it will qualify them to know ambition and designs of men; it will enable them to know ambition under every disguise it may assume; and knowing it, to defeat its views. In every government on earth is some trace of human weakness, some germ of corruption and degeneracy, which cunning will discover, and wickedness insensibly open, cultivate, and improve. Every government degenerates when trusted to the rulers of the people alone. The people themselves therefore are its only safe depositories. And to render even them safe their minds must be improved to a certain degree. This indeed is not all that is necessary, though it be essentially necessary. An amendment of our constitution must here come in aid of the public education. The influence over government must be shared among the people. If every individual which composes their mass participates of the ultimate authority, the government will be safe.*

As Chief Justice Earl Warren opines, until recently, Americans nearly uniformly believe that our citizens could not

> delegate to any or all of our governmental representatives the full responsibility for protection of our freedoms from the processes of erosion. Such protection can be had only through an understanding on the part of individual citizens of what these freedoms are, how they came into being and whether their spirit dominates our institutions and the life of our country.*

To fulfill our "enormous legacy," then-Senator Barack Obama reflects, requires us to "recognize our history [...] [because] understanding our history and knowing what it means, is an everyday activity."* Education reform is the lynchpin to preserving our freedom and equality. Because our educational system is failing to meet the needs of too many students throughout the entire educational spectrum, comprehensive and wide-ranging reform is needed. Instead of ignoring the Declaration and castigating America, our educators should provide all our students an excellent grounding in our form of self-government, including its historical and philosophical underpinnings—with a special emphasis on our First Principles. Our students should also develop the ability to fully and thoughtfully participate in the political process.

## K–12 Education Reform

To address this educational crisis, each State should establish and implement the American Citizenship Curriculum. The first obligation of our K–12 educational system should be to ground our young students in American history and civics, especially the First Principles. Our students should begin to learn our First Principles and American history in an age-appropriate fashion in kindergarten. This American citizenship curriculum should have specific, measurable expectations for students in each grade from kindergarten through the end of high school. Focusing on the Declaration, the Constitution, and our First Principles, the curriculum should comprehensively address civics, American history, and comparative political science.

Third or fourth graders should be able to identify (if not recite) the introductory portions of the Declaration. George Washington, John Adams, Abigail Adams, Patrick Henry, James Madison, Thomas Jefferson, Thomas Paine, Mercy Otis Warren, John Marshall, Susan B. Anthony, Elizabeth Cady Stanton, Abraham Lincoln, Frederick Douglass, and Dr. Martin Luther King, Jr., should become familiar figures in grade school. No later than the end of elementary school students should be able to describe the basic features of American government and the First Principles. The republican nature of our government, the separation of powers, federalism, the Bill of Rights, judicial review, and the sovereignty of the people should be well-understood concepts in middle school. No later than the end of middle school should our students comprehend the contours of American history, including the causes and effects of the Revolution, the War of 1812, Manifest Destiny and the fate of Native Americans, the Civil War, the Spanish–American War, the Progressive movement, World Wars I and II, the New Deal, the Civil Rights Movement and Great Society, the Korean and Vietnam Wars, the Cold War, the Gulf War, and the Global War on Terrorism. In high school, our students should be learning deep concepts, debating policies of all parties in light of the First Principles, role-playing, writing position papers, speaking in public, asking hard questions, conducting research, participating in public service, and even creating disciplinary knowledge.

Preferably, the American Citizenship Curriculum will be taught in a multidisciplinary way that truly engages students. It will emphasize the search for truth, critical thinking, collaborative learning, and self-directed, student-centered learning.* Properly leveraging Information Age tools and learning practices will dramatically enhance this effort.* The control exercised by textbook publishers should also be leveraged by establishing State standards that implement the American Citizenship Curriculum. Annual assessment and testing should also be a component of the curriculum. A focused, short test with online results would likely best serve educators and students. By coupling the American Citizenship Curriculum with annual testing for each grade, we can best ensure that American history, civics, and the First Principles receive the attention our students deserve.

In addition, many charter schools, nonpublic schools, and homeschool networks are already integrating a revival of classical education and American history and civics into their curricula. These efforts should continue and expand to benefit not only their students, but all students by placing competitive pressure on the broader system to reform its curriculum.

With the robust American Citizenship Curriculum, when it is time to vote and engage in the political arena, our high school graduates will understand the wonderful blessing they have by being citizens of the United States of America. When they are called upon to defend the country, they will have a heartfelt and reasoned understanding that such service is for something much different from conquest or vainglory, but for freedom and equality. If called to duty for something other than the defense of freedom or equality, those called will be well equipped to challenge the cause. Such an educational program will best fan the flame of freedom and equality for generations to come.

## Higher Education Reform

Although K–12 reform is indispensable, so is reform in higher education. Most political, cultural, social, business, and media leaders attend university, and all but abandoning our First Principles and history in higher education is a recipe for ignorant and destructive leadership. When attending the Continental Congress, John Adams wrote to his confidant, James Warren, that

> [o]ur great complaint is the scarcity of men fit to govern such mighty interests, as are clashing in the present contest. [...]
>
> Our policy must be to improve every opportunity and means for forming our people, and preparing leaders for them in the grand march of politics.*

To meet this challenge, all institutions of higher education should require at least one semester of coursework in American history. These courses should provide an intensive focus on the American Revolution and the Constitution. In addition, all college and university students should be required to attend at least one semester of American political science or civics. Like K–12 reform, these courses should focus not on seat time, but on quality. They should probe deeply into the American experience and principles, and students should become well-versed in the primary documents of the American Revolution, the Declaration, the Constitution, and the several civil rights movements. These courses should ensure that our most educated citizens are effectively prepared to meaningfully participate in our system of government. Students should be able to apply that foundational knowledge to today's controversies. Stanford University and Johns Hopkins University have adopted just such a semester requirement.

Institutions that currently struggle with these topics should follow the practices of those institutions of higher learning that provide exemplary education in such arenas through specialized programs and institutes or infusion into their required course load. Arizona State University's School of Civic and Economic Thought and Leadership; University of Florida's Hamilton School for Classical and Civic Education; Johns Hopkins University's SNF Agora Institute; University of Texas at Austin's School of Civic Leadership; University of North Carolina Chapel Hill's School of Civic Life and Leadership; The Ohio State University's Salmon P. Chase Center for Civics, Culture, and Society; the University of Tennessee, Knoxville's Institute of American Civics; Hillsdale College; and Ashland University's Ashbrook Academy are just several of the universities and colleges recognized for excellence in American history and civics.

Moreover, colleges and universities should create teacher training and community outreach programs dedicated to promoting deeper knowledge and research of American history and civics. One such program is Hillsdale College's Hoogland Center for Teacher Excellence, which hosts seminars for K–12 teachers to gain a deeper understanding of American history. Oakland University's Center for Civic Engagement hosts conferences and promotes intellectual exchange regarding the meaning of citizenship. Furman University hosts a week-long Teachers of Government program, which provides teachers with concentrated professional development in civics and related topics. Wayne State University's Center for the Study of Citizenship convenes conferences in citizenship studies and organizes several cutting-edge programs focused on strengthening communities. The University of Notre Dame's Center for Citizenship and Constitutional Government supports scholarship and education concerning the ideas and institutions of constitutional government. Today, these centers are rare. All universities and colleges need to establish and expand such efforts so that they become an integral part of any institution of higher education.

Law School Reform

Chief Justice Earl Warren alerts us that a "dedicated bench and a militant bar are the natural leaders" to preserving our liberties.* He explains

> [w]ithout an independent judiciary there can be no freedom.
>
> Without a militant bar to assert in court the constitutional rights of individuals regardless of how unpopular those assertions might be at the moment, such rights become merely "sounding brass and tinkling cymbals."*

Lawyers have a special trust and duty to maintain our freedoms and equality, and care must be taken to ensure that they are capable of fulfilling that task. The profound English parliamentarian Edmund Burke observes on the eve of the American Revolution that Americans possess a "fierce spirit of liberty" that was "stronger [...] probably than in any other people of the earth" in part because of Americans' widespread knowledge of the law. Burke notes that the study of law

> renders men acute, inquisitive, dextrous, prompt in attack, ready in defense, full of resources. In other countries, the people, more simple, and of a less mercurial cast, judge of an ill principle in government only by an actual grievance; here they anticipate the evil, and judge of the pressure of the grievance by the badness of the principle. They augur misgovernment at a distance, and snuff the approach of tyranny in every tainted breeze.*

What was once prized and thought to enliven our spirit is now ignored or derided in the very institutions that should celebrate it. Most law professors in their courses pay virtually no attention to American history, and many scorn the Founding Fathers. Likewise, the First Principles are generally ignored or, when noticed, distorted or denigrated. Legal education, especially at elite institutions, focuses on fashionable legal doctrines and trendy critiques or distortions of the Constitution. There is nothing wrong with exploring these doctrines and the shortfalls in American law, but to do so in the absence of a significant and fair focus on the First Principles and American history is misleading and undermines our system of ordered liberty.

Law schools must refocus their curriculum to include the First Principles and their historical genesis. Some might consider this beneath such institutions. On the contrary—constitutional law is often considered the most enlightened and elevated of legal topics. The real problem today is that such education is often devoid of any meaningful connection to the Declaration. As a very significant source of learning for our political class, law schools have a special obligation to ensure their students receive a comprehensive education regarding our constitutional order. Law schools should mandate at least one year of constitutional law (as almost all do). More importantly, law schools should require the extensive study of the Declaration and our First Principles, as well as the history surrounding the American Revolution, the adoption of the Constitution, and the civil rights movements. The American Bar Association should include such a requirement in its law school accreditation criteria.

In addition, state bar exams, the Multistate Bar Examination, and the Uniform Bar Examination should include testing on the Declaration and First Principles. No lawyer should be licensed to practice law without understanding that our nation was founded on the rule of law, unalienable rights, equality, the Social Compact, limited government, and the right to alter or abolish an oppressive government.

## Renewal of Nonacademic Institutions

Nonacademic institutions can play a vital role in renewing American history and civics. For example, in 2022, the US Chamber of Commerce Foundation and the Daniels Fund launched the National Civics Bee. In the first round, middle school students drafted essays regarding "Founding Principles"* and "Civic Virtues."* Modeled on the Scripps National Spelling Bee, the final round included twenty students in "a live quiz testing civics knowledge."* The Center for Civic Education hosts the annual We the People competition, which "culminates with simulated congressional hearings where students testify before a panel of judges acting as members of Congress."* The nonprofit Constituting America includes a range of education initiatives, including the *Constitutional Chats* podcast, "90-Day Studies" on various civics-related topics, the George Washington Speaking Initiative, We the Future Contest, and a book club. We need to increase such efforts dramatically.

## Armed Forces Education Reform

The military must also incorporate the First Principles, American history, and civics into its basic training, advanced individual training, and officer candidate school. As the premier force defending the Constitution and the republic, such knowledge is indispensable to ensure that the military itself is not corrupted and will defend freedom and equality.

## Education Reform Call to Action

Educational reform is a generational challenge. The problems in American education did not appear on the scene last month or last year. It is a many-decade-long degradation. It will take a generational renewal to revive the Declaration, Constitution, American history, and civics education. These changes will happen one classroom, one set of book purchases, one school board election, and one set of standards-setting at a time. Use your influence to engage your local schools, universities, legislatures, State school boards and superintendents, and other policymakers to take up the banner of education reform. The educational system is mostly complacent and entrenched in its current posture, but pressure from parents, political leaders, and taxpayers can push the system to fundamentally transform. In the past, such persistent pressure resulted in key education reforms, such as school choice, charter schools, and state standards and testing. Supporting educational alternatives will also directly help some students who attend such alternatives, as well as exert pressure on the dominant system to change. The effort will be long and difficult, but the alternative is too frightful to contemplate.

## Civic Calendar Renewal and Commemorating Patriot Week

An almost completely overlooked solution to restoring the Declaration is to revive our civic calendar. Unlike education reform, which is a long-term generational challenge requiring implementation (at least in part) by experts, this can be done right here and now by *anyone*.

But what do we mean by a civic calendar? As an analogy, all the great religions have an annual liturgical calendar requiring believers to halt in the hustle and bustle of life to renew their faith. Jewish holidays such as Purim, Passover, Rosh Hashanah, and Yom Kippur; Muslim holidays such as Ramadan, Eid al-Fitr, Eid al-Adah, and Mawlid al-Nabi; Hindu holidays such as Diwali, Krishna Janmashtami, Navratri, and Ganesha Chaturthi; Buddhist holidays such as Wesak, Losar, Magha Puja, and Dharma Day; and Christian holidays such as Ash Wednesday, Good Friday, Easter, and Christmas make believers put first things first. In a parallel fashion, America once had a *vibrant* civic calendar: Washington's Birthday, Lincoln's Birthday, Memorial Day, Independence Day, Thanksgiving, and Armistice Day. Why? To renew our faith in America. They should teach us the important things undergirding the United States—courage, sacrifice, personal responsibility, dedication, and the First Principles articulated in the Declaration and embedded in our Constitution.

The importance of the civic calendar is embraced along with the birth of our republic. On July 3, 1776, just one day after the resolution for independence is approved by the Second Continental Congress, John Adams presciently writes to his wife Abigail that the anniversary of Independence Day will be marked in a "great anniversary festival" including "pomp and parade, with shows, games, sports, guns, bells, bonfires and illuminations from one end of this continent to the other, from this time forward, forever more."* Over eighty years later, on July 10, 1858, Lincoln vividly harkens to the importance of celebrating Independence Day:

> We are now a mighty nation [...]. We run our memory back over the pages of history for about eighty-two years and we discover that we were then a very small people in point of numbers [...] with vastly less of everything we deem desirable among men,—we look upon the change as exceedingly advantageous to us and our posterity, and we fix upon something that happened away back [...].We find a race of men living in that day whom we claim as our fathers and grandfathers; they were iron men, they fought for the principle that they were contending for; and we understood that by what they then did it has followed that the degree of posterity that we now enjoy has come to us. We hold this annual celebration to remind ourselves of all the good done in this process of time of how it was done and who did it, and how we are historically connected with it; and we go from these meetings in better humor with ourselves—we feel more attached the one to the other, and more firmly bound to the country we inhabit. In every way we are better men in the age, and race, and country in which we live for these celebrations.*

Today's stark reality is that Independence Day is generally an empty excuse for a day off work, retail sales, parades, and barbecues. These activities usually lack any acknowledgement of the underlying importance of the holiday. Completely absent is Adams's expectation that Independence Day "ought to be solemnized."* Fireworks, hamburgers, and apple pie fill the day. The Spirit of '76? All but gone. When we bite into that hot dog, it is hardly a solemn occasion.

Memorial Day began as Decoration Day, on which women decorated with flowers the graves of those who had given their last full measure of devotion for the Union during the Civil War. Eventually, it expanded to include all of our sacred dead. Today? It is another empty excuse for family three-day weekend getaways, barbecues, carpet sales, and a signal to wear white for the season. Presidents' Day and Veterans Day (no longer Armistice Day) follow the general pattern. Although some academic gatherings and service activities mark Martin Luther King Day and

Juneteenth, that is the exception in which only a minuscule number of citizens participate.

Municipalities, schools, businesses, television, radio, podcasts, social media, sporting events, senior centers, libraries, churches, civic organizations (the Kiwanis, Rotary clubs, chambers of commerce, and so forth), theatre groups, movie theaters, and others should leverage the opportunities of each holiday and make them teachable moments addressing the origins, purposes, and importance of the holiday. For example, Independence Day should be accompanied by distributing complimentary copies of the Declaration. Readers of the Declaration should entertain malls, town halls, and parades. Television, radio, podcasts, and online platforms should play American Revolution and Declaration documentaries and educational presentations. The play *1776* should be standard fare along with the fireworks. Veterans should march proudly in parades on their special day. Lincoln–Douglas debate reenactments should pepper Presidents' Day, as should readings of Washington's Farewell Address. The "I Have a Dream" speech should ring boldly over the radio, television, podcasts, and the internet on Martin Luther King Day.

There are also opportunities for new traditions. In 2009, at a one-on-one lunch with my then-ten-year-old daughter Leah, I explain the importance—and demise—of the civic calendar. Outraged, Leah takes it to heart and immediately vows to do something about it. She pounds on the table and yells, "Dad, that's wrong! We need to do something! We need to create a new celebration for America!" Patriot Week is born.

Inspired by Kwanzaa's model, in which each day is dedicated to a specific principle, we agree that the celebration should be a week with key beginning and ending anchor dates. After some serious research, we select September 11 (the anniversary of the terrorist attacks, which has deep significance to this generation) and September 17 (the anniversary of the signing of the Constitution and Constitution Day—by federal law, schools receiving federal education funds are required to teach about the Constitution on that day).

Each day is dedicated to a First Principle from our Declaration, one or more of the Founding Fathers and other great Patriots that made the First Principle come to life, key documents and speeches embodying the respective First Principle, and historical flags that represent the First Principle. Because equality has been such a struggle for America, Patriot Week dedicates two days to that principle—one for racial equality and the other for gender equality.

Beginning in 2009, Patriot Week caught fire across the nation. As of this writing, bipartisan Patriot Week resolutions and proclamations have been issued by over fifteen governors and State legislatures, and various counties and municipalities. As of 2025, the US Senate has *unanimously* passed a Patriot Week resolution for seven consecutive years, cosponsored by Michigan Democrat Senator Gary Peters and Louisiana Republican Senator John Kennedy.

Over the years, Patriot Week participants across the nation include K–12 schools, colleges, law schools, senior centers, libraries, Kiwanis, Rotary clubs, businesses, banks, law firms, and many others. These grassroots participants tailor their Patriot Week efforts to best meet the needs of their circumstances and stakeholders. Activities include, among other things, lesson plans, school assemblies, book signings, panel discussions, guest speakers, essay contests, concerts, parades, picnics, "paloozas," 9/11 commemorations, gubernatorial debates, movies, and festivals. Currently we convene K–12 tours highlighting historical re-enactors to help inspire students to develop specific legislative proposals to lobby the Michigan legislature. The annual Patrick Henry Awards Dinner draws hundreds to watch Leah and others reenact Patrick Henry's "Give Me Liberty or Give Me Death!" speech. It also features historical re-enactors portraying Benjamin Franklin, Thomas Jefferson, George Washington, Abigail Adams, Abraham Lincoln, Alexander Hamilton, Frederick Douglass, King George III (including a debate between George Washington and George III), and others. Each year, it also honors several "Patriots of the Year." Dozens of lesson plans are available online for educators and students. Leah and I also produce the local cable program *Patriot Lessons* (which is capable of national distribution) with over 150 episodes and counting. The *Patriot Lessons: American History & Civics* podcast has racked up over one hundred thousand plays. We also have a set of "daily rituals" that anyone can do alone or with family and friends during Patriot Week. This unique, historically grounded, nonpartisan approach is desperately needed in our toxic political environment.

Patriot Week is just starting and has a long way to go to achieve its goals. Check it out at www.PatriotWeek.org and join us. We certainly need the help.

## Civic Calendar Renewal

Patriot Week has no monopoly on civic celebrations. We encourage everyone to participate in any celebration and commemoration that renews the spirit of America. Again, unlike education reform, everyone can participate in celebrating America.

There is a time when holiday commemorations were so commonplace that many doubted whether they were even necessary. Yet, even then, as Chief Justice Earl Warren* explains, they "still serve a purpose of rekindling the spirit evinced by" the Founding Fathers and Mothers "and in recharging our minds with the high purposes that impelled them to contribute so much to the society in which we live and to the institutions which guard our well-being. They afford us the opportunity to say in unison, 'Lest we forget.'"* These activities are meaningful, engaging, and thoughtful reminders of the exceptional nature of America and the blessings of freedom and equality we still enjoy. By routinely reinvigorating our understanding and the spirit of our First Principles and history, we will create a ready wellspring to preserve our republic in times of trouble and crisis.

**Time to Renew the Declaration or Risk America's Demise**

All that our nation has achieved is now at grave risk. We need not cite the numerous surveys that reveal that our political environment is toxic. Less recognized is the source of the danger: *We* are the threat—and not only from episodic political violence, riots, and flawed political leaders. Our gravest peril is the ignorance and disdain many hold for the Declaration, Constitution, and our First Principles. Paraphrasing Noah Webster, vacuity of the unalienable rights of individuals and our First Principles, joined with complacency and idleness in the face of threats, will doom our liberties and equality. As Abraham Lincoln reflects, as a nation of free people, "[W]e must live through all time, or die by suicide."*

Of course, there will often be disagreements regarding the application of the First Principles, our history, and the Constitution to specific policy questions. However, there was a time when we could disagree without demonizing our opponents. Even when passions overtake our better natures, we eventually reconcile behind what unites us. Like so much else, John Adams and Thomas Jefferson continue to teach us. When working in the Second Continental Congress, they were fast friends and allies. During the first and second post-Washington presidential elections, they faced off and became bitter rivals, their campaigns lobbing the most vicious of political attacks and insults.

Yet even after Adams (considered a Federalist) defeated Jefferson (a Republican) and, in turn, Jefferson then defeated Adams, they renewed their tender ties of friendship, including a famous decades-long correspondence. In large measure, they reconciled because they were always united behind the First Principles articulated in the Declaration and embedded in the Constitution. As Jefferson masterfully explained in his first inaugural address, "[E]very difference of opinion is not a difference of principle. We have been called by different names brethren of the same principle. We are all Republicans, we are all Federalists."* Today, if we are ignorant of or dismiss our First Principles, there is no unifying foundation to unite us. The politics of personal destruction become just that—the demonization of the enemy. There is nothing but personal animosity and hatred of the political enemy. We unravel. Furthermore, by failing to understand our philosophical and historical origins, we pave a wide-open path for demagogues, ungrounded populists, and rampant violations of the Constitution. This is the surest pathway to the death of America.

We must unite again behind the Declaration. If this book reveals nothing else, it is the uniqueness of the American experience. The Declaration removes all doubt that men and women, when dedicated to the truth and our First Principles, change the course of human history for the better in unimaginable ways. When the Founding Generation tossed off the yoke of British oppression and imperialism, little did they know it would spark in future generations the enfranchisement of all men and women, the emancipation of slaves, a universal belief that equality should be robustly protected, and a massive expansion of liberty. There were a few visionaries like Thomas Paine and Abigail Adams who so prophesied, but they were part of a tiny aberrant minority. As we have learned, for most of human history, unalienable rights, equality, limited government, the rule of law, the Social Compact, and the right to alter or abolish government were the exception. Supporting those principles is often treated as treason. We are the only nation in world history to be dedicated to all these First Principles. To be free and equal is a rare and precious gift. Our liberty and equality are the result of centuries of struggle, bought with the blood and struggle of our forefathers and foremothers. During the Cold War, we placed the entire nation and world on the brink of nuclear annihilation rather than submit to communist tyranny. If we turn away from ourselves, we must ask, "Why did we bother?"

All of us, Americans and citizens of the world, are the great heirs of this Declaration of universal principles. We need to revive and rely on it once again. History teaches us what awaits us if we do not: intolerance, discrimination, caste systems, feudalism, authoritarianism, dictatorships, absolutism, and totalitarianism—with their many horrors. Without the Declaration, we are doomed. These forces of darkness were cast off in 1776, and they can yet be repelled today. But only if we are willing to act and sacrifice on behalf of truth, equality, and freedom—that is, the Declaration. Make it so.*

# NOTES

To access the notes from this book, please scan the QR code below or visit RepublicBookPublishers.com/America250.

# ACKNOWLEDGMENTS

The patience and support of my wife, Shannon, is truly awe-inspiring.

My children, Alexander and Leah, are more than I deserve.

My friend since birth, Mike DeBruyn, is a truly remarkable editor.

Mike Brady's assistance is invaluable.

Bill Volz's title suggestion is genius.

The encouragement and support of the Patriot Week Foundation is tremendous.

The assistance of my agent, Diane S. Nine (introduced by the extraordinary Susan Nine, a friend of mine and Shannon [and the Wayne State debate program] for decades), is wondrous.

The support of Alfred Regnery and all at Republic Book Publishers is exemplary. The editors are fantastic. I am grateful to those who graciously offered their endorsements, an encouragement I consider received as a gift of Divine Providence.

# ABOUT THE AUTHOR

Emma Burcusel

Judge Michael Warren has served on the Oakland County Circuit Court in Michigan since 2002. He has taught constitutional and business law, is a former member of the Michigan State Board of Education, and has received many recognitions for his work, including induction into the Hall of Fame by the International Association of Top Professionals.

In 2009, with his then ten-year-old daughter Leah, he co-created the nonpartisan, nonprofit Patriot Week (www.PatriotWeek.org), which has been unanimously recognized by the US Senate and many states. He writes and co-hosts the *Patriot Lessons: American History and Civics Podcast.* He authored *America's Survival Guide: How to Stop America's Impending Suicide by Reclaiming Our First Principles and History,* alongside numerous law review articles, legal reforms, official proclamations, public reports, and scores of commentaries.

Judge Warren is married to the love of his life, Shannon. Together they have two adult children, Leah and Alexander, and a Westie named Dickens. Judge Warren is an avid marathon runner and Trekkie.